THE ARTIST AND THE GARDENER

THE ARTIST AND THE GARDENER

Sue Goodchild

ARTHUR H. STOCKWELL LTD
Torrs Park, Ilfracombe, Devon, EX34 8BA
Established 1898
www.ahstockwell.co.uk

ISBN 978-0-7223-4983-0
Printed in Great Britain by
Arthur H. Stockwell Ltd
Torrs Park   Ilfracombe
Devon

ACKNOWLEDGEMENTS AND BIBLIOGRAPHY

I am extremely grateful for the perseverance and endless patience of my good and dear friend Catherine Webstar, Robin Kempster and Steven Saris, in providing editorial advice. My thanks also to my cousin Victoria Lighting for taking photographs of my sister's garden prior to its considerable changes, and to my husband, Paul, for his patience and encouragement over the years of writing and painting for this book.

My grandfather and father's gardening books were invaluable in the research of plants. These include *The Smallholder Encyclopaedia* by John Hayhurst and S. A. Maycock, FRHS; *Gardening Book* by Arthur Hellyer; *The Gardener's Enquire Within* by A. J. Macself; also *Gardening Month by Month* by Percy Thrower; *On Gardening* and *Home and Garden* by Gertrude Jekyll; *The Well-Tempered Garden* by Christopher Lloyd; Gerard's *Herball*, David Austin's catalogue of roses, and reading BBC *Gardeners' World* magazine and listening to BBC's *Gardeners' Question Time* and Reginald Moule on the BBC.

INDEX

PROLOGUE

I have not attempted to write a guidebook as this is for those who love gardens and painting and for myself as a tribute to a loved sister, and as solace in a time of sadness at her untimely death. I combined my love of painting and appreciation of nature with Mag's expertise and knowledge, recording her favourite plants in paint. Mag knew the Latin names of plants; I knew their colours and shapes. Mag knew what plants needed, and cultivation was her primary motivation, whereas I love to compose and arrange and paint. Mag's plants were healthy and good-looking due to her preparation in soil, in compost and fertility and, being in England, benefited from rainfall in summer, while mine had to deal with drought in France and being an artist and amateur gardener and my learning the hard way about gardening. I have painted and written about plants and flowers more or less as they bloom, bearing in mind that climate and position in sun or shade can alter seasonal expectations. For example, in one year, after a cool summer, the yuccas flowered in November and in another year, after a hot spring, they flowered in May.

In wanting to learn about the nature, the history and the names of plants, I have studied plants, their habitats, many books and ultimately Gerard's *Herball*. As he would say, 'Nature maketh her plants not for meat and medicine only, but some be esteemed for beauty alone, and as garlands and crowns for pleasure.'

Miss Eleanor Sinclair Rohde in *The Old English Herbals* said of Gerard, 'His Herbal gripped the imagination of the English garden-loving world and it still retains its hold on us. There are English speaking people the world over who may know nothing of any other, but at least by name they know Gerard's Herbal.'

Gerard of Cremona, the great medieval scholar, built his knowledge and understanding on both the writings of Dioscorides and the Schools of Salerno and Montpellier. His translation of *Canon of Medicine* by Avicenna, an Arab physician, became a standard work which was still used in universities like Montpellier as late as 1650. The great amount of information that resulted from Gerard's work brought about a revaluation of medical teaching.

In the sixteenth-century the garden of Lord Zouche, 11th Baron Zouche of Harringsworth, in Hackney, London, became a centre for the increasing number of plant enthusiasts, and a collection point for plants and those bought back from Zouche's continental expeditions. Man's tendency to collect material became significant in England for the first time in horticulture, but the quest for the new and the curious was as much the expression of a genuine search for knowledge as it was a quirk of fashion. Economic botany, medical needs and herbal practice, horticulture and gardening for pleasure had a parting of the ways. Horticulture had come in the middle of the sixteenth century with the arrival on British soil of religious refugees from Flanders and France. They brought with them methods and skills in the cultivation of plants and the plants themselves. They settled mainly in what is now Norfolk and Suffolk, South-East England, and around London. Many cultivated their own physic gardens and became leaders in medical botany as well as foremost gardeners. Such a man was John Gerard, born in Cheshire in 1545, one of the most influential herbalists of the age, an apothecary and an ardent plants-man. Much has been written about Gerard's source material, doubts raised, dispelled and reasserted as to his accuracy and qualification of *The Herball*, published in 1597. His work is largely based on a list of plants growing in his own garden. This list was the first of its kind and has provided the only evidence available of plants, both native and introduced, under cultivation in England at that time. He also made field excursions into Kent and Middlesex, recording over seventy species of flora for the first time.

After Gerard, Thomas Johnson, 'the best herbalist of his age in England', edited and corrected *The Herball*, maintaining much of the quaintness of style so characteristic of Elizabethan botany, but carefully updating and correcting the text. The new version was published in 1633, twenty-one years after Gerard's death. He studied, identified and recorded flora found on trips in search of native plants. He recorded over 600 species in Kent and led the first botanical expedition to Wales, taking an interpreter with him! The poorer classes and peasants collected herbs from the fields or grew them around their cottages. Rural communities put every plant to some use, whether economic or symbolic. Medical services were costly, and it was Nicholas Culpeper who, in 1652, produced the first book designed to give the poor the information they needed to apply appropriate plant remedies.

The full title of his book was *The English Physician or an Astrologer-physical Discourse of the Vulgar Herbs of this Nation being a Complete Method of Physic whereby a Man May Preserve His Body and Health or Cure Himself Being Sick for Three Pence Charge with Such Things Only As Grow in England, They Being Most Fit for English Bodies.*

Culpeper sacrificed much wealth and reputation to serve the common people, and while in retrospect he is often regarded as a crank for the astrological aspect of his botany, he was merely playing to the gallery, as shown by the success of his herbal. In temperate zones, no one would dispute the astrological influence of seasonal effects on both plant and animal life. Vegetation is affected by phases of the moon, with increase in growth or proliferation of cells most marked towards the new moon. Throughout the thirteen lunar months of the calendar, growth is regulated or activated by the season and the moon, so there is very little growth of plants prior to the full moon in December, in the northern hemisphere, but much growth before the April and May full moon. 'The Doctrine of Signature' claimed supporters throughout the Middle Ages, and Culpeper, despite his academic ability, was an exponent of this theory, whereby certain plants were ascribed occult properties, parts of the plant representing that part of the body or condition for which they were intended. For example, the shape of the leaves of the pulmonaria was thought to resemble the lungs, so they were used in the relief of pulmonary disorders; consequently the plant is commonly known as lungwort. Likewise, the colour obtained from saffron suggested its use in the treatments of biliousness, and the felted leaves of coltsfoot and mullein were suggestive of mucus and thus used to treat haemorrhoids; the markings in the flower of eyebright suggested its use in the treatment of eyes, and the form of the walnut was likened to the brain and was recommended for headaches and madness. These early herbals were important travelling companions for the increasing number of English who were setting out for the New World. From the edited Gerard to the influential Culpeper, these handbooks of herbal remedies were regarded as indispensable in the New World, where many identical species of plants could be found, as well as genera then unknown to the new settlers, and new plants they had never seen before. It seems that results of these remedies were 'kill or cure'. When a patient recovered after herbal teas, this meant that the system had been restored. If not then it was regarded as God's will. New England gardens were planted according to Culpeper or Parkinson (the last of the great English herbalists and one of the first of the great English botanists), and many herbs which we regard today as growing wild in the New World have wandered from these early gardens. A great physic garden at Chelsea, founded by the Worshipful Society of Apothecaries in 1673, was first mentioned in 1674 when it was proposed that a wall be built around the existing garden. The wall was to be paid for at the society's own expense with the assistance of subscriptions. The apothecaries were to conduct 'herbarizings', which were walks in the country to collect or observe plants. It proved successful. The apothecaries had their own barge, which made its way from the City to Chelsea, where access to the garden was gained directly from the river. Funds were at a low ebb, but in 1722 a new lease was granted with the condition that apothecaries deliver to the Royal Society fifty specimen plants each year until about 2,000 specimens were assembled.

As botany turned more and more towards the cultivation of decorative plants and refined food plants, the pharmacists (modern-day apothecaries) remained the last practitioners of herbal lore, and the cultivation of herbs for cosmetic and medicinal use became a modern industry. In 1850, the principal crops were peppermint, lavender and chamomile, though aconite, belladonna, caraway, squirting cucumber, elecampane (inula), liquorice, foxgloves, lovage, angelica, hemlock, savin (juniper), poppies, roses and marshmallow were also grown. The most notable British herbalists between the two world wars were probably the partners Dorothy Hewer and Margaret Brownlow, who ran the The Herb Farm, at Seal in Kent. Dorothy Hewer began with an acre of land in 1926 and grew lavender, peppermint, rosemary, sage, angelica, lemon balm, thyme and marjoram, and she had her own drying sheds. Her garden was to become both a commercial proposition and a teaching establishment. One of her pupils, Margaret Brownlow, who later returned to Seal and became Miss Hewer's partner, made a worthy name for herself as a herbalist and an authoritative writer on herbs and became managing director of The Herb Farm following Miss Hewer's death in 1948. It was only the untimely death of Miss Brownlow herself that bought an abrupt end to the work at Seal. When her estate was settled, the nurserymen, Luxton and Bunyard, took over the herb nursery. Some years later, in 1971, their parent company, R. J. Cuthbert of Llangollen, North Wales, sold that part of the business to Bees Nursery of Chester, and the Seal farm was included in the sale.

Herb gatherers or 'simplers' went about Britain collecting many plants from the wild, in season, and selling their harvest to the herbalists, who in turn sold the dried herbs to the druggists or to the public. These simplers were the inheritors of the former 'green man', whose itinerant trade is still sometimes marked by inn signs as 'The Green Man'. The recent demand for herbs has been so great and the advances in growing, harvesting and storage techniques so rapid, that herb farming has begun to expand.

A plant may have numerous names. The botanical name may be difficult to remember, but is a universal identification system. Latin names give universality. Leonhard Fuchs's magnificent folio *De Historium Stirpium* was published in 1542 and the illustrations are botanically exact and are named in both Latin and German. Instead of plants being classified by long phrases, plants today have Latin names consisting of two parts. Botanists group all plants into families, then genera and then species. It is a surprise because the custom of using two-worded names, known as binomial-ism, is commonly credited to the Swedish naturalist Carolus Linnaeus in the mid eighteenth century. Before Linnaeus' binomial-ism became the normal form, in an effort to become as exact as possible botanists coined a descriptive name sometimes of six words or more for each plant. In 1753 Linnaeus published his *Species Plantarum* which listed all plants known at the time, giving to each names recognised today. Many of Linnaeus' names already existed, but their appearance in his book is taken as a new beginning. In order to deal with such a multiplicity of organisms it is essential to group them into explicable categories, and the search for a natural system has exercised botanists for centuries. While some of Linnaeus' terms and categories are still used, their post-Darwinian concepts are inevitably very different. Every plant can be said to be of a certain species; closely related yet distinct species can be grouped into a genus; and, in turn, related genera are grouped into a family, the name of which is usually derived from the most important genus in the group. Therefore a plant is known by its genus name and its species name; so, for example, *Eremurus* is the genus and *robustus* is the species. The species name is often descriptive. *Robustus* means robust; *pendula*, hanging; *japonica*, Japanese; *rontundifolia*, round leaves. A name may include an '×' which indicates that it is a hybrid – for example, *Eremurus × isabellinus*. The cultivar names (a cultivar is a plant selected for certain characteristics for cultivation) are encased in quote marks – *Eremurus × isabellinus* 'Cleopatra' – which is orange with a red stripe on the petal, or *E. × isabellinus* 'Obelisk' which is white with a green stripe on the petal. Mag knew the Latin names whereas I liked purely to enjoy the flowers, but now I too am learning the names.

INTRODUCTION

This book means more to me than the love of painting and plants – it is also a loving tribute to my sister, who was, among her many talents, a racing driver and a gardener.

It was June, a beautiful month full of colour and hope, and the garden flowers were at their showy best. Perhaps it was the best time for Mag to leave us, leave her beloved garden; nature is all about life and death. Margaret Dennis, my younger sister, Mag for short.

When I decided to capture the beauty of Mag's garden it was only with the knowledge of what she liked best, the plants we exchanged and seeing her garden only in the winter and as a tribute to a beloved sister.

I hardly noticed the garden on the day of her funeral in July, but I recall plenty of colour rather than individual plants. Cousin Victoria took some photos for me and I have painted with these in mind, from memory and from the plants in my own garden, some of which came from Mag's garden in the Thames Valley. I live in the north of the Loire Valley, so although we might grow similar plants, their growing conditions were different. In France the summers are long and dry and the winters can be damp with the occasional blast of cold from Russia, while the weather in England is moderate. In France the season could be three weeks ahead in the spring, but it also means a quick accession of flowers, which in England may last all summer. Bearing this in mind, flowering times have been left vague.

Mag loved and found plenty of sunshine in England and was as brown as a berry as she liked to garden in her bikini and boots – happy to be at one with nature.

Me and my younger sister, Mag.

Mag (Maggie) in her racing gear.

Apart from her love of gardening, Mag's other lifelong interest was racing. Until her children were born she and her husband raced motorbikes. Kart racing took over for forty-one years until her death. Her interest took in all areas of the sport – not only racing, but also administration and officiating. Despite much interest in her exploits, she actively avoided press, TV and radio coverage, avoided photos and magazine articles and gave away all her trophies as soon as she could. After much success, especially in the Isle of Man, which cemented her fame, and the death of her friend at Brands Hatch, where she was racing, she decided to leave work, stop racing and start her gardening business and to garden full-time. She was given a second greenhouse by a neighbour which increased her plant-production scope. She spent hours building small ponds, a stream and waterfall, moving rocks and stones to get just the right water noise. Her husband, Alan, supported her in all her pursuits.

I encouraged Mag to write about her experiences and at the end of her life she wrote in 2012:

January.

For the past nineteen years I have looked after up to twenty gardens as well as my own. In November last year I had to have an abdominal operation and the decision to retire was made for me.

The winter has been pretty tough in the garden but apart from sweeping snow off the greenhouses (yes, I have two) and disinterring the broccoli and cabbages from their nets, I have been unable to do very much outside.

All that will change next month with lots of veg and flower seeds to sow. For now I will settle for admiring the snowdrops, waiting in anticipation for the *Daphne bholua* 'Jacqueline Postil' and various hellebores to open their buds, then I'll know winter is finally to be kicked into touch.

The potato order arrived today (28.01). The earlies, 'Rocket', second earlies 'Charlotte' and maincrop 'Desirée', have now all been put in trays blunt end up to chit. The maincrop doesn't really need chitting but if left in the nets, their eyes grow through and then when emptied out, break off.

Went out to the shed to do a bit of tidying. Managed to throw a few old compost bags away. Why do I hoard them all? One less job to do in the spring.

I'm a bit worried about my cordyline. It must be all of twenty-five years old and fifteen feet, so has been through some pretty tough winters. This year not only have all the dead leaves come off, so have a lot of what look healthy green leaves. I guess the frost, snow and wind has damaged the crowns.

February.

Had a very productive day today. Pruned the roses, hibiscus and clematises (clematii?). I would normally shred all my prunings, but the hibiscus splinters up and gets wrapped around the shredder blades jamming it, so I had a bonfire on an empty path in the vegetable bed. Very satisfying.

I am continuing clearing the cordyline leaves. Have noticed that a couple of the trunks are wet and are exuding a pink substance – going to have to chop it down. Hopefully they will put up new shoots. The weather is still atrocious, but have made a start on preparing for seed sowing, getting flower and veg seeds in order of sowing – just need a good couple of weeks in March and I'll be up and running.

March.

I dug the heated propagator out of the shed and sowed some veg and flower seeds – plenty more to sow. The cordyline continues to lose leaves. Am going to cut them down and hope for new shoots.

April

Have been very busy pricking out seedlings. The potatoes planted out in early April have been earthed up several times already. The glorious weather has meant I have been able to sow carrots and beetroot in the veg patch. They are through now and will need thinning shortly. Put up canes for the runner beans and sowed runner and dwarf French beans over Easter.

Need to start pulling up the forget-me-nots now they are starting to set seeds.

Had a fantastic show of apple and pear blossom. There are that many apples and pears – will have to think about thinning them after the June drop (which usually happens in May). There are only so many apples you can eat.

Mag died in June.

THE ARTIST

Painting and growing these wonderful flowers and vegetables is a delight, as it has been all my life. Every season brings something of interest, in changing colours, in plant shape, in growth and in the distinctive seasonal characteristics of each month. Whatever the time of year, the garden can offer an inexhaustible source of ideas to inspire the artist. Discovering and developing ideas about a subject takes imagination and vision, only achieved as the result of hard work and experience. Leonardo da Vinci studied the structure of plants so as to fully understand his subject from both an aesthetic and a botanical point of view. When creating a painting, it is generally necessary for the artist to rearrange or adjust a three-dimensional reality into a two-dimensional plane along with a sense of rhythm, design and interest, reflecting personal preferences. Rarely does nature present a perfect composition.

To plan and plant a garden with painting in mind is to create a harmonious garden. The magic and flair comes with the inspiration of the gardener. When planting with the shapes of foliage and colour in mind, artistic sensitivity must combine with design and plantmanship. Groups of plants must co-ordinate with leaves and flowers, though the importance of foliage may not be so evident as colour takes over, making the leaves of secondary importance. Flowers are a wonderful source of inspiration. The shapes of open flowers are important, but so are the buds, leaves and stalks, which can be a very important part of the composition and provide contrast to the flowers.

Being a gardener as well as an artist, I witness first-hand the bright vibrant and endless colours of flowers. I am always moved when I see beautiful flowers with their different shapes, their colours and their perfume. Flowers are usually viewed as fragile and delicate, and I wish to capture this and their very essence. It is a joy to capture their true natural beauty, which is so transient. Painting flowers is such a pleasure. I am infatuated with natural beauty, tempered by an artistic desire to arrange and design shapes, colours and textures and a desire to enjoy my garden shared with my beloved husband, Paul, our wonderful dog, Belle, and Friska the cat, and friends who visit. There is nothing more pleasant than to wander around the garden, forgetting the toil, to sit and share a drink, exchange views, knowledge and plants.

Being an artist and a gardener I understand the needs of plants, making sure that they are planted where they will flourish given the right treatment. Also as an artist, it is important to understand how one colour will react when planted near another. As well as shape, size and colour, consideration should be made about harmony or vibrancy, in the flower or foliage, how fast growth will be, and whether it is a perennial, annual shrub or tree.

One of the pleasures of being an artist and a gardener is viewing the difference aspects, perhaps with one area and ideas forming about changing another. I do believe that a good garden is made by someone who loves growing, loves plants, and loves putting shapes, colours and textures together. To create a garden is to organise all the elements present and add fresh ideas, considering all the time the soil, the nature of trees, of shade, moisture and composition. Every part of the composition must be deliberately related right down to the last bulb. I like to think of the plants as paints, which composed properly will form the painting. A collection of plants is similar to a collection of paints on a palette and, as with painting, planning is the link to success. A garden is successful, as in painting, when the composition is planned, but this must relate to the plant's needs, to their shapes, textures, light conditions and moisture. It is the creative artist who forms the beautiful picture.

Sue Goodchild, the artist.

THE ARTIST IN THE GARDEN

As a gardener, I love to paint the flowers in my garden. There is nothing more exciting than finding a ready-made subject in the garden enhanced by sunlight. Sometimes there are only moments to capture the effects of sunshine on blooms or cast shade, and here a sketchbook is used. There is beauty in nature whether it is flowers, wildlife, water or weather conditions. Every season brings new delights in the garden and every day buds unfurl revealing their exquisite beauty. Artists paint from the soul, hoping to capture the heart and inspiration, the colours and shapes of the garden and flowers. The material for painting subjects is all around us.

My dream was to paint in the sun (or at least in the shade but surrounded by sunshine), but to achieve such I needed an income, so I created a painting school in France. As if designed, I met Paul, a chef, but was it his blue, sparkling eyes, his friendly nature or the sixth sense which overcame me and captured my heart?

A chef and an artist bought a large old farmhouse, with the help of parents and the bank. We learned new skills never before attempted – plumbing, electrics, plastering and gardening – and ran a school of art.

The origins of my garden are lost in the mists of time, when nature was wild and uncultivated and the fields were patches in the midst of untamed wilderness. Our forefathers loved to surround themselves with a garden with a fence between them and the outer world, but all had disappeared, no doubt trampled by animals as they lived in the abandoned house. All that remained were the fruit and nut trees, and the wonderful old oaks and the wild flowers which had moved in from the surrounding fields.

William Lawson was credited with making gardening popular for women with his book *A New Orchard and Garden* written solely for women. He lived from 1553 to 1635 and was the vicar of Ormesby, a country parish in Yorkshire. No doubt his gardening passion led him to be so long-lived for an age when most people did not reach fifty. Gardening was a national passion in the sixteenth and seventeenth centuries as more species came from abroad and interest in the useful qualities and medicinal virtues of plants grew. *The Country Housewife's Garden*, beautifully illustrated with charming woodcuts, tells the seventeenth-century woman everything she needs to know to have a productive and visually attractive garden. The concept of a 'pretty' garden would have been an anathema to most women of the seventeenth century, as gardens were primarily about producing food and herbs, except for the very rich, in which case the gardening was left to the servants. The seventeenth-century author of *The English Housewife*, Gervase Markham, claimed the 'complete woman' had skills in surgery, cookery, extraction of oils, banqueting, ordering of great feasts, preserving of all sorts of wines, distillations, perfumes, ordering of wool, hemp and flax, making cloth and dyeing, knowledge of dairies, of malting, of oats, of brewing and baking and all other things belonging to the household. Kitchen gardens were about supplying the table, and as much ground as possible was covered with edible plants. Every garden was different, planted according to the whims of the women of the household. William Lawson's book for the country housewife was designed to be read in conjunction with his *New Orchard and Garden*, thus giving women access to the idea of garden design for the very first time.

An artist must get to know the subject and choose the appropriate materials, whether it be pencil, pastel, oil, acrylic or watercolour. In most of the paintings here I have used watercolour. The artist must get to know the colours and what is possible to create starting with the primaries and, as one gains experience, adding new colours one by one, experimenting to discover the mix of the colours wanted. The basic colours could be a warm and a cool of blue, red and yellow. By looking at a colour wheel one can see that a cool yellow is close to green while a warm yellow is closer to red. Likewise a warm blue is close to violet, a cool blue close to green, a warm red is close to violet while a cool red is close to yellow. Suggested colours could be French Ultramarine (a warm blue), Cerulean (a cool blue), Permanent Rose (a cool red), and Cadmium Red (a warm red). Winsor Yellow is cool and Indian Yellow is warm. Variations could be substituted and others added. I like to add to the palette violet (warm), Burnt Sienna (warm), and Phthalocyanine Blue (cool), and sometimes a specific colour is needed. Each of these colours have properties in the pigments which can add to the visual qualities of the painting.

Colour is a most expressive element of painting, capturing emotion or mood. Working with colour means breaking it down into hue, value, intensity and temperature. The hues are red, green or blue. Red, yellow and blue are the 'primaries'. These cannot be mixed from other hues. 'Secondary' hues, such as green and orange, and 'tertiary' hues, such as blue-violet or red-orange can be mixed from the primaries. 'Complementary' colours are any two colours which are positioned directly opposite each other on the colour wheel. 'Value' is the relative lightness or darkness of a hue. The value of a hue can be adjusted in several ways, but when white is added to lighten it it is called a 'tint', and when black is added it is called a 'shade'. Tints might be lavender and pink while olive green and navy blue are shades. 'Intensity', also called 'chroma' or 'saturation', is the strength of the colour, but is often affected by surrounding colours. Hues of high intensity tend to advance while hues of low intensity retreat. Organising the paint in a working order means that dipping into a colour can become instinctive rather than random, giving freedom, and this is especially important when painting wet-in-wet.

When using watercolours, if too many colours are indiscriminately mixed on the palette, or too many layers of colour are built up on the paper, they may cancel each other and turn muddy and opaque. Freshness and transparency are essential to depict the delicacy of flowers. When mixing colours, I take care not to blend them so thoroughly that they become flat and lifeless. Colours which are partially mixed appear much livelier as with individual colours on damp paper and blending them just slightly so that they work together wet-in-wet.

I don't always paint wet-in-wet, but do in places where it is called for, where I want the paint to flow together or bleed to create soft edges. It is fun to drop a pool of colour from the palette into a still-wet wash and then tilt or bend the painting to steer the colour in the desired direction. It is fascinating to watch the paint trickle down the paper, but also being ready to tilt the paper in a different direction if the paint threatens to run elsewhere. Judgement and timing are important. This can be used in running colours together in individual petals or leaves.

I use good-quality paper, paints and brushes. I place the paper on a board at an angle so that the paint flows evenly. On a flat board the paint might create hard unwanted edges. I mix plenty of paint, especially when painting a wash. Running out of the mix may mean there is no time to mix more and the exact consistency may be hard to replicate. I charge the brush generously. When painting a flat wash, I begin at the top on dry paper and use strokes back and forth, slightly clipping the edge of the previous stroke. For a graded wash, I add more water with each stroke and do not retouch areas as this usually disturbs the paint and results in back blooms, and let the paint dry naturally, preferably at a slight angle.

DESIGN

Garden design is a combination of hard and soft landscape, paths, paved areas, arches and pergolas as well as borders and lawns. Plants reinforce the pattern with colour, form and foliage and lead the eye through a space and enticingly round corners. The basis of any good design is a permanent framework in hard structures and plants. Good framework plants give a strong and consistent presence throughout the seasons. A good structural framework anchors the garden and becomes a backdrop which can act as a foil for plants.

Autumn is a good time to view the garden and assess what is needed and if changes are required. This means pruning deciduous woody plants, moving shrubs and perennials while the soil is still warm and plants can still put down their roots and establish themselves before the cold of winter. When leaves fall the structure of the garden is revealed, and this is when the choice of plants can be the most important. Perhaps more than at any other time in the year, shrubs come into their own, providing much needed structure when the garden is bare. Large-leaved plants like fatsia attract attention, while smaller evergreen leaves might recede. The row of old gnarled oak trees frames the view down the hill and across to the beautiful fields and trees. This is a treasured view whatever time of year.

Within the garden there are views and vistas and these too can change as plants grow, so need to be assessed and even added to. I use large plants to create an impression of size and underplant with smaller plants. For rhythm and flow I use distinct plants with architectural interest, such as actinidia, which give height and form to the mixed border, and use other flower shapes and colours around them. Mag liked forget-me-nots and filled borders for a mass of colour. I'm not sure she would approve of my love of wild flowers in the borders. Many plants self-seed in unlikely spots, creating their own paintable designs. Foxgloves, poppies, larkspurs, honesty, columbines, periwinkles, violets, buttercups and forget-me-nots are prolific self-seeders. I like blue, lilac, white, pale pink and pale yellow in the shady areas, which sing out against the dark background. A dash of red among greenery can be enticing. This is all part of the design.

Another aspect in the garden is to have seating areas. I like to sit in shady places and paint, read, entertain or contemplate. At breakfast time the garden has a completely different atmosphere from that of lunchtime, when shadows retreat and everything is more vivid. The shade changes through the day, so I am fortunate enough to have a choice of inviting seating areas.

Introducing new points of interest can give the garden a new lease of life, a new focal point to entice and intrigue. Some of the most enchanting garden areas are in corners where incidental natural plants like poppies and foxgloves can create beautiful scenes, ready to paint. However, these corners can often be full of unwanted brambles and nettles, so this is similar to designing a painting, deciding what makes a good scene, what is wanted and what is not. Composition is primarily about colour, balance, shape, size, height and interest. In a similar way the power of suggestion is a subtle and effective way of adding interest, whether it be in a painting or a garden. Leaving a garden gate slightly ajar is an enticing invitation leading from one part of the garden to another. Here style is important as a simple wooden gate reflects a cottage-garden style, while a more elegant gate is more suitable for a formal setting. Steps in the garden create interest and a sense of mystery, leading the viewer on into another area of the garden. Curved steps add to the charm, as their destination is concealed, creating a sense of anticipation. They are strong design elements in themselves. Wide steps impart an air of elegance, while narrow steps are more intimate and suited to an informal setting.

The working area of the garden has a charm in itself. The garden shed is part of the design, painted a beautiful blue, which sits well with the greens of the vegetables. It is more than a place of storage for pots and tools.

My ideas are derived from nature and are painted in a realistic manner. I sometimes work on several studies of the same subject simultaneously, varying the compositional elements, vantage point, the colour and values, or anything else which is envisaged.

Style of painting, as in gardening, is not necessarily something the artist or gardener sets out to achieve as it is within the individual. It is inbred, but also one learns to express a personal style just by experience. Even good drawing and colour need an arresting design. Drawing is the most important part of the painting as it is a means of exploring and becoming acquainted with the subject. Drawing is the foundation of the picture and establishes the composition, which must be considered before proceeding.

Drawing en plein air brings a much deeper understanding of the subject than working from photos. Working outdoors is the greatest training of all. When working in the garden one can change position to gain the right composition. Also changing the eye level can alter the emphasis and changing light can alter the tones, highlighting one area against another. Shadows can be used to lead the eye into the focal point, and half closing the eyes can help to assess values and shapes.

Good painting has a magical quality which is impossible to explain in words as it is unique to the artist and in the same way to the gardener.

THE GARDENER

Garden design is personal and unique. My garden is different from Mag's and again from Dad's. It is tempered by individual personality, ideas gathered from different sources and the needs of the position of the site, its soil and also weather. Most gardens have a structure on which to build, be it paths, hedges and plants, but both my gardens were fields with oak trees and metal fences. It can be a bonus to have a ready-made garden, but may be time consuming and expensive to repair. Fortunately, I had freedom to start afresh and transform my ideas into reality.

My first garden at Le Petit Bois Gleu in France was a field with old pollarded oaks, a boundary close to the house and a dilapidated hedge of hawthorn, blackthorn, bramble, lilac and discarded metal objects.

This is one of my first paintings of the garden in its wild state showing the gap in the hedge used by the wild animals.

The boundary was close to the house, so we asked the owner of the field next to us if it was possible to buy more land. At that time the large field held only five cows, which when called at milking time ran down the hill to the farm below. The farmer cut the thistles and nettles with a sickle; he checked his cows each day dressed in recycled clothes. His daughter took two pairs of trousers and made one so that the back was a different colour from the front. His tractor was ancient and chugged up the hill to bring water to the cows if the well went dry. He had no protection from the sun, so was as brown as a berry. He retired at eighty and one time when I visited to buy eggs from him, I felt retirement hadn't come easily to him as I found him head down sitting on a plastic chair in his kitchen. He and his daughter lived in two rooms – the kitchen and the bedroom. Saddened by the death of his wife twenty years before, and also now that he could no longer tend his farm, he died soon after.

When the farmer died his daughter rented out the land to a neighbouring farmer and arranged for us to buy the plot close to the house as the slate beneath the shallow soil could not be ploughed and was no use for cultivation. This gave us a better shape to the garden and more incentive to take out the old hedge in the painting, which we did by hand. As we worked, the hedge sparrows moved further along to the other trees and we noticed the lack of wind protection. I fancied a plaited willow hedge along the new boundary, which was fine in the winter but by May was wilting badly in the dry soil and by June was dead. We then planted yew trees, but the new tenant farmer measured the distance to the limit and told us to move them as we were fifteen centimetres too close to the boundary! In France each neighbour must plant so far out from the boundary so as not to interfere with shading of crops or depleting the other side of sun or rain. We moved the trees.

We learned about the climate, changing seasons, soil in different parts of the garden, the plants, the ecology of the garden and the history of the place and the people. Various ideas emerged. The plan was to have sweeping drifts of the same plants along a border, creating flow and movement, with perennials, shrubs, trees and bulbs being the backbone to the plan from which new ideas could be developed. New inspirations and combinations to shape, texture and colour evolved, keeping ideas fresh and renewing the dream. The cows' concrete drinker became a fish pond, and the duck pond was planted with water lilies and irises and soon there were newts, frogs and dragonflies until the ducks arrived. Down the side of the pond we built steps and planted shrubs on either side, creating intrigue, hiding the steps and also giving shelter from the east wind.

The driveway used to be at the front of the house, so we dug out a bank by the roadside and made a parking area to the side of the house, then built a low wall and a hedge as protection against the north wind. We made a terrace at the south-facing front of the house, on to which open the doors of the hall, sitting room and bedrooms, which gives a sense of outside and it is a constant pleasure to look out on to the garden.

From our tiny garden in Devon, England, we had brought cuttings of roses, mallow and bergenia (elephant's ears). At the front of the house in Renazé were some ancient lavender bushes, from which I took cuttings for more plants, and mint, which was loved and still spreads happily in among its neighbours. A huge hydrangea blocked the steps to the main south-facing entrance, growing, surprisingly, in full sun and dry earth. The rampant vine had so much fruit that we cut off the grapes with shears and later pruned and tied it back so that it runs across the tops of the doors and windows. I planted an Albertine rose cutting, which grows up and around the dormer windows, giving us a breathtaking display of pink flowers in May and filling the house with its delicious scent. I later took more cuttings, which I grew with an actinidia, a present from friends from Devon. The combination of pink roses and the pink splash of the actinidia is stunning.

Cuttings were taken from the vine, a sweet white dessert grape, and grown on the north side of the house, where it now produces fine plump grapes until the birds and insects find them. I always marvel at the magic of germinating seeds and cuttings, which form roots and grow into wonderful plants. The Albertine and the vine, both sun-loving plants, thrive on the north side of the house, where there is more moisture. Eventually, herbaceous borders were created containing lilies, roses, echinops, dahlias, cosmos, lavender, mallow, buddleia, delphiniums and red-and-yellow red-hot pokers. Various focal points, such as sculptures, benches, water features and a summer house were placed amid the floral displays to create room-like areas where artists could enjoy painting. The planting is not symmetrical, but more of a free-fashion cottage-garden style. This changes as plants mature and more are added. Gardening is similar to composing living pictures in a multidimensional art form. Most winter jobs, such as laying on compost, are best done when the soil is in a workable condition. In a heated environment, seeds can be sown, but care must be taken that there is sufficient temperature and not too little or too much water. Seed potatoes are available in January and can be chitted in readiness for planting out in March. To do this, the potatoes are set out in single layers with the eye ends uppermost and kept in a light position in a frost-free place. This encourages the production of sturdy young shoots. The eyes should be limited so that shoots grow more sturdily. In some mild winters, many plants continue to grow, and in fact one February the bananas in my garden were still pushing up leaves until the north winds brought cold and ice. Snow can be good for the plants as they are protected from frost and cold winds. Mag wrapped her greenhouse in polythene to protect her plants, whereas I use mine more like a cold frame in winter. I have a polythene tunnel, where the temperature is maintained. I make sure that it is ventilated to allow for air circulation to prevent a stagnant atmosphere and disease. If the weather permits, some pruning can be done to summer-flowering shrubs, such as buddleia, davidia, caryopteris, *Hydrangea paniculata*, potentillas and hardy fuchsias. These are all shrubs which flower on young wood, which will grow over the next few months.

My love for flowers began with my grandparents, who loved their garden. Grandfather grew roses and sweet peas for Grandmother and huge cultivated chrysanthemums, which he sold to the local flower shop. Grandmother gave the beautiful blue hydrangeas, which grew magnificently in the border, with tea leaves. The wall of the house was covered in roses and the scent drifted in through my bedroom window. Wonderful memories of scent and the sweet song of the blackbird which sang from the branches of the roses.

LATE WINTER AND EARLY SPRING

Spring brings the promise of a new start with the air full of fragrance, the birds singing cheerfully and bees emerging to enjoy the first pollen in blossoms bursting forth. The perfume has been savoured many times before, but there is great pleasure when sitting in the garden drawing or painting these gorgeous flowers.

JASMINUM
Jasminum nudiflorum (winter jasmine)

The Painting

Painting and drawing outdoors can be the most exhilarating and exciting experience, but also challenging and unpredictable as the weather and light can change quickly, especially in winter. Painting en plein air can be difficult at first, but it is a more satisfying way of painting as the artist is directly involved with the subject. When painting outdoors and directly from nature, it is necessary to keep it as simple as possible. Working in direct sunlight can make it difficult to assess colour and tones, which can look completely different when back in the studio, but paintings are fresher and more spontaneous when painted outdoors.

Everything in painting is about relationships, so I judge each area by its relationship to the surrounding areas. Each petal relates to its neighbour. The bright sunshine brings out the vibrancy in colours and the varied, subtle shadows. The sharper contrasts provide a wider tonal field to give interest to the final image. Painting flowers is synonymous with colour and watercolour can be delicate, or saturated colour. This painting is of a deciduous shrub of loose, rambling shape, with glossy leaves. The yellow flowers are one of the best and most cheerful of midwinter-flowering, hardy shrubs, though they are scentless unlike summer jasmine.

The Gardener

Within the jasmine group there are winter-flowering and summer-flowering varieties. Some are scented, others odourless. *Jasminum nudiflorum*, the winter jasmine, has a wealth of bright-yellow star-shaped flowers on bare arching stems, though the young growth stays fresh green in midwinter, and is reliable whatever the weather from November to February. Each dangling shoot which touches the ground will root, forming another plant. It grows well in any position, even on a north-facing wall, trailing over banks and walls or trained up through a trellis. It is perhaps surprising that a large number of shrubs, plants and bulbs flower in the winter. Winter jasmine can be pruned as soon as flowering has finished. The old wood should be cut out, thin branches pruned and young green branches, which will produce new shoots and flowers, trained so that they are manageable within a framework. After pruning, a mulch of garden compost should be added. This stimulates the plant into producing a new crop of green stems, which root at the point of contact within a few weeks. If the old wood is not pruned it can quickly get out of order and become a tangled mass choked with dead shoots.

Jasmine was found in 1845 growing near Shanghai by Robert Fortune, who was collecting on behalf of the Horticultural Society, although jasmine was not on his list of plants to find.

In the language of flowers, jasmine is 'voluptuous love'.

Delicate flowers have more impact if grouped together and will last longer in winter than in summer and give so much pleasure and seem to welcome the arrival of spring. Plants chosen for their winter foliage – for example, hebe – will flower in summer, as will shrubs chosen for berries. Winter flowers are a reminder of how beautiful nature can be in the depths of austerity. The winter garden has aconites, snowdrops, hellebores, hardy cyclamen and small blue iris planted where perennials can take over once the flowers fade. The hardy cyclamen flowers from autumn followed by hellebores, aconites and snowdrops, then crocuses, anemones and daffodils.

DAPHNE BHOLUA
Nepalese paper plant

The Painting
Once I had established where the drawing of the flowers and leaves were to be, I wet around them and dropped into it various greens and blues so that the colours merged to give a soft appearance. When the wet-in-wet background was dry, I used the same greens in the leaves and darkened shadowed areas with violet, which was used in the flowers. These were painted with soft edges around the petals, darkening in the centres of each bloom.

The painting has the appearance of hovering in space, but I liked the effect and didn't want to complicate it with details of the rest of the surrounding plant. An idea would be to do a similar painting and experiment with more blooms and leaves around the central flowers.

The Gardener

This was Mag's favourite winter-flowering shrub. Its powerful intoxicating scent fills the air especially if planted in a sheltered place. It has a dense growing habit, is semi-evergreen with glossy foliage and clusters of flower buds which open to near white and last from December until March.

It is native to the Himalayas, from Nepal to Southern China. At lower levels it is found in forests and is evergreen, but at higher altitudes it is deciduous and found in pasture and grassy glades.

Daphne Bohlua is in the family Thymelaeaceae. It is one of a number of species which are used in traditional papermaking in Nepal, hence its common English name of paper daphne. The inner bark also has a fibre used to make rope. All parts of the plant are poisonous, but the bark and roots are used in traditional medicine in Nepal to treat fevers.

It would not like the conditions in my garden, which can be hot and dry in the summer and does not supply the steady supply of moisture in the growing season.

HELLEBORE

Helleborus niger (the Christmas rose); *Helleborus orientalis* (Lenten rose); *Helleborus foetidus* (stinking hellebore, bear's foot)

Paintings 1 and 2

Painting white flowers means looking carefully at the tones, so, for example, if the petals are against a dark background, the white will appear brighter and lighter. All surfaces, even those that are not highly reflective, will pick up some colour influences from the prevailing light and the surrounding colours. These hints of colour help to create the shape and modify the local colour. There may be traces of yellows and greens in the white and blue or purple tinges in the shadows and a touch of warmth where the sun catches on the outer edges of the petals. The flowers also cast shadows on the surrounding leaves helping to give the appearance that the flowers are in front of the leaves. Edge control, using both hard edges mostly in or near the focal point and soft edges helps the eye to move across the shapes and captures the

dazzling effect of sunlight on the most beautiful flowers.

The delicacy of the flower was accented by the complex dark background, which acts as a foil to the white petals. The grey-blue-purple of the background has varying degrees of cool and warm. This grey was diluted to use as soft shadows in the interior of the flower. While still wet a washy green was floated into the shadow. This acted as a link to the leaves. The minute spots on the inner petals meant careful and considered, delicate marks using the point of a fine brush.

The Gardener

As the sun warms the earth, hellebores bring colour to the slumbering garden and scent the air. Hellebores are one of the few plants which are at their best in winter, giving a bright, cheerful lift to the border. Most flower in winter or in very early spring. Different species can flower in succession from early winter to mid spring. They are hardy and grown mainly for their decorative foliage and striking heads of leafy bracts, and succeed best in well-drained soil. Home-made compost and leaf mould improves the texture of the soil and helps to promote new root growth, but they do not need manure or fertiliser. They are best in partial shade, and do not object to lime. Should they become very dry in summer, they can be either watered or given some mulch.

The Christmas rose (*Helleborus niger*) is the first hellebore to flower. It is a welcome beauty to the winter garden with its white bowl-shaped flowers and golden stamens, which may need protection to keep them unmarked. Neither the Christmas rose nor the Lenten rose are in any way related to true roses, but are herbaceous plants belonging to the buttercup family; the popular names have arisen because the flowers have a slight resemblance to single roses. It is this early flowering which makes them so valuable in the garden. Their attractive leathery leaves are deeply divided into seven or nine lobes and make slowly spreading clumps, thriving in shady places. These delicate-looking perennials are relatively easy to care for and come in many attractive shapes and colours. The 'petals' are sepals and are tough and protect the developing seed pods remaining until the seed ripens and falls. They grow best in part shade, but will tolerate full shade and should be left undisturbed for as long as possible.

The Christmas rose, named because its flowers grow with such purity and profusion during the shortest days of the year, is enshrouded in fable and legend of great antiquity. According to the Greek legend, the shepherd Melampus first realised its healing properties by observing its effect on his goats. Later, he is said to have used it successfully to cure the daughters of Proetus, King of Argus, of mental derangement by dosing them with milk of goats which had eaten the plant. The plant was formally known as Melampode after Melampus. Considerable ritual and ceremony attended the digging-up of roots in ancient Greece by the *rhizotomi* or root gatherers. A circle was made with the point of a sword around the plant and then prayers were offered while the black roots were lifted. Pliny, a physician of 1400 BC, used it to treat nervous disorders and hysteria. The Romans knew of the plant's curative powers. Belief in the plant's power to cure mania continued through the centuries and Gerard recommended it as 'good for mad and furious men, for melancholy, dull and heavy persons'.

The Christmas rose's round flower bud of blush pink forms deep in its crown in autumn and develops into pure-white flowers with clusters of yellow stamens at its centre from December to February, although it has been known to flower in my garden in late October. Its strong green foliage is itself attractive, even after the plant has flowered.

Propagation by seed is slow, but seedlings are more readily established than older plants and self-sown seedlings often succeed well. Strong, healthy stock can be increased by division of the roots, which should be done as soon after flowering as possible. Seeds should be collected and sown as soon as ripe.

The Lenten rose or Corsican hellebore (*H. orientalis*) has flowers varying from ivory white to deep maroon from March to April. Modern breeding has produced striped and spotted flowers, often flecked with crimson. Despite its name, it flowers from midwinter, sending up flowers and foliage on separate stems from February to May. It is a clump former with big, divided evergreen leaves.

The *H. viridis* flowers are few in a spreading, branched leafy cluster, half drooping, open cup-shaped and green. They are poisonous and violently purgative.

H. foetidus or stinking hellebore (an undeserved name) is also known by its various local names, bear's foot or setterwort. It is found growing wild in Europe. It is a tough architecturally handsome evergreen with finely divided attractive deep-green leaves, which make an excellent contrast to the clusters of numerous upright bright-green globular, bell-shaped flowers, sometimes edged with purple. It flowers in late winter and spring and is brilliant for early emerging bumblebees. It seeds everywhere. It has a floppy habit in northern climes, but is more upstanding in the Alps, so is best grown in partial shade so long as the soil is not too dry and is ideal between shrubs. They flower every year if left alone and given leaf mould after flowering.

All parts of the plant are poisonous. The poisonous glycoside persists in dried and stored plants. It was used in the past as a vermifuge and against lice, among other deseases.

H. lividus corsicus is evergreen with huge clusters of lime-green cup-like flowers which open as early as December or as late as May. In most years the stout flower stems above thick leathery leaves come into their full glory in spring.

Painting 3
Keeping a limited palette of the same pink, rather than adding yellows, has an harmonious effect. However, nature manages to put these colours together in a stunning way. A flat area of colour creates no particular spatial sense, but as soon as a second colour is added, there is an immediate reaction, which begins to suggest depth and shape. This may be an effect of light and dark with the lighter tone advancing from the darker tone, or a warm and cool colour contrast. The surfaces of petals and leaves, and the tonal modelling depend on how the light falls on them, and the direction, and the strength of colour quality. The quality of natural light changes according to the time of day and the season.

SPURGE
Euphorbiaciae, *Euphorbia*

The Painting

The painting process is a combination of wet-in-wet, wet-on-dry, glazing and alternating between warm and cool colours. Transparent paint and understanding the properties of the pigments are invaluable in making the right choices. The term 'artist's' attached to materials means superior quality. These superior pigments are incredibly strong and a little goes a long way. The colours are deep, luminous and wonderful to mix. Transparent paints are staining, which means the colours build much quicker when applied to dry paper. In this painting the dominant colour of green meant the subtleties in value changes were expressed in nuances of the different strengths of colour. The darker tones seemingly throw forward the lighter inner bracts, which are painted using thinner paint (more water) and a touch of yellow in the green. 'Contre-jour' means nearly everything in shadow with a halo effect of light. This also has the effect of merging and tonally blending the details, and shadows can be deep and full of colour. Light can be exhilarating, transforming the most mundane subject into a thing of beauty. Eugène Chevreul, the French chemist, observed that shadows are often tinged with colours complementary to the colour of the object casting the shadow. Chevreul's theory had a great influence on the Impressionist painters, who looked into shadow and saw a great wealth of colour.

The Gardener

The name euphorbia was given by Dioscorides, said by Pliny to have been given in honour of Euphorbus, physician to King Juba of Mauritania. There are 1,000 species widely distributed throughout the world, differing widely in habit and including annual and perennial herbs, shrubs and trees, many being succulent. The plants are characterised by a milky latex which exudes freely when they are damaged. It is often poisonous if taken internally and can be an irritant to the skin. The herbaceous euphorbias are native to warm temperate areas, especially the Mediterranean region, so are best grown in full or partial sun with sharp drainage and out of strong winds. They have striking foliage, which is all shades of green and yellow, white, purple and sometimes fiery red. The flowers are tiny and soon perish, but the raylet leaves, for which most euphorbias are grown, can generally be enjoyed for months.

Euphorbia cyparissas has little narrow leaves and turns bright yellow in the autumn. It loves hot, dry places, as does *E. epithymoides*, also known as

E. polychroma, and has lemon-yellow flowers in April which partner well with yellow primrose and yellow tulips or for contrast blue grape hyacinths, muscari and blue periwinkle.

E. griffithii has reddish-orange flowers in May and continues to flower throughout the summer.

E. sikkimensis has similar colour in the leaves and will grow in shady places. *E. helioscopia*, or sun spurge, is a usually unbranched annual with golden-yellow finely toothed leaves. *E. lathyris*, the caper spurge, is a robust biennial with a stout erect stem to one metre or more. The fruits are acrid and poisonous. *E. martini* is an evergreen with showy acid-green upright bracts and a red centre. Some euphorbias can become leggy, but this variety looks good even when not in flower.

E. wulfenii is a small shrub with large heads of yellowish-green flowers in April. They may contain both male and female flowers or be unisexual. The bracts are usually green or yellow but sometimes brilliantly coloured with the whole looking like a flower. They give a welcome show in winter being useful in the borders and rock garden, where they do well in dry places. Euphorbias like open situations, where after a few years they will form pleasing rounded clumps. Most flower in spring like *E. robbiae*, which has bright-green flowers and makes fine foliage. It is a good foil to mauve aubretias, blue forget-me-nots, purple heuchera, yellow primroses and orange wallflowers.

Most can be divided. They can be propagated by cuttings and will strike readily in heat. It is best to wear gloves as they have irritating sap. They can be raised from seed, but the capsules should be protected when nearly ripe as they are explosive and the seed can be shot quite a distance. The seeds have a drastic purgative action. They have been used as a fish or arrow poison in the past. Seeds are generally white or cream-coloured and are fragile so can easily be crushed. Water is absorbed into the seed at the time of germination. They need plenty of light and water when growing, but after flowering can be kept drier. They can also be propagated vegetatively, either by splitting the crown or by taking advantage of 'tillering', which is the formation of above-ground shoots from a node located at the base of the principal shoot. Watering must not be excessive, except after transplanting.

Painting 2

Smyrnium perfoliatum is a welcome sight in spring and a blessing for early insects, like bumblebees. This was painted with the leaves and flowers defined, but the background quite loosely in very limited colours – Winsor Yellow, Ultramarine Blue, and consequently green and Ultramarine Violet.

The Gardener

In spring, if the weather permits, hardy border plants which have not been disturbed for several years can be lifted and divided. This can be done by prising the root clumps apart by using two forks back to back. The small pieces of root are then transplanted in prepared ground, adding garden compost and, if possible, some fertiliser and bonemeal.

For most plants, the longer they are in leaf the better they will flower in the following year. Many spring-flowering plants and bulbs grow quickly in spring using reserves built up in the previous year. The plants use these reserves to flower and by letting the leaves go on as long as possible with adequate spring and summer moisture. If soil is moist in winter and dry in summer then plants from Europe and North America will do best. They tend to flower in spring before tree leaves shade the ground and are adapted to drier soil in summer.

In spring plants to divide include monarda, lupins, Michaelmas daisies, heleniums, rudbeckias, delphiniums, sedum, phlox, achillea, echinops, Shasta daisies and chrysanthemums.

SNOWDROP
Galanthus nivalis. Gala means milk and *anthos* means flower; *nivalis* means 'of the snow'.

The Painting

Watercolour is generally a transparent medium and transparency can depend on the amount of water used. The dilution of pigment with water enables the whiteness of the paper to show through and in doing so lightens the tone of the pigment. Snowdrops are predominantly but not exclusively white with green. To paint white flowers, the white of the paper is most important, but attention must be given to observing shadows and subtle changes in tone. The spaces between the flowers, leaves and stems are as important as the flowers themselves. They are referred to as 'negative spaces' and can provide sparkle and interest. There are many whites and they affect one another, as do all colours.

Painting from light to dark means properly relating one colour or value to another and not being confused by the white of the paper. I like to place an area of the darkest value so as to relate the lighter tones to it as I paint. Once the larger areas are painted it is easier to assess the values and concentrate on the details. There is simplicity in the sense of clarity, of thought and content, and this close connection with the subject gives a sense of intimacy. Even the most complicated compositions with enormous amounts of detail originate from a simple idea.

The Gardener
As in painting, white gardens needs careful planning as one white may make a neighbouring white appear grey or washed out.

The common snowdrop was given its title, *Galanthus nivalis*, by Swedish botanist Carolus Linnaeus in his *Species Pantarum* of 1753. Galtonia is the snowdrop named in honour of Francis Galton, 1822–1911, who advanced the fingerprint of snowdrop identification. Once a new breed of bulb was sold for £725.

They are closely related to hyacinths. Fragrances range from honey through almond to violet. They can be differentiated in three main ways: by their foliage, which may be applanate, plicate or convolute; by their flower form, which may be single or double; and by distinctive markings on their outer and/or inner petals. Snowdrop leaves contain an antifreeze so their cells do not collapse when they thaw after severe cold. The delicate-looking but weather-hardy snowdrops are one of the few plants that flower in winter indifferent to bleak surroundings. They represent hope as they are the first to announce the coming of longer and warmer days. They are natural plants of mountain and woodland, thrive in cool, moist conditions and cannot be coaxed to grow unless they choose, but once settled they will flourish and multiply. Snowdrops are most effective in drifts among shrubs or in glades of deciduous trees, where winter sunlight becomes available once the leafy canopy above them has disappeared. Then they lie dormant when the foliage regrows. A hundred snowdrops dotted about are almost invisible, lost in the undergrowth, but group them together and they become a drift of snowy-white flowers. Grouping them together is therefore practical as well as aesthetic. Where there is minimal competition from larger plants, they build up colonies by seed and multiplication of bulbs. Although associated with woodlands, snowdrops are just as happy in an ordinary garden and can grow and flower better when planted in a sunny area in fertile soil. They struggle if planted in dense shade under evergreens. It is one of nature's miracles that the snowdrop cleaves its way through bitter earth before winter is out. They have evolved to survive with the bulb storing enough energy to push through the soil. Over millions of years, snowdrops have adapted to cope with prevalent weather conditions. The snowdrop is a pendulous flower with inner sections protected from storm and winds and also offers protection to pollinating insects. The temperature inside the flower is degrees higher than outside, where the nectar is available and ripe pollen released. The stigma and stamens hang from the ovary and are protected by three inside petals, often with green, occasionally yellow, markings.

G. nivalis is the commonest self-naturalising type spreading through the garden. It is sterile, but increases from offsets, and because it does not produce seed the flowers last an extra-long time. *G.* 'S. Arnott' is exceptionally successful, being tough and strongly scented. They flower, set seed and hibernate. *G. caucasicus* is the earliest-flowering snowdrop and continues to flower even when clumps are left for years.

Snowdrops will colonise quickly of their own volition, either by seed or by their bulbs dividing spontaneously. Propagation is by clump division after flowering, replanting immediately, or sowing seed as soon as they are ripe. The seed will germinate in the spring. Hybrids often occur when several species are grown together. Another way to propagate is to take pairs of scales of the bulb and place them in a damp environment to encourage each set of scales to make new bulbs. Remove the outer brown scales and dead tissue, keeping the basal plate intact. Slice off the nose of the bulb with a clean sharp knife. Cut the bulb vertically in half, then quarters. Each section must have a piece of the basal plate attached. Peel back pairs of scales from each piece, cutting them free at the base with a scalpel, again with a piece of basal plate attached. Place in a plastic bag and fill with air before sealing and labelling. Place in a warm (21°C), dark place for twelve weeks. When 'bulblets' appear at the base of the scales, pot them on individually, covered with their own depth of compost. If the scales have become soft, remove them from the bulblets before potting on. If the scales are still firm, or have roots coming from their base, leave them attached to the bulblets.

Like a lot of spring flowers, snowdrops can grow in almost all soil types with a range of situations, but prefer a rich soil with plenty of humus and leaf mould. Snowdrops can be difficult to establish, but once started they need little attention. There are single- and double-flowered forms, some with scented blooms. They have solitary, bell-shaped flowers with short green-tipped inner petals and long pure-white outer petals. Not all are white – some of the most unusual are those with different colouring, such as 'Spindlestone Surprise', which is a pretty golden-yellow shade and 'Wendy's Gold', with yellow-tinged leaves and stems. Leaves also vary. 'Pewsley Vale' has tiny leaves while 'Marjorie Brown' has blue-green tulip-like leaves and 'Corkscrew' has twisted leaves. 'Dionysus' has large, chunky flowers, the inner segments heavily marked with green, 'Tutu' has a double form notable for its neat-and-tidy appearance with dainty flowers and heavily marked central segments. They have a faint perfume as aloof as the flower. *G. candicans* has long funnel-shaped fragrant flowers. Some species like the autumn-flowering forms, such as *G. nivalis*, *G. corcyrensis*, *G. elwesii*, and the early flowering form of *G. caucasicus* grow best in full sun.

Enthusiasts, known as 'Galanthophiles', are constantly seeking out new forms and such is the passion for novelty that rare varieties can change hands for substantial sums of money. Some notable varieties include 'Bell Bishop', which has big flower heads that stay closed in a teardrop shape; 'Richard Ayres', a tall, vigorous, large double; 'Walrus', a slow grower with long tusk-like narrow green petals; 'Blewberry Tart', with twisted green petals; 'Lapwing', with beautiful markings; and 'Warley Longbow', with pointed flowers. 'Mighty Atom' has leaves and flowers like brushstrokes, whereas 'White Swan' has tall, elegant stems with drooping flower heads.

To promote the expectancy of spring, I grow snowdrops in planters and place them on the outside window sill. As windows in France open inwards, it is not possible to have flowers inside on the window sill, but it is possible to appreciate the delicate, nodding snowdrops from inside the house looking out. I pot up some bulbs and keep them in a cool place before transferring them into a cold frame to flower in January. They will not tolerate this for long, so are best planted out soon after the flowers finish. An adventurous early bee searching for nectar may find the snowdrop worth the journey.

Leucojum vernum, or spring snowflake, is closely related to the snowdrop, *Galanthus*. It is a bulbous perennial with usually solitary, or rarely two, white nodding bell-shaped flowers with yellowish tips to the segments, borne on leafless stems, all rising from a large bulb. They thrive in rich, moist soils and are well adapted for naturalising in the same way as snowdrops. They are increased by offsets, which should be secured as soon as the foliage ripens, or more usually by seed. *L. aestivum* is more robust with flowers borne in a cluster on a tall stem. Both like the damp, so I grow them by the pond.

After snowdrops, come the crocus, scillas, narcissus, wood anemones and aconites, and under the fruit trees are clumps of sweet violets.

CANDYTUFT
Iberis sempervirens (garden candytuft, globe candytuft)

The Painting

I love this complicated and tricky plant to paint as each petal is minute but forms the flower head. I was careful to indicate the petals, but had in mind the whole beauty of the plant. Strong darks behind the petals help to give shape and a feeling of light on the flowers.

The Gardener

The spreading evergreen of candytuft can seem to deepen the colours of other plants, enhancing the intensity of yellows and giving a clearer refreshing appearance to forsythia, wallflowers and doronicum. White flowers can look dramatic in moonlight when other colours vanish in the darkness.

Originally from Iberia, the ancient name for Spain, hence the genus *Iberis*, candytuft is a vigorous, spreading dark-green plant with milk-white flowers requiring full sunlight. It is a welcome flowering plant in January and, in my garden, blooms well into May. Iberis tolerates dry conditions, so is good for rock gardens, which is where mine succeed so well.

Deadheading prolongs flowering, and immediately after flowering the plant should be pruned. It can be propagated by seed or softwood cuttings, taken in summer. To collect the seeds, pods need to dry on the plant. They self-seed freely. If they outgrow their space, they can be divided, after flowering.

ORNAMENTAL OR FLOWERING QUINCE
Chaenomeles speciosa. Chaeno means to gape and *meles* means apple.

The Painting

The best time of day is when the flowers are backlit – usually early morning or late afternoon, when the sunlight is behind them. This brings out the most dramatic light and colour. Just for a few moments the effect is amazing, when the light shines through the petals and shadows merge down into the centre of the flower.

Painting with watercolour is painting with light, but also each stroke should be deliberate with care and concentration. The application of paint needs to be confident, decisive and free from hesitation. Time spent thinking and planning could take longer than painting and then waiting for paint to dry must be observed as it is too easy to add paint at the wrong time and lose freshness and bloom. The paint needs to be completely dry before adding further washes.

In this painting I wanted to celebrate the fabulous colours in the petals and used pure Permanent Rose, washy in some areas and thicker paint in the centres of the flowers and where some petals were shaded. The bright-yellow stamens exaggerate the intensity of the pink petals.

The Gardener

These are deciduous shrubs, hardy and easily grown in open, sunny positions or against walls or as a hedge. They are not particular about soil. Their loose, unstructured growth can sprawl, growing to a height of one to two metres. The flowers are in shades of red, pink, coral, rose or white and scarlet-crimson with five petals and grouped in clusters and, provided they are not heavily pruned, will produce quince fruits in the autumn. The spring flowers can open as early as January and appear before the leaves. The small quince-like or tiny apple-like fruit turn gold in autumn. They have an aromatic scent and are edible and when cooked can be used to make jelly, jam, and liqueurs which are harshly acidic. In medicine its special reputation is that it relaxes the tendons and muscles. This probably came from the ancient concept that sour taste softens the liver, with the liver belonging to the wood element – hence the name 'wood fruit'. The tendons were considered to be under the influence of the liver system.

Chaenomeles are deciduous, retaining orange fruits alongside the scarlet flowers in late winter. They should be pruned immediately after flowering so that they make flowering spurs. If not pruned they can look like a hedge. They are propagated by seeds or by layering.

Chaenomeles lagenaria, commonly known as flowering quince, Chinese quince or Japanese quince, is native to Japan, Korea, China, Bhutan and Burma.

IRIS
Iris reticulata

The Painting

The stunning colours and shapes of the iris are bliss for the artist. The effects of sunlight and shadows mean constant change throughout the day, when I watch for unexpected opportunities and try to be bold. A slight change of angle can make a difference in the design of the image and indicate the needs of the painting. This painting needed to be vibrant with rich tones and textures in a realistic and detailed style. There is a range of blues, from warm Ultramarine, which contains red, through to cool, yellow-influenced Phthalo and Cerulean. Cobalt Blue is in between these pigments and is closest to a pure primary blue, but it is easily overpowered by other colours. Cobalt Blue is transparent and non-staining, so is ideal for glazing and cooling. Ultramarine is a warm blue, veering towards violet. It is a strong sedimentary pigment and mixes well with other colours to make strong darks, subtle greys and mauves. I chose several blues, mostly Ultramarine, Cobalt Blue and, for the lighter areas, Cerulean, and violet for the dark interior. The yellow stripe is Lemon Yellow with a touch of orange floated into it when wet.

The Gardener

Iris histrioides flowers from November to April depending on the weather, but generally the best flower in February, bringing an uplifting, exciting sense to rock gardens and containers with their bright flowers. The beautiful purple petals each have a line of stunning gold made even brighter against the purple. The flowers appear before the handsome foliage. They are delicately scented with honey-lemon-vanilla-like perfume.

Iris is the Greek word for rainbow. In Greek mythology, the goddess Iris used the rainbow as her personal highway as she travelled from place to place delivering messages of love. Because of this, the iris flower is also considered the symbol of eloquence, communication and messages. The iris has been a treasured flower since ancient times, often appearing in Egyptian works of art dating as far back as the 28th Egyptian dynasty, around 400 BC. A flower carved into the Sphinx of Giza in Egypt is believed to be an iris.

Even though the month of February is often cold and grey, Valentine's Day makes it one of the most romantic months of the year. Because the iris is the symbolic flower of the Greek goddess Iris, who was also the messenger of love, it seems fitting that the elegant iris is the birth flower of February. Flower colours have symbolic meanings. Purple iris denotes wisdom and compliments; blue iris symbolises faith and hope; yellow iris stands for passion; and white iris symbolises purity. Traditionally, the iris symbolises eloquence, faith, wisdom and hope, much as February carries with it the promise that spring will soon return.

CROCUS
Crocus

The Paintings

When working outside in the open one is more aware of the plants' surroundings and of perfume, movement of wind and changing light, unexpected insects, a bee or a butterfly landing on the subject. Even when painting flowers time and again, there is always something new to see and learn. I have to paint from the heart, to paint what I love. Painting honestly and being true to myself gives an ultimate sense of satisfaction.

Drawing is an important part of the process of looking and studying. When starting to paint, the first colour must be accurate as all other colours relate to it. This is more important than slavish detail, which does not necessarily make a better painting.

'Temperature' is the relative warmth or coolness of the colour. The family of cool colours are green, blue-green, blue, blue-violet, violet and red-violet. In these paintings the temperature is cool with the added warmth of the yellow, which is in the family of yellow-orange, red, red-orange, orange, yellow-orange, yellow and yellow-green. A powerful statement of colour, expressed through simplicity, is always effective. This makes for an interesting contrast without losing harmony.

The Gardener

Crocuses and snowdrops are invaluable for pollen and nectar needed for emerging queen bumblebees. Crocuses come from the mountainous regions of Southern and Eastern Europe and as far as China, so are hardy. They are some of the earliest spring flowers though there are several species that are autumn-flowering. The flowers are in yellow, blue, purple, lilac and white according to the species and variety. Some are only one colour, some are bicoloured and others are striped. All have thin green leaves with a faint white stripe. The leaves of the spring-flowering crocuses appear with the flowers. They are happy in the sun or dappled shade and, because of their natural habitat, will grow well in rockeries.

In his 1924 monograph, *Crocus and Colchicum*, bulb expert E. A. Bowles laments the fact that, of eighty species available, only three had then become favourites, all spring-flowering. He pointed out that Crocus *cancellatus* can flower in August, *C. speciosus* in October and both *C. sieberi* and *C. imperati* open in January. Crocus and colchicum are often confused. The crocus is an iris in the family Iridaceae while the colchicum belongs to the lily family.

Crocuses should be planted as early as possible in the autumn and thrive around the feet of deciduous shrubs or permanently situated herbaceous plants that cover a large space when in full leaf. It is very attractive to have a mass of differently coloured crocuses that have a fine effect, especially if planted in grass left unmown until the crocus leaves ripen. If planted deeply and permanently in such positions, dwarf-growing plants, such as saxifrages, may be placed above and the crocuses allowed to grow through. Their colours range from yellows and cream to pure white and pale mauve or violet-blues to deep purple. Some have distinctive markings of stripes or feather patterns.

Spring crocuses are useful for flowering in pots as long as the compost is free-draining. Placed in a light position in a cold frame and then outdoors or in a well-ventilated conservatory they will flower earlier than those in the open. Outside the picture window I have an attractive large blue pot into which I planted stunning white crocuses. As the snowdrops fade the fabulous blooms of crocus lift my heart, bringing another sensational display. *C. sieberi* 'Albus' is a lovely white species of crocus with long slender buds that open into a loose elegant flower with yellow anthers. They are especially effective planted in bold drifts. The individual flowers do not last long, but there is a succession which extends the season over a considerable period.

They can be propagated by seed to raise new varieties, but each year one or several young corms are formed either on top or by the side of the old ones, the latter annually dying away. For increasing stock, these may be lifted and replanted singly, allowing sufficient room for each in its turn to develop new corms. The following year more will be obtained by this method, which is better than if left crowded together.

Seed germinates freely and must be sown thinly, so as to allow the plants space to grow for two seasons in the seedbed without lifting. After the second year, when the leaves die down, the corms should be replanted and they will flower in their fourth year. In general the leaves should be left alone after flowering is over until they ripen, after which the corms need not be lifted and will develop naturally. Crocus seedlings descend about an inch and not always perpendicularly. They bury themselves deeper by forming a peculiar outgrowth called a starch root, which is a semi-transparent fleshy store of nutriment. The crocus at the ripening season loses the starch root, as its store of starch has been absorbed into a newly formed corm. The starch root withers and contracts and pulls the corm down lower into the space it once filled. The corms, by their mode of propagation underground, gradually become removed to a considerable distance from where they were first placed.

Crocuses have two seasons – late winter into spring, and the second in autumn. Some of the early group are *C. laevigatus* and *C. laevigatus* 'Fontenayi', sometimes flowering before snowdrops.

C. tommasinianus follows with its slender lilac-mauve flowers and is a good coloniser. The narrow leaves emerge in a papery sheath with a faint white stripe. The flowers are goblet-shaped and have six petals. As crocuses originate in mountainous regions of Southern or Eastern Europe, they are best grown in clumps on rockeries, but look good edging flower borders or in grass beneath trees, where they form groups.

In late winter months *C. chrysanthus* has bright-golden-yellow flowers appearing at the same time as the leaves. Numerous varieties are available with bicoloured petals in egg-yolk yellow, purple to smoky blue and bronze.

From early spring *C. sieberi* is pale mauve with a yellow throat. *C. ancryrensis* has rich yellow flowers in late winter and early spring. Birds often peck at yellow varieties, and mice and leatherjackets sometimes eat corms in the soil. *C. vernus* is the parent of the popular Dutch crocus, with colours ranging from white through silvery blue to violet.

Many of the species will grow well in the rock garden in soil which has a proportion of small stones intermixed, thereby ensuring good drainage.

In the wild, woodland trees, shrubs and flowers have an attraction for animals, birds and insects of all kinds looking for food, water, shelter and a place to breed. The domestic garden fulfils a similar need if it contains suitable plants. Living creatures will travel a long way in search of food and if a ready supply can be found in a garden, then it will become a hive of activity for many species and a fascinating source of interest and pleasure. Some of the traditional flowers, such as buddleias, known as the butterfly bush, are more attractive to bees, butterflies and other insects as they are rich with scent and nectar, unlike some more cultivated hybrid flowers with bigger and better blooms.

After the crocuses have flowered the early butterflies will visit alyssum, arabis, aubretia, polyanthus and wallflowers followed by honesty and sweet rocket, phlox, petunia, nicotiana, sedums, daisies and dahlias, all of which are attractive because of their abundant nectar.

Ladybirds may spend the winter clustered closely around older stems of roses. The lacewing, with its light-green, lace-patterned wings, is a pretty insect related to the dragonfly. Its larvae cover themselves with the skins of their dead victims.

GLORY OF THE SNOW
Chionodoxa

The Painting
The petals were wetted and Cobalt Blue and Ultramarine Blue dropped in, with the centres left without any paint to retain the white. When dry I lifted off colour down the centre of the petals so that they were paler, though not as white as the unpainted paper. Yellow was added to the middle of each flower head. I left the leaves simple so that the flowers stayed the main focus of the painting. The dark leaves help to show the paleness of the petals.

The Gardener
The flowers of *Chionodoxa* are similar to those of *Scilla*. *C. forbesii*, or glory of the snow, is a perennial in the family of Asparagaceae, subfamily Scilloideae. The name of glory of the snow is based on the flowers in high alpine zones when the snow melts in spring. The name glory of the snow is derived from the Greek words *chion*, meaning snow, and *doxa*, meaning glory. The genus is endemic to the East Mediterranean, specifically Crete, Cyprus and Turkey. They should be planted while dormant in late summer or early autumn. Racemes of star-shaped blue, white or pink flowers appear in early spring, the colour enhanced by the small clear white throat. The basal leaves are linear and mid green. In milder climates, they bloom earlier than in their native habitats. They require light when in growth, but can be grown under deciduous trees or shrubs, as their foliage dies down after flowering in early spring.

EARLY SPRING

Every day new pictures unfold as shoots emerge, buds swell and flowers stun with their beauty.

WILD HYACINTH
Scilla (squill or wild hyacinth)

The Paintings

Painting in natural light creates intensity and the play of light reveals the translucency of the petals and produces interesting tones. Apart from the pleasure I find in my garden, there is also a calmness which puts all worries into proportion. Gardening and painting blot out the stresses and strains of the real world. These lovely little pyramids of delicacy give so much pleasure. They were painted in much the same way as the chionodoxa.

Scilla has beautiful blue flowers. I started the painting with a light-green wash over the whole area, leaving the lighter petals as white paper, which were then painted with Cobalt Blue and Ultramarine Blue for the darker interiors and shadowed areas. The leaves were painted with the same green used in the initial wash, but in a thicker consistency, and a little Winsor Red was added for the shadows. The stems were a mix of red and green darkened in places. I then decided to deepen the interior shadows behind the leaves with Ultramarine Blue. This also acted as a link between leaves and flowers without it being intrusive.

The Gardener

Scilla is a genus of about fifty to eighty perennial bulbs in the family Asparagaceae, subfamily Scilloideae. *Galtonia candicans,* known as galtonia or summer hyacinths, are native to woodlands, subalpine meadows and seashores throughout Europe, Africa and North America. Their flowers are usually a penetrating blue, but there are white, pink and purple types known, flowering in early spring with a few flowering in autumn.

S. amoenia has bright-blue flowers and *S. peruviana* has white, red and lilac flowers known as 'Alba', 'Elegans' and Glabra'. The scillas are a varied group, ranging from the little Siberian squill, *S. siberica,* which has sprays of deep-violet-blue flowers in February. The scilla family includes the English bluebell, *S. non-scripta* and the Spanish bluebell, *S. hispanica*, which has larger, stiffer flower spikes of pink, blue or white. *S. tubergeniana* has pale-blue, dark-striped flowers and *S. bifolia* has loose racemes of nodding gentian-blue flowers or white flowers (*S. bifolia* 'Alba').

The hardy scilla are among the most beautiful of spring flowers, reminiscent of bluebells. They need to be planted in autumn in ordinary soil, in a sunny position, but will tolerate some shade, and any soil as long as it's not too wet. Do this when the bulb is resting. When they seed they naturalise in the borders, but do not become an invasive problem.

Other good ground-cover plants are violets in shady places and alpine strawberries.

ANEMONE BLANDA
Anemos means wind (windflower).

Painting 1

Painting flowers involves a whole range of technical and analytical aspects of tonal values, colour, form, light and space while at the same time drawing on the flowers' infinite diversity of shape, scale and colour. Apart from their beauty it is a whole learning experience observing the life cycle from bud through blossom to seed.

A group of blue blooms may have an effect of cold, but with the addition of yellow, the overall impression is now one of warmth and subtlety. In this painting the yellow of the stamens is echoed in the background. Plants in the foreground can be the main feature with the middle background toned down in tone and colour. The painting should be composed so that the main interest is in the focal area, and all supporting elements lead back to this point. The greater the tonal contrast in the focal point, the more interesting it becomes and therefore brings the eye back to that point. It is essential that there is no conflict of interest between the focal point and its surroundings. When painting quickly, an uncompromising fluidity results. Spontaneity brings a lively, fresh look.

Painting 2
One of the keys to success in watercolour is to understand how to mix colours. Combining only two colours preserves maximum transparency. A limited palette is essential as too many colours can confuse. Combining colours optically rather than physically in the palette, a composite and more complex colour is

created. The Impressionist technique was to paint wet-in-wet or direct painting, where colour is made by mixing wet paint – for example, blue mixed with yellow creates green. Optical mixing is based on wet-over-dry or indirect painting. Colours are laid down and then, when dry, another colour is scumbled over. If using blue and yellow, this does not produce green, but the two colours produce a unique colour as seen in the close view of the centre of the flower. The complementary colours blue and yellow give an appearance of green even though it is an impression.

There is an impression that artists reproduce exactly what they see, but great artists like Turner used complementary schemes as in *The Burning of the House of Lords and Commons*. The contrast of orange-yellow cloud against a bright-blue sky gives a brighter image because the colours are complementary. Complementary colours can create striking optical effects.

The Gardener
The unfurling leaves of spring are as exciting as the burst of colour when the flowers open for the first time. Starry blue flowers in early spring emerge from slender strappy leaves. They prefer a position in full sun or part shade in well-drained soil.

The greens of spring provide a wealth of delights. Anemones are spring flowers and thrive in sun in warm, open sites flowering from winter to spring, and if left undisturbed will form an intensive carpet. *Anemos* is the Greek for wind. All the windflowers have a short life. In classical mythology, Anemone was a nymph beloved of Zephyr. Jealous Flora banished Anemone from her court and changed her into a flower, which always blooms before the return of spring. Zephyr abandoned this unfortunate beauty to the rough caress of Boreas, the north wind, who failed to win her love but still disturbs her emotions, so that she blooms too early and therefore fades more quickly.

The red anemone, the flower of Holy Week, grew at the foot of the Cross on Calvary, and was believed to have been turned from white to red by the blood of Christ. It abounds in Palestine and is thought to have been the original of the 'lilies of the field' or 'flowers of the field' in the Bible. Umberto, Bishop of Pisa, who arrived in the Holy Land just too late to be of any use when the Crusaders were returning home defeated, determined some good should come of his enterprise and so filled his ships with earth from Palestine, carried it to Italy, and filled the Campo Santo at Pisa with it so that the dead might lie in holy soil. There, within the cloisters, the scarlet *Anemone coronaria* was seen for the first time in Italy, having been imported with the soil. It was regarded as a miracle and it is more pleasing to think of the pleasure given to the living. The blood-red *A. coronaria,* or the poppy anemone, has single or double flowers. It looks even more startling in the company of its smaller-flowered pale-blue relation *A. blanda,* which flowers in early spring.

D. H. Lawrence wrote of the scarlet anemones growing wild in Tuscany: 'one of the loveliest scarlet apparitions in the world. It is just pure condensed red, of a velvetiness without velvet and a scarlet without glow.' He also wrote about the violet-coloured anemone, so splendid a foil for the scarlet: 'They are curious, these great, dark violet anemones. You may pass them on a grey day or at evening or early morning, and never see them. But as you come along in the full sunshine, they seem to be baying at you with all their throats, baying deep purple into the air.'

The *Anemone* genus is of about seventy species of mostly small perennial plants. Travellers brought back many different kinds during the reign of Queen Elizabeth I. At that time it had not been given its Greek name of anemone, but was commonly called 'rose parsley'.

Wood anemones, *A. nemorosa,* grow well under oaks, where the soil is dry and nourishment is taken by the tree roots. The anemone sends out rhizomes underground, but above the tree roots. Japanese anemones, *A. hupehensis,* known also by their common name of windflower or thimbleweed, are also woodland plants and spread in the same way, by rhizomes. New plants can be propagated by root cuttings taken in autumn or winter. *A.* 'Scythinica' is a rich sapphire blue with pure glistening white within. There is also a rose-coloured form. A half-expanded flower showing the contrasting colouring is a beautiful sight. It is a fine plant for a sunny rock garden. In the rock garden this form not only thrives but seeds freely, and the young plants are as handsome as the parents. They need little care and attention and deliver psychedelic colours of cardinal red, purple, violet, white, shocking pink, and blue flowers ranging from lavender blue to deep ultramarine blue. It is best to buy when in flower to be sure of the colour.

Most anemones are hardy and will grow in ordinary garden soil. Some are better suited in a woodland soil. They are best planted in early autumn in an open, well-drained, sheltered position. Seed should be saved from the best anemones and as soon as ripe sown in a warm sheltered place in a well-prepared seedbed outside, or in pots under glass, covered lightly with sand and kept moist. The seeds are a little difficult to sow as the cottony down which adheres to them should be separated by rubbing them in dry sand. Successive sowings may prolong the flowering period.

PRIMROSE
Primula vulgaris

Painting 1
Exotic blooms and showy flowers make interesting paintings, and artists will always want to paint them, but beauty can also be found in the simplest flowers, as in primroses. The cool, acid greenish-yellows work well with plenty of surrounding green. Pure yellow works with almost anything, but too much yellow creates an unpleasant dazzle. Colour has many inferences. Certain strong colours or combinations of colour create a reaction. Van Gogh favoured strong complementaries, using red against green and blue next to orange, and in the painting of primroses and violas complementary colours give a lively but exciting combination. These are preferences and an expression of personality. The love of colour is a fundamental part of human nature and

is one of the most important components of visual communication. However, more colours do not lead to better paintings. Fewer colours are easier to control and more likely to create a harmonious colour unity. Complementary colours will create tension when placed next to each other as in the painting of yellow primroses and warm blue violets.

My garden has various features and areas almost like different rooms, each catching the light in a unique way which changes with the seasons. Having created the different areas, I still want to produce the emotion I feel and my own version in representational paintings. Often low level or dramatic light is of great interest. Morning and late afternoon sunshine emerging from the darkest rain clouds can be stunning, and to capture the drama is important, but these effects pass quickly. To analyse the colours I look for the properties of the yellow and surrounding green, further breaking it down to what type of yellow and whether it contains a touch of red or blue or whether it is a true yellow. This is called 'colour temperature' and is best understood by studying the base colour and determining how much red, blue or yellow is in the colour. In other words, whether the yellow leans toward red or towards blue.

It is always interesting that distance appears bluer than foreground, but it is necessary to understand the relationships between colours. This is very important. The pictorial arrangement of colour depends where the focal point is placed. If it is in the middle ground, then both the foreground and the background need to be carefully adapted to focus on the focal point. The foreground must be painted in a way that suggests its closeness, but leads the eye towards the middle ground.

The Gardener

The primrose is the traditional symbol of spring and represents early youth. Its common name comes from the medieval Latin *'prima rosa'*, the first rose of the year, but in fact it is not a rose at all. *Primula* is the botanical name of the genus, which is a group of about 500 species. The name derives from the fact that they flower early: *prime* means first – hence primrose means first rose. Many grow in nature at high altitudes in regions where there is a dryish autumn followed by a long winter, during which they remain dormant. After their spring flowering, wet summer conditions promote full development of their foliage. Primulas have rosettes of leaves paler on the reverse, which appear dusted with white, hence its common name of dusty miller, with flowers on individual stems coming from the base.

P. auricula comes in purple, green and white. Auriculas are descendants of *P. auricula* and *P. hirsuta*, known as *P. pubescens*. It is smaller with violet, blue, rose, milky-white or dull-red flowers and was initially bred by Flemish weavers, fleeing religious persecution in the sixteenth century. There was fierce competition between Flemish weavers, who placed their best primroses to decorate their shop windows. To achieve these showpieces they tinkered with their plants' chemistry. *P. juliae* makes low mounds of neat, rounded leaves with almost stemless magenta flowers.

There are two kinds of flowers, externally apparently identical but inwardly of different construction, and only one kind is found on each plant, never both. 'Pin-eyed' flowers have a green knob of the stigma, looking like a pinhead, whereas the 'thrum-eyed' have five anthers in a ring around the tube, but no central knob. In the pin-eyed flowers, further down the tube there are five anthers hanging on to the wall of the corolla tube, while in the thrum-eyed flower at this same place is the stigma knob. At the bottom of the tube in both is the seed case surrounded by pollen. It was Darwin who pointed out the reason for this is that only long-tongued insects, such as bees and moths, can reach the nectar at the base of the tube, which means while collecting the nectar the pollen is rubbed on the middle part of the proboscis from the anthers midway down the tube. This is repeated as the insect goes from flower to flower, and pollen in turn is transferred to the stigmas of both kinds of flower, causing cross-fertilisation. For example, a butterfly may visit a thrum-eyed flower wiping pollen off on to the top of its proboscis as it searches for nectar, which is then transferred on to the stigma of the next pin-eyed flower. On visiting a pin-eyed flower, pollen from the anthers halfway down the flower tube sticks to the middle of the butterfly's proboscis, which is then perfectly positioned to be wiped off on the stigma of a thrum-eyed flower.

They are slow to propagate but easily raised from seed, as are other primulas, and good forms may be reproduced by division of two or three old plants. The original woody parts should be discarded and the divisions replanted, watered with a liquid feed. It is essential that they do not dry out, though they need good drainage and good light but cool summer temperatures. They hate hot, dry weather, so are best placed in moist, woody loam or beneath evergreen shrubs or under thin tree cover. I grow them by the side of the pond and in shaded areas of the garden. In general primulas do best in some shade, especially in the hottest part of the day. When planted with other spring flowers, such as muscari, snowdrops, scillas, dwarf daffodils, anemones, violets, epimediums and pulmonarias, they make a wonderful show.

Polyanthus, meaning 'many flowers', refers to a plant with a stout stem carrying many flowers above the leaves like an oxlip or cowslip, from which they are bred. Both polyanthus and primroses are types of primula, the main difference between them being that primroses have one flower on one stem and polyanthuses have stouter stems each bearing a cluster of flowers. Primroses are graceful, but polyanthus make a more solid display. Primulas have a range of colours from white to cream, pale pink, lavender, deep orange, crimson and deep blue and both flower in spring. They are principally hardy and some, mainly larger herbaceous kinds, flower later in the year.

The primula season is a long one. There are many floriferous species that love a shady, moist place, and their foliage is usually bold and attractive after the flowers have faded. The primrose types are the primulas of spring, many of which are mountain plants and belong as single specimens in rock-garden crevices. The name polyanthus is used to describe hybrids of *P. vulgaris* and *P. veris*. Plants have up to twelve flowers held on a stout stalk, although the flat flowers, in a wide range of colours, may open before the stalk develops.

P. vulgaris and *P. veris* are woodlanders and ideal for block planting and are happy in country lanes and cottage gardens and climbing the banks of lanes and railway cuttings. They are at their most effective when planted with an almost mathematical regularity. The resulting flowering time is a carpet of blossom, and summer will see a continuous weed-smothering covering of green. By then the candelabra primula will be flowering. These carry their dainty flowers, red-purple or shell pink with dark eyes, in successive whorls up a long stem like a candelabra. They form a rosette of leaves around the upright flower stems. They spread by self-seeding.

P. japonica and *P. pulverulenta* both have magenta-crimson flowers and are excellent waterside plants.

The primrose has leathery, wrinkled, tongue-like, mid-green leaves. Pale-yellow, creamy-yellow or blue flowers flattened into five petals with a central eye nestle among clumps of leaves on frail stalks. They are successful self-seeders and grow in damp shaded places, in ditches alongside lanes, and flower as early as January, sometimes December. Seeds of this hardy, strong-growing species may be sown in the autumn in a frame or in pots outside and covered with sheets of glass. Most will germinate in the following spring, and when large enough the seedlings can be potted on and planted out the following August. They will be well established before winter and most will flower in the next spring. Strong-growing primulas and polyanthus primroses form large tufted crowns which can be propagated by division. It is easy to make more plants by this method in late summer, when the foliage is fully grown. Primroses have a rootstock, knotty with the successive bases of fallen leaves, and it has branched rootlets on all sides. I lift the plant and pull off individual plantlets where the leaves join the stem, making sure each has a root system and each has a terminal rosette of leaves attached. I then replant them immediately, into their new site, watering well, especially if the weather is hot and dry.

Both root and flowers of the primrose contain a fragrant oil, primulin. The whole plant is a sedative and in modern days a tincture of the fresh plant in bloom is used for sensitivity, restlessness and insomnia. Pliny speaks of it as almost a panacea used as an antispasmodic, a wormer, an emetic and an astringent. Culpeper said, 'The leaves of Primrose make a fine salve to heal wounds.' In ancient cookery the flowers were added to a pottage of rice, almonds, honey and saffron and called 'primrose pottage'. It is also said to be a soothing and very versatile herb that calms the nerves, eases headaches and acts as a mild sedative and tranquilliser. It is also thought to relieve lung congestion and ease bronchitis and to act as an anti-inflammatory.

Painting 2

The vibrant colours in the planting inspire the heart and the painting must capture this relationship. Sometimes yellow and pink do not sit well together, but with strategically placed foliage between these colours there is a sense of harmony. The yellows and blues appeal more to the excitement of a creative spirit and inspire the artist to paint more vividly with the background in soft muted colours. This means that the paint was thicker in the foreground and a lot more washy in the background.

A yellow garden can be varied as there are so many qualities of yellow, but they look wonderful together. The colour yellow shows up in the dusk almost as luminous as a white border, yet has none of the flatness by day. This painting was inspired by the brilliance of the yellow, while the darker leaves are more muted in the subdued light. I chose to use a dilute Lemon Yellow pigment, which is a cool yellow, and then added a thicker mix in some flowers. Lemon Yellow is a clear bright semi-opaque yellow.

Other yellows in my palette include Aureolin, known as Cobalt Yellow. This is an intense colour. Aureolin superseded Gamboge, the best bright Transparent Yellow, which was a gum. Less expensive and more light-fast Cadmiums were introduced in the late nineteenth century. New Gamboge is a warm yellow resembling the genuine and toxic Gamboge. Quinacridone Gold is a dark warm Transparent Yellow. Winsor Yellow is a warm yellow and semi-transparent, and Indian Yellow is a vibrant yellow.

The Gardener
Primula polyanthus is a hybrid of the primrose and the oxlip and is an enormous genus of hardy and half-hardy

46

perennials, but polyanthus are usually grown as biennials. It was developed from the common primrose, *P. vulgaris*, or *P. acaulis*, and the cowslip, *P. veris*. Plants of this cross are fairly common in natural situations where the two species meet, and are known as oxlips. It was not until coloured forms appeared, as distinct from the yellow form, in about the middle of the seventeenth century, that the polyanthus was produced. Its development was slow, but eventually rapid in the mid-eighteenth century. The standards set up by the old florists were rigid. The flower stems must be strong and elastic; the pedicels should be stiff and so proportioned that all flowers have room to show themselves without overlapping and form a close compact truss of not fewer than seven all alike in colour and form; the calyx should be large, quite round, perfectly smooth at the edges and lie quite flat. Its tube should be a fine yellow, perfectly round and well filled with six anthus, hence the name polyanthus. The eye should be a perfectly round, clear, bright, rich yellow forming a complete circle; the ground colour should be bright, rich and dark crimson. There is a wide range of colour from white to deep purple, giving a display lasting many weeks.

The old florists carefully pollinated their plants by hand, but present-day strains seed very freely and give good results and are reasonably true to colour. Seeds should be sown in June as soon as the plant is ripe. They germinate quickly and given a shady spot will flower the following spring. If sown later, then a season will be lost. Sowing in a seedbed kept moist in the open is best. If sown into boxes, the seedlings should be pricked out when large enough to handle and planted in their permanent places. They will be well established before winter and most will flower in the following spring. They grow best in rich, moist soil and partially shaded. However, in my dry garden they disappear in the summer and regrow in the autumn. They may be increased by division after flowering or in the autumn, but plants derived from seed show greater vigour and flower more freely. They are among the best plants for spring bedding and naturalising in wild places. Good varieties may be increased by division after flowering or in the autumn, though seedlings of good strains usually show greater vigour and flower more freely than plants derived from division. It has large blooms in compact long-lasting clusters on tall sturdy stems. It has retained the characteristic bright-green corrugated leaves of the primrose. Hybrids bred from *P. vulgaris* are smaller than polyanthus primroses, with clusters of often stemless flowers.

There is no mention of it prior to 1564, but during the next 100 years gardeners busied themselves in its culture. Many of the loveliest came from Ireland, where soil and climate provide all it needs. They grow in a wide range of colours – white, yellow, pink, peach, bronze, lilac, crimson, purple, scarlet and mahogany. They may be simple, double or frilled, but the beautiful laced varieties bred for show have disappeared. In their heyday in the seventeenth and eighteenth centuries they were cultivated with great care and patience by artisan florists. They had splendid names, such as 'Darlington's Defiance', 'Fillingham's Tantararara', 'Mason's Black Prince', 'Eckersley's Jolly Dragoon' and 'Heapey's Smiler'.

Cowslips, *P. veris,* first cousins of the primrose and probable ancestors of the polyanthus, bear a strong resemblance to their relatives, but grow apart. Local English names remind us of the image of a bunch of golden keys: Our Lady's bunch of keys, St Peter's keys (which became Peterkeys or Peterkin), paggle, pen gulls, and cuckooboots, culverkeys, galligaskins, herb paralysy, paigle, palsywort, St Peterwort, fairy cups, crewells, crowstripling, horsebuckle and herb Peter. From Tudor times and before, to Victorian days, children and maidens gathered cowslips for spring festivals to toss as favours, calling them 'cowslip balls' or 'tossies'. Cowslip, from the Saxon word *cuslippe*, was from a supposed likeness of its perfume to the breath of cows.

When Queen Elizabeth I ruled England, the cowslip was one of the most prolific flowers to spangle the meadows in spring. In Elizabethan days a few new forms seem to have been cultivated, some with two- or three-tiered flower groups along the stems and known as 'hose' or 'in-hose'. Gerard and Parkinson, herbalists and gardeners, speak of a double form.

It is the nectar enfolded in these 'rubies, fairy favours' that imparts the delicate flavour to the amber-coloured cowslip wine, a dessert wine. An advert for Mott's Leicestershire cowslip wine ran 'for dinner, dessert or evening. Purest, brilliant slightly sparkling, delicious, wholesome and stimulating'.

Old cookbooks offer recipes for cowslip wine, all suggesting varying quantities of flowers, sugar and water, some adding oranges, some lemons, others brandy or Rhenish wine. They also have recipes for cowslip conserve, cowslip cream, puddings and tarts. There must have been fields covered in cowslips to accommodate such usage.

Cowslips – or peagles, from the Scottish 'paigles', as Culpeper called them – are well known. Both wild and garden forms are well known.

Their main attraction has been as a cosmetic, a cream or toilet water supposed to remove spots and wrinkles from the skin, for sunburn and freckles, and to promote beauty. They were also supposed to remedy all infirmities, such as vertigo, palsies, convulsions and cramps. Gerard confirms this: 'A conserve made with the flowers, prevaileth wonderfully against the palsie.'

By the eighteenth century the cowslip was out of fashion as a garden plant, having given way to the larger and showier polyanthus. Today it remains a much loved wild flower seldom seen in gardens.

Candelabra primulas have long stems on which are whorls of outward-pointing flowers.

P. pulverulenta has rich crimson petals and the stems are beautifully dusted with a white farina. Mixed-coloured candelabra primulas are best when scattered about in informal drifts. The hardy moisture-loving clump-forming primulas flower in early summer. They form a rosette of leaves around the upright flower stems. Drumstick primulas include *P. denticulata*, with ball-shaped clusters of flowers on upright stalks with rosettes of leathery leaves. The flowers are lilac to deep purple and can be treated as an annual or biennial and spread by self-seeding.

Asiatic primulas prefer cool climates, but this species thrives and seeds where it is much warmer as long as it has shade and moisture-retaining soil. There is a shell-pink form called 'Bartley Strain', which is one of the most lovely of all garden plants. From seed, eighty per cent or so will have flowers of an identical pink shade, but the rest will be the usual red of the species. Hybridisation is rife, so to retain the pink remove the red flowers or plants before they set seed.

P. bulleyana is another which will thrive in warmer locations. Its flowers are more rounded and are a soft yellow.

BERGENIA
Bergenia stracheyi (elephant's ears)

The Paintings

Through drawing, the eye can be trained to an exceptional level of ability. Learning to see as an artist begins first in the mind before being transferred to the hand. Building drawing skills is the first step towards becoming a representational artist and is the foundation of a successful painting. I try not to put too much detail in the drawing as this leaves an area to discover and create with paint and can lead to 'happy accidents' and unexpected nuances which a more conscious approach would miss. Nature will always be the ultimate source of inspiration, but assessing the painting in the studio is equally important. My aim is to capture my love of nature and the emotions it evokes, with the studio a place to assess colour harmonies. I usually stand paintings in a prominent place so that each time I enter the studio I can see them with a fresh eye.

Painting these flowers reminded me of painting chaenomeles, with the pink petals and bright-yellow stamens, but here the pink was more subdued so I used Quinacridone Magenta and added a little violet in the shadows.

Quinacridone colours are synthetic pigments giving exceptional colour fastness and are transparent. Permanent Rose is a bright transparent rose violet and is a Quinacridone pigment. Opera Rose is a vivid magenta colour.

It is sometimes only possible to paint for a short time before the light changes and the shadows move. Sometimes it is best to observe the subject at different times of the day to select the most opportune moment. In this painting the light was above and behind the plant, casting shadows in the interior of the flowers.

I used a mixture of cool green for the leaves and warm pink for the flowers. The pinks appear brighter and warmer with the light on the petals more resonant when placed against a cool background.

The Gardener

The name *Bergenia* is in honour of Karl von Bergen (1704–1760), physician and botanist of Frankfurt. It is a genus of about eight species of perennial plants from the Himalayas. The genus is closely related to *Saxifraga*, in which group it was included. One very mild winter the bergenias flowered in December and, as light levels were low, the pale pink flowers appeared luminous, but whatever their flowering time they are beautiful. Bergenias are very hardy and tolerate most

49

but not boggy soils. Bergenias are perennial, evergreen with leathery, slightly glossy dark-green year-round leaves which are tinted red or purple in winter. In winter through to spring they have pretty clusters of shocking-pink, rose-pink or red flowers on tall, straight stems above the leaves, similar to those of *Saxifraga*. They are hardy, but the flowers of all species are susceptible to frost damage, so they are best planted near trees, shrubs or buildings to minimise the intensity of ground frost. They are an attractive feature for year-round ground cover and an evergreen edging. They are better planted in groups rather than dotted about. They make excellent under-planting for deciduous trees and shrubs. I like to use them along paths and in places where the flowers can be appreciated in the winter.

B. schmidtii is the earliest-flowering of this genus, producing its blooms in early spring. The strong, thick leaves give it the name elephant's ears. When leaves die back it is better to cut them off rather than pulling them off as they are attached so strongly that the buds and root may come away as well. The bergenia produces thick, fleshy stems which creep on top of the soil, increasing the plant's size, making good ground cover. When plants become congested they can be lifted and divided in spring after flowering or in the autumn. Split the plants into smaller portions, ensuring that each has some thick stem and some roots and leaves attached. Seeds germinate freely, but, as all species are infertile, seedlings will not come true unless grown away from other species, or are hand pollinated.

I often choose plants with good foliage as leaves last longer than flowers and their shapes and sizes produce bold patterns, especially in certain light effects.

B. cordifolia with its leathery evergreen leaves contrasts well with the softer variegated leaves of *Hosta undulata*. Another example of these textures is in a corner by the house, where I have yellow roses behind an acanthus with its fabulous shiny, architectural leaves, and next to this are the dramatic leaves of arum lily with its evocative white blooms, with purple heuchera, valerian, honesty, forget-me-nots and campanula tumbling over the foreground stone edges.

Mag hated bergenias and I have come across other people with the same strength of feeling – something I do not understand at all. Maybe this is because they are so successful and in small gardens may be regarded as invasive.

AKEBIA
Akebia quinata (chocolate vine)

The Painting

Tonal value is the name given to the varying levels of lightness and darkness. I look at the subject as a whole to evaluate the tonal structure. This might mean modifying the lights and darks to improve the tonal balance or even the design. Keen observation of tone was necessary in portraying the shapes of the flowers as well as the leaves and stalks. I enhanced the darks to give a sense of depth and a feeling of light. A mixture of soft, vibrant and dark greens can be just as dramatic as a blaze of colours. Pattern, texture and leaf shape are vital elements.

I usually mix my own greens, but in this case I did not need yellow or blue in painting the subject, so used a little Viridian and added yellow for the light areas and Winsor Violet, used to paint the flowers, for the darker leaves. Viridian is a very stable, powerful cold green with excellent permanence. It superseded a fugitive colour known as Emerald Green.

Ultramarine Blue contains red and makes subdued greens, whereas Phthalo or Winsor Blue produce the most intense green. Phthalo Blue is very strong and can bleed up through other colours painted over it. It can be used to mix vibrant, saturated greens or strong darks. It is not sedimentary, so can be built up gradually with a number of washes. Winsor Blue is very similar. Prussian and Antwerp Blues are also yellow-influenced blues, but lack the purity and intensity of Phthalo or Winsor Blues. Cerulean is similar in colour to dilute Phthalo Blue, but much less intense, and for this reason it is a colour for washes but cannot match Phthalo for strong, dark mixtures. Hooker's Green in its earliest form was a mix of Gamboge, later Aureolin, and Prussian Blue. The modern blend is of Phthalocyanine Blue and Cadmium Yellow.

For the flowers I used Winsor Violet, which is a transparent vivid mid-shade purple.

The Gardener

I enjoy colour, but equally the varying greens of leaf shape as well as the gorgeous flowers. Akebia is a vigorous, twining, semi-evergreen climbing shrub, with attractive palmate or trifoliate leaves. Being aware of what the plant needs, I have planted this akebia in full view from the house, so that the lovely flowers and interesting leaves are admired from spring through to autumn. The flowers come in axillary racemes, unisexual, but with both sexes on the same raceme; the females are few at the base and the males are numerous. Racemes are stalked flowers arranged singly along an elongated unbranched axis, with those at the base blooming first. The flowers are chocolate-scented, reddish purple with the leaves having three or five leaflets. The fruits are sausage-shaped pods which contain edible, sweet but rather insipid-flavoured pulp. It is eaten in Japan as a seasonal delicacy. The rind, with a slight bitter taste, is used as a vegetable stuffed with ground meat and deep-fried. In Japan, the leaves are made into a tea infusion. *Akebia quinata* has three leaves and is traditionally used for basket weaving.

To propagate, seed can be collected once the pods are ripe, and sown indoors straight away. Seedlings can then be transferred to a cold frame to 'harden off', at least a week before planting in the garden. Shoot cuttings can be taken from new spring growth, and placed in a humid, warm area to root. The plant should be controlled with regular pruning as it can quickly overpower other plants. These prunings can be used as cuttings. It is drought-resistant, but benefits from regular water.

In New Zealand, and several states in the Eastern United States, akebia is classed as an unwanted organism, since it is considered to be invasive.

PERIWINKLE
Vinca major and *Vinca minor* (trailing, creeping or running myrtle, old maid, church flower, ram-goatrose, big leaf and Magdalena)

The Paintings

There is nothing like working directly from the subject. The actual subject offers so much more than a photo in that a real emotional response to the subtlety of colour is more evident. Colour is one of the most powerful tools an artist can use in creating atmosphere and impact in a painting. When painting flowers it is necessary to focus on the big shapes of colour and to add details which are essential to describing the subject. Flowers need to be painted with the greatest economy so as to retain the transparency. I use mostly transparent colours which help to achieve the glow in the petals and once that glow is achieved the rest of the painting will fall into place.

The Gardener

Periwinkle is a tough hardy plant which will quickly occupy the whole border. The evergreen and spreading *Vinca minor* (lesser periwinkle) is a very hardy, prostrate perennial, trailing but covering large areas as it roots itself where it touches the ground, and is commonly grown as a ground-cover plant under trees and shrubs. It grows successfully in containers in part or full shade. It flowers spasmodically throughout the year, but is usually covered in flowers in spring.

V. major (greater periwinkle) has variegated silver and green leaves, useful for ground cover, but can be invasive. Both varieties remind me of friends. *V. minor* was given to me by a previous student in England, and French friends gave us a variegated variety, *V. major*, which is less invasive and very attractive. It was thought to have been introduced by the occupying Romans and can be found in copses and woods southwards from Denmark.

It is an accepted treatment of herbalists because as many as thirty-five alkalis have been isolated from the plant. The leaves of the periwinkle have astringent properties; ointments from them can be used in the treatment of ulcerated skin, bleeding haemorrhoids and eruptions and irritations of the scalp, also to improve cerebral blood flow and treat high blood pressure. A tisane or gargle made from crushed or chopped leaves alleviates throat ulcers. The sap is so acrid and astringent that it has been used in tanning. Its reputation in the past for warding off evil spirits accounts for its English name of sorcerer's violet and its French name, *violette des sorciers*. Its historical name of sorcerer's violet alludes to the times when its leaves were chewed to stop a nosebleed, its young tops were made into a conserve to prevent nightmares, and its long stems were twined and tied around a person's legs to allay cramp. In the language of flowers the periwinkle's meaning, 'sweet remembrance', was given to it by the French. Rousseau wrote of seeing the flowers again and being reminded of a previous walk. In Devonshire it had the nice name of blue buttons. It is still used medicinally for its astringent and tonic effects, and the leaves make a healing ointment if powdered in oil. Its name is a mystery as it bears no likeness to the winkle shell. Its use in aphrodisiacs has been recorded since the fourteenth century – further confirmation of its binding qualities. It is also under the influence of Venus, representing the love charm. In the eighteenth century white, red, blue, purple, double and even striped periwinkles were known, many of which have since disappeared. There are many forms of periwinkle, ranging from single blues to pink, burgundy, white and red, some double, some with green leaves and others with silver or gold markings.

The French names include *pervenche* and *pusellage*. Cultivation is simple, and once planted the periwinkle is difficult to eradicate. Its binding qualities can be exploited to stabilise banks of earth and to cover hedge banks and slopes. It is easily propagated by division, any single shoot with some root being potted in autumn or spring, and by cuttings of young shoots taken off as soon as the new growth begins in spring. The growing points should be taken off as the young plants are sufficiently established themselves to make them bushy. Rooting can take place if the nodes touch the ground. The flowers are produced on the young shoots as they lengthen.

V. major has large blue flowers, the colour a pure blue hard to find in other flowers. *V. elegantissima* is variegated. My favourite is *V. major reticulata*, which is also variegated with gold leaves and is very attractive. I have this variety growing in full sun at the front of the house, trained on wires so as to appreciate the beautiful blue flowers and fresh pale-yellow leaves, as a backdrop to spring flowers and summer planting. It also grows in shade and can lighten an otherwise dark area. If grown in dry poor soil they form stout, well-flowered tufts with only a few runners.

KERRIA
Kerria japonica (Jew's mallow, bachelor's buttons, Jew's mantle, Japanese rose)

The Drawing
Coloured pencils are easily portable and produce quick sketches though the individual separate colours need to be blended to give the depth of colour. Here a limited selection gave me various colours in the leaves and inner depth to the flowers.

Precise observation is vital, and spaces left between leaves, stems and flowers are important. I love to sketch and take the necessary time to improve, enjoying the entire process from inspiration to completion. Drawing develops the ability to select and emphasise the main attractions with the beauty of line that brings out the essence of the subject. Sometimes the drawings are finished pieces and at other times the base for experimentation evolving into paintings.

The Gardener

Kerria is named in honour of William Kerr, a young gardener and protégé of Sir Joseph Banks, the famous eighteenth-century naturalist and plant collector. In 1804 Kerr was seconded to the East India Company in China to search for undiscovered plants. Kerr introduced the cultivar 'Pleniflora', commonly known as bachelor's buttons. *Kerria japonica* is tall with weak arching stems and grows wild. The modern *K. japonica* 'Golden Guinea' is bigger and brighter than Kerr's original. It is a vigorous suckering plant, graceful and arching, slender-branched, twiggy, erect, hardy, deciduous with alternate leaves and a mass of bright-yellow blooms, and is one of the earliest and prettiest of spring flowers. It is happy almost anywhere and will brighten any place in the garden. It enjoys full sun or partial shade and needs well-drained rich soil. It can look dramatic illuminating a dark area or a north-facing wall. Kerria looks well surrounded by daffodils and primroses and a selection of blue blooms. There is a double form, but the single-flowered form is more elegant with a graceful habit.

It can be increased from semi-ripe cuttings in midsummer or layered shoots from mid spring to late summer, or by hardwood cuttings in late autumn and rooted suckers in spring or by division. These can be potted up and planted out in the following spring.

MID SPRING

HYACINTH
Hyacinthus

The Painting

This painting appears to be about colour, but is in fact about the light falling on the petals and soft shadows giving shape and form. Depicting light is one of the most basic principles of painting. Without light there would be no form. The way light hits the plant gives clues to size, shape, colour, detail and texture. Tonal value is one of the most important elements of design. Without tone all shapes appear flat and shapeless. It is the change of tone in each colour that turns the shapes into forms and separates the various components within the subject matter. Colour gives the painting beauty while the tonal value gives the painting depth and structure. Monochromatic paintings show how the absence of colour doesn't matter when the correct value is applied. If the colour of the subject is correct but the tonal value is wrong, then the painting will not read correctly, but if the tonal value is correct and the colour is wrong, the painting will still look right. Half closing the eyes enables one to evaluate tones more easily.

In this painting there are light edges against dark, which brings the light edges forward and it appears that the darker areas recede. This contrast accents areas where there is more activity and detail. All the petals were laced with light and interlocking shapes achieve a good shape. To keep the sparkle of the watercolour and the direction of the light, the whites had to be planned in advance of painting. The edges were treated with variations of tone from hard to soft and soft to hard.

The Gardener
The hyacinth is said to have sprung from the blood of the dead Hyakinthos, or Hyacinthus, who was a friend of the god Apollo. One day when the two young men were engaged in a game of quoits, Apollo hurled a quoit hard which went off course and hit Hyacinthus and killed him. Apollo did not have the power to restore his companion to life, but he changed him instead into the beautiful flower that has since borne his name. The French meaning is 'joy of heart'.

The hyacinth (hyacinthus) is native to the Mediterranean with a few found growing in tropical and Southern Africa and is related to *Scilla* and *Chionodoxa*. *Hyacinthus orientalis* is deliciously scented with elegant flower spikes in a wide range of colours: blue, pink, white and yellow. The flower heads grow in a very dense cylindrical form which appears slightly before the fleshy strap-like leaves. The large-flowered Dutch hyacinths have mostly replaced the wild species *H. orientalis*, from which they are descended. *H. amethystinus* can be distinguished from *H. orientalis* by its much more slender appearance and smaller, scentless, bright-blue flowers borne in a very lax one-sided cluster.

    The scent of fresh flowers indoors is a joy, but some fragrances can be overpowering and interestingly can change the bouquet of good wine. Many flowers lose their fragrance after a day. Often, though, it is difficult to recall the memory of the scent until the next time it is encountered. Many flowers, such as violets, sweet peas, wallflowers, roses, hyacinths, stocks and carnations, are so much better planted in sitting areas or near house windows, where their intoxicating scent can be experienced over and over again. A sense of smell can conjure vivid memories – more so than that of sight. The sweet perfume of crocuses, snowdrops, alyssum, hyacinth and narcissus recalls the scent of spring and the pleasures of warm sunny days.

GRAPE HYACINTH
Moschus, Muscari (musk grape hyacinth)

The Painting

The colour scheme is based on the dominant colour of the flower. Very often it is the colour harmonies which lead us to believe that colour is the principal influence of light in a painting. Most historical works of art relied on beauty of drawing, form, value and temperature to bring success. Once these skills are learned, then a limited palette can be developed adding more colours as confidence grows. This good structure can make the difference between a good or bad painting, just like a house with solid foundations. In this little painting the tonal values were assessed before starting. I used Winsor Blue for the lighter, cooler areas of the flowers, with Ultramarine Blue in the darker, deeper, warmer shadowed areas. Indian Yellow was used for the surround, and this warm yellow was combined with the cool blue to create the green. A touch of violet was used in the shadows.

The Gardener
Muscari is a genus of about fifty species. These are brilliant for pollinators, with each spike made up of numerous nectar- and pollen-rich flowers. Musk relates to the scent of some grape hyacinths, which are so called because of the short spikes of tiny pendulous, globular deep-blue or white flowers, which look like half-opened hyacinths, to which they are related. They are very hardy dwarf bulbs with few linear, fleshy, grass-like leaves. They spread rapidly and are excellent for a rock garden. They are native to the Mediterranean region and like sunny places and can form big

56

clumps. *M. atlanticum*, the grape hyacinth, is dark blue with white and out-curved lobes. *M. botryoides* is smaller and distinguished by globular flowers which are pale blue or violet with white lobes.

Propagation is by means of offsets and by seeds, the latter usually ripening freely. To obtain offsets the old bulbs should be lifted every second year in summer, but if left alone for a period they increase where they grow. Bulbs should be planted as soon as possible with a top dressing of good soil to aid flowering. They succeed in almost any soil and situation, but increase most freely in rich, open, well-drained soil. A top dressing of good soil may be given before flowering begins.

VIOLA
Viola odorata (sweet violet); *Viola cornuta* (horned violet); *Viola tricolor* (Johnny-jump-up)

The dainty viola is still adored for its simple beauty, colouring the garden and woodlands in early spring. If it is cut back after flowering it produces more flowers. It is ideal for edges and shaded borders. The leaves and flowers are edible and look beautiful adorning salad dishes.

The Paintings

Once the drawing was established I began painting starting with the flowers, putting in soft colours and building up to the darker more shaded areas, blending where necessary. I added more intense colour, then the leaves were painted being careful not to detract from the flowers, which are the main focus. Then I added the background. A dark background can emphasise a brightly lit area. After evaluating the painting by looking at it in reverse using a mirror, I added paint to areas to heighten colour and darken the darks to help the flowers appear to come forward.

Painting with a minimum number of colours to achieve maximum colour is a compositional discipline, allowing one colour to dominate while letting the others fulfil a supporting role.

Visualising the finished painting can instil a degree of confidence. A bold painting can only come out of a confident approach; where there is a risk of failure often come ideas, making the painting richer. The larger shapes become the foundation of the painting and include negative shapes, which are as important as the positive. Once the main shapes are formed, the more intricate ones develop. Smaller shapes are important and details follow, working as boldly and directly as possible.

Many edges may be lost to create mood and atmosphere. Where values are similar, the edge can be lost entirely. This will be mostly in the shadows, but can be achieved where an object in light meets another element of similar value. It is amazing how our eyes can finish describing in our minds what is actually not there.

The Gardener

Viola is the largest genus of flowering plants in the violet family, Violaceae. The flowers have five petals. Four are upswept or fan-shaped with two petals on each side, and one broad-lobed lower petal points downwards. Flowering is often profuse and may last through spring and summer. The native sweet violet has fragrant flowers. The sweetest-scented is the white double violet, which flowers twice a year. It is also one of the earliest flowers to bloom in late winter or early spring.

It grows in sun or shade and spreads by sending out long creeping runners, which produce plantlets, and it self-seeds freely. I find them growing in all corners of the garden. They flower all winter and well into spring until they set seed, casting them under the walnut tree – a cool, shady place where the grass doesn't thrive – but also creeping up into stone walls, in between paving stones and under the oak trees. The fruit is a rounded, slightly hairy capsule, which remains closed until it falls to the ground and splits into three sections to release small, shiny seeds. They may also be dispersed by ants.

Violas have an elusive scent, which temporarily desensitises the receptors of the nose, thus preventing any further scent being detected until the nerves recover.

Oil from the petals has long been used to make fragrances and flavourings, and both roots and flowers were used in ancient Greece as a sedative and as remedies for a number of ailments.

Bees seeking nectar follow the guidelines on the petals and become dusted with pollen from the stamens, completing pollination when visiting other flowers. Ants enjoy eating fleshy outgrowths on the seeds and so help dispersal.

Sweet violets are derived mainly from the European *V. odorata*. These have long stolons, by which they are propagated, leaves which are slightly downy when young, and scented flowers. *V. riviniana,* the common dog violet, is usually larger than the sweet violet, but is scentless. The term 'dog' refers to its supposed inferiority compared with the sweet violet. Nectar secreted in the flower spur attracts bumblebees, bee flies and hoverflies. It has deeply heart-shaped base leaves ending in a rosette of leaves and is the main food of the caterpillars of many species of fritillary butterflies. Stem tip cuttings can be taken or divisions made in spring or late summer, or they can be raised from seed sown in a cold frame in autumn.

The violet will tolerate dry shade or direct sun. The true violets are often plants of open woodland and do well among bushes or on the shadier sides of a rock garden. At the beginning of the nineteenth century several double forms, blue, rose and white, were cultivated alongside varieties of very large single flowers, for example the Russian viola, *V. suavis*, to encourage earlier and more profitable flowering and the benefit of even greater hardiness.

In ancient times, so highly regarded was the violet that it was made the symbol of Athens and both the Greeks and Romans wore it in wreaths and chaplets. Grecian ladies are said to have used the dye from the flowers to paint their eyelids. The Greeks called it *Ione*, as there is a legend that the god Zeus turned his lover, the princess Io, into a heifer to hide her from his jealous wife. He then created violets as a sweet treat for his amorous bovine to eat, which could be one reason the flower is indicative of constancy. Another legend tells how Orpheus sat down to rest, and where he laid his lute the first violet sprang. Pliny advised garlands of violets to ward off headaches, and Arabs flavoured sherbet with violets and prescribed it for the sting of the scorpion. It was used as a cure for wounds, bound round the head for headaches, as tea taken as a sedative, for cardiac disorders and gout, and made into wine. The Greeks and Romans endowed the flower with a variety of charms and there is little doubt that violets grew or were cultivated in the Mediterranean. The young leaves were fried and eaten with sugar and lemon juice. During the reign of Charles I and Charles II a violet conserve was made, and the flowers were sprinkled on salad. 'Violet plate' was sold by apothecaries as a laxative, probably compounded from the roots of the plant, which also have a strong emetic action. The pungent perfume of *V. odorata*, which is named from its sweet scent, was added to desserts, fruit salads and teas. A favourite French recipe *vyolette* was made from macerated, boiled violet flowers, which were used to colour rice flour then mixed with warm milk and sweetened with honey and sugar. Sometimes one finds this sweet referred to as 'violet paste', and it was largely consumed by 'persons of quality' with some enthusiasm because it was supposedly endowed with health-giving properties. Syrup of violets, for which quantities of violets were cultivated near Stratford-upon-Avon in England, has a chemical property whereby its blue colour is rendered red on contact with acids and green on contact with alkalis and can thus be used as a litmus. An oil obtained from the distillation of the flowers is used in perfumery.

The violet is still used in confectionery. Crystallised violets have for centuries been imported from France and can still be bought, though they are not too difficult to make at home. Pick the flower heads from the stalks, wash and drain them, then coat with egg white and crystallised sugar poured over the fresh flower. Stir until the sugar recrystallises and dry them off on floured paper, or aluminium foil, then dry them in a very cool oven or in a warming drawer. The same method is used for rose petals, orange flowers, almonds and orange peel. Candied violas are still produced in Toulouse, where they are known as *violettes de Toulouse* and are used as decoration for desserts. Viola essence flavours the liqueurs Crème Yvette, Crème de Violette and Parfait d'Amour. It is also used in Parma-violets confectionery.

In France the violet was the secret emblem of followers of Napoleon. During his absence they wore violet-coloured watch ribbons. It had been Josephine's favourite flower, always given to her by Napoleon on their wedding anniversary. Before leaving for St Helena he took a bunch of violets to her tomb. When he was banished to Elba, he vowed to return with the violets in the spring. During his exile, the flower was adopted by his supporters as an emblem, its name serving as a password. He was welcomed back with violets after his escape from Elba in 1815. He had a medallion containing a lock of Josephine's hair and some dried violets.

In the Victorian language of flowers, the violet is symbolic of modesty. Blue violets mean devotion and white violets mean purity. The violet is the traditional flower of Mothering Sunday. It reminds me of my grandmother, as I loved to delight her with gifts of violets. In those days I bought them from the flower shop as I didn't have a garden. I wish my grandmother could enjoy the violets in my garden today.

There are hundreds of viola and violette cultivars, many of which do not breed true from seed and therefore have to be propagated from cuttings. Violettes can be distinguished from violas by the lack of ray markings on their petals.

Perennial violas have profuse, intense violet and blue five-petalled flowers, but can also be in mauve, yellow, pink and white, although this is less common. They are close relatives of the annual summer and winter pansies. Violas and violettes have flat flowers with overlapping petals, but violettes are smaller than violas. Violettes have narrower petals with spurs at the back. The leaves are oval or heart-shaped and are often lobed. The violet has long procumbent stolons which, rooting at the ends, give the plant a prostrate habit. It spreads and survives the driest soils and severe winter frosts, but when cultivated revels in a humus-rich soil. Some of the daintiest-looking hybrids have been bred from tough alpine parents, making them very weather-resistant. Viola hybrids have fragrant flowers in various shades of blue, bronze, yellow, purple, mauve and near-black.

Its various local names are apple leaf, bairnwort, banwort, blaver, Bessy banwood and vilip.

V. biflora has bright-green kidney-shaped leaves and vivid yellow and violet flowers.

V. cornuta, the horned violet, is white, pale blue or soft lilac, some with three lower yellow petals and two upper violet-coloured petals. *V. cucullata* has heart-shaped leaves with white to violet flowers. *V. gracilis* is a deep-purple viola with long spurs and *V. major* is a clear primrose yellow. *V. hederacea* has violet-blue petals with white edges. *V. labradorica* 'Purpurea' has purple-green leaves and violet-mauve flowers. *V. lutea* is a mountain pansy with yellow flowers and brown or purple veins. *V. odorata*, the sweet violet, spreads by runners which root at their tips and flowers in shades of white to purple and is very fragrant. Pretty trailing *V.* 'Plentifall' has masses of winter-hardy blooms, ideal for a hanging basket. They are invaluable for winter baskets and containers. Their cheerful flowers add a colourful winter addition to foliage and bulbs. The leaves are rounded kidney-shaped with a heart-shaped base. *V. tricolor* (wild pansy, or heartsease) flowers are mostly tricoloured, usually predominantly violet with varying amounts of yellow and white, and variable in size. Petals are usually longer than the sepals. Leaves are heart-shaped to lance-shaped and it is an annual, biennial or perennial. *V. corsica* is hardy, tough and self-sows even in hot, dry places.

For self-seeding plants to come true without changes to colour or form, it is best to plant just one cultivar of the same species; otherwise they will hybridise. Different species of the same genus rarely cross. There are three main methods by which violets are propagated: by seed, by division or from cuttings. Once the flowers set seed, the plant will stop flowering, but if the faded flowers are nipped off, which can be tedious and time-consuming, flowering will continue throughout summer. The small purple and yellow violas in my garden seed freely into pots, in the rock garden, among vegetables and into gravel paths and in cracks wherever they can germinate. Collected seed can be sown in spring, then potted up and planted outside after hardening off. The plantlets can be used as colourful ground cover and informal edgings, falling over low walls and around shrubs, and are excellent in containers and window boxes. The most usual method is to plant out rooted runners, or divisions, in the spring or autumn in crumbly humus-rich soil. The plants will tolerate dryness or damp conditions, but their flowering quality is dependent on the condition of the soil prior to planting. Spring planting will often produce autumn flowers. Winter flowering can be encouraged by growing the plants in a cold frame and, provided that there is adequate ventilation, mildew will not affect them. Violets are hardy, but need fresh air and sunshine. The nectar of the violet is a favourite food source of both the male orange tip and the female white butterfly.

The flowers have a dynamic effect in that they demand viewing at close quarters while other flowers, such as Michaelmas daisies, are viewed as a whole. A viola is prized for its appealing individual bloom, whereas a single daisy may not have the same attraction.

PANSY
Viola (heartsease)

The Painting

In this painting the flowers have dark edges, so I have painted the background light and indistinct. I used bold colours – rich yellows complemented by deep purples. I thought carefully about the shapes using hard edges against soft, and only just suggesting background leaves in places. A magical interaction can take place by the emotional response to the flower. The bright colours can lift the spirits and, by suggesting the flower's perfume, the sunlight and dancing shadows, there can be a feeling of euphoria. The stunningly bright colours caught in the sunshine, the velvety purple darks against golden orange provide the complementary colours, yellow and purple creating a stunning combination.

To paint a pansy I start by wetting each area to be painted with clean water. This helps the paint to flow evenly. I began with the light-yellow centres, letting the yellows run together, then added a little red to Indian Yellow and stroked Rose Madder on the edges of some of the areas of the foreground blooms. Warm yellows are best when mixing oranges, as Lemon Yellow contains a little blue and can make the resultant colour appear more brown. When dry, I painted each petal separately using Rose Madder on the edges of some petals and then, while still wet, flooded in violet, pulling in the colour towards the yellow centres. Green was mixed from Ultramarine Blue and Indian Yellow, and then the area behind the petals was dampened to suggest leaves and stems. I darkened the green with a little red for shadows on the stems. When dry I added green to Rose Madder for the dark centres, stroking outwards into the petals.

Flowers depend a great deal on their high colour, but full-strength watercolour can look dull, almost opaque, so a light touch is needed, allowing the white of the paper to shine through, even when painting strong colour. Any subsequent colours can be added later.

The Gardener

There is little difference between violets, pansies and violas, but in general violas are more compact and usually smaller in the flower without the markings or blotches on the petals common to pansies, which almost always have two colours, one prominently blotched on the other, some frilled, some streaked with whiskers and some plain. The term 'pansy' is normally used for multicoloured, large-flowered cultivars, which are raised annually or biennially from seed.

Pansies have more compact growth than violets and have four petals pointing upwards and one downwards. Violas have two petals pointing upwards and three downwards. Violas have a less-extensive colour range than pansies, but are more heat- and cold-tolerant, therefore flower longer. Dedicated plant breeders continue to produce new and amazing hybrids. Apart from a number of species and variations under cultivation, there are several distinct types of pansies and violas which are of garden origin. These have arisen both from deliberate hybridisations as well as from selection of good varieties of flower. The modern pansy is the result of a breeding programme that began in 1800 on Lord Gambier's Buckinghamshire estate. Gardener William Thompson began crossing *Viola × wittrockiana*, the large flowering hybrid known as the pansy. The Victorians, inspired by the vast displays at royal residences, planted them in elaborately shaped beds that covered large areas. They are annuals or biennials, while violas are perennial.

The face of the pansy has earned it many names – Johnny-jump-up, three faces in a hood, ladies' delight, flamy (because its colours may be seen in the flames of a wood fire) and heartsease. In Scotland it was known as stepmother – so called because of the large lower petal with a 'daughter' on each side, and two upper petals which are the 'stepdaughters'. In many ancient herbals it was called 'herba Trinitas', dedicated to the Trinity because of its three colours – 'God is three distinct persons in one undivided Trinity, united in one eternal glory and divine majesty.' Pansies take their name from the French word *pensée*, meaning thought.

V. × wittrockiana is a group of mixed origin derived largely from the heartsease, *V. tricolor*, which varies largely in habit and flower colour, but having characters derived from *V. lutea* and possibly *V. altaica*. For centuries *V. tricolor* was esteemed for its quaintly marked flowers, but it had little horticultural importance and no change in size or colour until deliberate selection was made by English gardeners from 1810. William Thompson, gardener to Lord Gambier, who grew pansies on a large scale at Iver, Buckinghamshire, was chief worker and by 1835 about 400 named varieties were on sale. Selection in Britain led to the creation of a special group called show pansies, conforming to rules laid down by florists and pansy societies. The aim was to produce a flower as circular and flat as possible, not less than two inches in diameter, with a well-defined circular central blotch. These were derived mainly from *V. tricolor* and *V. lutea*. Meanwhile, selection in Belgium and France of pansies obtained from Britain resulted in another group, the fancy pansies, with a greater range of colours and a less formal shape. Botanically every member of this genus is a viola. In gardens the name viola is often used as a vernacular term with a restricted meaning for a group of plants. Tufted pansies were first raised in 1863 by James Grieve. In 1887 another prominent Scottish cultivator, Dr Charles Stuart, found among his seedlings one with small white flowers lacking the usual conspicuous rays. Circular or oval in shape, in a combination of colours with no markings, these pansies are bushy and derived from show pansies crossed with *V. cornuta*. Later seedlings of this type have become known as violettas, which are miniature types of garden violas derived from carefully selected crosses with *V. cornuta*. They are compact with very fragrant flowers borne erect well above the foliage. Some come fairly true from seed. A distinction is therefore made by gardeners between violets, pansies, violas and violettas.

Pansies are readily raised from seed, by layers and by cuttings. Propagation by cuttings can be taken immediately below a joint and all but the upper two leaves should be removed and inserted into sandy soil, placed in a cold frame and kept well syringed each day. They should be shaded from hot midday sun until they have rooted. Cuttings inserted in June and July will produce plants which can be planted out in autumn and will flower early the following spring. Autumn-rooted cuttings are best grown in a cold frame as the young plants may not be strong enough to stand the winter without protection. Seed sowing produces a large vigorous stock, but the plants will probably vary considerably. The seeds need to be sown in light, well-drained soil either in boxes or pots, and germinated in a cold frame during spring, then pricked out when large enough to handle, allowed to continue to grow under cool conditions in a frame and planted out when large enough. They will germinate freely outdoors, but a frame gives better protection. Cool treatment should be given, and in transplanting remove with as large a ball of soil as possible. Future growth depends largely upon an initial start with a good root system. Layering increases good varieties and old plants may be divided in August or September. Pansies do best in cool, moist soil and in a cool climate. With good cultivation and well-manured soil they can grow anywhere and produce large, good flowers over a long season. The beds should not be exposed to the midday sun nor overshadowed by trees. When watering in summer, it should be thorough as a sprinkling is often more injurious than beneficial. Spring planting should be done as early as possible, in February or March. As soon as the flowers begin to deteriorate they should be picked off. Early flowers can be produced by growing plants in pots. Strong plants from seeds, or from cuttings made in early August, should be put into pots. When rooted, about October, they should be placed in larger pots. The flower buds should be removed until good plants are formed. Flowering should begin in February and will continue into April.

The two main sections are fancy and show. Fancy varieties have various colours. The show varieties are much more formal. They have colours of black, maroon, primrose, white or yellow. 'White grounds' have a large central, dark blotch round the eye, then a ring of white, then an outer band, the belt of bronze, purple or maroon. 'Yellow grounds' are similarly marked, but have a middle ring of yellow instead of white.

Pansies are beautiful in a summer garden and equally in winter, and their perky warming faces cheer us on even the dullest day.

DAFFODIL
Narcissi, Narcissus (daffadowndilly)

Paintings 1, 2 and 3

There is a kind of magic about the dazzling brilliant yellow of the delicate daffodil. Simplicity is often better than adding too much detail. Here pure yellows straight from the tube were used. The morning light on the petals had just the right combination of direct light, partial light and shadow. The natural centre of interest of the flower was illuminated with an intense super-yellow. The petals of the daffodil were almost blanched out as they faced the sun, so the colour was a half tone, a fairly watery yellow with the sunlight glowing through the petals. These outer petals cast a little shadow on the base of the trumpet, and the interior of the trumpet appeared dark because of the strong, intense light of the entrance of the trumpet.

When painting outdoors, there can be overcast days, hazy days, sunny bright days and wet days, but the light holds true in each. Sometimes I will exaggerate the colour to add excitement. If these bright colours have areas of dark and light around them, they tend to glow more and create a stronger effect.

The Gardener

Narcissus is the Greek name used by Hippocrates and means to grow stiff, because of its narcotic properties. The French name for daffodil means melancholy and for narcissus, egotism or vanity. The family is Amaryllidaceae.

The more easily pronounced and undoubtedly prettier name of daffodil, for the scientific term narcissus, is a cheerful and indispensable addition to the spring garden, in window boxes and in pots. Daffodil is the English name while narcissus is the Latin. The correct botanical name for all members of the genus is narcissus, but those with trumpets are usually called daffodils. Trumpet daffodils have cups larger than the petals. There are now various varieties with colour combinations, mostly white and yellow.

Poets of Greece and Rome sang the praises of the daffodil 2,000 years ago, and in broken succession have provided further proof of the way in which the daffodil has commended itself to mankind in his pleasures and sorrows. Shakespeare, Milton, Herrick, Shelley, Keats, Wordsworth and Tennyson are a few of the great poets who have loved their beauty. Wordsworth's famous poem is always in the top five most loved English poems. His encounter with daffodils in the Lake District has become a romantic expression of our relationship with nature. They are radiant beauties that bring hope to the heart after the long winter months. A. A. Milne also wrote charmingly about daffodils laughing off winter in his poetry for children.

The daffodil is the national flower of Wales, though only since the nineteenth century, promoted by Lloyd George, who thought them more attractive than the leek, which was originally the national emblem.

Narcissus was named after a character in Greek mythology – a handsome shepherd boy who fell in love with his own reflection in a pool and drowned trying to catch the elusive spirit. The flower became a symbol of egotism or selfishness.

The word daffodil is such a thoroughly home-made English corruption of asphodel that it probably was applied to the wild species, the Lent lily, the true wild daffodil, associated with resurrection, but in Eastern cultures it is the flower of wealth and good fortune. It has been used throughout history as a medicine, despite being toxic. Today it is grown extensively in Wales as its bulb contains galantamine, a drug used in the treatment of Alzheimer's disease. They are hardy, spring-flowering bulbs with yellow or white trumpet-shaped flowers, found mostly in woodlands and meadows.

There are hundreds of hybrids that are classified according to their flower shape, size of the cup or trumpet, corolla, and the outer petals and parentage from which they have been bred. Genetic cultivation and plant technology have extended the natural flowering season with varieties blooming earlier or later than usual. The first narcissus flowers open in late winter, the last in early summer, so with a selection it is possible to have flowers for several months. Flowers are white or yellow, solitary or umbellate, drooping or inclined. Hybridisation in gardens as well as among the wild plants, where several species are in the same area, has given all gradations from one extreme to the other. Growers have introduced double blooms with ruffled, split central cups and the natural yellows and golds have been strengthened, paled and new colours added, such as pink in the trumpet. A great impetus was given in the latter half of the nineteenth century through the raising of seedlings by a few enthusiastic growers. They showed that a great variety of forms and colourings could be secured by this means, especially when different forms were crossed. Some hybrids were known from wild sources, but many more were soon raised in gardens. Size has been greatly increased by efforts of the Narcissus and Tulip Committee of the Royal Horticultural Society, who have preserved the balance between size and form.

The great majority are easily grown, and once planted may be left undisturbed. For garden purposes the narcissus has been grouped by the RHS into eleven divisions to accommodate not only the species, but also the numerous hybrids to which they have given rise.

Painting 4

Orange-yellows can be soft and warm verging to apricot and towards red and brown. Yellow can suppress and lend subtlety to white and the effect that white has on other colours. When painting flowers, one of the main considerations is the green of the foliage. Colour mixing for greens has many pitfalls because of their variations in temperature. Ultramarine Blue mixed with Lemon Yellow can result in a slightly warm green because of the red in the blue, while mixing the same cool yellow with a cool blue, such as Cerulean Blue, will produce a cold, fresh green. A minimum of tone was required to emphasise the trumpet-like quality of the daffodil.

The Gardener

Large-cupped narcissi have cup-shaped corollas about a third of the length of the petals. Some are yellow or white, some with orange or apricot cups. The small narcissi have small cups, being less than one-third the length of the petals. These usually have one flower to the stem and are best grown in borders or for naturalising in grass.

Daffodils will grow in almost any soil and situation except dense shade. The wild species can have a grace of their own and many can be grown in grass or between shrubs. July is the best time to plant.

The depth of planting depends on the size of the bulb, which should be covered by soils one and a half times as deep as the length of the bulb. A natural look may be had by scattering the bulbs haphazardly over the planting area and planting where they fall. In borders and beds they may safely be left for three years undisturbed. By the end of the third season, they have usually increased to such an extent that the bulbs may be overcrowded and should be lifted and divided. It is best to do this when the foliage has died down. This ensures that the leaves have fed and developed the bulb. Daffodils are affected by the previous growing season when they store up supplies in their bulbs. Abundant moisture in May helps promote free flowering in the next spring. The flower in the bulbs will be well developed for the next year as early as May. The successive flowering of most bulbs can be traced back to the weather in the previous spring. A dry spring may cause 'blindness' in the next year, and a series of dry periods can cause bulbs to die out completely.

Not only do bulbs make beautiful flowers, but they generally require little maintenance and will, if left undisturbed, steadily increase in number over the years. They will also grow in semi-shade where many other plants may struggle to grow. They can be planted around the bases of trees and in rock gardens, and can be moved without difficulty.

Bulbs, corms, tubers and rhizomes store food in underground organs. The bulb is composed of a number of thinnish layers while both corm and tuber are quite solid. Bulbs and corms appear to have evolved the capacity to store food in underground organs to avoid the effects of extreme climatic conditions. Bulbs and corms spend a lot of energy in setting seed, but by removing dying flowers the bulb's energy is redirected into producing bulbils or corm-lets.

Seeds can be collected and grown on, but I prefer not to allow the seed heads to form as I believe this takes a lot of energy from the bulb and may affect the flower in the following year. However, seedlings are not difficult to raise. The seeds should be collected as soon as the capsules burst. They should be sown soon after collection in sandy loam in the open air or in a cold frame. If sown thinly, the seedlings, which appear in the following spring, may remain over another year in the seed pans and then be transplanted after the foliage dies down. Small species will flower when three or four years old, with larger flowers when five to seven years old. The seedlings are not at their best in the first year.

Double-flowered narcissi have double-scented flowers and are best planted in borders. They are fifteen to thirty-eight centimetres high with two or three flowers. *Narcissus jonquilla* has several small sweetly scented flowers, sometimes with swept-back petals, and grows in a sunny, sheltered spot.

N. cyclamineus is a Lilliputian among daffodils and a very dainty little flower. It has pendent flowers with long, narrow, frilled, trumpet-shaped cups and swept-back petals. The perianth, or outer calyx, or sepals, is narrow and stands up close and erect. These narcissi are best grown in a rockery. They are easily pleased as to soils and position, although better in an open sunny site. They are best left to naturalise unless they become overcrowded.

N. triandrus is the name of a very distinct species with comparatively small trumpets, but the funnel-shaped cups appear long because they are narrow, while the perianth segments grow back in the opposite direction to that of the trumpet. Narcissus species have flowers in a variety of shapes and sizes, mostly dwarf and best grown in a rockery.

Shrubs and spring bulbs add structure and early interest to herbaceous borders which are based on roses, lilac, buddleia, foxgloves, golden rose, mallow, daisies, lilies, nicotiana and poppies. The dying foliage of spring bulbs is hidden by the new growth of perennials and summer annuals. The dead foliage of the bulbs can be cleared away, with care taken to stake plants so that they do not smother other plants. Some clumps may need dividing in autumn or winter so as to maintain vigour and produce more plants.

Where informal effects are aimed at, good-sized irregular groups of one variety should be planted. This makes a much more pleasing effect than mixtures of varieties. Narcissi in borders and beds may be left for three years undisturbed, and by the end of the third year they will have increased to such an extent that they may be overcrowded, and they should be lifted when the foliage has died down. A proper development of the bulb depends upon healthy foliage. Lifting should be done carefully as the bulbs can bruise easily. They should be carefully dried in a cool, dry shed and on no account laid out in the sun to dry, for their temperature would be raised sufficiently to kill the exposed part and much damage often results. When dry the bulbs should be checked and any showing damage rejected, and offsets large enough to be separated easily from the parent bulb separated. The bulbs may then be graded into sizes and stored until planting time.

Many varieties are well suited for growing pots, boxes or bowls for early flowering. The successful cultivation of narcissi for early flowering is largely dependent upon the condition of storage of the bulbs from the time of lifting until they are planted, for although the bulbs appear to be dormant, profound changes can occur, conditioned largely by the temperature of storage. The best temperature for the development and progress of the flower has proved to be low. A high temperature at the time of lifting, and immediately after, has been found to retard flowering markedly. Storage at a comparatively low temperature at lifting until the bulbs are planted in mid September, however, results in very early flowering. Cool conditions through the summer and cool conditions for the rooting period may bring the bulb into flower by Christmas.

EARLY PURPLE ORCHID
Orchis mascula

The Painting
The intricate shapes of each flower along the stems meant making close observation and a detailed drawing and careful painting using the tip of a fine brush. I used Quinacridone Rose and Quinacridone Violet for the main flowers and Winsor Violet for the shadows and stems. The dark leaves are a mix of Ultramarine Blue and Winsor Yellow with a touch of rose to darken. More rose and violet was added to the green for the dark spots.

The Gardener
Orchis is from the Greek for testicle and *mascula* is from the Latin for masculine or virile, referring to both the underground parts of the plant and the erect phallic appearance of the spur at the back of the flower. The French meaning is 'fervour'.

This is a wild orchid and its appearance every year is a delight. The early purple orchid is usually found in grassland, grass banks or woodland. The flowers have two side lobes with crenellated edges and a central lobe and a spur behind the hood curving upwards and rounded at the end. The sepals spread upwards. There are between ten and fifty flowers when fully open in colours ranging from magenta and light purple to violet or pink. The orchid has no nectar, but attracts pollinating insects as the flowers mimic other species. The flowers smell of honey when fresh, but after pollination smell of urine perhaps as a sign to insects that pollination has already taken place. The basal leaves have large dark-purple spots, which against the green appear almost black. The number of blotches is variable, some having none.

The starchy tubers are one of the most concentrated plant foods known and were eaten by sailors on long sea voyages. Before the advent of coffee the plant was also used to brew a popular aphrodisiac drink called 'salop', which was also a refreshing tonic. Salop houses sold salop made from powdered root.

CAMELLIA
Camellia sinensis (Japan rose)

Painting 1

Two colours, no matter how refined but of the same value – for example, Cadmium Red and Cerulean Blue – result in interesting flickering between the two. Here the light has changed the white petals into a series of warm and cool colours, giving a tonal difference but also a stunning image. The dark background gives drama to the flowers and leaves. Painting is manipulation of paint. This means there should be enough pigment in the brush so as to flow on to the painting surface and by watching and controlling the flow create beautiful paint configurations. Painting this way has the potential to lift the soul, usually because the image touches the heart and brings about a sense of empathy.

The Gardener

The French meaning is 'pride'. Few shrubs can rival the perfect blooms of camellias, with their handsome glossy foliage. There are eighty species native to Asia and thousands of varieties, many of which have been cultivated in Japan and China for centuries. The first species of camellia was introduced into Europe in 1792 and into the US in 1797. It was named for the seventeenth-century Moravian Jesuit and pharmacist George Joseph Kamel, 1661–1706, who travelled in Asia and wrote an account of the plants. They were once treated as tender and exotic and lived in glasshouses, but during the First World War it was realised that they can survive severe winters. All camellias are slow-growing, generally hardy, evergreen shrubs with beautiful late winter to mid-spring flowers and have dark-green, shiny foliage and large, showy flowers in pink, white and red with numerous stamens. Camellias dislike lime and chalky soils and do not like hot, dry places, but will grow in sun or shade given the right conditions. The elegant flowers can be damaged by frost so a sheltered spot, preferably west-facing, is best. Planted in the partial shade given by oak trees it suffers less damage to its flowers by frost than when fully exposed.

The commonest species in cultivation is *Camellia japonica*, of which there are many cultivars. It is hardy and has showy flowers in scarlet, crimson, rose, pink and white with semi-double and double flowers. The fine glossy green foliage makes it one of the most decorative of evergreens when not in flower. Camellias have shallow roots and can be vulnerable to drying out, which may not be evident until the following season when they lose leaves and may not flower well. Care must be taken that they suffer neither from drought nor from standing long in water through poor drainage, both of which result in bud drop. Camellias thrive in a compost of light loam with the addition of some well-decayed leaf mould and sand, avoiding touching the main trunk, to ensure free passage of water, which is required in liberal amounts. They can be grown in pots of fibrous loam mixed with peat, leaf soil and sand. They do not require frequent repotting as quite large plants can be grown in comparatively small containers. However, the best time to repot is before they make fresh growth or before the buds are fully formed; otherwise there is danger of them dropping off. They should be assisted by frequent applications of weak liquid manure. As they complete their growth and the flower buds become visible, they should be kept slightly drier, and when the buds are set, more water may be given. Established camellias will thrive in much drier positions than rhododendrons, although both require similar conditions. Camellias often appear quite fresh and unaffected by a long drought while rhododendrons nearby may be limp and drooping. I have them planted in the partial shade near oak trees, which give shelter, and so they suffer less damage to their flowers from an unexpected frost.

Camellias can be propagated by layers, cuttings, budding and seed. Layers may be put down at any time except when the plant is making young growth. Cuttings are best made from ripe wood, towards the close of the growing season in late July or early August. The cuttings should be supple but not soft and inserted into sandy leaf soil and placed in a cool place. When they have 'callused' they may be given slight bottom heat, which will hasten rooting. In bud cuttings, a piece of stem with leaf attached is taken as a cutting in late summer or early autumn and is an excellent way of quickly increasing stock. If there are long shoots, several cuttings with two leaves can be made. Remove the lower leaf and halve the upper one. Then make a long, sloping cut with a sharp knife, right across the wood at the base of the cutting. This should be well below the lower leaf bud. Bottom heat will accelerate rooting, but even in an unheated frame the cuttings should be struck by the following spring, when they can be potted on.

C. williamsii is more open in growth, with single shell-pink flowers and double flowers in pink. *C. reticulata* is tall and has large flowers. *C. sasanqua* has smaller flowers in winter and spring and both are tender.

Camellias and rhododendrons gradually increase in size, resulting in a huge bush taking a lot of space and perhaps fewer flowers. If this happens, then cut back the previous season's growth when growth starts in spring and all risk of frost is over. This leaves the plant smaller and flowers are more in proportion to its size. Ideally, pruning should be before buds open, so that energy is directed into the remaining stems. Trace each main branch to find its lead shoot – usually the longest and most vigorous – and cut this back to a couple of leaves. I do the same for vigorous side shoots and remove any that are congested, opening up the shrub. This has the added advantage of cutting off spent blooms on shrubs that have flowered earlier in the spring.

In Victorian times the camellia was known as the Japan rose. Henry Phillips in his *Floral Emblems*, 1839, conveyed the message 'Beauty is your only attraction' because the camellia has beautiful flowers but no scent. A vivid red camellia is a major force in the garden in spring.

Painting 2

Waiting for a flower bud to open can seem to take a long time, so when painting that long-awaited bloom I try to capture that same vitality. Since the blossoms are the focal point, I want other elements in the composition to be understated. The leaves and stems take second place to the flowers, but their directional lines provide movement and enliven the composition. The exciting and inspiring element about the watercolour is its spontaneity. The colour can flow and blend in its own mysterious way or be tightly controlled in other areas.

Cool light produces warm shadows and warm light produces cool shadows. This means discerning how warm or cool a colour is compared to that which is next to it. Comparison is the key to accurately painting the subtle nuances of temperature in colours as revealed by the temperature of the light. These subtleties can capture the distinctive qualities of light, time of day, weather conditions and atmosphere of the scene.

LATE SPRING

CORN LILY
Ixia (wand flower, African corn lily)

The Painting

Ixias are beautiful shades of blues and violet with white centres. I am moved by the way the light affects everything it touches, uncovering hidden colours and illuminating the subject's own unique character. There is a beauty in all flowers, in all things, large and small, simple and complex, but it is the hidden intricacies within each bloom which are so attractive.

The Gardener

The Greek name, ixia, meaning bird lime, refers to the clammy sap. Ixias are South African plants with slender stems with bright colours and fragrance. As they are not quite hardy they need to be planted in a sunny, well-drained border or under a south wall. They need good drainage and protection against frost. Growing in pots is a good idea, requiring little water in winter and fully exposed to light as the flowers need strong sunlight to open well.

Ixias are sterile and do not set seed. They increase by offsets from the corms, which can bloom in their first or second year. They are fragrant and good for bees and butterflies.

WALLFLOWER
Erysimum cheiri

The Drawing

In this sketch the colours are a clear orange and yellow which is extended into the unopened buds. The leaves are of a dark dull green, tinged with brown-bronze, picking up the colours in the flower, and a touch of purple.

Shadows need to have colour within them and reflected light – not grey or black, which can make them appear heavy and solid. Every mark, every stroke, is based on decades of continuous drawing and painting. It is joyful, wondrous and sometimes surprising how it evolves, but it is the expression of the inner self, the individual and unique creativity which makes the difference.

The Gardener

Spring is full of the promise of regeneration, of warmer days and the air full of fragrance. The fragrance of spring blossom never fails to heighten feelings of pleasure. In spring, purple and lilac aubretias mix well with arabis and dazzling wallflowers, being among the most richly scented of spring flowers. They have a fine range of colours, from yellow to apricot, orange, red, white, cream and purple. I plant them near the house and by benches where we might sit and enjoy their sweet fragrance. They can be grown with the colours mixed, in beds or blocks of the same colour, or patterns of different colours and look wonderful among bulbs and early flowering border perennials. The wallflower is related to the cabbage and was introduced from the Eastern Mediterranean; it was seen naturalised in the wild in Britain as long ago as the sixteenth century.

Erysimum cheiri, the English wallflower, is not in fact English but native to the Eastern Mediterranean, whereas *E. × marshallii,* better known as *E. allionii*, Siberian wallflower, is not Siberian but a hybrid first raised in England! English and Siberian wallflowers can be distinguished botanically by differences in their fruit and stigma and in their colour. Siberian wallflowers are orange, apricot or yellow and at their best later than the English wallflower, which has a broader range of colour from creamy white through yellow and orange to red, purple and brown, and they have looser flower heads.

Wallflowers fall into two groups – perennial or shrubby and spring bedding plants. The perennial wallflowers – the Mediterranean species – mature into evergreen shrubs up to a maximum of about ninety centimetres high and wide. They revel in sunny well-drained conditions and can flower for months; they love full sun. The foliage varies from fresh green to grey-green. The best-known so-called perennial wallflower is 'Bowles Mauve', whose long flowering season is legendary. At the base of a wall it may flower all year, but after a year or two may decline. Tip cuttings root easily in a gritty soil mix.

Spring bedding wallflowers are treated as biennials, meaning that they grow in their first season and flower in the second, but there are also wallflowers which will flower within sixteen to twenty weeks, making them ideal for sowing from early and late summer for a continuous show in beds or containers. The seed is sown outside in summer and the young plants moved to their flowering positions in autumn. As wallflowers are of the cabbage family it is best to avoid sowing in any area where any member of the cabbage family has grown before as clubroot can stay in the soil for up to fifteen years. They will grow in land which has grown potatoes in the previous year. The seed should be sown in shallow drills, and when the plantlets are large enough can be potted on or transplanted. Wallflowers produce sturdy, branching plants with fibrous rooting systems, ensuring prolific flowering especially if the growing tip and the base of the taproot are cut back.

Saved seed can be sown straight away or let the plants seed around naturally. Self-seeded wallflowers have a sturdiness in the lower portions of the half-woody stems.

They are hardy plants and are often found on sunny sites on walls and poor soil – hence their name. After flowering I cut back the head to encourage a second flush of flowers. This also stops the plant becoming leggy and untidy.

There is a hardy herbaceous perennial alpine wallflower, *E. alpinum*, related to the biennial wallflower. It has grey-green foliage and clusters of sweetly scented pale-yellow or mauve flowers. *E. capitatum* has larger creamy-yellow flower clusters.

Traditionally wallflowers are planted with tulips or, for a cooler effect, interplanted with clouds of forget-me-nots, such as *Myosotis* 'Blue Cloud' or *M.* 'Musik'. These have the added bonus of screening faded wallflower foliage. Another exciting combination would be pale-yellow wallflowers among mounds of purple-leaved *Heuchera* 'Plum Pudding'. Other combinations could be to use complementary colours with narcissus or doronicum (leopard's bane). The range of colours now available is superb and as wallflowers have a wonderful perfume, are easy to grow and combine with other plants, they are an excellent choice for spring.

Painting 2
One of the keys to success in watercolour is understanding how to mix colours. I keep all mixes to a combination of only two colours because this preserves maximum transparency. I prefer to work with transparent colours to retain luminosity in the petals. Light areas need very subtle transitions of colour and value to avoid complication.

The petals were painted first using a washy purple, deeper into the centre of the plant with some petals tinged with darker colour to suggest veins. The highlight on the petals was left as pure white unpainted paper and the unopened buds painted with a purple-brown. The background was a washy green darkening into the centre so as to give more impact to the light on the petals.

LAMIUM
Lamium maculatum (spotted dead-nettle)

The Painting

Watercolour is fascinating as it is an expression of tonal values, colour temperature capturing light, transparent, rich, dark and atmospheric hues. Including too many colours can be confusing and unbalanced, but if colours are used in a controlled range, harmony results. An effective way of creating harmony in a painting is to focus on a small selection of colours which lie next to each other on the colour wheel. These are called analogous colours, which work well together since they share a common base colour. Examples of colour schemes might be blue, blue-green and blue-violet and the pink sits well with the violet. Here the subtle pink sits well with the soft green, giving a gentle, attractive but interesting arrangement.

The Gardener
Like me, Mag didn't like weeds; unlike me, she liked to see freshly dug earth. I have to temper myself to see the whole area rather than focus on just the weeds. Years of adding compost and ground-cover plants help to conserve moisture and eventually the plants cover the ground where weeds would have grown. Sometimes, though, they are

beautiful flowering weeds, which I appreciate, but I don't let them seed and so spread in a later season.

Ground-cover plants make a good foil to other taller plants in the border. The ideal ground-cover plant is one which has good foliage all year and spreads across the earth surface so thickly that no weed could possibly find a place to grow. Beautiful lamium is such a plant, with its pink flowers and variegated foliage. *Lamium maculatum,* the spotted dead-nettle, has attractive variegated leaves and pinkish-purple flowers, which are very welcome in early spring to autumn. The flowers are hermaphrodite, meaning they are self-fertile, having male and female organs, but they are also pollinated by bees and lamium is noted for attracting wildlife. Seeds germinate at any time of year and the plant is hardy.

In Mag's garden with higher rainfall, lamiums grew anywhere, in sun or shade, but in my garden lamium prefers the shade. It pegs itself down as it travels around the border and soon covers otherwise difficult areas.

PULMONARIA
Pulmonaria saccharata; *Pulmonaria officinalis* (lungwort)

Painting 1

A careful drawing made the painting process easier. I drew around the white spots on the leaves and left them unpainted. This close-up study of the pretty flowers is a mixture of Crimson, painted lightly with plenty of water and then, when dry, the same colour but thicker added in the centres. The blue flowers are a mix of Ultramarine Blue with touches of violet and Crimson. These same colours are added to the green for the shadows on the stalks and leaves. With a limited palette there is not a limiting of hues as all colours can be mixed from Aureolin, Indian Yellow, Quinacridone Crimson, Quinacridone Violet and French Ultramarine. In other paintings Winsor Red, Winsor Blue and Transparent Orange can be added.

Painting 2
The same technique was used for this painting as in the previous, using the same colours but adding a blue background. Ultramarine Blue (my favourite colour along with violet) is a fabulous, absolutely permanent and non-toxic blue pigment. Synthetic Ultramarine is chemically identical to lapis lazuli, a

precious stone found in Central Asia which was brought to Venice on Arab boats during the Renaissance, hence the name 'overseas' or 'ultra-marine'. Blue and purple came to be associated with royalty because of its rarity.

The Gardener

A hairy, leafy, rather weak-stemmed perennial with pink funnel-shaped flowers is held on purple-brown calyxes or elongated stems, and is decorated with small silver-spotted stem leaves. The flowers open rosy purple and turn violet and violet-blue. The flowers are in dense short clusters, which scarcely elongate after flowering. The basal autumn and spring leaves are oval and often heart-shaped at the base with white spots.

CERINTHE

Kerosanthos (honeywort) *Keros* means wax and *anthos* means flower.

The Painting

Edges are not all soft or all hard; they are varied. Each painting is a learning process and sometimes the best learning experiences are when tackling a different format – perhaps a challenging one. Here the idea was to retain the softness without losing the depth. The first wash provided the source of light that comes through from the background. When dry, more colours were added, but most of the initial background wash was not touched again, leaving it as if out of focus. I like to work first from direct observation, then respond to my initial impression. Being inspired by the subject is the first step. This must be complemented by the vision, which means planning to capture that first impression. It also means having a picture in the mind before beginning and then improvising to make a personal statement. Painting is about communicating passion. It is an expressive way of communicating feelings and reaction to a subject. Practical skills must be part of the process, but are pointless if the painting is not painted from the heart. This emotion translated into paint will produce a painting full of passion; however, it is important to have a clear vision of how the painting will develop. Both sides of the brain come into play using the creative side plus the skills of technique and concentration from the other side.

The Gardener

Cerinthe and also pulmonaria are related to borage. Cerinthe is a genus of about seven species of annual or perennial herbs native to the Mediterranean region, with glabrous, glaucus foliage and terminal leafy racemes of tubular bell-shaped, drooping pink then lilac and blue flowers and occasionally white flowers with attractive sage-green foliage speckled with white. Cerinthe is a strong spreader and the hairy leaves deter slugs and snails, and bees are said to obtain pollen from the flower.

The Doctrine of Signatures advanced the theory that certain plants were ascribed occult properties. Parts of the plant represented parts of the body or conditions for which they were intended. For example, the leaves of pulmonaria were thought to resemble the lungs in shape and so they were used in the relief of pulmonary disorders; consequently the plant is commonly known as lungwort. Its country names seem to stress its appearance rather than its properties. The Latin is *pulmo*, meaning lung, referring to the spotted leaves of *Pulmonaria officinalis,* which were supposed to resemble diseased lungs. The majority of its vernacular and old names cling to religious associations and its appearance. Children of Israel, sage of Bethlehem, spotted Mary, Mary's milk drops and Lady's milk sile (sile meaning soil or stain) all refer to the blotched leaves. Jerusalem cowslip refers to the shape of the flowers and the double names Joseph and Mary, Adam and Eve and sometimes soldiers and sailors refer to its flowers of bright blue and deep pink, particularly when the two colours appear at the same time on the plant – reminiscent of the colours of early military uniforms. It flowers very early and it often produces a few blooms in autumn as well. It grows best where it doesn't dry out.

The annual species of cerinthe is hardy and needs only ordinary soil. The seed should be sown in a sunny place in spring. The perennials need a dry sheltered position with thorough drainage lest the fleshy roots rot in winter. Once introduced into the garden, self-sown seedlings will mean that it rarely disappears.

SNAKE'S HEAD FRITILLARY
Fritillaria meleagris (Chess flower, frog-cup, guinea-hen flower, guinea flower, leper lily, because its shape resembled the bell once carried by lepers, Lazarus bell, chequered lily, chequered daffodil, drooping tulip)

The Drawing

The pencil is an expressive, versatile, economic and most neglected medium. With creative handling the graphite pencil can produce more varied effects than any other black-and-white medium. One of the advantages of using pencils is the spontaneity and freedom experienced when drawing directly from nature. Distinctive drawn lines can be made by sharpening the lead point differently, and the various grades of lead, from very hard to very soft, produce even more variety, both in line and tone. Pencil is also compatible with a wide variety of paper surfaces, whose textures can add a great deal of interest to a drawing. An accurate drawing establishes the composition, using hard and soft-grade pencils from 2H to 4B, which give a fine, sensitive touch on smooth, hot-pressed paper. Hard grades, such as 4H, can scratch the surface and don't layer or blend well. Pencil grades softer than 4B provide depth of tone, but can smear easily.

A good working drawing means the plant has been observed and analysed. Sketches show how the composition will develop and also maintain the original response of excitement and interest in the plant. Drawing quick thumbnail and value studies will help clarify thinking about shapes and design. Value is more important than colour. Colour is more intuitive and far more fleeting, but appreciation of value is merely training the eye, which everyone ought to be able to acquire. Drawing well is an extension of seeing well. There is a saying that one can only paint as well as one can draw. Drawing with graphite pencil means concentrating on the main elements; and because colour is not an element, it is easier to focus on contour, texture and important qualities. The process of learning to view a subject selectively, to analyse and interpret its essential forms, is an important experience that can be gained through drawing and is often thought of as a preliminary to painting rather than a self-contained finished image. Drawings do stand as works of art in themselves.

The Gardener

Fritillaria meleagris, the snake's head fritillary, is so called because of its unique, exquisite, pendulous strikingly beautiful nodding flower bells carried on slender stems, spotted and chequered like the skin of a snake. The flowers come in a patchwork of mauves, pinks, purples, greens and whites; some are pure white, others richly pink. They have a 'teardrop' gland within the base of each segment. Fritillaries flower from April to May and thrive in loamy soil and partially shaded places and can be naturalised in grass that is not cut until midsummer.

It was grown by Gerard, who knew it as the 'chequered daffodil' or 'ginnie hen flower', which suggests that it was a rare native. Fritillary is also a wild flower. The name may originally have been used to describe the chequer pattern on the flower in the mistaken belief that *fritillus*, meaning dice box, also meant chessboard.

CROWN IMPERIAL
Fritillaria imperialis

The Painting

Getting the tonal values right is essential because they describe the light source, and the lighting is one of the main keys to defining the particular time of day and weather conditions surrounding the subject. The light source also helps to identify the forms and structure of the individual objects within the scene.

Tonal value is the name given to the varying levels of lightness and darkness on the subject regardless of colour. Tones are sometimes called values. The eye goes first to the biggest area of the lightest light and then to the secondary light levels. The light on the petals and the shade in the interior of the flower give shape and the white stamens add to this effect.

The Gardener
All *Fritillaria imperialis*, crown imperials, do not show visible shoots until the new year. They have stout, upright stems each with a thrusting terminal cluster of large red, orange or yellow flowers like a ring of bells surmounted by a bunch of greenery in pineapple style. Each cluster of flowers has a crowning tuft of leaves. It has an unpleasant smell. It is best grown among other herbaceous plants in a border or as a focal point. Left undisturbed they will increase and make the most splendid feature.

AMELANCHIER
(snowy mespilus, shadbush, shadwood, shadblow, service tree, sarvisberry, sarvis, Juneberry, saskatoon,
sugarplum, wild plum, chuckley pear; historically it was called pigeon berry)

Painting 1

I carefully drew the flower's petals and stamens as I wanted to reserve the white of the paper. The lightest things in nature are whiter than white paper and the darkest are much darker than black paint. This means that the tones must relate to each other; and as paint dries lighter than when wet, each value must be darker than that required when it is dry.

As the stamens are a particular feature of the plant, I masked them with fluid and then washed in Ultramarine Blue and a mix of green further down behind the flowers. This was to create a contrast and to show up the white of the flowers. I used a washy Ultramarine Violet for the shadows on the petals and mixed some of the violet over the green to darken the lower leaves.

Painting 2

In June, colourful berries form. The berries were painted with a mix of Magenta and Ultramarine Violet, and Ultramarine Blue was added to the mix to give the dark shadows. Highlights were reserved, unpainted paper. The background was kept simple and washy, hinting at greenery behind the berries.

The Gardener

Amelanchier is a genus of twenty-five species of deciduous shrubs and small trees, native to North America, Europe and North Asia. Being of the Rosaceae family, they have five petals surrounding the stamens. They are easily cultivated and very hardy; they like a sunny or dappled-shade site and a rich loamy soil. They prefer a moist, well-drained soil, but are tolerant of drought. Amelanchiers have four seasons of interest, beginning with their flood of white, star-shaped flat to saucer-shaped fragrant blossoms, giving the illusion of snow when seen from a distance; summer fruits; leaf colours of red and orange; and, in winter, smooth greyish bark with striped fissures and shallow furrows when young. This changes to a spangled appearance when older. *A. lamanchier* is among one of the first trees to flower in spring, with its clusters of white flowers which bloom before the leaves appear. There are varieties in shades of red and yellow. The bronze-coloured leaves open coppery-red, making a beautiful contrast with the flowers. In June red berries form (giving it the name of Juneberry), which mature to purple-black in July. These are edible and can be eaten fresh or used to make jams or jellies. They contain small seeds at the centre and have a sweet flavour with a hint of apple, and when cooked in puddings and pies the seeds impart an almond flavour. The fruit is rich in iron and copper. Birds feast on the fruits and may strip the tree before the fruits ripen. The foliage can be eaten by swallowtail and other butterfly larvae. Amelanchiers produces more and better-quality fruits when grown in the full sunshine needed for fruit ripening. In autumn the leaves turn a brilliant orange, gold and red.

Plants are hermaphrodite, being asexual, and as they do not need to be pollinated they may be hybrids. Propagation can be by seed, which germinates quickly if sown fresh. Seed is best harvested when green though fully formed, but before the seed coat has hardened, and then sown immediately in pots outdoors or in a cold frame. When the seedlings are large enough, prick them into individual pots and grow them on in a sheltered outdoor position. Grow them on for two years before planting them out in winter into their permanent positions. It is beneficial to fertilise young plants in spring with compost or a tree plant food. Generally older plants do not need fertilisation.

Rooted suckers can create more plants. Shoots with a few roots often develop at the base. These can be cut off and potted on in spring.

My little shrub is important to me as I gathered the berries while walking with my sister in Saville Gardens in January 2012 just before she died. It was absolutely freezing, but we enjoyed being together and sharing the fresh air and the gardens. A special memory to me.

PASQUE FLOWER

Ranunculaceae, Pulsatilla vulgaris (Easter flower, windflower, prairie crocus, meadow anemone)

The Painting

The complementary colours of yellow and purple were the attraction to painting these pasque flowers. The flower centres were painted with Winsor Yellow and, when dry, dots of Winsor Orange were added so that the paler yellow suggested pollen. The greens of the leaves were a further contrast, showing the nature of their growth, adding to the composition without being too important.

Each painting is part of the process of being an artist. The process must be enjoyable, otherwise it becomes a task and creativity disappears. The process is constantly in flux and growth and ever evolving. The act of painting has true value and the reason to become an artist. A beautiful garden is a place of calm, a place to lift the spirits. Like Monet said, "I need go no further than my garden to find a perfect subject to paint."

I like busy, complicated scenes, but they must have a calm area. The key issue is to concentrate on the focal point, which will put all the other details into a supporting role. An exciting way to achieve contrast is through colour, though a painting which is entirely warm or entirely cool in colour can be bland. By contrasting cool and warm colours, neutral and intense colours or complementary colours, the painting can be brought to life and have greater impact. Constable used this technique by using small patches of warm and cool greens placed side by side to break up the area, as did Monet. When colour and value contrast are used together, the result can be stunning.

The Gardener

Pulsatillas have tufted clumps of ferny leaves, from which slightly nodding goblet-shaped flowers appear in mid spring. Colours are rich mauve-purple with other varieties having pale-mauve, pink, red or white flowers. They have prominent centres of golden-yellow stamens. When the flowers fade, pretty silken seed heads develop. These resemble the seed heads of clematis.

The brightly coloured flowers bloom around Easter time, hence its common name, pasque flower. Gerard claims to have christened it 'pasque flower'. The link with Easter is probably of some antiquity, more accurately relating to the pre-Christian dawn goddess, Eastre, the Teutonic goddess of dawn, spring and fertility. She is also called Ostara, with sunrise celebrations centred on growth and renewal. Her male consort was the sun god and rites of spring were celebrated in her honour on the first day of spring. The full moon represents a 'pregnant' phase of Eastre, passing into fertility to give birth to the sun's offspring. Prayers to Eastre assured abundant crops and eggs were exchanged and eaten as talismans. The earth in spring is full of fertility and awakening, so the egg is an obvious symbol and has been a symbol of rebirth since ancient times. The Egyptians and Greeks buried eggs in tombs of the dead as a sign of resurrection. Eggs were decorated and given as gifts, and dyed eggs were part of early rituals in ancient civilisations, probably being the first Easter eggs. The word east is related to her and the female hormone oestrogen is named for her.

In the south-east of England the pasque flower is known as the Danes flower. Previously it was known as *Anemone pulsatilla*, but it differs in some botanical detail from other anemones. The name pulsatilla was first given by Mattioli, meaning 'shaking in the wind'.

Their hairiness makes them shrink from the dampness of winter, so they need really good drainage. The generic name may indicate that the drying effect of the wind is beneficial to them in ridding their silky calyxes and foliage of excess moisture.

FORSYTHIA
Forsythia intermedia (golden balls or golden bell bush, Easter tree)

The Painting

A spray of forsythia looks like a firework exploding with yellow sparks, vibrant and full of movement and colour. Value and design are the most important tools in composing the picture. Early morning or late afternoon is the best time to capture strong shadows. Morning light has cool tones while afternoon light has warm, golden tones. A high level of detail is very labour-intensive and one of the main requirements is to remain interested and challenged throughout the process of painting. I have found that small drops of masking fluid can capture the highlights on each petal. Darker areas can be painted over the fluid once it is dry. When the fluid is removed by rubbing gently with the finger, the highlights can be washed over with pale yellow. A dark background of the plant is an advantage to enhancing the brilliance of yellow.

The Gardener

The sun-loving forsythia is one of the first shrubs to make a big display of magnificent starry golden-yellow massed flowers, which are a delight in spring with their bright colours shrugging off the sombre days of winter. Great sprays of heavily massed golden-yellow flowers are borne along the branches either singly or in groups. The best flowers are produced on strong one-year-old stems, so pruning out old flowering stems improves the quality of the flowers, which are tubular at the base opening out into long petals. Forsythias respond well to hard pruning after flowering has finished. This allows time for the growth of new branches, which will mature before winter sets in and provides the flower buds for next year's spring flowering. As many of the older branches as possible should be cut out as well as the younger ones which have already flowered. Cuttings of bare wood put into a sheltered border in October will root easily. They will also root in water and should then be potted into compost and placed in a cold frame. Forsythia grows very slowly through the winter, waiting for better light and more warmth. Forsythia can be grown anywhere as a specimen shrub, against a wall or trained as standard trees.

The genus is named after the eighteenth-century British horticulturist William Forsyth, superintendent of the Royal Gardens, Kensington, and author of a book on fruit growing.

FORGET-ME-NOT
Myosotis sylvatica or *Myositis scorpioides* (scorpion weed, love me, mouse ears, snake grass)

The Painting

The compositional drawing established where the shapes and colours would be. I used Cerulean Blue and Phthalocyanine Blue, a cool blue for the forget-me-not's petals, darkened here and there with Ultramarine Blue. The greens were a mix of Winsor Lemon and Cerulean Blue, giving a cool green; Ultramarine Blue and Winsor Lemon created a warmer green. The centres of the flowers were Winsor Lemon, and when dry a dot of Winsor Orange was added. This complementary colour accentuated the different blues.

Cerulean is named after the Latin word *caeruleum*, meaning sky or heaven. It is a highly stable and light-fast greenish blue, although it lacks the richness of Cobalt Blue, which is an expensive but wonderful blue. Phthalocyanine Blue is very powerful, appearing almost black when applied thickly. It has other trade names, which include Monastral, Winsor and Phthalo.

The Gardener
Henry IV adopted the forget-me-not as his symbol during his exile in 1398, and retained the symbol upon his return to England the following year.

Newfoundland used the flower as a symbol of remembrance of the nation's war dead. This is still in limited practice, though alongside the Flanders poppy. The flower was popularised by Coleridge in his poem 'The Keepsake' in 1802, in which the flower is both a love token and a memento.

The Victorians, who were great travellers, used to go out of their way to see myosotis in its greatest beauty and abundance by the banks of a small stream in Luxembourg called the Fairies' Bath or the Cascade of the Enchanted Oak. The forget-me-not was woven in ribbons, embroidered on cushion-covers, embossed on valentine cards, painted on china, lithographed for ornamental texts and painstakingly reproduced by young ladies in albums accompanied by a few appropriate lines. It headed notepaper and menus, and was top favourite on birthday cards, and its pink and blue flowers were cleverly reproduced in velvet to adorn many bonnets.

Myosotis means 'mouse ears' in reference to the shape of the leaves. Its common name was from the French *ne m'oubliez pas* and was first used in England in 1532. Forget-me-nots represent 'true love' and get their name from a German legend in which a young man dies in the act of picking forget-me-nots for his sweetheart. As he slipped and fell into the river beside which they were growing, he threw the flowers at her feet with the parting words "Forget me not." In another legend, God thought he had finished giving the flowers their colours when he heard one whisper, "Forget me not." There was nothing left but a very small amount of blue, but the forget-me-not was delighted to wear such a light shade of blue.

Freemasons began using the forget-me-not in 1926 as a symbol, well known in Germany, as a message not to forget the poor and desperate. In later years it was used as a means of recognition by a handful of Masons in place of the square and compass design. This was done across Nazi-occupied Europe to avoid any danger of being singled out and persecuted. Today it is an interchangeable symbol with Freemasonry and some also use the forget-me-not to remember those Masons who were victimised by the Nazi regime. In English Freemasonry it is more commonly now worn to remember those that have died as a symbol that they may be gone but not forgotten.

The forget-me-not was one of Mag's favourite flowers and always reminds me of her. A drift of the jaunty, tiny branched flower panicles of pure sky blue or pink, each with a yellow or white centre, borne on tall stems above the basal leaves, looks wonderful with bulbs or for edges and in containers. They are traditionally planted with tulips, wallflowers, pansies and polyanthus. They also look wonderful in drifts under roses. They are best grown in sun, provided there is sufficient moisture in the soil, and will tolerate some shade. Forget-me-nots are annuals that complete their whole life cycle within one year. The seed germinates, grows, flowers, sets seed and dies, sometimes not in the calendar year, but always within a period of twelve months.

The nectar at the base of the very short tubular flower attracts butterflies, long-headed flies and bees, but if pollinators do not visit the flowers they are usually self-pollinated.

Myosotis capitata has brilliant dark-blue flowers while *M. traversii* has pale-yellow flowers.

M. scorpioides (scorpion grass, or water forget-me-not) is a rather weak, leafy, ascending perennial often rooted below, forming spike-like clusters of short-stalked bright-blue flowers in spring to autumn.

The forget-me-not is a biennial and a member of the borage family. It sheds seeds that germinate everywhere and once in a garden will always give a fabulous show.

DOG'S-TOOTH VIOLET

Erythronium 'Pagoda' (fawn lily, trout lily, dog's tooth violet, adder's tongue)

The Painting

There is no colour without light, and lighting can play a significant role in creating interest. Not only does light emphasise the transparency of petals, but it creates an interplay in the background. The colours of nature are richer and more varied than they appear to be from a casual glance. Even on a grey day the sky contains all the primary colours – red, yellow and blue – in a dilute form, which enhances that feeling of colour. I sometimes exaggerate strong colour to add excitement, and a cool background helps the glow of the petals and creates a special effect. In this painting of the erythronium I chose a close view of a small flower, which gives the appearance of a large flower but I felt it was exciting. I glazed over some areas with a light tint of colour to adjust hue and value and washed clear water over some areas to soften and tie shapes together. I am also aware of the negative shapes as well as the positive, which enhance the beauty of the flower. Some edges were sharpened to direct attention to the centre of the flower, which is the centre of interest.

The Gardener

The common name of erythronium is dog's-tooth violet because of the shape of long, pointed canine-like bulbs. It is an attractive spring-flowering plant with delicate white, yellow or purple-pink flowers with upward-curled petals often with contrasting marks in the centre. Erythroniums have two leaves, which may be either glossy green or marked with conspicuous mottling. It is a native of woodland, requiring moist humus-rich soil and a cool, shady place among shrubs, ideal under rhododendrons. The European species, *Erythronium dens-canis,* has pink-purple, violet or white flowers patterned inside with contrasting zones, and jagged green leaves blotched grey or brown. Only two species have pink flowers and bronze leaves.

    E. revolutum is ideal for naturalising in woodland, *E. revolutum americanum*, or trout lily, is the parent of a number of garden varieties with yellow, white or pink to purple flowers. *E. tuolumnense* is the most vigorous and has bright-yellow drooping flowers and pale-green leaves, named after California's' Tuolumne river, where the plants grow wild. It increases rapidly by offsets. *E.* 'Pagoda' has sulphur-yellow nodding flowers that carpet the ground in dappled shade. *E. giganteum* has upward-curled shaped flowers of palest-straw colour, almost white, and has large leaves. The flowers grow singly or in pairs, on tall stems with throats beautifully marked and golden-anthered stamens. Their colours range from yellow to pink and purple.

E. californicum, or 'White Beauty', has creamy-white flowers and mottled foliage and increases into clumps. *E. oregonum* is white and is propagated by offsets and can also be increased by seed distribution. *E. evolumnense* is a vigorous butter-yellow-flowered species and increases rapidly by offsets.

They require cool conditions, unlike their relative the tulip. The bulbs should be planted in autumn without delay as they have no protective outer skin and are therefore prone to drying out if left exposed. The bulb soon forms a good clump and is good ground cover. They smother new weed seedlings before they get a chance to establish. It is important that they do not dry out completely in summer as they need moisture even when seemingly dormant. They can be propagated by division after flowering, and care should be taken not to expose them as they can dry out. They should be planted with the more pointed end upwards and with at least six centimetres of soil above the tip. Once they are planted it is best to leave them to build up clusters, as this is how they are most effective. If they become too crowded, they can be lifted in late summer, divided and planted in a previously prepared area. They benefit from a sprinkling of potash in autumn and spring. They look good planted with hellebores and anemones.

TULIP
Tulipa

Painting 1
Sometimes I like to paint a flower when it is at its peak, the moment of glory before it dies. Full-blown tulips have a magnificence, with bold colours and sometimes curving stems and pointed leaves which make a composition interesting. I like to make lots of preliminary sketches, which means careful observation. Drawing is actually learning to look at proportions, relationships between sizes and shapes. It is important to study how the light and consequently the shadows fall on the subject. The tonal values within and around the plant dictate the contrast, and this is what gives the painting depth.

Painting 2
The twisting and turning of the petals and the light shining through and the all-important shadows make the plant look three-dimensional in the painting. To achieve an interesting composition, I overlapped several flowers to create a sense of depth, and having one of the flowers in shadow balances the painting. I kept the background simple since there is a lot of detail in the flowers and leaves.

Bright colours can be stimulating, expressing vitality both to the eye and to the soul. Colour can influence mood and atmosphere, lift the spirits and play a large part in the interpretation of the subject, and it can be manipulated to create an effect, just as in gardening.

This painting is much more an impression with blocks of red and pink against a wet-in-wet background. Once the red petals were dry, a wash of clear water was carefully painted around the flowers and then colour applied into the wet. The most beautiful and atmospheric effects can be produced when colour is dropped on to wet paper and allowed to mix, rather than mixing the colours in the palette. The colours spread and merge gently together and dry in a unique way.

The Gardener

The charm of the tulip as a garden flower is greatly enhanced by underplanting with dwarf plants such as forget-me-nots, wallflowers, violas and daisies. Yellow tulips look wonderful with flame-coloured wallflowers, and purple heuchera are gorgeous with purple tulips and violas. Pink tulips sit beautifully with forget-me-nots.

Tulips are notoriously difficult to keep going from year to year, especially in cool, moist climates and heavy or moisture-retaining soil, and if they are allowed to become crowded. Although foliage of spring-flowering bulbs may not appear above ground until late winter, root production begins in late summer and the earlier they can be planted the better. The only exception to this is the tulip, which is best planted in early winter. It is a good idea to emulate the growing conditions from which the bulbs originate, adding grit especially when planted in pots. In mixed borders the bulbs may be left in the ground, but the leaves should not be removed until they have withered. They require plenty of leaf mould, grit and burnt refuse, and in spring potash. Placing the bulbs on the soil surface before planting ensures even distribution. When planted early they can be attacked by frost or by a fungus disease called 'fire'. As the flowers go over, the seed head should be broken off so as to prevent the withered petals and stamens from falling into the ground, which may encourage the 'fire' fungus, which could be a problematic source of infection in the following year.

One of the best ways to help tulips to multiply is to remove spent flowers. Once the plants finish blooming those that have been fertilised form seed heads. If the seed is allowed to develop, the food made by the leaves is then wholly directed to the seed instead of developing the bulb, which sustains their growth and flowering in the following season. By leaving the bulbs in the ground, clusters of new bulbs form around the parent. These can be divided and replanted immediately. When tulips which have been grown in pots have finished flowering, I plant them in the garden to rest and to grow and flower again in the following year. Tulips, unlike daffodils, are resilient. If a daffodil is knocked down by wind and rain, it stays down while tulips, with their swanlike necks, can turn so as to face upwards again.

No wild species has been identified as the species from which the garden tulip has been developed. The tulips came originally from Turkey. *Tulip* is Turkish for turban. It is probable that the introduction of the garden tulip into Europe is due to Ogier Ghiselin de Busbecq, who was ambassador of the Holy Roman Empire to Suleiman the Magnificent. He first saw them at Adrianople when on his way to Constantinople in 1554 and introduced them to Europe in 1572. In 1559 Conrad Gesner, the Swiss naturalist, described some tulips he saw growing at Augsberg. From the description it seems probable that these were seedlings of *Tulipa suaveolens* (dwarf tulips), not *T. gesneriana*, which is similar to garden tulips.

The English writer Richard Hakluyt wrote in 1582, 'Within these four years there have been brought into England from Vienna in Austria divers kinds of flowers called Tulipes and these and others procured thither a little before from Constantinople by an excellent man called M. Carolus Clusius.'

Richard Hakluyt promoted the British colonisation of North America and his writings were a source of material for William Shakespeare and other authors. He also encouraged the production of geographical and historical writings.

In 1593 Clusius became professor of botany at Leiden and took with him tulip bulbs. Unfortunately for him they were stolen and they were soon distributed widely over Holland, but apparently they were not the first to be grown in Leiden. In 1590 John Hogeland grew tulips at Leiden from bulbs possibly obtained from George Rye, a merchant of Mechlin, who himself had acquired them from an Eastern merchant in Antwerp. In 1574 Selim II sent an order to the Sheriff of Aziz for 50,000 bulbs for the royal gardens. High prices were sometimes paid for tulip bulbs in Turkey, and the Sultan directed the Mayor of Stamboul (officially named Istanbul today) to fix their prices, those who sold at higher prices than those fixed being sentenced to expulsion from the city. The cult of the tulip became as extravagant in Turkey during the reign of Ahmed III (1702–1720) as ever it did in Holland during the tulip mania from 1634 to 1637. In both Holland and Turkey fabulous prices were asked and received for special tulip bulbs and much speculation went on in Holland, not for their food value, although the bulbs have been eaten from time to time, but to supply the enormous demand for bulbs for spring flowering, which grew up in many countries.

The pointed petal was the ideal in Turkey, but was little valued in Europe, where the rounded broad end to the petal was valued. Various forms have been developed. Both English and (mostly) Dutch raisers have played a part in attaining the present strains. New varieties are obtained by seedlings, which are not difficult to raise.

The nineteenth-century tulip only flowered in late spring and had cup-shaped flowers with no other colour than white or yellow in the base of the flower. Others were grown in gardens derived from the same general source, but they gained little recognition as flowers worthy of the fancier's attention and care. The tulip is still valued for its perfection of shape and clear colour, but many other forms are grown widely. There was confusion over varieties until 1913, when a Tulip Nomenclature Committee was set up by the Royal Horticultural Society and comparative trials were instituted in its garden at Wisley. English and Dutch growers co-operated in sorting out the varieties and in preparing a report, which was published in 1917. Meanwhile, other strains of tulips were being evolved in Holland and trials were begun in 1929 at the headquarters of the Algemene Vereniging Voor Bloembollencultur General Dutch Bulb Growers Society of Harlem, and the committee was reconstituted to settle the questions of classification and to draw up colour descriptions of the numerous additional varieties which were grown there or appeared at exhibitions. In 1929 a 'Tentative List of Tulip Names' was published as a result of co-operation between the two bodies represented on the committee with a supplement in 1930, and in accordance with the resolution adopted at the International Horticultural Conference held at Rome. From this 1935 list come the names of garden varieties of tulip. Other new varieties were considered since and the two societies co-operated in producing the 'Classified List of Tulip Names', published in 1948, containing over 4,300 names, of which about 500 are synonyms.

The robust Darwin tulips with square-based flowers were introduced in 1899, and this group has provided many of the most well known and most widely grown of present-day varieties. They are highly bred artificial cultivation, the work of three centuries of breeding. The vast number of large-flowered hybrids vary according to the flowering time, plant shape, flower size and form. Most have lance-shaped leaves.

Nature has evolved a multitude of ways for plants to survive, but bulbous plants fall technically into several different categories. Whether or not they are true bulbs, corms, tubers or rhizomes, they are all storage organs, in which food is stockpiled by the leaves during the growing period before dying back to a resting period. Tulips are colourful, sophisticated and easy to grow, a welcome splash of colour in spring, and give endless and lovely combinations. Each bulb contains a ready formed flower. Tulips need to be planted deeply to avoid the too early emergence of the young tender shoots. Single early tulips have rounded petals, forming small deep cup-shaped single flowers which sometimes open flat in full sun. They are among the earliest tulips to flower in spring. The difference in flowering times means a succession of blooms. Pinks and scarlets combine well. 'Vermilion Brilliant' will provide a feast of colour followed by 'Brilliant Star', which flowers a little later and is slightly taller. In my garden the beautiful single tulip is 'De Wit'. It is a glowing orange with stipplings and veinings. 'Fred Moor' is even brighter and a first-rate early deep scarlet is 'Artus' followed a week or two later by 'Crimoisie Brilliant', ' Chrysomera' (a golden yellow) and 'Mon Tresor' (a deeper yellow). Double early tulips have large double flowers resembling peonies. These follow on from the singles. They don't fare well in wind and rain, so need a sheltered position.

The two most usually grown groups of botanical tulips are the Greigii and Kaufmanniana hybrids. Tulips in these groups will continue in soils which otherwise would be most inhospitable to the genus. Kaufmanniana hybrids, or water-lily tulips, are so named because of their open, distinctive flowers. They are creamy white with red shading on the exterior of the outer petals. They are the first hybrid species to flower.

Greigii tulips are short, have purple-striped leaves and giant flower heads and are most effective in rock gardens or containers. They are distinguished by their broad leaves, which are prominently marked and streaked with dark brownish purple. The best is 'Red Riding Hood', which is bright scarlet. *T. praestans* has long red flowers with blunt petals in early to mid spring. Each stem carries between two and five flowers with attractive broad grey-green leaves. *T. tarda* has flowers with narrow petals with a yellow base in mid spring. Up to five petals are carried in a cluster on each stem. *T. linifolia* is brilliant scarlet with narrow leaves, recommended for the rock garden or a hot, well-drained place. Fosteriana tulips flower a week or two later than the 'botanicals' and are the basis of the Darwin hybrids. 'White Emperor' is the best and is a longer-lasting, tall, white tulip. *T.* 'Cantata' is vermilion and 'Candela' is yellow. The Parrot tulips are a later garden-raised group, perhaps from the variety of *T. gesneriana* called 'Dracontia'. The Cottage tulips vary greatly in form with four well-marked types: the true cup type as in 'Bouton d'Or'; the long, pointed type, often with a distinct waist; the type with pointed reflexing segments; and the long egg-shaped type.

Some of the best scented tulips are the orange tulips, such as lily-flowered 'Ballerina'. The lily-flowered tulips are the closest to the original Turkish tulips that ignited the Dutch passion for the flower in the seventeenth century, and although they appear to be fragile this is not the case.

MAHONIA
*Mahonia japonica (*Oregon grape)

The Painting

Colour may be divided into warm and cool colours. Warm colours are brilliant red, crimson, orange, peach and warm yellow. Cool colours include stark brilliant white, bluish pink, magenta and purple-reds with an element of blue through shades of green-yellow, cool blue, and green, although within each are warm and cool. For example, Ultramarine Blue has some red, which makes it a warm blue. The cool greens of the glossy mahonia leaves accentuate the bright-yellow flowers, a complementary colour against contrasting blue-green. When looking from the yellow flowers to the blue-green foliage the eye becomes saturated with colour, so that the blue-green can appear luminous and refreshing. Mood is created by using a limited palette of subdued, harmonious colours and careful use of values and colour. Dramatic light means being ready for the fleeting moment when the sun appears. Capturing light as it flows over the subject creates dramatic tension, rhythm, the life and breath of the scene.

This close up view of the mahonia shows the detail of the flowers, which were painted with Lemon Yellow. I used Raw Sienna for the centres of the flowers and shadows on the buds. A touch more blue was added to the top leaves as the blue helps to complement the yellow and make it appear brighter.

The Gardener

When the family lived at Greendoors, near Windsor, we had a big garden with mahonia grown as a hedge along one boundary. Now, with them planted in my garden, I am reminded of my childhood delight in these plants. Mahonia has attractive evergreen glossy foliage, showy racemes of flowers followed by attractive grape-like clusters of berries loved by birds. The sweetly scented bright-yellow flowers are grouped together. The handsome glossy leaves are similar to a holly, from which it derives its specific name. The genus is named for nineteenth-century North American horticulturist Bernard McMahon.

Mahonia is a form of the Oregon grape and belongs to the barberry family, which also includes berberis and epimedium. There are over seventy species of mahonia worldwide, originating in America and Asia. The American species are generally dense and spreading, with clusters of yellow flowers in spring. Asian mahonias are usually more upright, with dramatic blooms from November to March. The holly-like leaves turn rich red and purple in winter and there are sprays of perfumed soft-yellow flowers in mid spring followed by small purple berries. The Chinese *Mahonia japonica* has the very best fragrance, reminiscent of lily-of-the-valley, and prefers a sheltered position with protection from winds. *M. japonica* has a long flowering season which lasts for six months. Its lily-of-the-valley fragrance is a joy and the sprigs of yellow flowers are uplifting in winter. No regular pruning is needed, but after several years long vertical shoots on bare wood can be pruned back after flowering in April. This also means it does not become leggy. New shoots will grow from the old wood and flower in their next season. They can be invasive, putting out new shoots in all directions.

MAGNOLIA

Painting 1

A familiar scene can be transformed from mundane to sensational by a particular quality of light. The elegant flowers of *Magnolia stellata* (star magnolia) are plump, almost leathery and yet elegant and beautiful. The magnificent blooms of the magnolia are a cheerful and evocative sight in early spring. Being white, it means looking carefully at the colour values within the shadows and their relation to each other. It is crucial to look for strong lighting effects, especially where the light glows through the petals. In my painting, the tones in the petals were built up with light washes, in certain areas defining the curve and leaving the white of the paper as the sunlit parts. Darker washes were used to give depth, making sure that the edges of the petals were given distinct separation and that they did not flow together. No pigment or white paper comes anywhere near the brightness of natural light, so, in the painting, everything around the light area has to be made darker to achieve a convincing sense of light.

Painting 2

M. 'Leonard Messel'. The background was soaked with clear water, avoiding the magnolia petals. Immediately Ultramarine Blue and Sap Green were dropped at random on to the wet surface, dispersing and merging and the blue granulating in places. When dry I used a minute amount of watery Ultramarine Violet, Opera Rose and Ultramarine Blue to shape the petals and then rose in the centre of the flower. The branches were lightly painted with Burnt Sienna darkened in places with a little violet and kept washy so that they almost disappeared at their extremes.

The Gardener

The name magnolia was given in honour of Pierre Magnol, 1638–1751, director of the Botanical Gardens, Montpellier. *Magnolia* is a genus of about eighty species of trees and shrubs, natives of North and Central America, East Asia and the Himalayas. *M. stellata* is deciduous with white fragrant flowers which are later tinged with rose. They come early in spring and have been known to flower in the autumn as well. All early flowering shrubs need careful placing in sunny or lightly shaded positions sheltered from strong winds. In the evening dark colours will almost disappear and lighter colours become less vivid, but white becomes relatively more luminous and is the last to disappear from view.

This is a slow-growing deciduous bush rather than a tree. It has fragrant pure-white starry strap-petalled flowers in spring. To encourage flowering, an application of acidifying fertiliser, similar to those applied to rhododendrons and azaleas, can help. I take soft-tip cuttings from late spring to early summer. Layering is more reliable, but takes longer. To do this peg down shoots from spring to late summer and detach rooted stems a year later.

M. 'Galaxy' has tulip-shaped buds of reddish purple which open into fat goblet-like flowers revealing a white and pale-pink inside, highlighted by a protruding cone of brown carpels and pink stamens. The flowers arrive before the leaves. The tree shape becomes wider and more conical as its arching branches droop with age. The large oval leaves turn yellow in autumn.

Most magnolias thrive in moist slightly acid soils and a warm, sunny position and benefit from a top dressing of leaf mould. Cold winds and late frosts can disfigure the flowers and even damage young growth.

In autumn magnolias have long distinctive seed pods resembling exotic-looking cones, which spread open to reveal bright-red berries. Inside are the seeds, which are attractive to birds and squirrels, who relish the tasty fruit.

BLUEBELL
Endymion (wild hyacinth)

The Painting

The secret of successful watercolour painting lies in the artist's ability to control the right amount of water used with the right amount of pigment and allowing the washes to settle and dry without interruption. This means that the washes may evolve on their own, and this is one of the dynamics of watercolour. Technical ability, once acquired, is for life, though one can continually improve upon it. Paint application is not a random act – decisions about colours and their placement are decided beforehand. The main objective is to concentrate and learn a little every day.

In the bluebell painting the background shapes were encouraged to flow around the flower shapes, leaving the white of the paper untouched. When the wash had dried, I painted the flowers and stalks, building up depth with stronger colour. Accurately placing a single brushstroke demands intense concentration, but not all the details are explained; some things can be left to the imagination.

Wet-in-wet is one of the most beautiful and expressive techniques in watercolour painting. When colours are applied to a wet or damp surface they merge gently into each other and dry with a soft, hazy quality, blending colours naturally on the paper without leaving a hard edge.

Practical Use of Watercolour Paper

For soft, watery application of this kind there needs to be an understanding of how absorbent the paper is and how it will respond. Some types of paper are not very absorbent, so the paint sits on the surface and may not give the effect envisaged. I use cold-pressed paper and mostly transparent watercolours. It is important to use good paper and lay down washes only once, which makes for greater luminosity. For a wet-in-wet technique it is best to use a heavy-grade paper which will accept water and paint without wrinkling. The paper is moistened with water using a large brush or spray. No water should lie on the surface or underneath the paper, so if the board is tilted slightly any excess water will flow downwards, as will the colours when added. If the board and paper are laid flat, there is danger of washes running inwards or backwards, creating unwanted blotches and water marks, or 'blooms'. The colours will diffuse of their own accord and should not be touched. It is important to mix plenty of paint as running out of colour during a wash application can cause problems, as the colour already applied can dry, and a further application will not merge smoothly into the first, causing blooms and lines. I use plenty of colour as the wet surface of the paper will dilute and soften, and as the wash dries will appear to be lighter and paler.

Rough paper is made on a screen that allows the wet pulp of the fibres to bulge through in the little humps that exist after the paper has dried. Smooth paper is passed between warm metal rollers while still wet. This process irons the paper, smoothing its surface. This is why the paper is often called 'hot-pressed'. The polished rollers smooth the surface of the paper, but also compress the fibres, so that the resulting paper is almost always less absorbent than rough paper. This means that paint can be removed more easily, if need be, and can look fresher and cleaner with sharper edges. Greater detail is possible by this means. Rough-brushing on smooth paper cannot be achieved in the same way as on rough paper. Speed and a very dry brush will provide some rough-brush effects. Smooth paper responds well to colour – unlike rough paper, which tends to neutralise colours, losing intensity as the humps in the paper cast individual shadows.

"Exaggerate the essentials and leave out the obvious."
Vincent Van Gogh

The Gardener

In my garden between the oak trees and spreading outwards into the flower borders and lawn is a multitude of bluebells. Their blue seems to reflect the sky, but it is a more complex blue than that overhead, running rich azure to the palest tints and shot with delicate pinks and rich purples. Bluebells, *Endymion non-scriptus,* used to be known as wild hyacinths and the French still call them *jacinthes des bois,* since they are almost always found in woodland glades. The sight of a wood carpeted with bluebells is magical and has often inspired poets. Tennyson memorably likened bluebells to the sky breaking through the earth. English bluebells have flowers which hang to one side of the slightly bent stalk, are scented and have creamy white pollen. *E. hispanicus*, the Spanish bluebell, is similar to *E. non-scriptus*, but the flowers are erect or ascending in a conical cluster and not one-sided. The flowers are unscented and the petal tips flare outwards and curl back. The pollen is pale bluish green. They are invasive and crowd out the native *E. non-scriptus*.

LEOPARD'S BANE
Doronicum pardalianches

The Painting

The artist as well as the gardener needs to be observant and interested in the changes in nature and must follow them attentively. I wish to capture the fabulous shapes and colours of nature and the ever changing light and fleeting atmospheric conditions. My paintings tend to be detailed, but I want my compositions to be uncluttered, so in this painting the flowers are the main feature. The background was a wash of Ultramarine Blue running into green with the plant detailed. Primary colours are pure, natural, are not made and cannot be mixed from any other colours. Primary colours are the basis of all other colours and are mixed in varying proportions to produce every other colour known. Pure yellow was used for the petals, a touch of red mixed into the yellow to produce a pale orange for the centres, and blue was added to the yellow to make green for the leaves.

The Gardener

Doronicum has big bright-yellow daisies on thickened rhizomes and, being one of the earliest flowers, continues from March and into May. It is very good for nectar-eating insects. It is a perennial native to Europe and temperate Asia. *Doronicum plantagineum* is one metre high; *D. cordatum* is best for edging, being only a third of the height. *D. pardalianches*, or great leopard's bane, has yellow flowers, sometimes three or five to a stem. They have one leaf extending from a bushy rosette of rounded heart-shaped leaves. They are hardy and thrive in most garden soils, in sun or partial shade, going dormant in summer. Their tuberous underground stems should be divided every second or third year and are easily propagated by division in autumn.

They look magnificent surrounded by the blue of forget-me-nots, cornflowers and periwinkles. The cluster of flowers included self-seeded pink aquilegia. The aquilegas are best among lilac and purple irises, creating a quite different combination, resulting in effective matching or contrasting colour.

EARLY SUMMER

WISTERIA
(Japanese or Chinese wisteria)

The Drawing

Drawing focuses the eye and the mind to notice subtleties in value changes and nuances of colour shifts, which may not be apparent before starting the drawing. Time taken to study the subject of the painting develops skills of observation and gives a more intimate knowledge – in this case of the shapes, colours and values of the wisteria flower. Morning sun intensifies the colours, but also filters through the petals, giving them a sense of luminosity.

Coloured pencil is a translucent medium, so colours laid down first will show through subsequent layers built up over them. The basic strokes are laid down, one colour on top of another to develop hues and tonal values with varying degrees of pressure, but never heavily. This would cause an unpleasant shine. A light touch is needed in the drawing of the delicate flowers.

Close-up details of nature are inspiring. The closer to the subject, the more there is to discover.

The Painting

Each weather condition and each time of day has a unique atmosphere that affects the mood and lighting. The best time is early or late in the day. It is important to anticipate how the weather, clouds and direction of the light can affect the painting. The light can change an everyday scene into something quite striking. Painting direct from nature can awaken the senses and feed the soul, but requires patience and a willingness to be at one with nature. I find watercolour is the easiest medium to use as it is so portable and the transparent colours let the paper glow through the veils of colour washes. The choice of pigments changes throughout the year with fresh greens in spring, violets and blues in shadows in the summer and winter, and yellows and reds in autumn.

In this painting, the mood is achieved through the use of particular colours combined with a chiaroscuro effect, which is the dramatic contrasting of light and shadow. Many plants have only two main colours, but a wide range of hues. There

is always an excitement when starting a new painting. As the painting evolves it is possible to see how it will finish, but I constantly question whether the colour is warmer, cooler, lighter or darker. I used a warm Ultramarine Blue for the flowers, with a little purple mixed in for the shadows. The same blue was used in the mix of green for the leaves, with a paler more dilute mix for the background. The yellowy-green background worked well as a complement to the blue and gave a light airy feel at the same time as suggesting more growth behind the flowers.

The Gardener

Wisteria is a most beautiful, vigorous, twining deciduous climbing plant that can grow to many metres. The flowers are similar to those of the pea plant on long trails in blue, lavender or mauve, pale pink and white.

They are tolerant of poor soils as their roots can fix their own nitrogen. If they are planted in a rich soil they can often produce more leaf than flower. The woody stem twines around anything it reaches. *Wisteria floribunda* (Japanese wisteria) grows in a clockwise direction, while *W. sinensis* (Chinese wisteria) grows anticlockwise. The millions of gracefully cascading flowers open gradually from the base of the plant upwards at the same time as the leaves emerge. The shimmering pendulous sprays of pale-lilac flowers cascade down and act like a perfumed curtain over our arbour. Smaller racemes appear in the summer in a secondary flush of blooms followed by pendulous pods full of large seeds. It flowers better if pruned twice yearly, creating stubby spur-like side shoots, which bear masses of spectacular scented blooms in spring. To keep them tidy and encourage flowering they should be pruned during the height of summer, taking all the whippy new growths back to two buds or five leaves. This will induce spurs for the following year. Summer pruning is for flowering, and winter pruning is for growth. Every winter it should be cut back nearly to the old wood, leaving spur shoots for future flowering, but I do find it best to trim long shoots every week through spring and summer. To have some form of control, a hard prune in the dormant season stops tendrils reaching into unwanted places. This also allows sunlight to reach and ripen the wood on which the following year's flowers should form.

I cannot be sure from which variety I collected the original seed, but it is very vigorous, so is probably *W. sinensis*, which has a huge trunk and long racemes with fabulous marvellously scented purple flowers. It has obviously spread its roots under the path and found plenty of moisture as well as profiting from a warm, sheltered site. I have learned from this first plant that its offspring need careful management early in life so as to appreciate the beauty without too much work.

Propagation in summer is by layering stems, which is securing stems to the ground so that they take root. I now have wisteria growing along the top of a fence, but have to control it as it could easily overrun a climbing rose. I once planted a layered stem close to the house – too close – and had difficulty removing the long roots which had grown down under the house.

Applying potash can inhibit a plant's uptake of nitrogen, which makes the plant grow lushly. This growth check is effective on plants like wisteria and many other crops, such as tomatoes.

CHOISYA
Choisya ternata (Mexican orange blossom)

Painting 1

When the weather is clear the sunlight will be strong and give the effect of direct light shining through the petals, giving a glow to the delicate flowers and bouncing inside the open heads and forming intricate shadows illuminating their shape and structure.

In the first painting there are limited colours, yellow and blue. The yellow was used for the stamens and the blue for the shadows on the petals. The blue shadows help to give shape to the flowers and push some flowers and some petals backwards. The same effect was achieved with the blue on the leaves, which were painted with a mix of the two colours.

Painting 2

The same process was used in this painting except a thin violet was used for the shadows instead of blue and the yellow stamens were ringed with orange. A little orange was also mixed into the green to give the darker green in the centre.

The Gardener

Named in honour of J. D. Choisy, 1799–1859, a Swiss botanist, *Choisya ternata* was discovered in Mexico by Aimé Bonpland in 1804. This is a charming fast-growing evergreen shrub native to Mexico with shining trifoliate, glossy and light-green leaves. It has a delicious pungent scent, smelling lightly of citrus when crushed, and clusters of dazzling starry-white scented flowers, which have five petals with a prominent little clump of yellow stamens in the centre. They are similar to the flowers of the orange tree. The fragrant flowers last for weeks. The leaves grow in groups of three at the end of the branches.

C. ternata is the original plant and can produce a second flush of flowers in autumn. *C. ternata* 'Sundance' is less likely to flower a second time, but the benefit is the beautiful lime-green colour of the foliage. British nurseryman Peter Catt explained: 'This very popular plant started its life when, in 1978, I spotted a very small leaf, low down on an old *Choisya ternata* from which I was taking cuttings. I took the cutting on which this small leaf was and rooted it. When it came into growth, I removed the shoot from the top, which encouraged the side shoots. These I also removed. This forced a growth from the leaf that I had spotted which was about the size of my small fingernail and had a white edge. I encouraged a white edged variegation. To my amazement out came a golden shoot and having cleaned it up in a micro-prop lab, the plant was launched at the Chelsea Flower Show in 1986.'

Sometimes it reverts to plain green, which outgrow the yellow. These green shoots must be removed. It can bleach in scorching sun, especially on dry soils and in dry summers, and does not like drying winds.

C. × dewitteana 'Aztec Pearl' is best in full sun and lower growing and is the hardiest of all choisya varieties. *C. dewitteana* 'White Dazzler' has long, thin dark-green leaves, and pure-white flowers with prominent golden-coloured stamens at the centre. *C. × dewitteana* 'Aztec Gold' is similar to 'White Dazzler', but has lime-green/yellow foliage. It enjoys good, well-cultivated soil and a sunny sheltered position, but can accept extremes of heat and cold. It grows well in light or dappled shade, but if there is too much shade the plants look spindly and do not flower well. I have mine planted near a fence, which is the perfect backdrop for its white fragrant flowers and it is wonderful for attracting bees. It needs no pruning and is easily increased by cuttings of half-ripe shoots in gentle heat or older shoots in a cold frame.

Choisyas are easy to grow, tolerant of most soils and need no pruning. A wonderful garden plant with fabulous scent and beautiful leaves.

HONESTY
Lunaria annua 'Albiflora'

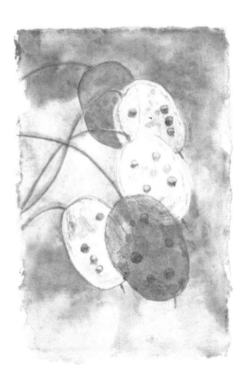

Painting 1
I particularly enjoy painting flowers in their natural surroundings rather than in formal arrangements in a vase. The form of the flower can change dramatically according to the viewpoint. In this painting of honesty I have included flowers, foliage, stems and the start of the transparent seed pods, all of which change within days. There was a hint of yellow in the stamens, useful as a complement to the violet, so this same yellow was repeated in the background, giving a harmonious and lively contrast, enhancing the vivid violet flower colour and giving a feel of sunshine.

Painting 2
Often it is the seed pods that one thinks of when talking of honesty. The opaque, papery seed pods needed a slightly darker background and very little shadow, which could make them appear too solid. The background

was wetted with clear water and blue, violet and Magenta dropped in immediately so that the colours dispersed and merged. It is especially important to do this quickly as Arches, hot-pressed, is smooth and paint sits on the surface, rather than sinking into it. Lack of attention can easily lead to unwanted water marks.

The Gardener

'We call this herbe in English, "Penny floure", or "Mony-floure", "Silver plate", "Pricksong-wort"; in Norfolke, Sattin, and white sattin; and amongst our women it is called "Honestie".'

Gerard

Honesty has a misleading botanical name, *Lunaria annua. Luna*, the moon, refers to the silver, oval, 'moon-like' seed pods, known as silicles. Honesty is sown in one year, germinates and flowers in the next. The common name, honesty, arose in the sixteenth century, and may relate to the translucence of the seed pods. In South East Asia it is called money plant, and in the US it is called silver dollars, Chinese money or Chinese coins, because the seed pods look like silver coins. In France it is known as *monnaie du Pape* or the Pope's money. In Denmark it is known as *judaspenge*, meaning coins of Judas, referring to the story of Judas Iscariot and the thirty pieces of silver paid for betraying Christ.

Honesty has many wonderful rosy-lilac, lilac or white flowers, which make a fabulous display in spring followed by the seed heads, which have a white surface with pearl-like luminosity, often used for decoration. The abundant seeds can be rubbed free from the papery surround or allowed to fall to perpetuate the display in the following year. It is easy to grow from seed, grown as an annual or biennial, in full sun or partial shade. The plants are prolific reseeders, so once established there is no need to seed again. It can be considered invasive. I have noted that they grow extremely well after a wet winter, cold early, followed by a very warm late spring. Honesty develops thick, tuber-like, deep storage roots, in common with other brassicas in the mustard family. The roots can be eaten boiled or raw. *L. annua* will cope in most situations, growing in the flower or vegetable borders, preferring damp conditions. Plenty of good home-made compost and leaf mould should be incorporated when planting, but manure should be avoided.

There is a white form, 'Alba Variegata', which has creamy-white variegated leaves.

RIBES
Ribes sanguineum (flowering currant)

The Drawing
Coloured pencils are ideal for sketching and on-the-spot drawing of colour studies, which can be developed into finished drawings or paintings. Drawings don't have to be laboured, but can be a graphic expression concentrating on the important

factors. Most subjects are seemingly complex, but with selection grows sharper observation. Observation is advanced when a critical eye is used rather than drawing what the mind assumes to be there. Objects don't always conform to expectations, and colours should never be used without really seeing and understanding. The form of the flower can change dramatically according to the viewpoint, which can be very individual.

Ribes is an attractive plant with bright-red and pink flowers. I made sure the coloured pencils had sharpened tips so as to get the sharp edges. The leaves were started with yellow-green with dark green added to suggest veins and shadow.

The Painting

The intense study needed in the drawing led to easier understanding when painting the plant. I used Quinacridone Magenta, in various degrees of strength, for the flowers and a mix of Aurelian Yellow and Cobalt Blue for the leaves with Aurelian Yellow in the veins. The background was a wash of the mixed green, to suggest leaves, Cobalt Blue, for some sky, and hints of Magenta to indicate more flowers.

The Gardener

The flowering currant is a vigorous ornamental shrub with clusters of rose-pink or magenta-red flowers which bloom each year. The variety 'King Edward VII' makes a compact, upright plant that has dangling dark-red racemes of flowers, blooming at the same time as the leaves, which have a strong resinous scent. Plants can be left unpruned, but, for the best blooms in the following year, it is worth cutting the branches that have flowered back to a strong pair of buds just after flowering. It will grow in almost any soil and in sun or shade and is restricted to temperate parts of the northern hemisphere.

The genus *Ribes* is divided into two big groups: the gooseberries and the currants. Gooseberries and currants used to occupy different genera. Gooseberries were believed to belong to the saxifrage family, but now they are recognised in the genus *Ribes*. Most people think of gooseberry bushes as having spines while current bushes don't. Also gooseberry bushes usually produce flower clusters, or inflorescences, of only one to three blossoms, while the inflorescences of currant species usually hold four or more blossoms. In autumn the flowering currant produces a dark-purple edible fruit, but it is fairly tasteless and people generally don't bother eating them; but they but can be made into jams or wine. The songbirds certainly appreciate them.

When warm showers fall the air smells sweeter and feels warmer. Plants glisten with silver sunlit droplets, and flowering shrubs herald the arrival of spring with the soft pinks of the camellias, the bright yellow of forsythia and mahonias, the white fragrant flowers of choisyas and viburnums, rhododendrons and azaleas, berberis, honeysuckle and lilac. They are followed by philadelphus and buddleia, caryopteris and mallow.

SWEET ROCKET

Hesperis matronalis (dame's rocket, damask violet, dame's wort, dame's gilliflower, night scented gilliflower, queen's gilliflower, rogue's gilliflower, summer lilac, mother of the evening, winter gilliflower and sweet rocket)

The Painting

Each painting has a life of its own. I contemplate different possibilities until I reach a desirable outcome. My paintings are a combination of observation, exploration, imagination, reinvention and technical skill.

I wanted to keep this painting loose with limited colours. I used Ultramarine Blue, Ultramarine Violet and Cobalt Blue for the flowers and tiny amounts of each were mixed into the greens where darks were wanted. Dilute blue provided the shadows on the white flowers.

As the days lengthen and become warmer and the light stronger, white flowers appear crisper and their scent heavier, blending with the perfume from other flowers. Painting among this beauty is inspirational, exciting and such a pleasure.

The Gardener

This is one of my favourite flowers. It is of the Cruciferae or mustard family. *Hesperis* is Greek for evening and this plant was probably given the name because the delicious scent of the flowers is stronger towards evening. It is an herbaceous plant with flowers of various colours, which are short-lived perennials and biennials. In the first year of growth the plant produces a mound of leaves, with flowering following in the second year. The foliage has short hairs on the top and bottom surfaces, which gives the leaves a rough feel. The many four-petalled flowers are showy and range in colour from different shades of lavender and purple to white and pink and some have mixed colours. Warm weather greatly shortens the flower's blooming time. Deadheading will prolong flowering or they may be left to set seed. The seed can be sown in trays, making sure that light is not excluded as it is required for germination. When large enough, the seedlings can be potted on. I prefer to scatter seed or let the plants self-seed in the flower borders, where they care for themselves, and it is a wonderful surprise to find the plants in unexpected corners of the garden.

Hesperis, a cultivated plant, grows best in full sun or partial shade. It is undemanding and self-seeds quickly. It can also be propagated from cuttings or division of clumps.

Bees and butterflies adore the loose clusters of deliciously scented flowers, with hesperis being host to caterpillars of several butterfly species, including the orange tip, large white and small white, and various moths. The flowers can be sprinkled over summer salads, giving an enticing effect.

Hesperis can be confused with phlox, which has similar flower clusters, but they are distinguished by foliage and flower differences. Hesperis has alternately arranged leaves and four petals per flower while phlox has opposite leaves and five petals.

CAMASSIA

Liliaceae, *Camassia quamash* (quamash, the North American Indian name of the plant, Indian hyacinth, camash, camas, wild hyacinth)

The Painting

I chose to paint the close-up of this glorious flower, drawing the complicated centres and masking out the stamens so that I could paint freely with washes of purple darkened in the centres. I started painting the petals with Ultramarine Blue and as the unopened buds were darker, more blue was added. Without these darks, there would be no suggestion of depth. It is not the little things that make a strong painting, but the big shapes, overall design and confident handling of the medium.

The Gardener

Of this genus of five or six species, *Camassia quamash* is the shortest and neatest. The stems are covered with individual starlike flowers that combine to create a shimmering cloud. Colours are pink, lavender, deep purple, blue-violet and amethyst purple with attractive yellow anthers. It is possible to have a succession of flowers by planting the dark-blue Caerulea Group followed by the pale-blue 'Electra' and then the ivory *C. leichtlinii*. *C. leichtlinii,* sometimes called Leichtlin's camass, was named in honour of Max Leichtlin (1831–1910) of Baden-Baden, Germany, who introduced many plants into cultivation, notably from the Near East.

Unlike bulbs, camassias flourish in well-drained damp soil, high in humus, and will grow on the margins of ponds and streams. They grow naturally in moist meadows, but naturalise well in gardens. Camassias were an important food staple for Native Americans and settlers in parts of the American old West. Many towns are named after the camassia. After flowering, the bulbs are pit-roasted or boiled. A pit-roast camassia bulb looks and tastes similar to baked sweet potato, but sweeter. They can cause flatulence due to their containing inulin and other oligosaccharides. When dried, the bulbs could be pounded into flour. In the Great Basin, expanded settlements accompanied by turning cattle and hogs on to 'camas prairies' greatly diminished food available to native tribes and increased tension between Native Americans and settlers and travellers. Though the once immense spreads of 'camas lands' have diminished because of modern developments and agriculture, numerous 'camas prairies' and marshes may still be seen today.

When planting in autumn, it is best to dig in plenty of good compost or leaf mould as this helps plants to survive long periods of drought. The foliage is long, narrow and grooved. After flowering the foliage should die back naturally. The plants can be divided in autumn after the leaves have withered. When established they will self-seed freely, which gives the best means of propagation as they do not produce offsets unless wounded. These will bloom in their third year. If no more plants are needed, the seed heads should be cut off. These bulbs thrive on competition as they would in their natural habitat in North America.

There are no insects or disease problems and the plants are strong and need no support.

EXOCHORDA
(the bride, Korolkowii, pearl bush)

The Painting

A beautiful plant with a mass of flowers, which had to be suggested rather than each flower painstakingly drawn. I used masking fluid to retain the white of the paper and, when dry, I laid in various greens, keeping the blues in the background and the yellows in the foreground to give a sense of space and depth. I washed on a little yellow-green on one side of the exochorda and a darker cooler green on the other side. When the fluid was removed I washed over a small amount of blue in the shadowed areas to give a sense of shape and shadow.

The Gardener
Exochorda is a very beautiful but little-known genus with masses of exquisite large pure-white flowers. This is a special plant for me as I collected some seed from under a bush in Saville Gardens, Windsor, when out walking with my sister a few months before she died. She loved the gardens, but it was January and very cold; but she was determined, as she was in all she did, to complete the walk despite her obvious pain. My plant is growing and is now flowering in late spring. Exochorda is a very beautiful bush when in flower, its branches festooned with short spikes of white blooms which last for only about a week. It needs plenty of space and plenty of sun and an annual pruning after flowering.

Apart from by seed, exochorda can be propagated by cuttings taken in summer or by digging up suckers bearing roots.

VIBURNUM
Vibernum opulus 'Roseum' (snowball tree)

The Painting

The white flowers are, in fact, unpainted white paper with hints of blue and yellow in places which represent shadows on the delicate petals. The background was most important in that it provides the contrast for the white petals. The background was kept loose and washy, just enough to show up the flowers. I didn't worry about the water marks or random spots of colour as this indicates leafy growths around the flower head.

The Gardener

There are a lot of viburnums, all of which make good garden shrubs. *Vibernum opulus* grows wild and is known as guelder rose. It is very beautiful, especially when covered with shiny scarlet berries in the autumn. There is a shorter variety called 'Compactum', which is a better garden plant. *V. tomentosum plicatum*, the Japanese snowball tree, has smaller but more numerous flower clusters and *V. tomentosum* 'Mariesii' has flat clusters of white flowers all along its branches in May. *V. fragrans* has very fragrant clusters of pinkish-white flowers in winter. *V. carlesii* is even more fragrant. *V. tinus* is evergreen and has pink-and-white flowers from November to April. *V. × burkwoodii* has pink-budded tubular flowers, which open flat and waxy, pure white and sweetly scented. *V. tinus laurustinus,* a winter- and spring-flowering species, is evergreen and of bushy habit with ovately lance-shaped dark-green leaves. It has flat pink buds and white flowers. *V. davidii* is an excellent low-growing evergreen, which grows in sun or shade.

Viburnums are easily cultivated, but will adapted to dry situations and poor soil. The flowers are exceptionally fragrant, but the wood can be evil-smelling when bruised. No fruit is produced.

AZALEA

The Painting

When watercolour flows across the surface of the paper there is merging and softening of colours. In this painting the background is a mix of wet-in-wet and wet-on-dry, which gives two different effects. The stamens, which are against the darker background, were masked out so as to allow the free flow of the washes. When the background was dry, the mask was removed and then painted. Azaleas have delicate shapes and colours. Backlighting often intensifies colours and creates interesting shadows. Light creates the most fascinating colours, where light and shadow meet the translucent pigment can glow. Painting the shadow means using a number of pure tones of the same base colour.

The Gardener

Friends gave my husband a birthday present of an evergreen azalea, which I have nurtured. It didn't like our dry garden, so after struggling for a while it is now in a pot and has recovered very well and flowers beautifully. In spring the flowers are of moderate size, appearing before the leaves have unfolded or are still quite small, but there is so much blossom that not a leaf or twig remains visible. The leaves are a brilliant green.

Some azaleas bloom in spring and some, like the hardy varieties of *Rhododendron indicum*, flower in summer. There is a huge range of charming colours and differing growing habits. Deciduous azaleas are immensely beautiful, with clusters of fragrant flowers in a wonderful colour range, including yellow, orange, pink, scarlet, crimson and intermediate shades, and they are daintier than rhododendrons. In some varieties the leaves turn copper and crimson before falling in autumn. Azaleas are hardy, free-flowering and easy to grow in soils that contain no chalk or lime. They will grow in full sun or partial shade.

Evergreen azaleas or Japanese azaleas are valuable for their flowers and foliage, which are among the showiest of all shrubs when in flower and, being evergreen, give substance to the winter garden. Colours range from white to crimson, but with none of the yellow shades that characterise the taller, more open-branched deciduous azaleas, and with greater emphasis on pinks, scarlet and carmine. It is not usual to find evergreens providing autumn colour, but all the new leaves stay on the bush and are wholly evergreen, while older leaves change colour at the approach of autumn and either fall after a few weeks' brilliance or may stay on in burnished tones and revert to green in spring.

Azaleas can be transplanted at any age, in common with most rhododendrons. This means that small plants can be grown fairly close together and later, as they grow, thinned out and planted elsewhere.

In my opinion azaleas don't sit well next to rhododendrons with their yellow, orange, flame and scarlet flowers and the bright green of their young foliage. The French name of the *azalée*, refers to *joie d'aimer* – joy of loving.

RHODODENDRON
Japanese azalea

Painting 1

Colours express vitality and spark interest and stimulation. Colour can influence mood, create atmosphere and lift the spirit. There is usually something of interest in shape or colour, which attracts the attention. A painting is more interesting if there is an area that holds the eye and emphasises the focal area. If highly saturated colours are used all over the painting there is confusion and the eye doesn't settle.

Certain flowers change their shape when viewed full face as against side or rear elevation. Looking at flowers from unusual angles can give what appear to be abstract shapes. Some complicated flowers, such as rhododendrons, are best when there is detail in the focal area and less in other areas (or at least undefined) so as to direct attention to this area. If there is the same level of detail elsewhere in the painting there could be confusion. Other forms can be developed around the main shapes.

It took careful study to work out how each flower related to the next. The crinkly petals made interesting patterns linking one with another, but also cast shadows which helped determine the shapes. The inner shadows helped to show the stamens. Colours used were Permanent Rose on pre-wetted areas, dragging the colours into the centres of the flowers so that some areas were left unpainted, hopefully suggesting the delicacy of the petals. Violet was used for the darker shadows.

Painting 2

Perception of colour changes according to distance from the subject; in the foreground colours can appear warmer than those in the background. To create depth, the colour needs to be cooler and the value lighter so that it recedes into the distance. Colours in soft focus merge and diffuse into the background affected by water vapour in the atmosphere giving a slight blue cast. This makes red appear slightly mauve, or even purple. Warmer tones come forward. In this painting a cool colour was washed over the underlying colour to modify it and give a sense of distance, placing some flower heads behind others. The 'glazing' method is particularly suited to transparent watercolour, but can be used with other mediums, such as oils and acrylics. Coloured pencils can be used in the same way. This is known as 'burnishing'.

Daylight has a cold effect on colours depending on the sunlight, which can appear warm in colour. Although white flowers can appear cold, I saw a lot of colour especially in the interiors of the blooms and the centre of the plant. The light caught on the upper sections of each flower and this was complemented by using violet in the shadows in and around the blooms. Pink stalks warmed the centre of the painting as well as linking to the violet. I left the stamens pale against the darker interiors and used all colours – yellow, violet and pink – mixed together to give strong darks.

The Gardener

The name rhododendron is from the Greek *rhodon*, meaning rose, and *dendron*, meaning tree. In the language of plants it is linked to 'elegance'. The first rhododendron was introduced into Britain in 1656. The much more abundant *Rhododendron ferrugineum* was introduced in 1752. By the nineteenth century there were fifteen species. An important acquisition from Northern India in 1815 was *R. arboreum*, but the first cultivation came in 1849–1851, when Joseph D. Hooker explored the Himalayas. Hooker's introduction provided an entirely new conception of the rhododendron. Hybridisation introduced the first red-flowered varieties. Subsequently more species were found on the western side of China, proving to be the richest rhododendron area on the globe. French missionaries sent back botanical material in the dried form, but very little seed, although some arrived in Paris as early as 1889. The first genuine attempt was made in 1899–1900 by Messrs Veitch of Chelsea, when they sent out E. H. Wilson. From that time onwards until 1939 and from 1946 onwards, a band of collectors introduced a continuous stream of new species they had discovered.

Rhododendrons are semi-evergreen ericaceous shrubs bearing profuse clusters of funnel-shaped flowers. The most spectacular of flowering shrubs, and none are surpassed by the hardy hybrids for sheer display. Rhododendrons are easy to grow and flower freely every year.

As with the azaleas, rhododendrons remain slow-growing in our garden due to lack of rainfall, but even so they flower beautifully. Hardy hybrid rhododendrons have spectacular colours ranging from white to scarlet, deep red, mauve, maroon and purple, deep pink, rose red, gold and, for the rock garden, light blue and rose pink. They have ten stamens whereas azaleas have five.

R. obtusum amoenum have magenta, crimson, mauve and pink flowers and look wonderful when planted together, but isolated from other flower colours. *R. calostrotum, R. saluenense* and *R. keleticum* have large flowers of reddish purple. The plum-coloured *R. campylogynum myrtilloides* and the pale-yellow *R. hanceanum* 'Nanum' prefer cooler conditions and are both slow-growing, while the white *R. leucaspis* has striking brown anthers. Although these plants do well in full sunlight, they can look better in broken or dappled light. *R. impeditum* and *R. scintillans* have violet and blue small flowers in clusters and will grow in full sun.

Like all rhododendrons, they require lime-free, acidic, open, well-drained soil and need to be away from direct sunlight, but need a bright position. A top dressing of decayed leaves or bracken helps to retain moisture. The mulch has the effect of keeping the rhododendron roots cool and moist right through the summer. This is important as the roots are near the surface and can be affected by drought. However, if they are kept compact and healthy they should not be allowed to become cluttered with dead leaves in winter. In my garden the oaks give plenty of shade and, as they are deeply rooted, are not in competition with the rhododendrons. Few shrubs are more easily and safely transplanted than the rhododendron, as their root system is usually so close to the stem and so dense that it can be removed entirely. This is best done in spring or autumn.

Propagation can be by seed, grafting, layering or cuttings. All large-leaved varieties should be raised by either seed or layering. Once the flowers have faded the trusses should be picked off to prevent production of seed and so concentrate the energies of the plant on the new growths and the forming of the following season's blossom. The dead flowers should be broken off with finger and thumb, being careful not to damage the buds at the base. If the stems become leggy and bare, they should be cut back in spring.

Painting 3

The colours of flowers exert great influences on us, but their greatest impact is when associated with surrounding greens. The bright colours of the flowers need the coolness and restfulness of green nearby and are therefore much more effective by contrast.

The 'found' edges are those which remain prominent and the 'lost' areas are those which are allowed to become obscure and undefined. The lost edges take the eye through the painting and often around corners of objects forming the framework of the painting. By wetting the paper and letting washes flow and run harmoniously, edges become extremely important. It is often a good idea to leave some of these washes to mingle on the surface because it is not good to define every single feature. Lost edges can be soft colours against more pronounced areas or where the depth of colour has been faded out.

Optical mixing is using two separate colours placed next to each other. This was used in the painting of the rhododendrons. A washy Winsor Yellow and Cobalt and Ultramarine Blues with a little Quinacridone Rose all merged together in the flower interiors. The closer the colours in tone or value, the more easily they will mix optically to create a third colour. The further apart the colours are the more the two colours will remain distinct; and if two complementary colours are used side by side, the more they will shimmer and vibrate. It is interesting that if one stares at a colour for a long period of time and then looks at something white or pale in colour, an after-image appears in its complementary colour. As the receptors of the eye are given time to rest, the illusion vanishes. Ultramarine Violet was washed into the shaded areas, especially in the furthest petals and background. All colours were mixed together in varying proportions to make a dark green.

Painting 4

The play of light can be very exciting and create completely different effects. The mostly pink flowers of the rhododendron were turned almost blue in the cool morning light. Even the interior of some flowers in the sunshine had blue shadows. Later in the day, the light is warmer and hence the colours are changed again.

MALTESE CROSS

Lychnis coronaria; *Lychnis chalcedonica*; *Lychnis fulgens* (ragged robin)

The Painting

I was inspired by the effect of light on the crimson flowers and silvery-grey leaves and chose to silhouette the stems against a washy background. I mixed yellowy green with violet with added Crimson. I used the same colours in the plants: Crimson for the flowers with violet shadows in the veins of the leaves. Adding a touch of the same yellow to the violet, the complementary colour, darkens the colour without destroying its chroma. Colour can achieve mood and atmosphere. I don't aim for a photographic likeness, but aim for accurate shapes and values and to capture the magic and the initial feeling so that it is not ordinary and predictable.

The Gardener

Lychnis is the name used by Theophrastus from *lychnos*, meaning lamp, referring to the ancient use of leaves of a woolly species. *Lychnis chalcedonica*, or Maltese cross, as the flowers form a shape similar to that of the Maltese cross, has numerous common names, such as Jerusalem cross, burning love, dusky salmon, flower of Bristol, fireball, flower of Constantinople, gardener's delight, meadow campion, nonesuch, red robin, scarlet lightning, scarlet lychnis, catchfly (based on the sticky stems) and tears of Christ. It has brilliant scarlet cross-shaped flowers on drumstick-like heads. It grows in hot, dry places and in relatively poor sandy soil. Red flowers can be difficult to place in the border so as not to clash with other colours, but I have it in a corner next to the pond. This splash of colour is a welcome, happy sight with the green of the fatsia behind it, and is especially precious as the seed was sent to me by a previous student from America.

It is easily grown in good garden soil, but will grow in poor sandy soil, in a warm, sheltered position, especially where *L. coronaria* and *L. fulgens* are concerned. *L. coronaria*, or rose campion, has white, woolly, densely leafy non-flowering shoots at the base with purple or white flowers. Rose campion has grey leaves, and I love the magenta-crimson flowers from spring to late summer. It is sometimes known as *Agrostemma coronaria* (rose campion, dusty miller, crown pink, mullein pink, lamp flower) and is easily grown from seed.

L. chalcedonica and *L. fulgens* have bright-Scarlet flowers that look splendid with white (perhaps Shasta daisies) and also yellow, blue and purple flowers. Red campion often hybridises with white campion to produce pink flowers. They set seed freely and can be propagated by division in spring. These dazzling flowers have velvety-green foliage and crimson single flowers, which appear in late spring. It likes to bake in the sun, but in my garden will also grow in the shade.

The genus is closely related to *Silene*, differing in the flower of *Lychnis* having five styles while there are three in *Silene*. The seed capsules of *Lychnis* have five teeth whereas there are six in *Silene*.

ACTINIDIA
Actinidia kolomikta (Chinese gooseberry). *Aktin* means ray-like, referring to the style of the spokes of a wheel.

The Painting

First I make a quick, simple pencil sketch, a thumbnail, to determine shape, size, perspective, light and shade, and once this is clear then painting can begin. A painting which is initially well draughted and drawn already has solid foundations from which to work. I try to stay focused on what it was that attracted me to paint this subject in the first place. It becomes a very personal involvement, trying to study the subject and impart a dramatic and exciting experience.

Once satisfied with the composition, I mask out those areas which would be difficult to retain when using a wash. The fine details of the tiny flowers and the stalks were masked so that the background could be painted freely in contrast to the detailed foreground. To ensure colour unity, a wash of local colour was laid down around the leaves which I wanted to remain unpainted. When dry the edges of the leaves were refined, tonal contrast was added and the pink in the veins and some leaves added.

The Gardener

Actinidia is a graceful plant with beautiful heart-shaped pink-tipped leaves which merge into white and dark green. The tiny flowers are hardly noticed as it is the stunning leaves which outshine everything. There are usually five sepals and petals with numerous stamens, and anthers which are mostly yellow or purple. The fruit is a juicy edible berry containing many small seeds. It is a hardy twining deciduous climber, usually reaching about three metres and best grown against a sunny wall. Propagation is most successful by taking cuttings in summer and bringing them on in a propagator.

LILAC
Syringa vulgaris

The Painting

This is a high-key watercolour, where the light tones and colours give a feeling of brightness. High-key paintings often convey a cheerful, bright mood or an atmosphere of softness and delicacy. Even in the darkest shadows, the tones will be lightened by reflected light on a sunny day. If they are painted too dark, the tonal unity of the painting could be destroyed. A low-key painting is at the darker end of the tonal range and can evoke feelings of mystery, can be sombre and powerful. Light can modify the perception of colour. I prefer to use white paper as it allows light to reflect off the surface and gives the watercolour washes full transparent brilliance. My favourite paper is of good quality and texture and takes washes well, although it is easily stained. I use a large brush for big areas and a small brush for small areas. The larger brush encourages bold strokes and the smaller brush is used for details.

The first opening flower head was interesting as it was a mix of opened blossoms and tight buds, giving shapes which the light caught in different areas and ways.

Double flowers proved to be complicated in that the flowers caught the light differently. The close-up sketch was more open than the view from a distance. Colours used were Quinacridone Rose and violet for the deeper-shadowed areas. Quinacridone colours are a family of high-performance synthetic pigments with exceptional colour and lightfastness.

I deliberated as to whether to add the blue sky, but made a light wash of blue and another of light green behind the lower leaves. I tried to keep the background loose and washy.

There has to be passion for the subject, for the unknown, to embrace surprises and the undiscovered and for another way to paint the subject. A painting will be meaningful if the artist is passionate about the subject.

The Gardener

The fragrance of lilac is an exquisite pleasure. Purple lilac expresses first emotions of love, which is especially important since our lilac was a present from my parents. The lilac's chief beauty lies in its beautiful plumes of flowers and their rich, heady scent.

Lilac came originally from China, Persia and the North Balkan Peninsula, arriving in Vienna by way of Turkey. Sir Thomas Hanmer cultivated three different varieties in 1659: the common blue or violet, the white and the rare red.

There is confusion over the name as the lilac is really syringa and the flower we know as syringa is really philadelphus. This happened because Gerard, the seventeenth-century herbalist, called the purple lilac 'seyringa', from the Greek *syrinx*, meaning pipe or tube; the blue he called 'the pipe tree', because its stems, when the pith is removed, are hollow like a pipe; and the mock orange, or philadelphus, he called 'the white pipe tree', so when the white form of lilac was introduced it was given the same name. Country names are laylock, lelaps, lily-oak, mayflower and ducksbill because of the rolled edges of the flowerlets. In the language of flowers it is called 'friendship'.

This deciduous shrub will grow practically anywhere, but in good, well-cultivated soil and a sunny position flower trusses will be encouraged. No pruning is needed, but if possible the faded flower panicles should be cut off to prevent wastage of vigour in seed development. If flowering is over-prolific in one year, the shrub may become exhausted and may need a rest year. For bigger trusses in the subsequent year this must be done along with pruning of weak or overcrowded shoots and suckers at the base.

Propagation is by seeds, cuttings or layering, which is the surest method. Cuttings can be made from half-ripened shoots.

Syringa persica, the Persian lilac, is another species with particularly fragrant flowers. There are a number of improved garden varieties with larger flowers, double in some, and in a range of colours from white to deep purple. Lilacs can look their best when grown as half-standards. For the first two or three years they can be disappointing, but then they make great rounded heads covered with flowers and are easy to prune.

Lilacs flower early and can look uninteresting for the rest of the year. Even with splendid flowering, some plants can be without flowers for months and so can be interplanted with dahlias, cannas, gladioli, roses, chrysanthemums, etc., to give a boost when needed.

WEIGELA
Weigela diervilla

The Painting

Dramatic tonal contrast and warm and cool colours, quality of light, variations in size and shape, contrast, texture and careful drawing provide interest. The artist must train the eye to look at shape, form, colour, tone and dimension, then the brain interprets the information so that it is transformed on to paper. The brain is amazingly adept at decoding the messages it receives from the eyes and can create complex images from very little information. I have trained my eye and mind to look and register more carefully. Making rapid drawings every day develops a skill and speed even with the most complicated subjects, also learning to study and understand the object. Studying nature gives a kind of vision and a discipline, being absorbed in quiet concentration.

Once the drawing was done I painted the flower petals with Crimson, deepening the centres but leaving the white of the paper for the delicate stamens. This Crimson was added to the greens for the darkest areas – just a few colours in all.

The Gardener

Weigelas are native of East Asia. The genus is named after the German scientist Christian Ehrenfried von Weigel. The first species to be collected for Western gardens, *Weigela florida,* was found by Robert Fortune and imported to England in 1845.

Weigelas are large hardy deciduous shrubs in the honeysuckle family. They have long arching stems which are wreathed in little trumpet-shaped flowers in multiple shades of pink to red and white with pale-green leaves, yellow, variegated, golden, chartreuse, bronze-chocolate to deep purple-black. Also known as *W. diervilla*, these pink or crimson flowering deciduous shrubs are easily grown in almost any soil and position. They flower best in open, sunny places in early summer and sporadically into autumn. They are best grouped together in mixed colours of white and pink and crimson.

W. 'Looymansii Aurea' has rosy-pink flowers and light-golden leaves. One which is especially worth growing is *W. florida variegata* with pink flowers and cream-edged leaves. One of my favourites is 'Midnight Wine', low-growing so ideal for the front of the border. It has dark burgundy-purple foliage and is attractive, but even more so when the pink flowers appear. The white bell-shaped flowers of 'Date Night Tuxedo' are stunning against the dark foliage. *W.* 'Monet' is inspired by and named after the French Impressionist artist.

Weigelas require very little if any pruning, and do not need deadheading. For large flowers and healthy foliage, flowering stems should be cut back to non-flowering shoots as soon as the flowers fade so as to restrict the size of the plant. Propagation is easy from hardwood semi-ripe or softwood cuttings.

IRIS
Iris reticulata

Painting 1

The stunning colours and shapes of the iris are bliss for the artist. The effects of sunlight and shadows mean constant change throughout the day, when I watch for unexpected opportunities and try to be bold. A slight change of angle can make a difference in the design of the image and indicate the needs of the painting. This painting needed to be vibrant with rich tones and textures in a realistic and detailed style. There is a range of blues, from warm French Ultramarine, which contains red, through to cool, yellow-influenced Phthalo and Cerulean. Cobalt Blue is in between these pigments and is closest to a pure primary blue, but it is easily overpowered by other colours. Cobalt Blue is transparent and non-staining, so is ideal for glazing and cooling. Ultramarine is a warm blue, veering towards violet. It is a strong sedimentary pigment and mixes well with other colours to make strong darks, subtle greys and mauves. I chose several blues, mostly Ultramarine, Cobalt Blue and, for the lighter areas, Cerulean, and Quinacridone Violet for the dark interior. The yellow stripe is Winsor Lemon with a touch of Winsor Orange floated into it when wet.

Watercolour is ideal for the interpretation of flowers as the subtle variations of colour and tone, and bold fluidity, reflect the nature of the subject. Watercolour is a very direct, spontaneous medium and, when used with aplomb, can produce the most wonderful effects. Pure watercolour can create wonderful effects and can be the most sensitive of mediums. By dropping water or dilute pigment into a drying wash a marbled pattern can be produced. This can be repeated adding other colours so that they merge or the water pushes the pigment to the edges and makes subtle shadings and delicate outlines. There are hard edges where the paint was used dry and soft edges where the flow of water has blurred shapes. In this painting I was careful not to let the paint run over the iris blooms and major leaves. These were painted in a loose manner, but in their small contained areas. To succeed I needed to capture the folds of the petals, blur the background to enhance the detail in the flowers and keep interest on the flowers. The three outer petals bend down and the three inner petals are upright. The 'beards' are often in contrasting colours to lure the bees into the heart of the flower.

Painting is a journey into the unknown with successes and disappointments, but failure is a valuable opportunity to learn. There is no right or wrong way. Each artist must formulate their own paths free from dogma and ideology, which makes painting so exciting. Often the inspiration for a painting comes from something as simple as an unusual light. The effect of sunshine on flowers is wonderful, and naturally bright colours are exciting and can be exaggerated for full impact.

The Gardener

The iris, the flower of light, and in the language of flowers 'tender-heart', is one of the earliest cultivated plants and may be seen in bas-relief at Karnak. It was imported into Egypt some 1,400 years before the birth of Christ. The iris was named after the Greek messenger of the gods, Iris, who bridged heaven and earth with her rainbow. In Greek mythology, the goddess Iris used the rainbow as her personal highway as she travelled from place to place delivering messages of love. Her name was given to the flower because of the numerous colours of the iris, and because of this the iris flower is also considered the symbol of eloquence, communication and messages and represents faith, hope and wisdom. Purple irises were planted over the graves of women to summon the goddess to guide the dead in their journey. The iris has been a treasured flower since ancient times, often appearing in Egyptian works of art dating as far back as the 28th Egyptian dynasty, around 400 BC. A flower carved into the Sphinx of Giza in Egypt is believed to be an iris. The Greeks used it for perfume, make-up and medicine. Many historic varieties remain, varying in height, colour and bloom time, but all possess a perfect form with three inner petals, called standards, and three outer petals, called falls.

Florentine iris provides the orris root, which is a corruption of iris root. In Greek and Roman medicine, orris was used in ointments and oils. The rhizomes are lifted in August, once they are mature, cleared of rootlets, stripped free of their brown outer skin, and dried. Although the fresh roots have no particular scent, on drying they are delicately perfumed of violets and the sweet odour strengthens if they are kept for a year or two. Chalky in appearance, they are ground and used in dentifrices and toilet preparations. Orris is an ingredient of potpourri as it improves and helps to retain and bind the perfumes.

From Dante we learn that the ancient arms of the city of Florence depicted a white iris on a red ground, indicating the importance of the commercial cultivation of the iris. It became naturalised in Tuscany, having been introduced from Macedonia, its home. The fleur-de-lys, which became the emblem of the French royal house, was based on the iris flower. In Europe the iris was cultivated by peasants on the tops of houses. It is the state flower of Tennessee, the fleur-de-lys being the emblem for the city of New Orleans.

Iris germanica, London flag or purple flag, has rich blue-purple falls with a white beard and light-purple upright inner petals (standards). They are sweetly scented. Hybrids come in a range of yellows, creams, whites, purple and blues.

Painting 2

I was careful that the yellow centre was not too strong, as the complementary colour, violet, can be invasive. The background remained indistinct, using the same yellow in the green and a touch of blue and violet to link with the flowers and to give depth. The foreground leaves contained more yellow to bring them forward. A variety of leaf shapes and sizes provide interest and texture. Smooth, glossy leaf surfaces reflect light in different ways, thus affecting the visual colour and impact. Nature is filled with the influences of surrounding objects reflecting colour, but in this case the main local colour of the iris is in isolation. One has to learn the ways and nature of plants through experience as well as theoretically.

Watercolour has a reputation for being difficult to use and control, but it need not be with forethought and planning. Watercolour has a unique attractiveness and brilliant colours and the seductive atmosphere created by the use of water. Using good-quality paper is important and a contributing factor to a successful painting. A painting should have life, love and beauty, painted from the heart. If there is no excitement felt when painting then this will be apparent in the finished work.

Laying down the first washes of watercolour is exciting after much consideration. When a colour is dropped into a wet area, and another immediately into it and allowed to blend, it will create an exciting mix. This blending of colours is one of the many joys of painting with watercolour. Watercolour is very challenging, but the effects are very exciting and sometimes unexpected. The essence of the painting process is a constant search for the intrinsic vitality and mood contained within the subjects.

The challenge was to capture the silky smoothness of the petals and the delicacy of the beautiful flower while enriching the cool colours with the warm sunshine which shone through the petals. I used the warm yellows of the flower against blues in the background. Watercolour provides a glow from the paper, creating an optical mixture of colour. When a transparent colour is laid around a previously painted yellow suggestion of flowers, the two do not mix. If the two were mixed, then the effect would be to neutralise the intensities and could create a grey. When these colours are viewed side by side, the eye emphasises their differences and the colour contrast between them appears stronger.

The Gardener

There are two distinct types of iris, one with rhizomes and one with bulb-like corms. The yellow iris, *I. pseudacorus*, is one of the most distinctive plants in marginal vegetation throughout Europe, covering watery meadows and banks of rivers and canals. In my garden I have them on the edge of the pond, but have to divide them every few years as they increase their rhizomes, spreading quickly. The young foliage rising out of the water is very beautiful and the flowers last well. The seed pods need to be cut off so that they don't float and eventually form another colony of seedlings.

For hundreds of years the yellow iris has been used as a dye plant. The rhizomes produce a black dye and the flowers provide yellow, the commonest colour obtainable from vegetable material. The roots were also used to scent and starch laundry, and the powered root, orris root, was mixed with ordinary hair powder and sold as violet powder for the hair. It was suppose to cure toothache, suspended in beer casks to prevent the beer becoming stale, and in wine casks to give bouquet. The common blue flower was mixed with alum by the monks to produce a green pigment for the illuminations of manuscripts.

In the south of England it was called levers, from 'laefer', a flag, and sometimes flag-flower, dagger-flower and dragon-flower. In Scotland it might be luggs or waterskegs, or segg, a corruption of 'sedge', a small sword. Because of its sword-like leaves it is the Japanese emblem of a warrior.

In the past 'flags' along the riverbank indicated a ford, for the creeping roots or rhizomes, broken and torn by hooves and wheels, drifted downstream and established themselves in the shallows to root again. The yellow iris has the most interesting history of all the irises for in the sixth century Clovis, the first king of the Franks, discovered a ford on the Rhine indicated by yellow flag irises and bought his army to safety from the overpowering Goths, near Cologne. Quite naturally he adopted the flower as his emblem. Its three large petals symbolised faith, wisdom, and valour. In the twelfth century Louis V of France adopted the fleur-de-lys emblem during the Crusades. Thereafter it was emblazoned upon the escutcheons of the kings of France. When Edward of England claimed the crown of France, the fleur-de-lys was added to the English coat of arms and remained there until 1801 – nearly 250 years after Calais had been reclaimed by the French. The symbol was outlawed during the French Revolution, in 1792, and hundreds of men and women found wearing it were condemned to death. It was reinstated with Louis XVIII in 1814 and it was continued with Charles X and again outlawed in 1830, when Charles was dethroned.

In England, the Plantagent standard bearing the fleur-de-lys of France is the emblem on the arms of Eton College, founded by Henry VI. Edward III added it to the arms of England. It was not until 1800 that George III replaced the fleur-de-lys with the shamrock.

The name lily when applied to the iris is merely a confusion of common usage, dating back across the centuries to biblical times, referring to 'lilies of the field'. It seems to be a collective name for any showy flower, as was the name rose.

Fleur-de-luce

The common 'Floure de luce' hath long and large flaggy leaves like the blade of a sword with two edges, amongst which spring up smooth and plaine stalks two foot long, bearing floures toward the top compact of six leaves joyned together, where of three that stand upright are best inward one toward another; and in those leaves that hang downeward there are certaine rough or hairy welts, growing or rising from the nether part of the leafe upward, almost of a yellow colour. the roots be thicke, long and knobby, with many hairy threds hanging therat.

Gerard

Painting 3

As the paper dries it loses its shine and back runs can occur, this causes a hard edge where the surrounding water stops, leaving a deposit of pigment at the edge. The resulting bloom can be a bonus or an ugly mistake. Sharp-edged shapes and lines can be added to the dry paper by slowly introducing more intense and darker colours, resulting in soft, hard or blurred edges.

In this painting, while the paint floated on the wet paper and colours merged one into another, exciting things happened, taking all my concentration at this most creative moment. All depends on how much water and paint, the wetness of the paper, the speed of the brushstrokes and the pressure of the brush. As the painting is in between very wet and very dry, it is at its most vulnerable state.

Painting is an exciting, challenging and sometimes maddening process of discovery and exploration. All we can do is accept the challenge with commitment, enthusiasm and energy.

The Gardener

The bearded irises are a large group of irises that spread underground by means of rhizomes. They have thick, flat, fan-shaped leaves and beautiful flowers with tufts of hair (beards) on the three outer petals (falls). Tall bearded irises come in amethyst, rich yellow, black, pale yellow, pale blue, chestnut brown, flamingo pink, golden yellow and gold, and red-brown. The bearded irises, or German or flag irises, are best in sunny, well-drained soil, containing some lime and planted so that their rhizomes are partly exposed on the soil surface. The vast number of varieties of bearded iris which have been raised in gardens from the latter half of the nineteenth century onwards made classification a necessity. At first an endeavour was made to group them with the wild species to which they bore most resemblance, but it was soon found that the crossing between the species which was taking place closed up the gaps between the wild species and caused this method of classifying the varieties to be inadequate. About 1920 the British Iris Society and the Royal Horticultural Society devised an artificial mode of classifying which was found of much value in basing the main groups solely upon the colour of the flowers.

Bulbous irises are a group of bulbs unlike bearded and beardless irises which are rhizomatous. *I. histrioides* has bright royal-blue flowers with a yellow central ridge on the falls and flowers in early to midwinter. It is hardy and tolerates dappled shade. *I. histrioides* flowers from November to April depending on the weather, but generally the best flower in February, bringing an uplifting, exciting sense to rock gardens and containers with their bright flowers. The beautiful purple petals each have a line of stunning gold made even brighter against the purple. The flowers appear before the handsome foliage. They are delicately scented with honey-lemon-vanilla-like perfume.

There are three hybrid bulbous irises. Dutch hybrids flower in spring and early summer with colours in white, yellow, blue and purple. English hybrids flower in midsummer with the largest flowers in white, blues, pink and purple. Spanish hybrids flower in early to midsummer and have larger fragrant blooms in smoky shades of white, brown, blues, purple and mauve. The variety 'Chrysolora' is a good clear yellow and there is a white form. 'Thunderbolt' has a fine massive flower, bronze and orange shot with purple. They flower after the bearded iris. *I. ochroleuca* is yellow and white – the yellow contrasts beautifully with pure white. They need good, rich soil, plenty of moisture and sunshine in the growing season. The bulbous species form offsets, which is a good way of increase, though the offsets may be very small and need two or three years to reach a flowering stage.

Shakespeare called the golden-yellow flower 'flower de luce'. Other English names are legion-flag, flagons, Jacob's sword, laister, levers, lug, maiken, yellow saggan, seggs, water seg, seggin, shaldon, skeg, sword lily, fliggers (referring to the movement of the sword-like leaves in the breeze) and cucumber (which is descriptive of the seed capsule).

Even though the month of February is often cold and grey, Valentine's Day makes it one of the most romantic months of the year. Because the iris is the symbolic flower of the Greek goddess Iris, who was also the messenger of love, it seems fitting that the elegant iris is the birthday flower of February. Flower colours have symbolic meanings. Traditionally, the iris symbolises eloquence, faith, wisdom and hope, much as February carries with it the promise that spring will soon return. The dark-blue iris symbolises faith and hope; the purple iris denotes royalty, wisdom and compliments; the yellow iris is a symbol of passion; and the white iris symbolises purity. Irises may also express courage and admiration.

STACHYS
Stachys byzantina (lamb's ear, woolly hedge nettle, woolly betony, lamb's tongues)

The Painting
I wanted this to be a lively, loose painting with just a few colours. Different brushes will give different effects depending upon the way the brush is held and the speed with which it is drawn across the paper. The proportion of water to paint in the brush and on the paper can also be controlled to create distinctive effects.

I used violet, green and pink and left some areas, like leaves and buds, unpainted. The darker background helped to explain the shapes, and the loose brushwork hinted at other plants surrounding the stachys.

The Gardener
Stachys is native to Turkey, Armenia and Iran and is naturalised as an escapee from gardens. It is often termed under the names *Stachys lanata* or *S. olympica*. Most silver-leaved plants come from the Mediterranean climates, where plants are exposed to many months of sunlight along with drying winds and dry, well-drained soil. Their felted leaves allow them to withstand high wind and low rainfall.

Stachys flowers in late spring and early summer. The flowers are small and either white or purple-cerise, which makes a splash of colour when planted en masse. They are short-lived perennials with tall tongue-shaped leaves heavily covered with silvery-white velvety hairs. As silver-leaved plants are short-lived it is useful to propagate them from cuttings taken from semi-ripe growth in summer. This can be done by making a cut immediately below a leaf joint and stripping off the lower leaves, inserting into compost and gravel mix and placing in a shady place. Cuttings should be rooted by autumn, but are best left in a cold frame until spring.

They are named lamb's ears because of the leaves' curved shape and white, soft, fur-like hair coating. They are often grown in children's gardens, as they are easy to grow and the thick felt-like leaves are fun to touch. It is also used as an edging plant. In Brazil it is used as an edible herb, called *lambari*. It has sometimes been used as a medicinal plant. A number of cultivars exist, including white flowering forms – plants such as 'Big Ears', with leaves very large; 'Cotton Ball', a sterile cultivar that does not produce flowering stems and is asexually propagated; 'Primrose Heron', with leaves yellow in spring and pink flowers; 'Sheila McQueen', which is sterile, low-growing and has large leaves; 'Silky Fleece', a tall plant with lilac-plum flowers and smaller white woolly foliage; and 'Silver Carpet', which is sterile and has grey leaves.

The plants tend to be evergreen, but can die back during cold winters and regenerate new growth from the crown. *S. lanata* is a wonderful ground cover with its cerise flower spikes, but the rosettes of silver leaves are equally attractive even through winter. Silver-leafed stachys is effective as a foil among brilliantly coloured blooms, which are best separated by foliage plants that harmonise with both.

Stachys is special to me as Mag gave me the original seeds from her garden.

<h2 style="text-align:center">KING SOLOMON'S SEAL</h2>

Rhizoma polygonati (polygonatum, Siberian Solomon's seal)

The Painting

Whatever the subject, painting is a theatrical process. There is always the potential to create an interesting narrative through the way the subject is lit. Reading the proportions properly is necessary to create a likeness. However, the relationship between the object and the light is more important than a likeness.

Paul Gauguin said, "In painting as in music, one should ask for inspiration more than description."

The imagination and inspiration do not alter the basic features of the subject, but add aesthetic and personal feelings; otherwise it might as well be a photograph. Close examination of the subject helps to invigorate the imagination, which hopefully is carried into the painting.

The minute flowers were masked so that the darker background leaves could be painted without fear of losing the white for the flowers. Very few colours were used – Sap Green for the foreground leaves, a more washy mix to the sides and a little Winsor Yellow added in places. I made sure that some of the dark green, mixed from Sap Green and Ultramarine Violet, was behind the white flowers so that they showed to good advantage. The flowers were shaded with a very dilute green. More darks were added behind the flowers and leaves.

The Gardener

The name *polygonatum* was used by Dioscorides – *poly* meaning many and *gonu* meaning knee joints, referring to its characteristic knobbly rhizomes. The scars of cut or broken rhizomes bear impressions like ancient seal marks, which has been said to account for the plant's vernacular name, though the word 'seal' is also a reminder of the plant's use in the past, when a mucilaginous dressing was made for broken bones. Gerard suggested that the root could be pulverised and used to brew ale, which 'soddereth and gleweth together the bones in very short space but very strongly, yea, although the bones be but slenderly and unhandsomely placed and wrapped up'.

This indicates the limitations of medical skills in the sixteenth and seventeenth centuries, when plants like Solomon's seal and comfrey were used in plasters.

The true official plant is *Polygonatum officinale*, a British native of limestone woodland, but it is also found in localised areas of Europe and extending to North Africa, the Western Himalayas and China. The species indigenous to Europe is *P. multiflorum*, which is clump-forming with arching round stems, grown in gardens for many generations. *P. verticillatum* is an erect perennial, with angled stems and flowers in pendulous clusters in the leaf axils. *P. >× hybridum* is a hybrid between two European species, *P. odoratum* and *P. multiflorum*. *P. ordoratum* is similar to the common *P. multiflorum*, but is shorter and found in woods and rocky places. It is a highly ornamental species related to asparagus. It has angular stems reaching a height of sixty centimetres or more and is found naturally occurring from Europe to Eastern Asia. They prefer a brightly shaded location as too little light will result in poor flowering and a limp habit of growth. Seed collected and sown fresh in autumn will germinate the following spring if provided with cold treatment or division of the rhizomes in early spring before growth begins. Slugs may be a problem particularly when young shoots appear. Rabbits and deer may also graze on them despite their mildly toxic leaves.

Many species have long been used as food in China. Leaves, stems and rhizomes are used raw or cooked and served with meat and rice. The rhizomes are also used to make a tea or soaked in wine or liquor to flavour the beverages. They are also fried with sugar and honey to make sweet snacks. An American species, *P. biflorum,* referring to the flowers, which grow in pairs, has a starchy root that was eaten like the potato, and the dried rhizomes can be ground and added to flour to make bread and supplement food staples. The shoots of some polygonatums can be boiled and used like asparagus.

In spring, the fresh green leaves are borne along the arching stems before the tubular white flowers, green-tipped, appear in pairs which dangle beneath the arched stem. By the time the dangling white flower bells are strung beneath them, they have forfeited much of their youthful bloom. These are followed by seed pods. The flowers are attractive, but so is the foliage, which turns a golden yellow in autumn. They should be grown in the cooler part of the garden.

LILY-OF-THE-VALLEY
Liliaceae, *Convallaria majalis* (the perfumed pearl, May lily, the queen of flowers)

The Painting

The leaves grow in pairs enfolding the stem, from which hang tiny rounded bells of white flowers. I look for darks behind the flowers so as to show the white against the green. The light catches on the leaves, and in places they appear slightly blue and in others yellow. A base green is mixed, to which is added a cool blue – either Cerulean or Winsor Blue – with a warm yellow, Indian Yellow, added to the green for the lighter areas.

Once the view is selected, the light effect should be firmly fixed in mind, as the light will change, continually, from moment to moment. The best outdoor paintings are masterly portrayals of light, capturing the jewel-like essence of nature. By deliberately playing light against dark, then depth, realism and interest are added. It is light and shade that enables us to see the shapes of things, or to determine space, distance and atmosphere.

The Gardener

May lilies, as they are popularly called, have an intense sweet perfume. They flourish in shaded corners and borders that never face the high sun. Through the centuries, lily-of-the-valley has been associated with spring festivals, especially Pentecost. They are regarded as the symbol of a return to happiness, being associated with purity and gentleness. In many European countries, lily-of-the-valley is customarily presented to ladies on the first day of May. An old custom in Germany was to go to the woods to gather bunches on Whit Monday, so it came to be called May bloom. In France, especially in Normandy, similar festivals are held with picnics and carnivals when floats and carts are decorated with flower spikes in elaborate designs. Its provincial names vary between the queen of flowers, Our lady's tears or Mary's tears (because it grew from the tears the Virgin shed at the foot of the Cross), lily of May, little May bells, muguet fairy cups, May lily, wood lily, convallaria, lily-conval, conval-lily, 'lilly constancy', 'liri confancie', mugwet (which is a Middle English corruption of the French muguet) and valleys. Another medieval name, probably given by the monks, was ladder-to-heaven, from the step-like placing of the flowers on the stem.

'The Latines have named it "lilium convallium".'

The flowers were used to decorate churches, and when Lady chapels were built to honour the Virgin lilies were placed there whenever possible.

Nicholas Culpeper recalls the usefulness of lily-of-the-valley in a variety of treatments for widely differing ills, saying that distilled water of the flowers in wine restores lost speech, helps the palsy, is excellently good in the apoplexy, comforts the heart and 'vital spiritual'. The effective medicinal element is convallatoxin, a digitalis-like drug that similarly acts upon the heart. It can be extracted from all parts of the plant, which, unlike many, is richest in its product during the flowering period. Unlike digitalin, convallatoxin is non-poisonous. In herbal practice, an infusion is considered to be a good remedy for the restoration of speech following cardiac arrest, and a tisane of flowers and leaves is said to soothe a sore throat. The leaves yield a green dye.

The wild flowers were planted in gardens by the middle of the sixteenth century. There are five species in white, pink and striped and some double. Mrs Gaskell wrote in *Wives and Daughters* of plans for a picnic in the season when they flower in Hurstwood, where they grow wild.

Lily-of-the-valley is a perennial with creeping rhizomes and short, erect, curved stems bearing a one-sided cluster of very sweet-scented, pure-white, bell-shaped pendulous flowers above a pair of elliptic leaves. The pale-green radical leaves grow in pairs and enfold the flower stalks. The tiny rounded bells of white flowers hang down around the stem. They will grow outside in almost any situation, but are best in shade and plenty of moisture. When established, the crowns increase and the larger ones flower annually without any attention except an annual autumnal top dressing of manure or rich soil. As the plants are not overly ornamental, except when in flower, a place should be found for them where they will not be too prominent in other seasons.

PEONY
Paeonia

Painting 1

Chinese artists loved the peony, as did Monet, Manet, Renoir, Augustus John and the seventeenth-century flower painters. In this painting, the intention was to try to capture the intricacies of the stunning, satiny, tightly packed petals, and this was done by reserving the thick stamens and carefully painting each petal. The design must convey the essential spirit of the flower. Peony flowers are large and bold, so I wanted it to dominate the space. I selected a large brush relative to the petal size and painted in one stroke. While still wet, a slightly stronger colour was touched on to the point where the petals join the centre of the flower. This will create a gentle gradation. The juxtaposition of colour will bring a low-toned harmony into life. In some areas I enhanced the blue or red within the petals and echoed the yellow-green of the centre of the flower in the background.

Not knowing the outcome of such an experiment can lead to fear of mistakes, but it also expands the imagination, deviating from the usual process, and is a learning opportunity. Stepping out of the comfort zone in a painting is apt to show in the painting. The stimuli can give the painting a fresh, different look.

The Gardener

The Ancient Greek name was used by Theophrastus, who was the first physician to use the plant medicinally. A magnificent plant with often fragrant flowers, it is the oldest of all garden flowers. It is called after Paeon, the physician to the gods, and its Latin name, *Paeonia officinalis*, is indicative of its connection with the apothecary's garden. A robust, poisonous perennial plant with large red flowers and stalks and red stamens, *P. lactiflora* 'Festiva Maxima', Chinese peony, is the main parent of many hybrids in single, double or semi-double bowl-shaped flowers. The peony has been cherished around the world since ancient times as a source of food, medicine, magic claims and beauty. The single peony appears to have been the earliest known, and it is native to many parts of Europe. The wild peony is known as the male peony, and the garden peony is the female. The male flower is probably an escape from ancient monastery gardens, where it would have been grown for medicinal purposes. There are at least eight varieties grown in herb gardens, and they were said to cure no less than twenty diseases. The old double white was introduced to England in the sixteenth century. Paeon, the physician, is said to have first used the plant medicinally.

The peony belongs to the buttercup family and is surrounded by many ancient beliefs and superstitions. The seeds were gathered during the waning moon and hung about the necks of children as a protection against the evil eye. In Mongolia the seeds were used instead of tea and the Saxons used them for flavouring. The kernels were eaten as a condiment and the roots made into broth.

The most flamboyant of flowers, sweetly scented, yet easy to grow and very hardy and long-lived, there herbaceous perennials will grow equally well in sun or shade. The colours of the flowers are more intense when they are protected from strong sunlight and the flowers last longer in shade. Colours range from pure white through shades of pink and purple, rich shades of magenta, burgundy, white, peach and red, and many have prominent golden stamens. They come with ruffled or rounded flowers with glossy deep-green leaves. The common peony, *P. officinalis*, has large, very full double blooms, crimson in the variety 'Rubra Plena', and white in 'Alba Plena'. The Chinese peony, *P. lactiflora*, has fragrant single, semi-double and fully double varieties and there are many more. They should be planted with the tips of the buds below the soil surface, making sure that the roots are not exposed. They require moisture and cold for dormancy, needing a period of chilling in winter, which they do not get if planted too deeply. They generally have three to five 'eyes' or buds on the end of a long carrot-like root. They should flower in their second year after planting. As the plant dies down the foliage is attractively tinted and the seed heads very ornamental. A partially protected position is best and they prefer a rich, limy soil. Most do well in slight shade. Ample space should be allowed as they have a spreading habit. A mulch in summer will be beneficial. Division is the best means of propagation, but should not be done too often as the plants need some time to become established and are best left to form good clumps. Seed is readily produced by most and, if sown as soon as ripe, usually germinates freely in a cold frame, in most instances coming true to type.

No other plants will make such a magnificent display, or require so little aftercare, provided they are planted in a good, rich, deeply dug soil. As soon as the buds are formed, they should be staked with a cane; otherwise the blossoms become heavy after a shower and are liable to touch the ground and be damaged.

The plant can live for 100 years or more if left undisturbed, and its flowers improve with age.

Painting 2

Light creates form, colour and texture. On the shadowed side there is less light, so less form and texture are visible with the colour more muted, which in turn enhances the feeling of light. On a sunny day it is usually easy to differentiate between light and shadow, direct light (which is warmer) and pure light (which is cooler). Since the sky is the greatest reflector of light, its blue reflection is the source of cool light in shadows. Direct sunlight has less of the bluer wavelengths and is therefore warmer. On a clear day as the sun approaches the horizon there is much more atmosphere for light to traverse and so some of the blue wavelengths are lost. This is what causes the low-intensity blue at the horizon to appear high-intensity blue/purple overhead, where there is less atmosphere. The shorter wavelengths of light (blue and violet) have more energy and tend to bounce around in the atmosphere and scatter or reflect some of the blue light, which is directed back towards earth. Sometimes the penetration of warm light through the atmosphere contrasts with blue in the shadows. Blue has a great influence on white, purifying it and increasing its luminosity. The best moments are those when the painting flows effortlessly. It's natural to want to succeed and the most successful paintings are quick responses to the subject, which retains the freshness and spontaneity and luminosity of watercolour. Creativity, exploration and risk-taking can lead to the expansion of possibilities. This means venturing into the unknown, risking failure – but then watercolour is exciting. A drop of colour into a wet wash produces a magical diffusion, intense colour, variety and vibrancy.

CEANOTHUS
(Keanothus, a name used to designate a spiny plant, native of North America, chiefly California, Californian lilac, wild lilac, soap bush)

The Drawing
Observational drawing is important, as are measuring proportions, heights and lengths of shapes and noticing how one shape relates to another. Good drawing is absolutely essential because it's the structure for all painting. All drawing is based on measuring. This is all part of a classical drawing theory, but applicable to all subjects, and this the artist must practise always. Each stroke has to be applied with meaning, confidence and purpose in order to achieve an impression of vitality and freshness. Since light is the central character in the drawing, areas left pale maximise the

impact, giving a sense of form and shape. These pale areas represent the highlights, using the shadows as a unifying force. To represent the light, I think about the shadows. I focus on letting the shadows define the image. By drawing outdoors, I am better able to capture the atmosphere of the moment. Monet set up several canvases, and as the light changed so he moved to the appropriate canvas for that particular effect, returning to previous canvases when the light changed. Outdoor painting is usually completed in one session and then adjusted in the studio. When working in the studio, I stop now and then to check progress by looking at the image in a mirror held over my shoulder. The reverse image reveals any mistakes or imbalances, which can be rectified before proceeding.

The Gardener

The ceanothus has a special attraction as its blue flowers are one of the rarest colours among hardy shrubs. They are sun-lovers and benefit from being planted near a sunny wall. I like to plant ceanothus so that its clouds of blue mingle with the deeper blue of a clematis. The majority are evergreen with some hardy deciduous and near-hardy evergreen flowering shrubs, which perform best against a sunny wall in open ground or in deep pots. If planted in the ground, they should be mulched in late winter or spring with organic compost, away from the base of the shrub. To encourage new growth, add a general fertiliser. They like good, well-cultivated, well-drained soils. Many are drought-tolerant.

Ceanothus velutinus is the most common and widespread. They are fast-growing, but may be short-lived. *C. arboreus* or *C. thyrsiflorus* var. *griseus* can live twenty-five years or more. The evergreen varieties mostly flower in spring and deciduous ones flower in summer and early autumn. The sweet-smelling flowers are small and numerous in large, dense, showy panicles in colours ranging from pale blue to bright blue, deep blue, indigo blue and rose pink.

Pruning is not needed, but to promote growth the soft tips can be pinched out. Overlong branches can be pruned after flowering in summer, never cutting into old wood as it may not regrow. Spring flowers bloom on shoots produced in the previous summer. Summer flowers bloom on the current year's growth. Deciduous ceanothus blooms on new shoots each year. Pruning generates many strong new shoots each year. Overgrown evergreen ceanothus does not respond well to renovation pruning. It is better to take semi-ripe cuttings from midsummer to autumn with deciduous shrubs from softwood cuttings taken in late spring to midsummer. Shoots can sprout from roots and stems, which can be taken as cuttings. To propagate from seed, following scarification and stratification, the seeds need to be soaked in water for twelve hours followed by chilling for three months.

Ceanothus is a genus of about fifty to sixty species of nitrogen-fixing shrubs in the family *Rhamnaceae*. The name comes from the Greek word meaning spiny plant. It is endemic to North America, with some found in the Eastern United States, South-East Canada and as far south as Guatemala.

Ceanothus is a source of nutrition for deer and the flowers are important in attracting birds, butterflies, bees and other beneficial insects. Early pioneers used the plant as a substitute for black tea.

PINCUSHION FLOWER
Scabiosa

The Painting

This was a great exercise in complementary colours – violet and a hint of yellow. The flowers were painted carefully as the forms of the petals were quite complicated. The delicacy of the plant meant careful observation and a light painterly touch. The violet paint was diluted to indicate the papery appearance of the petals. A slightly thicker violet, but still light, was added in places and then another thicker violet was used so as to show the layers of petals. The centres were painted with pale yellow and Yellow Ochre was added around each pale circle. The stalks were an important part of the design, painted in light green and then darkened in the shadow areas.

The Gardener

These are fragrant, long-lasting annuals and perennials for the front and middle of the flower border. They are very attractive to butterflies. Beautiful flowers in blue, rose, purple and yellowish white. They grow well in ordinary soil and may be increased by seeds or division. *Scabiosa atropurpurea* has several names – mournful widow, sweet scabious, pincushion and Egyption rose.

Knautia arvensis, field scabious, is a little branched hairy perennial with long-stalked, bluish-lilac, hemispherical flower heads with the outermost flowers distinctly larger than the inner. Basal leaves are often entire, forming an overwintering grey-green rosette, with the stem leaves deeply pinnately cut into oblong lobes with an elliptic terminal lobe. It is very pretty and useful in my dry garden.

S. lucida, or shining scabious, is distinguished by its almost hairless, somewhat glossy leaves and rose-lilac, violet or deep-mauve flowers. It is a perennial from the Alps, Pyrenees and Carpathians. *S. graminifolia* is the grass-leaved scabious, distinguished by its grass-like linear, acute, silky-haired leaves, mostly basal, and its large lilac-blue flowers, which are globular and long-stemmed with the outer florets longer than the inner. It is a softly hairy, tufted, woody-based perennial which flowers from June to August.

MOCK ORANGE
Philadelphus

Painting 1

There is no short cut to becoming a good painter, only practice. I find that making sketches or studies is the best way to learn without thinking of finished pieces. Practising with sketches, experimenting and repeating techniques, helps with mastering basic skills. What is important is the experience.

I used a pencil drawing to work out the composition for a finished painting, sorting out where the lights and darks would be. Determining the tones is most important.

In the painting, I used the drawing as a guide, keeping the greens cool and the shadows on the petals warm, using warm blue, violet and in places some green. The stamens were the same warm yellow as used in the mix for the brighter greens, while the blue was in the mix for the cooler greens.

Painting 2

Philadelphus virginalis has double flowers. The positions of the flowers is very important; and when the blooms are repeated throughout the painting, unity and balance is created. Sometimes a flower appears more attractive if the heads are tilted at an angle instead of face on. The stems were important as well as they look as if they can support the flower heads. A painting, like a flower, ought to be a perfect picture of harmony, and a flower represents perfect harmony in its petal forms, its exquisite soft shapes, its colour and fragrance, all of which can evoke an emotional response. An artist sees what is invisible to others and must capture those elusive moments of beauty before they pass.

The Gardener

Philadelphus is the ancient Greek name meaning brotherly love. The beautiful white flowers have prominent gold stamens and a rich, fruity perfume which can scent the whole garden. White flowers create a cool mood, fresh during the day and a luminous quality at twilight. Their fabulous strong fragrance and white flowers give the plant the common name of mock orange. Certain scents and sounds recall summer with the whirr of the lawn mower and the scent of bruised and cut grass drying in the sun as well as the scents of the flowers. It is therefore best planted near a walkway or patio, where scent can be appreciated. The plant can look dull after flowering. Philadelphus can be pruned as soon as flowers have faded and pruning should consist only of removal of branches which have flowered; otherwise it can grow into unmanageable thickets. Cutting the larger stems encourages vigorous growth from the ground, making the shrub full at the base, and improves the flowering as more light reaches the interior of the plant. It roots easily from cuttings – softwood cuttings in summer or hardwood cuttings in autumn and winter.

LOOSESTRIFE
Lysimachia (yellow loosestrife, purple lythrum, yellow pimpernel)

The Painting

The impact of colour may be much greater when focused on one particular plant as the eye is drawn to the bright colour. Also, working with a limited palette is an exciting challenge, simplifying colour choices. By limiting the colours, the focus is on tone and temperature contrasts to enhance the rhythm and drama of the painting. A focal point works better when corresponding shapes and colours are a counterbalance, not a distraction. Adding soft and hard edges adds depth to the painting. Sometimes it is necessary to exaggerate certain edges and play down others. I didn't want to explain every edge, so to create interest the main flowers were painted clearly and sharply with hard edges with the strongest contrasts saved for the focal point. The background is subtle, using a wet-on-wet technique, which gives beautiful blended colour flows, creating a diffused effect in unexpected ways. If subsequent areas need to be softened then a damp brush, possibly a stiff brush, will lift some colour. Colour is important, but tone must be paramount.

Sargent said, 'Colour is an inborn gift, but appreciation of value is merely training of the eye, which everyone ought to be able to acquire.' The two must work together to achieve colour relationship.

The Gardener
The plant was useful to both man and beast, being used by the herbalist Nicholas Culpeper, 1616–1654, to treat nosebleeds and stomach complaints, to keep flies away from animals and as a yellow dye. The genus name *Lysimachia* is derived from Greek words meaning loosing strife, hence its common name.

L. vulgaris is an erect, softly hairy, rhizomatous perennial with clusters of golden-yellow flowers in June. *L. punctata* has larger yellow flowers. Loosestrife (garden or yellow loosestrife) has lance-shaped mid-green leaves and whorls of bright-yellow starry-shaped flowers and gives a welcome splash of colour in the garden. The flowers have no nectar or scent, but several species of wasp and a tiny solitary bee, *Macropis labiata*, are attracted to the abundant pollen. The leaves provide food for moth caterpillars.

The plants are suitable for garden borders as long as they are regularly divided to avoid compaction. The divided clumps of rhizomes will produce more plants.

Plants grow up the house walls, with large windows giving the feeling of being outdoors. The studio and garden are the places where I prefer to spend as much time as possible. The garden is an extension of the house, or is it the other way round? All downstairs rooms have doors which open into the garden, and upstairs the rooms have large windows looking down on to the garden. Our covered eating area is like a garden room draped with wisteria, honeysuckle and roses. They are all beautiful and scented, making it a perfect place on a sunny day, and in the evenings this creates a romantic atmosphere.

BERBERIS
(barberry)

Painting 1

Wanting to create a highly believable scene, I think about warm and cool colours before starting the painting. The warm reds in the berries were balanced well with the cooler purple in the leaves. I also think about how the light catches the delicate flowers, dramatically silhouetting them against some darker leaves and a hint of sunshine behind. The shapes and colours were so enchanting. I concentrated on painting the wonderful colours against the light falling on the leaves.

Shadows enhance the feeling of light and are best painted with a combination of cool and warm colours, which give a more luminous effect. The stronger the light, the deeper the shadow. Shadows are one of the most practical and best ways of creating a three-dimensional look. By painting a shadow, tones are immediately introduced which give the object volume and depth. Shadows can enhance the drama and beauty in the painting and if kept transparent can be evocative and mysterious. To produce luminous shadows, the complementary colour of the object is used – for example, orange will cast a shadow with a bluish tinge while a red will cast a shadow with a greenish tinge and yellow will cast a violet shadow and warm yellow will cast a blue shadow.

Technique should be subordinate to expression, but after many years of painting it becomes more developed and part of the skill, allowing personal expression to be more vital.

Painting 2

These fabulous yellow flowers invited an array of different warm and cool colours in Indian Yellow, Winsor Lemon and Winsor Orange and, in the shadowed centres of the flowers, a touch of Quinacridone Magenta mixed into the yellow. The leaves were also interesting to paint, in that various shades of green provide a useful contrast and complement to the yellow. The blue was Cobalt, neat in places, and mixed with the yellows for the greens. The cool yellow and cool blue made a bright green and with the warm yellow a richer, warmer green. A touch of Magenta was added to the warmer green for shaded areas, and this also helped to give depth behind the flowers.

The Gardener

Berberis is a large genus of deciduous and evergreen shrubs. Berberis is commonly known as barberry. It has ornamental leaves and tiny rich-yellow scented flowers. There are numerous different kinds, some of which are evergreen, comprising about 450 species, of which some 280 belong to the Asiatic group, found in India, the Himalayas, Tibet, China and Japan. There are a few which grow in Africa and Europe, with two from the Americas. Nearly all have spines on the stems, and the flowers are solitary or in panicles. I have and adore the hardy deciduous species with their fabulous purple-red colouring in autumn. In spring sweetly scented yellow or orange solitary flowers make a fine display, followed by red or purple berries. They are especially good for my garden as they tolerate dry conditions. Unfortunately all the stems have spines, which is bad news for gardeners. Many deciduous species have attractive pink or red autumn colour with some *B. thunbergii* having dark-red to violet foliage. The name comes from the Dutch botanist Carl Peter Thunberg, 1743–1828, who identified this species in Japan in 1784. Charles Darwin named a Chilean species, *B. darwinii*. It was first recorded by him on the *Beagle* in 1835. *B. darwinii* is hardy and not frost-tender, is an evergreen shrub with dense, dark, glossy green leaves all year with drooping racemes of rich-orange flowers tinged red in bud, from April to May, followed by blue-black berries, ripening in summer. The fruit loses its acidity when fully ripe although there is a lot of seed compared to the amount of flesh. Many species have spines on the shoots.

Berberis, or 'berberys', is the Arabic name of the fruit, which is a small berry ripening red or dark blue, often with a pink or violet waxy surface bloom. The edible berries are rich in vitamin C, but have a sharp acid flavour, which loses its acidity when fully ripe. They were used in Europe in a similar way to citrus peel, but are little used now, but in Persian cuisine berberis was used to flavour rice pilafs and poultry meat. In Russia it is used in jams as the berries are high in pectin, which makes jam congeal as it cools after being boiled. It is used as flavouring for soft drinks and sweets.

Traditional medicine dates back more than 2,500 years. American Indians used barberries to treat scurvy and a decoction has been used to treat gastrointestinal ailments and coughs. It also reduces the risk of heart disease, and supports a healthy liver. The dried fruit of *B. vulgaris* is used in herbal medicines as it contains alkaloids, the most prominent of which is berberine, which is an antimicrobial, killing bacteria and parasites, is anti-inflammatory, hypotensive (lowering blood pressure), sedative and has anti-bacterial properties. Barberry root has been used for sores, burns, ulcers, acne, itch, ringworm, cuts and bruises. Historically yellow dye was extracted from the stem, root and bark for leather and hair.

Propagation may be by suckers, layering or cuttings. Cuttings of half-ripe wood can be taken in summer or of mature wood in autumn. Seed should be sown when ripe, placed in a cold frame, and should germinate in late winter or early spring. Seed from overripe fruit will take longer to germinate. The seed should be kept well ventilated as they are subject to damping off. The seedlings should be potted individually and kept in a cold frame until the following spring before planting out into a sunny position which encourages fruiting. Seeds germinate freely, but may not be good specimens. The plant is self-fertile, having both male and female organs, and is pollinated by insects. It can grow in semi-shade or full sun, but prefers a moist, well-drained soil. It is pollinated by insects, being noted for being attractive to wildlife. Berberis is a food plant for the larvae of some Lepidoptera species, including the barberry carpet moth.

Berberis is often used as a hedge as the long arching branches are attractive when in flower or bearing fruit. Plants can be pruned and will re-sprout well from the base. It was believed to have formed part of the crown of thorns that Jesus wore.

Common names are michay, calafaten quelung and holy thorn.

POPPY
Papaver eschscholzia (Californian poppy)

Drawing 1
This little ink drawing helped with understanding the shapes of the flower heads and the seed heads, the twists and turns of the stems and the intricate foliage, and the natural composition made a pleasing design.

Painting 1
I grow poppies in my garden and each year I am amazed at their beauty and strength of colour. I study them closely and try to reflect their clean lines in my paintings. Red poppies flash their colour like fire enhanced by the surrounding greens or enhanced by accompanying cornflowers, as complementary colours next to each other make their colours seem brighter. Our eyes read contrast – a red will appear more intense when it is placed next to a green. The petals do not last long, but the sculptural seed heads offer another painting opportunity.

The intensity of the poppy colours is stimulating. If the subject is exciting to the artist, it will come through in

131

the painting. Spontaneous, lively, fresh and stimulating. Outdoor painting is an emotional response to our surroundings and must express feelings which are experienced at that moment.

It is sunlight and nature which inspire me, capturing the dazzling effect of the transparency and texture of the petals, the delicate qualities of reflected light and the incredibly subtle variations of colour. The eye will be drawn to the strongest contrast of colour and tone, but also to the most intense detail or textural interest, so these elements need to be in the focal area. Bright colours can create a considerable impact when seen in the context of a mid-tonal-range painting, but care should be taken not to overstate.

Colour, shape, form, light and shade, and texture have to be interpreted from a three-dimensional form on to a two-dimensional surface when the mind is encouraged into recognising and believing in the object. The shapes have to be manipulated into forms using the effects of light and shade, which give the illusion of solid objects with some parts in light and others in shadow. Observing the growth patterns of the plant is essential. I begin with simplified shapes of leaves and flowers, establishing the character of the plants, and then develop these with colour, focusing on a good range of values and a simple palette. The temptation is to mix too many colours, which can result in muddy mixes, so keeping the colours pure gives a much more interesting and stimulating effect.

A colour is as intense as it can be when used straight from the tube, but this level of intensity can be changed when another colour is placed next to it. In this painting the red looks stronger where it is placed next to a complementary colour, such as green. Our eyes are automatically drawn to these contrasts. The intensity in the focal point stands out more because the green does not compete, but is secondary to the red.

The Gardener
The single poppy of the cornfields, the white, red and purple blotched opium poppy, the brilliant yellow poppy and the black-centred oriental poppy all have silky petals and retain their creases until they drop. Neither sun nor rain changes this.

Vessels looking like upside-down poppy capsules, thought to be used for poppy wine, as well as pipes for smoking opium, were found amid the ruins of Knossos in Crete. They have been found mixed with ancient Egyptian barley grains and among human remains in a Spanish cave dating back to Neolithic times (around 4,000 BC). Whether opium was used for recreational or ritual purposes in these ancient cultures is uncertain, but there is strong evidence that the ancient Egyptians used opium medicinally, both as an analgesic and as a sedative. Greek and Arab physicians advocated the use of poppy wine, not only as a painkiller, but also for conditions such as colic, diarrhoea and persistent coughs. Historically, poppies have been used in several ways. Gerard recommends using the seeds 'to season bread or serve at table with other junket dishes and is delightful to be eaten'. The seeds themselves contain no opiate but provide oil. Poppies have been cultivated in France and Germany for their seeds, which are not narcotic, but used instead of olive oil. A syrup was produced from the petals which was only slightly narcotic, and its juice used for colouring medicine. As a dye it was unreliable, and therefore unsatisfactory, although it has been used in the making of red ink. As a hot fermentation, poppy heads can be used to soothe sprained joints, toothache and neuralgia. Oils in the seeds were used in cooking and in creating paints. In various parts of the world, the incision made in the capsules to drain off the precious drug differs in shape and position, but the end product is opium. This incision has to be precise and should not penetrate the wall to the seed cavity. The juice flows out as a creamy-coloured liquid with a narcotic smell and dries to a brown colour and a gummy consistency. It can be scraped off with a knife and collected.

The field or corn poppy is *Papaver rhoeas,* the Latin name meaning a flow or falling-off, which is descriptive of both the latex and the falling petals. On the edges of my garden, where the land is disturbed by the plough but the seeder falls short of the boundary, there are often poppies. The common poppy needs recently disturbed soil to be able to germinate. These are annual poppies, but will distribute seed and grow in the garden. Their scarlet blooms are an attractive sight in the countryside in early summer. Farmland provides a habitat for many wild plant species such as poppies, capable of colonising disturbed soil. However, these garnets of the cornfields are no longer so plentiful among the crops since the advent of chemical herbicides.

The capsule, or poppy head, sprinkles its hundreds of seeds like a pepper pot. This beautiful and bee-friendly flower has a notorious history. Where poppies grew before farms and fields existed remains a mystery, but they were probably once confined to unstable habitats such as open ground, dried-out pond margins, sand dunes and crumbling clifftops, where many are still found today.

Painting 2

Light in the landscape is as important as light on the flowers. When composing the painting, line and form, placement of the main objects, tone, texture and

colour are all of equal importance. Even so, take colour out of the equation and a well-balanced painting should still be interesting. Unlike the other elements, colour is not essential. Having said that, there is an emotional response to colour and red is one of the most powerful.

Eugène Chevreul, a French chemist, noted that shadows are often tinged with colours opposite to the colour of the object which casts the shadow. His theories had a huge influence on the work of the Impressionist painters, who started to look closely at the colours in shadows. It is because of the way the Impressionists worked that now shadows are seen in terms of colour. Sometimes the colour of a shadowed area is simply a darker version of the local colour of the object. Where there is bright light, such as outdoors on a sunny day, shadows tend to pick up the colours around them. In painting the greens, some of the red is added into the green to convey shadowed areas beneath the flowers. This darkens and subdues the green compared to the yellow-greens in full sunlight.

Atmosphere is a major factor in painting outdoors. It is important to understand how it affects objects in order to control the illusion of depth. In the distance the atmosphere will cause colours and values to change with the range of values lighter and restricted, appearing softer and blurred as if out of focus. Dark values become lighter as they recede into the background and colours will have less intensity than those in the foreground. During the day, the effect of the sky will also make everything appear cooler or more blue into the distance, while the foreground will be sharper and clearer and have more contrast in value and colour.

To create depth in the painting, the nearest flowers are painted in sharp focus with crisp edges to emphasise their closeness, while those further back are less defined. Letting some of the flowers touch and overlap also helps to create the illusion of three dimensions. Some flowers are painted as simple shapes while those in the foreground have more detail.

These beautiful poppies were growing in my garden. The composition was ready-made with the Scarlet against the different shades of green. I used Quinacridone Red-orange for the flowers and a wash of Indian Yellow in the background, which was overpainted when dry with washy Ultramarine Blue, which was then washed in with Indian Yellow for the trees and both colours formed the greens, with yellow accenting stems and leaves in the foreground.

The Gardener

The English vernacular names for the poppy are numerous – cockrose (because the flowers unfold at cockcrow), soldiers, canker, cankerer rose and redweed.

'Nature rarely spreads red around, it took man to create fields of poppies.'

Painting 3

Field poppies create stunning pictures with the scarlet flowers against their complementary colour, green, in the grasses. This was quite a loosely painted painting, essentially to capture the transient nature of the poppies.

The Gardener

The scarlet field poppy is forever linked with battle, for it was from the cornfields that John Tradescant, gardener and soldier, fighting the French under the Duke of Buckingham, brought the first seeds back to England. Growing in profusion only on cultivated land, the poppy blazed a scarlet trail throughout Europe, running for miles along the straight poplar-lined roads and vineyards of France. It is revered by poets, artists and photographers. It has replaced the rosemary plant as the most famous symbol each November, recalling the killing fields of the First World War, where it acquired its other common name – Flanders poppy. The poppy is distinguished by its seed capsules; at the slightest breeze, the seeds are shaken through the perforations around the top of the capsule. Many seeds are deeply buried and can remain buried alive for hundreds of years until the land is disturbed. This is why enormous number of poppies covered the Flanders battlefields after the First World War. The massive disturbance caused by shell holes and trenches provided ideal conditions for the germination of millions of poppy seeds – a spectacular phenomenon still recalled by the wearing of red poppies and buttonholes on Remembrance Day. The artificial poppies sold for 11 November are made by the blind of St Dunstan's. In 1970 a number of young people brought white poppies to Whitehall as a symbol of peace.

The British artist Sir Cedric Morris contributed to the variations with a dusky-pink variety, named 'Cedric Morris'. He developed many plants named

Cedric Morris, including rose, geranium, narcissus and canna as well as the poppy. Cedric Morris is best known for his flower, landscape and portrait paintings. During the war he joined the Artists Rifles, but before embarking for France was declared medically unfit for action, due to a failed operation during childhood. He studied plants and painted watercolours, walking around the fields and hedgerows, searching for softer-colour variants in poppies. He became friendly with many artists, including Barbara Hepworth. Lucian Freud was his student. He painted two large flower murals on board the liner *Queen Mary*.

Poppies live for one season, flowering and seeding, shedding large numbers of seeds before they die, but the seeds germinate within twenty-four hours, which is why they clothed the battle-torn fields and desolate farms of Flanders in red after one season of calm following the Battle of Waterloo and the First World War. Now in Flanders fields the poppies grow between the crosses, row by row.

The name *Papaver* is from the Latin *pappa* or *papa*, a breast, probably because of the soporific milky fluid that exudes from the plant, and it was said to have been administered to fractious infants. It is also said that the ancient Latin plant name was derived from the sound made in chewing the seed. The Anglo-Saxon name, *popig*, became 'pop' in English, but the poppy has many names in the countryside, including cheese-bowl, corn rose, wind-rose and headache, as the scent was supposed to cause pains in the head. It was also known as telltale, because a petal crushed in the hand told whether a lover was true or false. If the petal squeaked, he was true.

The poppy used to turn the landscape from green to red, beautiful against blue cornflowers, but with chemicals and sprays the farmlands are now poorer in colour. Although the poppy is not plentiful in crops it is still a universal plant. It is native to Europe, has been introduced into North America, New Zealand and Australia and is parent to the Shirley poppy, which was originally raised by the Reverend William Wilks, a former secretary of the Royal Horticultural Society. He selected seeds from the wild and bred and named them after his parish in Shirley, Surrey, England. Colours are white, pale or dark pink, and 'Picotee' has dark edges.

Gardeners welcome poppies as beautiful, dramatic flowers. They have has wiry stems and bright-scarlet cup-shaped flowers with a dark blotch at the base. The flowers have no nectar, but honeybees collect protein-rich pollen as food for their larvae.

It is the white poppy that is the true poppy of sleep. Brought to Europe from Asia, the opium poppy has been in use since Neolithic times, and its virtues were known and noted in many ancient manuscripts. *P. somniferum,* whose Latin name is derived from Somnus, the Roman god of sleep, is the oldest species in cultivation – a plant of immense antiquity, originating from the Middle East and known around the Mediterranean in medieval times. It is an erect glaucous annual with large deeply lobed leaves and very large white, lilac or purple flowers with dark basal blotches. Opiate juices from its unripe green seed capsules hold both opium and heroin. It is the source of morphine and codeine. When smoked or chewed, opium causes intoxication and it is an addictive drug. This narcotic drug was introduced across the ancient trade routes to China by the Arabs. This led to opium smoking, which became a scourge in China, but was common practice. The importation of opium into China was prohibited in 1729 by Emperor Yung Cheng. This ban, and other restrictions on trade, led to war with Great Britain – the Opium Wars of 1839 to 1842 – and ultimately to the growth of home production of the opium poppy. This in turn began to reverse the trend and China also began to profit from the export of opium. A world conference was held in Shanghai to control world production of the trade in opium.

By the end of these wars British trading companies had accumulated vast amounts of wealth. In the nineteenth century, morphine was isolated from opium, named after Morpheus, the Greek god of dreams. Morphine was found to be a far more potent painkiller than opium, but when it was used extensively during the American Civil War another characteristic it shared with opium became apparent – it was highly addictive. In 1898 heroin was produced from morphine and marketed as a superior cough medicine and painkiller. Ironically, it was also thought to be non-addictive, but turned out to be five times more addictive than morphine. Heroin-laced cough medicine was still available in 1917.

In Britain during the nineteenth century, laudanum (opium dissolved in alcohol) was widely taken by people in all levels of society. It was also used to quieten hungry children, leading inevitably to many unfortunates becoming addicted. However, these same addictive chemicals have also given us analgesics such as codeine and morphine, while the oily seeds, which do not contain narcotic substances, are widely used in baking and also in the paint-manufacturing industry.

Poppy-seed oil, extracted from the ripe seeds, known as mawseed, is a fine edible oil quite free from opium, and it is also used as a drying oil in paint making.

P. somniferum is an annual, has grey-green foliage and the flowers are white, pink, red, purple or rich burgundy. Some have double flowers, resembling peonies. There is something magical about the gentle unfolding of the delicate petals from a tiny bud.

Drawing 2

This is an ink drawing, using a brush, made on smooth paper. There's something exciting about the directness of ink. The flying seeds gave a sense of movement, echoed by the curves of the stems and looseness of the brushstrokes.

The Gardener

P. aeoniaeflorum, the opium poppy, has been grown in gardens since the Bronze Age for its morphine content and related chemicals. There are various popular cultivars, including 'Black Peony', which is in fact dark purple, and 'Scarlet Peony'. *P. laciniatum* has double flowers with petals which appear to be shredded and ruffled. Some favourites are 'Crimson Feathers', 'Rose Feathers' and 'Swandown'. *P. triniifolium* is a biennial for the rock garden. It has pale-red beautiful rosettes. *P. atlanticum* is a perennial with orange flowers in summer. *P. pilosum* from Asia Minor is a perennial with bright-scarlet and orange flowers also in summer. The single-flowered opium poppies are closest to the wild form. These come in all sorts of colours, from purple to white. Some are grown for their decorative 'pepperpot' seed capsules, which, after flowering, are dried to a pale-buff colour and can be a precious crop. They are also used by flower arrangers. Others, such as 'Bread-seed White Persian', are specifically grown for their seeds used in baking.

For many gardeners the Shirley poppy holds a far greater attraction. It is so called because it was bred in 1880 by the Reverend W. Wilks in his garden in Shirley, Surrey, where he discovered this new form of annual poppy growing in his garden. The flower had a narrow edge of white around each petal and no blotch. He sowed the resulting seeds and continued to select from subsequent generations until he had a group of poppies with single, tissue-paper-like petals, no dark blotches at the base and colours ranging from pale pink to lilac and mauve, as well as red. Other gardeners over the years made selections from their plantings of Shirley poppies so that now there are double and semi-double forms and 'Picotee' flowers with lighter or darker edges.

Cultivars flower from June to September and reach a height of thirty to sixty centimetres.

Part of the delight when sowing mixtures of these annual poppies is that the combinations of flower colours and petal edgings is undetermined.

Painting 4

The scarlet poppy is stunning, but there is a gentleness about the pale pink made dramatic by the purple-blue centre. This helped to establish the main flower in the foreground and brought the light on the petals to the fore. There is a wonderful freshness and delicacy of texture about every sort of poppy, with the oriental poppy complemented to perfection by the huge black blotches at the base of each petal, and by the velvety purple blackness of their stamens. I chose to paint a dark background to enhance the feel of the delicate, soft petals. Some of the dark blues in the stamen were washed into the background and used as shadow areas. I tried to keep the painting light and elegant, so as to capture the fragile and graceful appearance of the petals. I used a fine brush to depict the veins in the petals.

The Gardener

Despite the delicate crêpe-papery appearance of its beautiful flowers they are quite hardy. The blooms are held singly on hairy stems and may need staking. The deeply cut leaves form a clump and die down in winter. Colours range from pink, pale pink and salmon pink to white, off-white, flesh pink, orange-vermilion, deep scarlet, deep orange, orange-scarlet and mauve-pink. *P. bracteatum* is more robust, forming dense clumps, and has several leafy bracts under each bud. The huge flowers are truly beautiful, but are short-lived and tend to fall over. When untidiness becomes intolerable they can be cut back, and regular deadheading can induce fresh new leaves and there can be a second flush later in the season. They are unlikely to self-seed, but can be propagated by root cuttings taken in autumn. Native to Turkey, Iran and the Caucasus, they are therefore hardy, thriving in the hottest sun and poor, dry soils, but need good air circulation to avoid damp weather causing botrytis, a fungal disease.

There is evidence of oriental poppies found in Egyptian tombs that are 3,000 years old. The wild form has scarlet flowers with a dark purple blotch at the base of each petal. It is native to the meadows and lower mountain zones of West and Central Asia, notably Armenia, Iran and Turkey. Because of its beauty it has spread all over the world. A survival mechanism allows the plant to survive the summer droughts in its native habitat of Central Asia. Its flowers are very attractive to bees, which aid their pollination.

It was in North America that the original poppy, poppy oriental, was found by the French botanist Tournefort. Seeds were sent back to Paris and introduced into Europe in the eighteenth century, but the plant was not very popular as bare patches were left when it finished flowering in summer. In spite of this, enthusiasts were intrigued with its beautiful blooms and began to work on its colour range. Through two more centuries it was cultivated as a garden plant before the famous colours appeared.

A nurseryman named Perry did some outstanding work, producing hybrids such as 'Mrs Marsha', which is striped crimson and white; 'Mrs Perry', a salmon pink; and 'Lady Frederick Moore', which has very large salmon blooms. The nursery sold a number of plants which were supposed to be pink, but when a customer complained that the plants flowered white Mr Perry went to see the plants and delightedly exchanged pink flowers for the long-sought-after white ones.

Selective breeding has produced hundreds of cultivars, singles, doubles, without blotches, with fringed petals and in many colours from white to salmon pink and light orange. The heavy blooms need support to prevent them from bending over and snapping. This led to hybridisers producing semi-dwarf cultivars with small pure-red flowers. A smaller plant 'Pizzicato', unlike most oriental poppies, comes true to seed. It has single blotched flowers in a wide range of colours, from dark red to white. Some suitable for rock gardens are lemon-yellow Japanese poppy, *P. miyabeanum*, and, from Morocco, *P. atlanticum*, with pale-orange flowers and the alpine *P. alpinum* with white or yellow flowers. All three are perennials, but are short-lived so often grown as annuals.

Painting 5

There is something evocative about blue Himalayan poppy flowers, especially with the yellow stamens against the blue. I used various blues – a cool Cerulean Blue for the petals in the light and a warm Ultramarine Blue for those in shade or turning away. Purple enhanced the blue in the shaded areas, stroking it gently and merging all the blues together with a hint of dilute red to give a pink glow. A warm yellow was used for the stamens and in the leaves along with the Ultramarine. At the back of the flower turning away, a little red was washed outwards from the stem into the blue, and all three primary colours were mixed together to form a strong dark for the background.

Painting the illusion of three dimensions on a two-dimensional surface is thoroughly intriguing and fascinating. It is very important to use the imagination to add emotional impact to the work. Add to this an understanding of technique and a love of the subject plus the initial inspiration. The ability to recognise tonal relationships within the subject is absolutely paramount to successfully depicting the subject.

The Gardener

Meconopsis, the blue poppy, originated from the Himalayas. In the late spring of 1922 a British Himalayan expedition, led by legendary mountaineer George Leigh Mallory, discovered the plant on their failed attempt to reach the summit of the then unconquered Mount Everest.

Blue poppies have a reputation for being difficult to grow, but can be grown successfully in a rich well-drained soil in an area of partial shade away from strong winds. They need to be watered regularly through the summer and a liquid fertiliser applied once a month, which keeps the plants vigorous and healthy. In autumn I apply a mulch. *Meconopsis*

'Lingholm' is a reliable perennial with pure blue blooms. *M. baileyi* 'Hensol Violet' has bright-violet-purple flowers with a hint of red. The name is so called for its origins from Hensol Castle, South Wales, United Kingdom, where it was discovered by Lady Henderson. *M. cambrica*, the Welsh poppy, is easier

The Iceland poppy, *P. nudicaule*, is a perennial not from Iceland but from Asia. It undoubtedly cross-pollinated in the wild and in gardens with a few of its closely related species, including *P. radicatum*, which actually is from Iceland. It has some of the most stunning of all poppy flowers and, unusually for a poppy, makes good cut flowers. Colours range from orange to red, pink, white and yellow. The Iceland poppy is short-lived and is often grown as an autumn-sown biennial.

COLOUR

The Artist

The creation of the illusion of objects is accomplished by tone and the interaction of colour. I'm increasingly intoxicated from the flush of excitement which comes from painting and drawing, with the first few brushstrokes which create a sense of purpose. Colour is very personal. No two artists will use the same mix of colours even when they might be painting the same object. We all react to colour to some degree, with most of us having a colour preference. Colour is complicated, but is made easier by being selective and simplifying the number of choices. I usually choose a warm and cool version of each primary and perhaps some earth colours, such as Yellow Ochre, Burnt Sienna and Raw Umber. From these basic colours most mixes are possible. I keep the colours in groups, in the same order, so that it is easy to automatically dip into the right place. I put all the reds together, blues together, etc., as in a spectrum.

We all make colour choices in our daily lives and are affected by the colours we see around us. It is not by chance that traffic 'stop' lights are red; however, most of us are fairly conservative about the colours we choose to live with on a daily basis. We dress mainly in restrained or neutral colours accessorised with brighter accents. We look for harmonies and muted hues.

Colour helps us to define space and form. We respond consciously or subconsciously to its emotional appeal, and hence we have learned to use it with great variety and invention. We associate certain colours with other influences. Orange and purple together may seem brash, but blues and greens are more restful and relate more sympathetically to nature. Few people wear all yellow, yet it evokes images of sunshine and a cheerful atmosphere. Expressing mood and emotion through colour is a relatively abstract exercise dependent on all sorts of personal preferences. However, a person with normal colour vision is capable of identifying up to 10 million variations of colour values. Three types of cone-cell receptors in our eyes pick up colour, each detecting one of the three primary colours – red, yellow or blue. None of us can be sure that we see colours in exactly the same way as anyone else.

The ways in which colours are used together contribute to the mood, atmosphere and expressiveness of the final image. The choice of colour scheme can express the artist's feelings about the subject. Sometimes it is challenging to invent colours which make the image more personal in effect; a personal interpretation of the visual world. Artists need to find a way of sifting the essentials and explaining them visually. This means sharpening colour perception and the ability to analyse various colours and effects.

The Colour Wheel

There are millions of pure hues and tonal variations of colour; therefore the range of colour values that can be identified are more or less infinite. However, in the artist's paints there are some distinct colour groups – red, orange, yellow, green, blue and purple. An infinite number of hues can be mixed from different combinations of the six: red-orange, yellow-green, blue-green, blue-purple and so on. Hue is the name of the colour, as in red or blue. Chroma refers to the hue's degree

140

of brightness or intensity. Value is the relative degree of a hue's darkness or lightness. Temperature describes whether the hue leans towards cool colours, such as blue or violet, or towards warm, red or yellow. Comparing Cadmium Red with Alizarin Crimson, the Cadmium Red appears to have a touch of yellow in it while the Alizarin has a bluish tint. This makes Cadmium Red a warm red and Alizarin Crimson a cool red. Cadmium Yellow is a warm yellow while Lemon Yellow is cool as it leans towards blue. Ultramarine Blue leans toward red, so is warm, and Cerulean and Cobalt Blues are cool. By mixing two primaries that have the same temperature, a bright, intense secondary, such as orange, green or violet, is the result. If the two primary colours have opposite temperatures, the resultant mix is more muted; however, Alizarin Crimson (cool) and Ultramarine Blue (warm) yield a bright purple. When two colours that are opposite each other on the colour wheel (complementary) are combined – for example, yellow with purple, orange with blue, or red with green, a neutral or grey is created. Understanding the effects of complementary colours is important as they neutralise each other. This can be useful to modify the intensity of a colour. For example, if an orange is too bright it can be muted by adding a touch of blue.

I like to use warm and cool versions of each primary colour, some earth colours, such as Burnt Sienna and occasionally Raw Umber, and, my indulgence, Ultramarine Violet. I arrange the colours in my palette in the same order as the colour wheel: purple, blue, green, yellow, orange, red and earth colours. It is easier to have the colours in the same order so that they can be dipped into automatically, and this is especially important when a quick response is needed. Paint at its most basic is composed of three elements – the pigment, the medium and the diluent. The pigment provides the bulk and the colour; the medium is added to the pigment particles so that it adheres to the support; the diluent is added to give the paint a workable consistency and flow. In water-based media, such as watercolour, gouache, acrylic and tempera, this is water; in alkyd it is Liquin and white spirit; and in oil it is linseed oil and turpentine.

Transparent colours can be mixed with others to make more radiant hues. They appear quite dark in their concentrated form in the palette, but can be diluted to the palest tint. Transparent colours used include Ultramarine Blue, Permanent Rose, Alizarin Crimson, Winsor Violet, Indian Yellow, Aureolin, Burnt Sienna, Permanent Sap Green and Quinacridone colours. I use a lot of Indian Yellow, as it is a warm, luminescent golden yellow and appears almost fluorescent in sunlight. It is not a replacement for Cadmium Yellow, which is opaque and has totally different characteristics.

There is also a whole range of opaque and semi-opaque colours renowned for their brilliant hues and their covering power. These colours appear lighter in their concentrated form in the palette than do their transparent counterparts. They deliver bright, vibrant colour and include Cadmium Red, Indian Red, Cadmium Yellow and Lemon Yellow. Opaque colours can be used to replace lost highlights, as being opaque they cover the colours beneath. I do not use Titanium White, Indigo, Sepia or Paynes Grey as I use the white of the paper and mix my own greys.

Red is a colour which can dominate most other colours, especially in the brightest and purest hues. It occurs frequently in nature. The extensive colour range of reds passes from the dark-toned, earthy red-browns and rich purples to the lighter values of orange-reds and clear vibrant pinks. A warm red contains an element of yellow, so an Alizarin shade cannot be created with the same clarity. Permanent Alizarin Crimson is a cool stable red. It is a superior, clear, transparent and light-fast red colour biased towards purple. It was originally named after the organic dye Alizarin, found in the root of the madder plant – hence Rose Madder Lake and the related synthetic lake pigment Alizarin Crimson. It is beautifully transparent, and when mixed with some Quinacridone Gold produces a warm red approaching a primary red such as Cadmium Red, but remaining transparent. Cinnabar was one of the earliest red pigments produced from hard red rock, varying from a liver colour to a scarlet. It was the only bright red of the ancient world and was traded extensively around the Mediterranean.

Strong-coloured minerals were highly valued and became articles of commerce; however, many minerals are rich in colour, but relatively few make useful pigments. For example, ruby becomes a white dust when powdered, as do many other stones.

Vermilion is a version of Cinnabar and was an important red for many centuries. It is a toxic mercury compound. Vermilion suffers from permanent darkening on exposure to the atmosphere, especially when high levels of ultraviolet are present. This happens particularly in watercolour or gouache. It is usually reliable as an oil or acrylic paint. Genuine Vermilion, which has a habit of turning black and is toxic, has been superseded by Vermilion Hue. Modern pigments are both less expensive and less toxic. Cadmium Red is the best substitute for Vermilion. The inclination of Vermilion towards orange meant that clear violets could not be mixed as any added blue will give only dull colours. This led to manufacture of 'red lake' pigments. Crimson Lake, or Carmine Lake, was originally produced from the cochineal beetle, as was Purple Lake. Rose Madder is fugitive when exposed to light. It is generally superseded by Quinacridone pigments, which are lightfast. Winsor Orange, between red and yellow in the colour spectrum, is secondary to both these colours and shares some of their visual characteristics and emotional impact.

All Cadmium colours – the yellows, orange and reds – are from the same basic family and are very close in make-up. They share the same admirable qualities: strong, bright colours which handle well and are absolutely lightfast. Cadmium Red is made in a variety of shades, ranging from oranges to a deep red. The more cadmium selenide is added, the redder the colour, but it is toxic, opaque and expensive. It is the most permanent bright red available, but may fade in damp conditions. Cadmium Red light is by far the most versatile as it can be darkened with a blue-green to give darker versions. Bright cherry reds were very popular with earlier artists and were often contrasted with the complementary green, with black or a very dark colour. A common approach was to lay down opaque Vermilion first and glaze over it with a transparent violet-red such as madder lake, Carmine or Brazil-wood. Brazil was a red produced from a particular wood, powdered and boiled to extract the colour, so highly esteemed it led to the naming of the country, Brazil. Today it is possible to lay down Cadmium Red light in the underpainting and glaze over it with transparent Quinacridone Violet. Quinacridone Red is an excellent pigment all round, because of its transparency and good mixing characteristics. It makes both vibrant oranges and purples. In watercolour it dilutes into flowing washes that dry slightly textured. Mixed with Winsor Yellow it gives a clean, sharp orange, and by mixing this with Permanent Rose gives a similar colour to Cadmium Red, the difference being that it is transparent. With a little more orange, it can imitate Vermilion. Quinacridone Red is lightfast even when thinly diluted or mixed with white. Red can look very different when placed next to white and again next to black and most striking when next to green. In oil, it is good as a glazing colour. Quinacridone Red has a high oil absorption and dries at an average speed to give a hard and fairly flexible paint film, so is best used in the upper layers of the painting. In oil, Cadmium colours give a more opaque, buttery colour. It is always best to use the best quality paint as 'student' colours give inferior results. These are usually identified by the use of the word 'hue' or 'azo' following the name. Many of these imitations are produced from very poor materials and the colour fades quite quickly. Today the artist has a greater variety of permanent red pigments available than at any time in history.

Blue is a primary colour and one with a strong presence and a wide range of hues and tones. French Ultramarine Blue is much more intense than Ultramarine Blue and is more expensive initially, but will far outlast a tube of plain Ultramarine. Ultramarine is a complex naturally occurring pigment. The name comes from the Latin *ultramarinus*, meaning beyond the sea, as the pigment was imported to Europe from mines in Afghanistan by Italian traders. It was often used for paintings of the robes of the Virgin Mary, and symbolised holiness and humility. *Lapis lazuli*, the original source of Ultramarine, was a rare and valued mineral pigment, but synthetic pigments have greatly increased the range. Its granulation gives texture. It is useful for mixing greys, when mixed with Burnt Sienna. French Ultramarine Blue is a warm sedimentary blue ideal for violet mixtures with Permanent Alizarin Crimson, or for rich strong darks with Alizarin Crimson and Quinacridone Gold. In watercolour, the pigment particles dry to a pleasant flocculate texture. When oil is added to French Ultramarine, wax and other substances are added. It has a high oil absorption, is slow-drying, is a good mixing colour and is beautifully rich and transparent, making it an ideal glazing colour. Ultramarine Purple, my favourite colour, is a secondary mixed colour, combining the properties of blue and red – the strongest primaries – so can be a powerful rich colour sensation. Because of the red element in the Ultramarine, it will not make a sharp green when mixed with any yellow.

Winsor Blue has alternative names of Phthalocyanine, Monestral and Intense Blue, sometimes called Prussian Blue. There is a red shade and a cool greenish blue. It is wonderfully transparent and permanent. Phthalocyanine Blue is a cool primary blue, bright and synthetic, and is non-granulating because the pigment particles are extremely small. Its intense tinting strength can easily overpower other colours in a mix. Its transparency makes it a useful glazing pigment. It was created to replace capricious and less-reliable Prussian Blue. Prussian Blue has an extremely strong stain, so a small amount goes a long way. Cobalt Blue is a cool blue which makes bright greens. It is stable and lightfast and can be a substitute for Ultramarine in its brightness and evenness and is compatible with all other pigments. It is toxic if inhaled or ingested. Cobalt Blue is totally stable in watercolour, but dries very quickly in oil, which can cause cracks when painted over layers which have not dried sufficiently. It has a much longer history than most pigments in use today. Cobalt Blue is unique and expensive and is often approximated by using cheaper Phthalo and French Ultramarine blues, but they cannot equal Cobalt Blue's undertone when mixed with other colours. It has excellent lightfastness, is semi-transparent and non-staining with a bias towards purple and granulates slightly. When mixed with Lemon Yellow, which leans towards green, a hint of grey is produced in the green as the Cobalt Blue leans towards purple. Mixed with Alizarin a rich purple can result. As Alizarin is a lightweight pigment and Cobalt Blue is heavy, they can separate to give an optical sparkle to the mix. Cobalt Blue is made by calcinating the powders of cobalt oxide and aluminium oxide in high temperatures. In oil painting it can yellow in time because of its high oil absorption, particularly if more oil is added when mixing. It dries reasonably quickly to give a hard and fairly flexible paint film. When applied unmixed it is better used in the upper layers of the painting. The dry paint may look dull, but freshens when varnished.

Cerulean or Caerulean Blue derives from the Latin *caerulum*, meaning heaven or sky. Cerulean is a lovely truly greenish blue, first produced in England in 1805 and introduced to the artist by George Rowney in 1870. This expensive pigment is valuable in painting skies because of its hue, its permanence and its opaqueness. It is not recommended for use in watercolour painting because of its chalkiness in washes, and will not blend with the under-colour to make a clear third colour as a transparent colour would, but in oil it keeps its colour better than any other blue. As its oil absorption is high, it is better used in the upper area of the painting.

Cobalt Turquoise is a marriage between Cobalt Blue and Cerulean Blue, with a dash of chromium oxide added. This is done in chemistry so that the result is a mono pigment and gives a good, clean mix. It has Cerulean's opacity and is mid toned and will not make a dark colour. The Cobalt influence prevents a really bright green when mixed with Lemon Yellow, but is a useful fresh spring green. Mixed with Gamboge, which has an orangey bias, far less acid than Lemon Yellow, it creates a more subdued, softer green. Raw Sienna and Cobalt Turquoise give a very neutralised grey-green, but it has a fullness from mixing only two pigments. When mixed with Vermilion, an unusual plummy colour is produced, not purple. A better purple is made from mixing with Alizarin Crimson hue. A full-blooded purple cannot be produced because of Cobalt Turquoise's greenish tendencies. A dark grey can be mixed with Burnt Sienna and Burnt Umber to give a dark brown or bluish grey. In watercolour it is opaque and granular. In oil paint it is medium- to fast-drying and has a very high oil absorption, making it unsuitable for underpainting when using multilayers. It is not used in pastels as it is toxic and the dust could be breathed in.

Cobalt Violet is slightly mauve, but adding Cobalt Blue takes it towards violet, combining the stability of blue and the energy of red. It symbolises power, dignity, nobility, luxury, royalty and ambition, conveys wealth, quality and extravagance and is associated with wisdom, independence, creativity, mystery, magic, peace, calm, femininity and truth. Violet/purple is the colour of luxury; it indicates sensuality, passion, and depth of feeling. This lavish colour creates an unusual atmosphere and provides an unexpected essence. Those liking violet tend to be unique, highly sensitive and observant, creative and artistically talented.

Indigo used to be a fugitive pigment, but is now synthesised by mixing blue and purple and adding a touch of yellow. A colour close to black can be made by adding a touch of yellow to a dense purple. Shadows are never black, but consist of a number of warm and cool colours, which create depth and mood in a painting.

Prussian Blue, ferric ferrocyanide, is an intense, dark-value, translucent, high-staining pigment. It is also known as Berlin Blue, Paris Blue, Persian Blue, Chinese Blue, Turnball Blue, etc. The generic name is Iron Blue. Although Prussian Blue is a deep blue, it can have reddish or green undertones, depending on the preparation conditions, oxidising agents and temperature. The pigment was first discovered in Berlin around 1704 by German colour maker Heinrich Diesbach. While in the process of making a red-lake pigment, he unwittingly used potash contaminated with animal oil that had been supplied by the alchemist Johan Konrad Dippel. The result was a very pale mixture instead of the expected strong red, and attempts to strengthen the colour failed – first he achieved a purple and finally a rich deep-blue colour. Both Diesbach and Dippel soon found the value of their 'mistake' and further experimentation led to the discovery of Prussian Blue, which became available as an artists' colour in the early part of the eighteenth century. At that time reliable dark-blue pigments were scarce, so the colour became highly popular. Indigo and Azurite were fugitive, the magnificent Ultramarine was more expensive than gold, and Smalt was not an easy pigment to work with. Prussian Blue was widely used by such masters as Pieter van der Werff, William Blake, Antoine Watteau and Pablo Picasso during his blue period, and endured well into the twentieth century until the discovery of Phthalo Blue. Despite its complex structure, Prussian Blue is cheaply and easily produced and, although it is prepared from cyanide salts, is non-toxic and safe to use. With the addition of Lemon Yellow, Cadmium Yellow or Hansa Yellow light, a range of greens can be mixed. By adding a dab of Quinacridone Magenta a beautiful dark green can be achieved. Prussian Blue also makes a lovely violet when mixed with Quinacridone Magenta, and with Cadmium Red or Burnt Sienna creates a lively near black.

Cyanine Blue is made by combining Cobalt Blue with Prussian Blue

Modern technology has provided the largest range of high-quality pigments ever enjoyed by artists. All are derived from two major sources: organic, from matter that has been a living entity; and inorganic, from mineral sources. Inorganic pigments are subdivided into natural and synthetic. The natural pigments include earth colours such as yellow and Red Ochres and Raw Sienna, high in iron-oxide content, and Umbers that contain manganese. These pigments create useful reds, Raw Sienna and Burnt Sienna, Light Red and Venetian Red. Natural pigments are very reliable as they are generally lean, extremely lightfast and good driers. Chemical dyes used in modern watercolours give us vibrant permanent colours unlike many of the mineral and vegetable-based pigments of the past. These colours simplify the mixing process and allow for better colour harmony.

Raw Sienna is a beautiful, transparent orange-yellow, similar to Quinacridone Gold or Quinacridone Gold Deep, and valued as a glaze, but can look heavy when applied thickly. It is similar to Yellow Ochre, but darker, more brown due to its higher silica content. It can be brightened by adding Lemon Yellow, to give a soft golden colour. Mixed with transparent Vermilion it gives a soft, warm orange; mixed with Cerulean it gives a soft green; and with Ultramarine it forms a grey-green. It doesn't mix well with blue, so is useful when these colours are required to remain separate. A Raw-Sienna-type colour can be mixed from orange with a small amount of green added. This opposes the reddish element in the orange and partially neutralises it, breaking its brightness. As both the orange and the green are secondary mixes, there are effectively four colours in the mix.

Yellow occupies a narrower band of the spectrum, being highly reflective and naturally light-toned, providing a sense of illumination. Whereas most colours will darken with increased saturation, yellow tends to appear brighter as it gains intensity. Quinacridone Gold is a warm, extremely transparent compound yellow. Indian Yellow is also extremely transparent and can be used instead of Quinacridone Gold. It used to be made from the urine of cows fed on a special diet of mango leaves, but is now replaced by synthetic alternatives. Indian Yellow is a deep mustard yellow, a more saturated yellow, but not as permanent as Quinacridone Gold. The beauty of either of these yellows is their transparency. They can be added to dark colours and will influence the colour without lifting the tone. Most other yellows when added to a dark mixture will lighten the colour's tone and go muddy.

Gamboge, Rattan Yellow or Wisteria Yellow, is an organic pigment made from tree resin. It is warm, golden and transparent, but has poor lightfastness. The resin was tapped from ten-year-old trees, *Garcinia hanburyi*, by making spiral incisions in the bark so that the milky yellow resinous gum drips out, which congealed leaving the raw Gamboge. When pulverised, it forms a bright-yellow powder, which is mixed with binders to make paint. In thick layers it shows a gloss because of its resin content. It is not lightproof, and due to its toxicity it was replaced by new Gamboge, which is lightfast and is more staining than Yellow Ochre. Rattan Yellow is the literal translation of the Chinese name for the pigment and Wisteria Yellow is translated from the Japanese. The name of Gamboge derives from its country of origin – Cambodia. Other names are Gummi Gutta and Drop Gum.

Yellow Ochre, also known as Gold Ochre, is a warm yellow, but is semi-opaque. Used on its own it is delightful, but when mixed with blue it creates dull greens. It is in a family of earth pigments which includes Yellow Ochre, Red Ochre, Purple Ochre, Sienna and Umber. Yellow Ochre is a natural earth pigment containing iron oxide-hydroxide, which gives ochre its yellow colour. It has been in constant use since the days of the cave painter. It is lightfast, a soft, dulled orange. The pigment was developed in the 1780s by the French scientist Jean-Étienne Astier from Provence. It is found in various parts of the world with the best quality from the Perigord area of France, where it is carefully washed, refined and graded. A similar synthetic colour called Mars Yellow is more brash. The raw clay was extracted from open pits and mines, washed, drained, dried, cut into bricks, crushed, sifted and classified by colour and quality. The best quality was reserved for artists. In Britain, ochre was mined at Brixham, Devon, and became an important product for the British fishing industry, where it was combined with oil and used to coat sails to protect them from seawater. It gave them a reddish colour. In watercolour its low tinting strength means it can be usefully used in washes. Mixed into Phthalo Green, it produces a beautifully subdued range of rich greens.

Benzimidazolone Orange is a modern synthetic known as Winsor Orange. It is a clean orange that gives an even wash, is strong and fairly opaque. Cadmium Orange is similar, but more opaque. It replaced the more toxic and less permanent Chrome Orange. It has excellent lightfastness, a slow drying speed and high oil absorption, so is better used in the upper layers of the painting.

Aureolin Yellow, sometimes called Cobalt Yellow, is an expensive pigment. It is transparent, lightly staining, light-valued, but intense.

Cadmium Yellow (Aurora Yellow) is brilliant and has good permanence and tinting power. Cadmium Yellow lacks transparency, but is powerful. It makes semi-transparent oranges when mixed with Quinacridone Red. Hansa Yellow is a good replacement. Mixed with Viridian it gives a bright, pale green called Cadmium Green.

Yellow with Other Colours

Sap Green is no longer made from the sap of buckthorn berries but from yellow-bias Phthalo pigments, and Hooker's Green is made from blue-shade Phthalo pigments. Olive Green is a dark yellow-green. Viridian is a dark-green pigment of hydrated oxide, more green than blue (*viridis* means green in Latin). Cadmium Green is a light-green mixture of Cadmium Yellow and Viridian. Chrome Green is chromic oxide (a rare mineral), is permanent and opaque and is a less toxic alternative to Emerald Green. Emerald Green is particularly bright and light with a faint blue cast. The name derives from the appearance of the gemstone emerald.

Terre Verte, or Green Earth, and Verona Green are derived from the minerals celadonite and glauconite. High-quality deposits can be found in England, France, Cyprus, Germany and Verona, hence the name. The colour ranges from neutral yellow-green to pale greenish grey to dark matt Olive Green. Phthalocyanine Green, or Monestral Green, is a bright blue-green. It has very high tinting and transparency. Ultramarine Green is French Ultramarine before final roasting. It is a bright bluish green, but becomes a dull greenish blue on continued exposure. Hues of the final product vary from pale greenish blue to violet depending on the silica–alumina ratio. An Olive Green can be made from orange and green. The more green that is added to the mix, the closer the colour veers to oxide of chromium. The more orange in the mix, the closer it approximates to Olive Green.

Quinacridone colours are transparent, vibrant and permanent. Quinacridone Rose is a cool red (Permanent Rose), Quinacridone Violet makes good purples mixed with warm Ultramarine. Quinacridone Magenta makes oranges and reds when mixed with warm yellows and with blue creates purple. Quinacridone Burnt Scarlet is a replacement for Brown Madder and an alternative to Indian Red; and Quinacridone Orange is similar to Burnt Sienna. Earth colours are usually named after the place where they were found, so Burnt Sienna comes from Sienna, Burnt Umber from Umbria. Indian Red is a reddish-brown colour resembling the red soil used as body paint by American Indians. Burnt Sienna was originally created by roasting Raw Sienna, turning the ochry colour to a fiery red-brown. Burnt Sienna is the clearest and most transparent of all the earth colours. It has weak tinting power, is granular and is one of the most useful colours in watercolour. It can be mixed by using a fair amount of orange broken with a small amount of purple. Burnt Umber is a warm brown leaning towards orange, while Raw Umber is a cool brown leaning towards green. The use of earth as pigment goes back to the dawn of man. Raw Umber can vary in tone and colour, depending on its area of origin. Some sources have a greenish undertone; others have a yellow or purplish bias. It is a granulating semi-transparent pigment and can look flat if used thickly. Raw Umber's greenish undertone can be imitated by mixing green and Permanent Rose. Burnt Umber is made by roasting Raw-Sienna pigment in an oven, making it darker, more transparent and redder in bias. It is a deep brown and granular. To make a colour similar to Burnt Umber, green is mixed into a fairly strong purple. Most paintings, however colourful, need neutrals such as greys, fawns, browns and earth colours. Rather than seeing them as dull, they can be seen as rich, complex and interesting. Some earth colours are synthesised and are known as Mars colours. Mars Violet, or Caput Mortuum, is the darkest red earth colour with a distinct violet undertone. Mars Violet is based on Mars Yellow which has been roasted in an oven. It is a dull brownish violet, superb in pastel colour especially in the paler tints, or in mixes with other colours. Indian Red is deep in tone with a purplish character which, when mixed with Ultramarine, makes good shadow colours.

Certain pigments have a tendency to separate out when mixed with others in a wash and allowed to dry undisturbed. Speed is more important than accuracy when applying washes and overpainting is to be avoided; however, watercolour can create effects independent of the artist and this can be exciting or frustrating. Learning to let accidents happen is part of advancing and learning. Sometimes accidents are the best part of a painting. This separation is caused by the different physical qualities of the pigments. The earth colours are coarser by nature than most other colours. As the wash dries, tiny granules of the course pigment floating in the water settle on the raised tooth of the paper, and the result is an area of flat colour with a natural granular texture which can be used to great effect. A mixture of Burnt Sienna and Ultramarine creates a very attractive grey which dries with a subtle granular pattern. Pigments which granulate include Yellow Ochre, Burnt Umber, Manganese Blue, Cobalt Blue and Ultramarine. This granular effect is unique to watercolour.

It is important to know that the colours are permanent when painting for exhibitions, sale or commission. Permanent colours include Cerulean Blue, Cobalt Blue, French Ultramarine, Cadmium Yellow, Cadmium Red, Bright Red, Permanent Alizarin Crimson, Burnt Sienna and Burnt Umber. This refers to both artists' and students'-quality paints. Transparent colours include Aureolin Yellow, Indian Yellow, Raw Sienna, Permanent Alizarin Crimson and Burnt Sienna. More-opaque colours include the Cadmium Reds and Yellows, Naples Yellow, Lemon Yellow, Light Red, Sepia and Indigo.

There are half-pans, whole pans and tubes to choose from. Watercolour pans are convenient when painting outdoors and tubes are useful for large washes. It is convenient to have the larger pans in the colours most often used. Tubes dispense the paint more readily, so are quicker and easier when mixing washes. I use both. It helps to wet the surface of the pan before starting painting. This softens the paint, making it easier to use. The same can be done with paint already squeezed from tubes where the surface has dried.

The light reflecting off white paper is an integral part of watercolour painting. I do not use white paint in watercolour, preferring to reserve the white of the paper, which is the most effective way of creating pure, sparkling highlights. This means that planning is necessary with highlights reserved by painting around them. Too many whites could be overemphatic, but subtle shadows help with tones and values. Hard edges can be effective around reserved white, but can be softened by adding more water or using a damp brush to lift a little paint. I use Arches paper, which is very absorbent, but other papers, such as Cotman, Bockingford or Saunders, are less absorbent and hence it is easier to lift paint off. Some colours, such as Phthalocyanine Blue, act like dies, staining the paper, and can never be lifted or blended easily once applied.

Titanium White is a non-poisonous, good covering paint useful in all techniques. Titanium White is medium-toned, being neither warm nor cool, and has tinting strength superior to all other white, including Zinc and Lead White. Zinc White is non-poisonous, permanent and doesn't yellow in its pure form. It is compatible with other pigments, but in watercolour is destructive to the permanency of colours and accelerates fading, though this does not happen in oil paint. It can crack if laid down thickly.

Different Hues

When two adjacent colours are similar in hue, they both appear duller in colour. When two adjacent colours differ in colourfulness, the more colourful of the two seems more vivid, while the less colourful looks duller. When two adjacent colours differ in tonality, the lighter of the two appears even lighter, while the darker looks even darker. If two objects are of equal lightness, that which is surrounded by the greatest darkness will appear the lightest. An area of a lighter colour tends to look larger than a same-sized area of a darker colour. It is possible to modify the intensity of a colour – for example, if an orange is too bright, add a touch of blue; or by placing complementary colours next to each other, the colours can seem brighter. It is important to continually compare warm and cool colours. This comparison is relative as a colour is only warm or cool when compared to the colour next to it. Because of the way our brains read contrast, a red will appear more intense when placed next to a green and a purple looks brighter next to a yellow.

As soon as two colours are placed side by side, an optical reaction will make them shimmer and vibrate. Equal proportions of colour usually vie for attention and eventually cancel each other out. It is important to allow one colour to dominate, deciding on the main primary colour and using it in small areas surrounded with muted more-neutral versions of its complementary colour – for example, primary red with muted green. The eye receives the light reflected by colours on a spinning disc in such a way that it is unable to separate them, so all are blended as a single optical mixture. The effect was observed many centuries ago by Ptolemy of Alexandria, who commented that the gaze of the viewer 'falling on all the colours, cannot distinguish between the original one and the most recent, nor between those which are in different places; for all the colours, spread over the whole disc, seem to be one colour at the same time, and what is in fact made up of a mixture of colours, appears one uniform colour'. Visible light waves are the colours of a rainbow. Each colour has a different wavelength. Red has the longest wavelength, and violet the shortest. When all the wavelengths are seen together, they make white light.

Isaac Newton experimented with spinning discs in the 1670s, but it was not until the mid nineteenth century that James Clerk Maxwell established that optical mixing obeys the same colour theory as the mixing of coloured light. A disc divided equally into red and violet sectors will, when rapidly rotated, appear a dull magenta; rotating red and green sectors will yield a dull yellow, and so on. Subsequently, this colour mixing was popularised as 'pointillism', which allowed individual brushstrokes to be blended as an optical mixture. Instead of using spinning discs, the artist has to consider the relationship between viewing distance and the smallness of the dots used. Georges Seurat realised that the technique of painting directly from paintbox to canvas allowed the light from each brushstroke to be preserved, and there was no darkening of colours when mixed on the palette. This creates subtle colour effects, which contribute to a high-key luminosity. The effect comes close to imitating the manner in which nature itself mixes colours, whether by leaves on a tree, grass in a field or ripples on the surface of water. Two adjacent colour spots are optically mixed to form a third colour. This is called optical mixing or broken colour. This is not mixing colours on the surface as they remain separate and mix only in the viewer's eye. The result of mixing two saturated colours is a third, less-saturated colour, giving the painting luminosity and colour vibrancy and visual interest to otherwise flat areas of colour if painted conventionally. Chevreul's original researches were prompted by his work at the Gobelins tapestry factory in Paris. The pointillist transposes the colour skills of the weaver into paint on canvas, and today's computer artist uses the same methods and colour theories explored by Chevreul, Maxwell and Seurat over a century ago.

Complementary colours placed next to each other can make a colour seem brighter. Red and blue can create just as strong a colour contrast as red and green, next to each other, just as blue and orange has a dazzling effect and purple looks brighter next to yellow. Refer to the paintings of hibiscus (red and green) and sunflowers (yellow and blue), where each pigment influences our perception of the other. A bright colour will only be intense if there are complements or neutrals nearby. Complementary colours alongside each other will add vitality to each colour. An underpainting of red will add vibrancy to green foliage allowed to show through. Overlapping a thin layer of colour over another colour can modify colours. Glazing is well suited to watercolour, but can be used in oils, gouache and acrylics and coloured pencils where a lighter colour can be layered over another, blending the colours. This is called 'burnishing'. A cool colour only recedes if there are warm colours which appear to move forward. A bright colour will look stunning if surrounded by complements or neutrals nearby to show off its intensity. Each new colour added affects the colours surrounding it. Colour harmony must be considered.

Two separate colours applied, but not blended, create optical mixing to create a third colour, whereas the further apart they are, the more the two colours will remain distinct. Therefore, a colour is influenced by surrounding colours and this should be considered to create 'colour harmony'. The colour of the object should also be considered as well as surrounding colours, the light hitting it, reflections from other objects and any cast shadows. The harmonies in most paintings can be categorised as monochromatic (values of single colour), analogous (colours close on the colour wheel), split complementary (complementary with a split to adjacent hues) or triadic (colours forming an equilateral triangle on the colour wheel). The saturation of a colour is its degree of richness, purity or greyness. Saturated colours are all the pure colours found around the outside of the colour wheel. They are either primary colours or a mixture of no more than two primaries. Other commonly used terms for saturation are intensity or the chroma of a colour. Tertiary colours are a mixture containing all three primaries, all the browns, ochres, etc.

Perception of colour changes according to the object's distance from the viewer. Colours appear warmer in the foreground than those receding into the distance, which appear cooler and greyer. Even white objects appear greyer and cooler in the distance, so warmer tones are reserved for objects in the foreground.

Colour is an effect of light. Colour influences the way light is perceived in paintings, but its effect is essentially supportive, adding to the main tonal structure of the image. Being attracted to paintings by their colour harmonies, it is understandable that we sometimes mistakenly believe that colour is the principle influence of light in paintings. But, as in music, harmonies without definite key or tonal arrangement to set them against remain discordant and meaningless. A range of colours depends upon the quality of illumination created by the available light, but the colour is a real phenomenon, not an illusory or transitory effect. Each object reflects certain light wavelengths and absorbs others, and its ability to do this is inherent. A red object, for example, does not suddenly turn blue under blue light conditions, but it will not appear red if it is not receiving light which includes red-light wavelengths. The light source can affect the object so that it appears either warm or cool. The temperature of the shadows will always be the opposite of the temperature of the light source. In warm sunlight the shadows will appear cool and vice versa. The sky at sunset takes on a radiant glow which even the brightest pigment colours cannot hope to match; but by introducing cool colours next to the warm colours, the warm will appear brighter. When warm pinks and golds are interweaved with cool blues and violets, they vibrate against each other and create a radiant glow. Evening light is a special light emphasising colour, texture and shadow. Natural light is fleeting, and when the effects of that light turn intensely dramatic, then is the time to capture that irresistible moment.

In the shadows I incorporate purple into the base colour and towards the brightly lit area I add more yellow up to the highlight, which may be white. Reflected light affects only the properties of the shadows. The reflected or secondary light is not strong enough to overpower the main light. Anything that receives light will reflect its light into a lesser light and everything is relative to what is next to it. There is always a danger of using a dull grey for shadows, losing a valuable opportunity to use bright, positive, lively colours. Once form, colour and tone in shaded areas is seen properly, a feeling of depth and sunshine is portrayed. The vitality of the painting can be created from the tension between the various elements in the painting, including colours, pushing and pulling against one another. Creating atmosphere requires flowing colours and delicate nuances, and with a multicoloured wash the separate elements become one fluid unity. Laying one wash over another is a technique which requires immense care in choosing pigments and judgement.

A flat wash allows an area of colour to read at its maximum strength, but colour composition can be upset by colour dominance attracting too much attention so that it is difficult to see the whole painting; or some passages in the painting could be too similar so that it is hard to look at one without being distracted by the other. Modifying the colours towards the same hue, saturation or tone brings them closer, and the opposite will create more contrast – for example, working two reds together, Vermilion and Scarlet, which are both yellow-shade, or Crimson and Magenta, which are blue-shade reds, or Ultramarine Blue, which is red-shade and Phthalocyanine or Cobalt Blue, which are yellow-shade. This avoids a warm/cool combination. For example, mix a clean violet with a blue-shade red, or mix Magenta with a red-shade blue, Ultramarine Blue. To mix a clear, bright green, I use a cool yellow on the blue side, Winsor Yellow, mixed with Phthalocyanine Blue, a cool blue on the yellow side. There is no red in either of these pigments.

Colour is one of the most powerful and influential tools for creating mood, atmosphere and impact. It lifts the spirits and enhances creativity. Colours can be passionate and powerful. Good, rich colours were only available fairly recently. Artists like Rembrandt relied on value. His earthy palette was a result of the time in which he lived. Artists have more tools today than artists working in the past.

The Gardener

The most interesting part of a painting is the personality of the artist, and this is the same in the garden. It is the signature of the artist, the signature of the gardener. Painting and gardening are things we can learn to do, but they are also a search to express that which already exists within – the inner voice. It is important to learn the techniques which enable the creative spirit to be accessed, nourished and allowed to grow and blossom. The garden is fundamentally a place of rest and refreshment for the mind, with a constant succession of beauty in one form or another throughout the year, but a garden can be very artificial in that it often includes a great many favourite plants, each providing different but complementary planting. Decisions about colour should always be made with blooming times in mind. It is best to have sufficient flowers in each season rather than all in a peak period. By thinking out colour schemes, a border can be stunning. Introducing too many gaudy or conflicting colours can bring the eye to focus too acutely on each particular area. The exquisite beauty of flowers holds a whole world of colour. Unexpected colour combinations appear in nature, such as green flowers and red leaves. The use of one plant, be it a tree, shrub or bulbs planted in drifts, is more alluring than a rainbow of colours and has greater appeal than a conglomeration. The strategic use of good foliage plants is one way to avoid conflicts of colour, and by using white-flowered plants clashes of colour can be avoided. Just as in painting, if the values are right, the garden will be successful. It is easier to capture the correct values in grey and white than in colour. When painting in oils and acrylic, it is possible to lay down the values and build up to the colour by overlaying the appropriate transparent glazes. This is not possible when using transparent watercolour as the white is the white of the paper and needs much planning. I like to paint white flowers because of the colours within the shadows; and just as this needs planning, so does the garden composition and choice of plants. White flowers look magical in moonlight, when other colours disappear, and have a cooling effect on hot days and can be used to very best effect in more shaded areas, where they can be seen more clearly, whereas hot colours have the best effect in bright sunshine. It is a good idea to plant summer-blooming white flowers by seating areas or where they can be seen from the house. Gardens with all white flowers can be restful, but may be monotonous; but this can be improved when they are blended with another colour. When white flowers are grouped with other colours the virtues of each are highlighted. White flowers enhance a border of silver foliage, glistening and reflecting light. Clumps of daisy-like osteospermum, stately pure-white delphiniums and phlox, together with lacy, leafy *Centaurea gymnocarpa,* give a stunning effect. Silver- and grey-foliage plants have delicate colour and a soft velvety texture, which comes from the thin covering of hairs they have developed to help them withstand drought and hot conditions of their native lands. Different growth habits and varying leaf shapes can look extremely effective. The splendid herbaceous flowering period is limited and for many months gaps can occur when flowers have faded, but with planning these can be interplanted with dahlias, cannas and annuals.

Purple foliage brings richness and excitement to the border, but should be used sparingly as it can look heavy if planted in too big a drift. They are better offset by silvery-white underplanting – so, for example, *Berberis thunbergii* makes a wonderful companion to *Euonymus fortunei* 'Silver Queen'.

Green plants come in an enormous range of colour variety, in blue-greens, yellow-greens, grey-greens, dark and yellow-greens. Cool greens appear to recede in the planting, while yellow-greens stand out against more sombre shades. As well as colour changes, leaf textures add further interest in smooth, rough, hairy and glossy surfaces, reflecting light in different ways, thus affecting the visual colour of plants. The growth habits of different plants allow sunlight to penetrate, creating patterns of light and shade. This can be very exciting when painting, but may be fleeting as the sun moves and the shadows change.

Just as in painting, using the colour wheel helps the planning and composition to be strong rather than chaotic – soft colours for a quiet corner, and vibrant, hot colours to create lively, exciting areas in the garden. Harmonious colours sit adjacent to each other, though one colour may be dominant. Harmonious colours could be violet, magenta and red, or yellow, yellow-green and orange, or green, blue-green and blue. Complementary colours are directly opposite each other on the colour wheel. These colours can be dynamic, each making the other more stunning, but not harmonious. Colours might be orange and blue, yellow and violet, and red and green. Accent colours may be a combination of harmonious and complementary, such as an orange accent among blue and violet colours. These are techniques used in painting, but I usually avoid clashing colours, such as red and yellow. This is a personal choice, but in nature these colours seem to work beautifully, as in red-hot pokers, with their red-and-yellow flowers.

Yellow is a cheerful, sunny colour, often associated with certain flowers, like narcissi, primulas, forsythia, sunflowers, mahonias and winter jasmines. After white, yellow is the most eye-catching colour in the garden. It is luminous and stands out distinctly at a distance, giving the appearance of being closer. For maximum effect, yellow flowers are best planted in bold drifts and clumps rather than dotted about in small patches. Set among fresh green foliage, yellow flowers give a restful feel without detracting from the excitement. Yellow foliage is like white, drawing attention to its luminosity especially when there is a darker background to enhance the colour and in late afternoon and evening light. Golden foliage can be used to brighten dark corners, giving a feeling of lightness where little light reaches and can give a longer-lasting display than yellow flowers. The darkest days of winter can be brightened by the sight of winter jasmine and early narcissi, followed by daffodils, cowslips and primroses, and then azaleas and rhododendrons, and golden roses, laburnums, yarrows, and, in autumn, rudbeckias, heleniums, dahlias and chrysanthemums.

The vibrant reds and oranges of dahlias, cannas and crocosmias make a stunning statement, and by placing oranges, reds and yellows together the image is more harmonious than putting opposing colours together. Red can be a powerful, even aggressive colour, so is best used in small areas surrounded by plenty of green or grey foliage plants. It seems that too much red can tire the eyes. Red gives the impression of coming forward, so can make a garden appear shorter. Also red flowers do not show well in the evening light, so are best mixed with paler flowers. Red flowers, such as scarlet tulips, glow against a backdrop of fresh green foliage and perhaps white flowers like honesty and summer snowflake. In the autumn, the spindle tree, *Euonymus europaeus*, has soft yellow tints with huge very attractive clusters of seed capsules which weigh down the branches. Also the spectacular firethorns, pyracantha, have dependable orange-red fruits, good for wildlife as well as being a welcome splash of colour. Scarlet flowers can look fabulous when placed next to blues and purples – lychnis next to agapanthus or delphiniums, or flamboyant *Salvia splendens* partnered with startling red coleus and bronze marigolds, for example.

Pale-pink flowers appear luminous in fading light, especially against dark backgrounds. Darker pinks and bright reds seem to vanish at dusk, so planting schemes should take account of the different flower colours, shapes and textures, setting pale colours against slightly darker ones. Many annuals and biennials are in single shades such as rose-pink snapdragons (antirrhinums), tobacco plants (nicotiana) and perennials like pink-flowered yarrow (*Achillea millefolium* 'Red Beauty'). Pink and white work well together, especially in the evening light. Pink shows up well in the diffused light of overcast days and at dusk, while white brings freshness and glows at twilight. These colours are enhanced by green foliage. The silvery-pink blooms of bergenia make a striking contrast against their large leathery leaves, and complement the flowers of *Anemone blanda* 'Pink Star'. White roses, such as the glossy leaved 'Iceberg', look even better when underplanted with the deep-cut mid-green leaves and pink flowers of *Geranium endressii* 'Wargrave Pink'.

The blaze of colour from summer flowers can be made even more alluring when backed by dappled light from trees. The summer greens can also be refreshing and restful. There is is an art in co-ordinating colours in the garden, perhaps by blending oranges with purples, yellows with blues, and pinks and whites with silver and green foliage. A single-colour theme can look stunning. In a white border there could be daisies, roses and lilies, while sunflowers, marigolds and rudbeckias form dramatic yellows, and red roses with red hydrangea, pelargonium, fuchsia and gazania create a stunning display.

A blue theme could include perennial delphiniums, which come in all shades of blue, agapanthus, catmint (*Nepeta* × *faassenii*), blue salvias, larkspurs, hydrangeas, Russian sage (*Perovskia atriplicifolia*), with its mass of violet-blue flowers, purple alliums, hibiscus and misty-blue forget-me-nots. Winter blues include pansies and the little blue *Iris histrioides* and *Iris reticulata*. The darker and more purple the blue, the more they appear to recede. The quality of the light has a great effect on our perception of colour. In a blue border, a variety of campanulas, Canterbury bells, lupins, honesty and sweet rocket give the cottage-garden effect. Blues grade gently into mauve and purples and violet and pink touched here and there. Lavender blue is in the colder range of pale purples with an inclination towards grey. Blue and mauve flowers vary from cool and crisp to near-purple and rich midnight blue, from cornflower blue to deep-purple iris. There are no blue roses or tulips, despite many attempts at cross-breeding. Dark-blue flowers make little impact from a distance, but can be exquisite close to, or in pale surroundings. Blues mix happily with most other colours. Light blues, surrounded by grey or silver foliage, become more luminous, making them good plants for around a patio. Irises and lupins make perfect partners as their lilac-blue blooms complement and the very different blue-green sword-shaped leaves of the iris support the floppy, complicated-shaped green lupin foliage. All blues, especially the paler tints, are recessive, so are invaluable for giving the impression of extra depth. Plantings of delphiniums and caryopteris make the garden appear longer. Subtle effects can be achieved by combining delicate mauve ageratums with the frosty-looking deeply cut foliage of silver-leaved *Senecio cineraria*. These blue flowers can create a pleasant combination when next to yellow. They sit well together as these colours, when mixed together, make green. Blue and yellow flowers can be a stunning combination. A blue clematis looks magnificent against a wall of yellow roses and the hardy annual *Convolvulus tricolor* has brilliant-blue flowers with centres marked with white and yellow stars, beautiful with golden-yellow Californian poppies (*Eschscholzia californica*). Another stunning combination is the satiny blue flowers of *Geranium ibericum* with the tiers of creamy-yellow tubular *Phlomis russeliana*. These complementary colours enliven one another and few combinations are as powerful as in the purplish-blue flowers of clematis with orange-yellow honeysuckle; in spring, refreshing and cooling primroses with grape hyacinths, daffodils with bluebells; in summer, golden doronicums with blue delphiniums and campanulas, or rich golden rudbeckias with metallic-blue globe thistle (*Echinops ritro*); and in autumn, blue caryopteris alongside yellow dahlias. Such brilliance can be toned down by choosing a lighter tint of one of the colours – for example, pale-blue petunias with hot-orange French marigold 'Paprika'. Plants with purple foliage contrast well with green, yellow or variegated leaves. Purple plants complement paler flowers and foliage. Green in its many variations is a colour that should have the closest attention in the garden. Flowers come and go, but leaves, whether evergreen or deciduous, last longer than any plant can hold its blooms.

Blue and pink are good partners as the two colours harmonise, as in pale-pink tulips and blue forget-me-nots. Dark blue can look sombre, but be changed positively by pale-pink flowers alongside, such as pink peonies against the blue of ceanothus, and rich-blue sprays of *Anchusa azurea* and rose-red foxgloves. Another idea is soft cerise-pink flower clusters of *Phlox paniculata* teamed with the statuesque white-and-purple spikes of *Acanthus spinosus* and backed by blue larkspurs. Mauve is one of the more gentle colours in the garden, ranging from pink-blue to pale purple. Several rhododendrons have mauve flowers and the stately foxglove (*Digitalis purpurea*) gives a regal feel to the border when teamed with mauve delphiniums and, as a foreground, Magenta *Geranium psilostemon* and frothy pink bells of *Heuchera sanguinea* 'Scintillation'. *Acanthus spinosus* (bear's breeches) continues the theme along with purple-pink mallow and hollyhock, and the mauve lacecaps of *Hydrangea villosa* with purple-leaved *Berberis thunbergii* 'Rose Glow' as a backdrop. Another wonderful mauve flower is *Liatris spicata*, which resembles a small red-hot poker, all looking dramatic when against green foliage. Putting colours together is one of the most exciting aspects of gardening, but is more difficult than for the artist as flowers are constantly changing. However, gardeners can adapt and change plants and their visual effects. A plant or shrub should be assessed by its character, its foliage, colour, shape, size and texture as well as its flowers and its flowering and fruiting period. I use grey-foliaged plants as a foil for brightly coloured flowers. Plants like senecios, lavender and nepeta act as a base for soft pinks and mauves and crimson using a few flowers with allied and related colours together. In nature there are few base hues, but a vast range of saturation and value – for example, greens darkening reds. This intermixing produces greys from blue-greys to orange-greys and this leads to outstanding colour harmonies.

Complementary colours lie opposite each other on the colour wheel and share no common colours. They are fascinating when placed side by side because their contrast is stunning and vibrant. Yet if they are mixed together they produce grey, which is the ultimate neutral. Both in painting and garden design, it is essential to understand complementary colours in that they are either contrasting or neutral. By mixing yellow, orange and red paired with their complementary colours of deep purple, blue and green, the range of greys is vibrant rather than flat-looking and neutral. By controlling the temperature and value of greys, objects can appear to recede or stand out.

Variety in monochromatic planning can be achieved by utilising different shades of the same colour or a contrasting colour. Decisions about colour should always be made with blooming times in mind. A plant that is magnificent for a few weeks could be planted near a plant which will attract attention as the first loses visual interest. There is a temptation to have too many plants in the garden. It is best to limit the choice of plants to their culture, the soil condition and their colours. When plants bloom it is a good idea to note any discrepancies, or ways of improving harmony, so that they can be rectified at a later stage. Most flowers seen in sunlight turn their heads towards the sun, and consequently there are cast shadows behind them. As the planes of light on the objects change direction, there is a change of colour. It is worth remembering this when planning the planting. Secrecy, seclusion and subtlety are vital to the romantic ideals. A sense of mystery and seclusion created by enclosing boundaries, wreathing walls, enticing vistas, enclosed areas and cloistered corners, draws the eye to a focal point. The aim is not for fussy correctiveness and clipped edges, but aim for a little control in formal symmetry, softened by informal planting, with colour, fragrance, shape and form being more important than neat stripes in the lawn. The most visually striking and pleasing colour combinations come from repetition or mass planting rather than a patchwork of different colours. Gardening is a continuous artistic venture where dreams and ideas become reality. The journey of self-discovery is an endless journey as there will always be more to express, new ideas and new ways to paint and plant in the garden. The journey may be elusive and challenging, but always an emotional quest where the artist grows and blossoms. Plants can be like paints set out on a palette so that they form a beautiful picture as one colour flows into another, from cool to hot and back again. Painting and drawing is like watching a plant grow: from a seed of an idea in a sketchbook, a painting can grow and blossom into something wonderful. Each artist, each gardener, expresses those things they need to express and in an individual way which is right for them alone. Gertrude Jekyll was an artist before she turned to gardening, and the development of the mixed border, which in time gave rise to the herbaceous border, is largely the result of her sensitivity to colour and form.

MIDSUMMER

STOCK
Matthiola (gillyflower, night-scented stock)

The Painting

Each scene has its own unique subtle lighting effects, some more complicated than others. What better pleasure than the play of light and shade, the movement of the wind, the warmth of the sun on my back and the fragrance of the flowers, of buzzing bees and the song of the birds! However, I sometimes bring plants into the studio to study and understand the complexities, and as I have a south-facing studio there is often dramatic lighting where the colours are intensified by light and shade.

When passing from warm-coloured flowers, such as the red and violet, to the cool of the white, the eye receives a wonderful surprise. I like to bring some of the background colour into the mid distance, and warmer foreground colours to the background. All the colours are used in mixing the greens so that they harmonise, and in this way achieve unity and the best effect.

A complicated and detailed painting which started with a drawing as a guide was then given a light wash of rose on two flower heads and lilac on the other two. Ten-week stocks are like a pyramid of flower. I used Quinacridone Magenta for the main flowers, reserving the centre of each flower for the yellow and green stamens. A little violet was used to darken between the petals and this and the Magenta were washed into the background to suggest other flowers. When dry, darker tones were painted around the flowers with a size-4 brush. A light green was added to the centres and around the white flowers. When using watercolour, sunlit subjects can look pale and insipid, so I exaggerated colours to give the impression of depth. The light and shadows change continually when working on location. It is important to step back and check colour and tone relationships. Back in the studio I added details, emphasising certain areas with colour and tone, but still retaining the highlights.

The shape, pattern and colour of the shadows are crucial elements, which sometimes means putting shadow in the foreground to achieve a powerful effect. Mixing complementary colours together creates a chromatic grey, which then harmonises throughout.

The ratio of water to pigment is crucial. For deep darks a minimum of water and lots of pigment is important, but for a wet-into-wet technique plenty of water is needed. If there is more water in the brush than on the paper, unwanted back-runs can occur. Technique should be handled with confidence. It does not make a good painting on its own, but is a good tool and with experience the technique improves. Technique without inspiration results in a painting without soul.

The Gardener

The stock has no affectionate country name except gillyflower, which it shares with carnations and wallflowers. The name matthiola, after the Italian botanist Pierandrea Mattiola, is a little more distinguished.

The ten-week stocks were developed from the sea stock gillyflower, discovered and grown by John Tradescant. The Brompton stock was developed by London and Wise, the famous nurserymen, whose business was founded at Brompton in 1681.

Exotic clove-scented stock releases its perfume at night, so is best grown near a window or where the scent can waft into the house. It has compact or double flower clusters in pretty shades of purple, pink, crimson and white with grey-green foliage. There are two main groups: summer stocks and winter stocks. Summer stocks are also known as ten-week stocks, since they flower in ten to twelve weeks from sowing the seeds, usually in March or outdoors in April. The March sowing should be pricked out into boxes of light, rich soil as soon as they are large enough to handle and given plenty of air, as stock seedlings are very apt to be attacked by damping-off fungi, especially in seed pans. These seedlings should be ready to transplant to the flower border in May. Ten-week stocks need rich soil with a leaf-mould mulch during hot weather. If the soil is poor they will flower prematurely. Winter stocks are those sown in one year to flower in the next. They include the Intermediate, East Lothian and Brompton stocks. Brompton stocks are highly fragrant. There are single and double blooms which bloom in spring and last through to late summer, but may not flower in the hottest summers. The Emperor or Perpetual stocks also belong here, but if sown in March will usually flower in the autumn of the same year. The normal time for sowing these types is June or early July. The Brompton stocks are robust, vigorous plants, branching and good for flowering in May and June. Perpetual stocks, also vigorous and branching if treated in the same way, will flower in June. The Intermediate and East Lothian stocks are shorter. Stocks are more apt to suffer from excessive damp than from low temperatures, but anything colder than 10°C may damage the roots.

Double stocks are more lasting and have no stamens and no carpels, so no seeds are produced. Double stocks can only be produced from single flowers belonging to a strain apt to produce double flowers.

The night-scented stock is a small plant with insignificant flowers which are shut by day and are intensely fragrant at night. Virginia stock is also a small plant with many tiny flowers.

HONEYSUCKLE
Lonicera (woodbine)

Painting 1

Honeysuckle has beautiful variations of soft yellow, pink and orange. In fact *Lonicera japonica,* which flowers in summer and autumn, opens white on its first evening, but changes to yellow the next day. The delicacy of each flower and the intricate details are defined by light, and close study is necessary to understand the plant. The stalks and leaves were of various shades of spring green and pink against a slightly darker background. Some of the choices are those of value or tone, editing, simplifying forms, colours and shapes. Understanding the light, and taking into account that it can change with clouds passing and time of day, and having a clear image of how I want the finished painting to be, makes planning easier and the chances of success greater.

Painting 2

When planning a painting the composition, tones, colours and shapes should be assessed. Painting is continual preparation and planning expressed in the chosen medium. Just as Shakespeare had no interest in leaving a legacy of published work, so the artist must reach the hearts and minds of the people.

In this painting I liked the way one form led to another and how the main yellow was tinged with pink, leading the eye back to the buds. I started with pale yellow, building up to a warm pinky yellow and eventually a touch of red in the centre of the flower. The background was wetted, avoiding the flowers, and a blue-green mix dropped in and allowed to spread. The same green was used for the leaves, darkening some in places. I aimed for beauty and harmony in the sweeping lines and the harmonious colours.

The Gardener

Honeysuckle enjoys good, well-cultivated soil, but will grow in most soils either in full sun or in shade. As honeysuckle flowers at night the change in colour is more likely brought about by pollination than by the effect of light or temperature. Their fragrance is best in the evening, attracting night-time pollinators, such as hawk moths, which rely on scent cues. Although physiological changes associated with ageing may have an influence, the colour of the flowers can serve as a cue to pollinators as there is more reward in older flowers, which change from white to gold and then to deep gold. Daytime pollinators, such as bees, butterflies and wasps, rely on vision and scent. The yellow-coloured flowers are sweet with the richest nectar, and the unopened flowers have almost none.

They all climb vigorously by twining clockwise, so should be provided with wires or trellis, pergolas, archways or trees for support, where tying is rarely needed. The common honeysuckle has two varieties – early Dutch, flowering in May and June, and late Dutch, flowering from July onwards. Both are fragrant. The Japanese honeysuckle (*L. japonica*), also very fragrant, has smaller creamy flowers in summer. There are several varieties – 'Aureoreticulata', with leaves spotted with yellow, and 'Halliana', with white flowers changing to pale yellow. There are many new varieties in orange, purple and scarlet. The scented honeysuckle can be complemented by the scentless varieties, such as the bright-orange types, which lack the sweet fragrance of the native honeysuckle. The scarlet trumpet honeysuckle (*L. brownii*) has very showy, brilliant-scarlet-red flowers, but no scent, and nor does *L. tellmanniana*, which has abundant clusters of bright-orange-yellow flowers. These like shade and can be pruned after flowering, but no regular pruning is needed.

Honeysuckle symbolises the 'bonds of love' through its twining stems, and no doubt the term 'connections', in the language of flowers, refers to this twining habit. It has whorls of beautiful sweet-scented trumpet-shaped flowers. The honeysuckle has an abundance of leaves and the delicately perfumed flowers have long tubes, darker in the bud and buttery yellow when opened.

The generic name was dedicated to the sixteenth-century German botanist Adam Lonitzer, 1528–1586, by Linnaeus. Country names are woodbine or woodbind, from its twining habit, ladies' fingers, and sometimes caprifoly, meaning goat leaf, from a belief that the leaves were the favourite food of goats. Each flower has a two-lipped mouth and protruding stamens, often tinged with red or purple. After pollination the flowers change from white to yellow, and then round, glossy red berries appear in clusters, each fruit containing up to eight oblong seeds – a welcome source of food for birds. The red berries or seeds from the shrivelled fruits are eaten by blackbirds, robins, thrushes and blue tits. Both nectar and scent at the bottom of the flower tube attract pollinating moths, especially the large elephant hawk moth. The leaves are food for the larvae of marsh fritillary butterflies and the rare white admiral, foster mother to the cycle of caterpillar, chrysalis and butterfly. Birds often strip the loose bark from old branches to use in nest building. In the edges of woodlands the roots of honeysuckle can be cool and shaded and the plants can climb through shrubs into full sunshine, blooming better than in shade and fruiting much more freely, with berries of red, yellow, black, purple, blue and white. The berries germinate in deep shade and then the plant climbs to reach the light.

Cuttings can also be made of moderately firm young shoots in summer and given gentle heat. Firmer cuttings can be dibbled into very sandy soil under a cloche outdoors. As the honeysuckle is so vigorous it needs pruning twice a year.

PIERIS
(lily-of-the-valley bush, Japanese pie, Japanese andromeda)

The Painting

Drawing is the gateway to painting, and observation is where it all begins. Observation, perception and contemplation open the door to the entire creative process. Learning to see properly is a skill that must be refined and improved upon if there is to be progress. I want to paint the beautiful scenes, recalling how wonderful life can be and also those scenes which give a thrill and appeal aesthetically, always bearing in mind that an artist must also be a perpetual student. There is always something new to learn.

In this watercolour painting the dark background gives a full range of values as this is the darkest area and the unpainted white of the paper is the lightest. When using watercolour, the background is painted first and subtle shading added to the white flowers on the unpainted paper to give depth and suggest shape.

The effect of colour depends greatly on how much is visible. A very small patch of colour in a large expanse of white may not be significant, yet the reverse can have impact and make the white appear whiter. With the deepest values established, the white petals become truly luminous.

Studying the subject is important. By sketching the subject various ideas of value and colour ranges can be explored as well as a fuller understanding of the elements involved. The more dramatic or contrasting the elements of line, shape and colour, the greater the impact of the painting.

The Gardener

Pieris originates from the southern regions of the Himalayas through to parts of China. It is a beautiful shrub with pure-white urn-like shaped lily-of-the-valley-type flowers, which hang in clusters along pendulous stalks.

Pieris forrestii is an especially beautiful form with bright-fiery-red young leaf growth.

The white species, *P. floribunda*, sometimes called the snowdrop tree, has flowers which resemble those of the true snowdrop.

Little pruning is needed, but if the branches grow too long they can be trimmed. Propagation can be by simple layering in the autumn or by cuttings in late summer, rooted in sand or peat mixture, or in autumn when they should be put in a propagator, also by seed or offsets.

ALLIUM

Painting 1

To draw the allium, I think of the basic round shape of the flowering head. Drawing is an essential component of any painting, which is really a continuation of the drawing. I spend a long time planning and a shorter time painting. Without this planning it is like building a house without any foundations. This gives the initial guideline as all the flowers and buds fit into the circle. The flowers were painted with Winsor Violet and Quinacridone Rose, and the stems with a mix of Winsor Yellow and Ultramarine Blue, with Winsor Yellow on the stamens. The shadows on the flowers were violet, added when the first application was dry and also run into the green while the green was still wet. It is better to concentrate on fine-tuning rather than dramatic effects. Smaller areas of detail then become more significant and effective.

Painting 2

I enjoyed experimenting with this painting, making it different from the previous ones. I wanted to emphasise the backlighting, which created dazzling shapes and glowing colour with light shining through the intricate seed heads.

I started by working out the positions of the seed heads and lightly drew them before preparing the various colours. I then wet the paper and dropped in the colour, keeping the yellows and oranges in one area and the darker blues, violets and reds in another. Where some colours were overlaid the second colour pushed out the first and created interesting effects. Other colours, such as Ultramarine Blue, granulated, giving a speckled effect. In places I dropped pure water, which pushed the colours sideways. I then let the whole painting dry before sharpening up the shapes of the seed heads, adding shadows to give them a three-dimensional look, but without them being too distinct. I wanted them to be part of their surroundings.

The Gardener

The onion and leek are both alliums and some of the ornamental species, grown for their handsome flower heads, have a similar odour when crushed. Ornamental onions have two main groups: those with round heads and those with flowers which hang. Among the most decorative are *Allium ostrowskianum*, with globular heads of lilac-pink flowers, and *A.* 'Purple Sensation' has large heads of purple rose. *A. christophii* has enormous spherical flower heads of metallic blue-mauve. *A. cernuum* is more pink and is best among the shorter perennials at the front of the border. *A. neapolitanum* has looser heads of white flowers and *A. moly* has yellow flowers. *A. rosenbachianum* has very large heads of purple flowers and *A. sphaerocephalon* has small heads of plum-purple heads, similar to chive flowers but larger and brighter. *Ornithogalum umbellatum* has sprays of white flowers and is known as star of Bethlehem. All are suited to a sunny position and ordinary soil and produce globular heads of white, yellow, purple or blue flowers.

After flowering the seed heads hold their shape and remain attractive for months.

BUDDLEIA
Buddleja davidii (butterfly bush or summer lilac, orange-eye)

Painting 1

This was quite a complex painting, where I wanted to show the structure and how colour changes from palest pink to deep purple. This needed careful observation to achieve the shadowed interior, giving depth and shape to the flower head. Sometimes it may take longer to develop the precise colour relationships than to paint the picture. It is a question of painting what is seen and not what is perceived to be there, and to establish links from one area to another to see what is essential. I start a watercolour in a traditional way by laying down the palest tints and gradually building up to the darkest tones. Interesting things happen in the complicated areas behind the flower heads. Even when studying a single flower head a warm colour with a darker cooler colour behind gives each more impact. To make a colour appear less dark, surround it with a darker tone.

Painting 2

The background was left very washy to suggest other flowers on the bush. The main flower head was painted with little dabs of pale Quinacridone Purple, darkened between the tiny blooms with violet and then, with a fine-pointed brush, violet was used to indicate the centre of each flower. The shadows on the leaves were darkened with a little violet, so keeping the colours harmonious.

Painting 3

Buddleja globosa. Looking at flowers from unusually depicted angles throws up strange abstract shapes which have entirely new rhythms and possibilities. Some areas need to be disentangled in order to produce a kind of logic. By taking a single flower and studying it carefully, the mind's eye begins to see the separate forms emerge and excitement rises.

The Gardener

B. globosa, the orange ball tree, is a large shrub growing to five metres. It has sweet-scented bright-orange-yellow ball-shaped flowers in loose clusters at the branch tips.

B. davidii has various common names, such as the butterfly bush, and summer lilac. The species was named after the French missionary and naturalist Armand David, who discovered it in Asia in the nineteenth century. The name of the genus derives from the English botanist the Reverend Adam Buddle, 1660–1715. It is a genus of some seventy species of deciduous or evergreen shrubs.

The beautiful nectar-rich purple spikes of flowers are a great attraction for butterflies – peacock, painted lady, tortoiseshell and red admiral – the hummingbird hawk moth, hoverflies, and after dark the nocturnal moths. Butterflies are attracted to brightly coloured flowers with their promise of nectar, but when laying their eggs they become sensitised to the colour green and at this stage it is only the green leaves of the specific native host plant that matter. Most butterflies and moths return to the same species that fed them in their earlier stages as a caterpillar, so planting the food plant of a particular butterfly in certain areas can increase their population. Oak trees support hundreds of species, while the stinging nettle feeds and shelters red admirals, the small tortoiseshell and the peacock, as well as moths. Plants like buddleia provide copious supplies of sugary liquid and ivy produces nectar in autumn from its heavily scented greenish flowers – an essential source of late-season energy for red admirals, commas, painted ladies and other insects. Foxgloves have long flower tubes so that only long-tongued bumblebees can reach the nectar. This variety of plants encourages other wildlife, such as thrushes, ladybirds, dragonflies, spiders and the larvae of hoverflies, which consume aphids, snails and other creatures. With diverse planting, nourishing insect life provides food for birds and larger animals.

Buddleias are large, branching shrubs growing to five metres. They will grow practically anywhere, even in poor chalky or limy soils and in dry, rocky places, and do best in full sunshine. The purple buddleia is the most popular. It has long, conical, spectacular spikes or panicles of honey-scented fragrant flowers in shades from deep purple to pinks, lavender and white.

Buddleia are vigorous growers, but can be cut back to the main stem or even hard back to the ground and will throw up new shoots and encourage fabulous flowers in the next season. If pruned in spring, they will flower in late summer and autumn, providing nectar for butterflies before hibernating. Those that blossom on the current season's growth may be pruned almost to the ground in winter as the flowers are borne on the new growth, which grows quickly in the spring. This also keeps them in better shape. It is better to deadhead immediately after their first flush, which encourages them to flower again. The semi-evergreen *B. globosa* has a wealth of globular golden balls of flowers which are wonderfully fragrant and a honey feast for bees. It can become large and ungainly and will not produce further blooms unless pruned immediately after flowering, as it flowers on wood ripened in the previous summer.

Propagation is by cuttings from short side shoots in summer or by seeds. The flowers are hermaphrodite, having male and female parts.

By watching and listening to birds and insects, one can learn so much. Different species of striped hoverflies, bees and butterflies visit flowers for pollen and often return to the same plant within a short time. In the garden, there are plants which flower month after month and are always covered with many different butterflies and hoverflies. Verbena is a good example.

Wrens call and robins sing out their beautiful songs followed by the blackbird, and there is great excitement in spring when the hoopoe announces its arrival and the nightingale sends out its sweet melodies. Blue tits nest under the leaves and there is constant activity. The grapevine, wisteria and climbing roses give them cover and attract insects for food. Always there is the sound of birdsong.

DICENTRA
Dicentra (Lamprocapnos) spectabilis (coeur de Marie, lyre flower, lady-in-the bath, bleeding heart, Dutchman's trousers, Venus's car)

The Painting
The background was soaked with clean water and then blue, pink and green were dropped in and allowed to disperse into soft, misty images of flowers and leaves. When completely dry the mid-distance flowers were added, but the paint was very dilute so that they had only slightly more colour than those in the background. I didn't worry about details in these first stages, but was more concerned with carefully painting around the white petals of the flowers in the foreground using Permanent Rose.

The Gardener

Dicentra are graceful plants with ferny light-green leaves and pendent heart-shaped flowers. They are in the poppy family, Papaveraceae, and are native to Siberia, Korea, Japan and Northern China. The first specimens were introduced in 1816, but before any kind of commercial cultivation the plant died out. Dicentra was reintroduced more successfully by Scottish botanist and plant hunter Robert Fortune, who was sent to bring the plant back by the Royal Horticultural Society.

The largest is *Dicentra spectabilis*, or bleeding heart, from the shape of the outer, nodding, heart-shaped bright-fuchsia-pink flowers that 'bleed' white petals, resembling droplets. They are rhizomatous herbaceous perennials with delicate attractive divided fern-like leaves on fleshy green to pink arching stems with up to twenty gracefully pendent flowers in spring and early summer.

As they are woodland plants they prefer moist soil and need protection from wind and frost, so full to partial shade under trees is ideal, but they will grow in a wide range of soil types. They flower best in morning sun and afternoon shade. In very hot summers, the plant may stop flowering, but resumes in cooler weather. Moist soil is difficult to maintain in my garden, so consistent watering is necessary. To prevent diseases I am careful to avoid wetting the foliage. When the foliage turns yellow and dies down in summer, it should be removed to keep the plants looking fresh. In autumn the foliage should be cut back to soil level and a winter mulch applied.

Dicentra can be propagated by sowing seed in a cold frame as soon as ripe, or plants can be divided in early spring or after the leaves have died down. Root cuttings can be taken in winter. The roots are very brittle and easily damaged; but once established in the ground, the plant needs less maintenance. Seeds need a period of freezing. They can be sown in pots and stored in a freezer for six to eight weeks and then placed outdoors. Slugs and snails may eat the new growth. Clumps remain compact for many years and do not need dividing. In autumn the plants should be mulched with compost or leaf mould. The plants take about five years to attain their full height.

HYPERICUM
Hypericaceae (St John's wort, rose of Sharon)

The Painting

The flowers and stamens were drawn carefully and then the stamens were masked out. Drawing is the bedrock of all great realistic art. Its importance cannot be overestimated. Drawing and painting are fun, but it is a serious pursuit and requires devotion, perseverance and hard work. In this little painting I wanted to include all the details which describe the flower, so it was necessary to study the shapes and intricate changes between petals, leaves and stamens. When confronted with a lot of information, colours, shapes, tones and textures need to be simplified. In order to evaluate the tones some detail must be ignored or played down in favour of the light and dark tones. In this painting the leaves are supplementary to the more important flowers, and the darks within the leaves and inner plant act as a useful foil to the lighter stamens, which are more visible against the dark background.

Lemon Yellow was used for the flower petals and Yellow Ochre for the shadowed areas. The same yellows were used in mixing the greens, making sure to darken around the centre and near petals. Lemon Yellow was used for the stamens once the masking fluid was removed.

The Gardener

Hypericum is a small clump-forming perennial shrub with numerous bright-yellow star-shaped flowers with pincushion stamens. It has common names of rose of Sharon and St John's Wort.

It was named after St John's Day, 24 June (Midsummer's Day), when it was picked for ritual and medicinal use. Bee flies visit the flowers for the accessible nectar. Propagation is by taking cuttings of the new season's young shoots in late spring or early summer, or by division. The black seeds may be sown in a cold frame in early spring or outside in April. It is a useful plant for dry shade or difficult situations.

Some are large shrubs and some are small, neat plants such as *Hypericum coris* and *H. polyphyllum*, which have bright-yellow flowers, but there are smaller varieties. The flowers have five petals coloured bright yellow with conspicuous black spots. These appear at the end of the upper branches in spring and early summer. Common St John's wort (*H. perforatum*) is a medicinal herb with antidepressant, antibacterial, antioxidant, neuro-protective, and potent anti-inflammatory properties. Clinical evidence supports the use of St John's wort preparations as a treatment for depression and certain other conditions. *H. perforatum* is indigenous to Europe, but has spread worldwide as an invasive species. Other names include Tipton's weed, rosin rose, goat weed, chase-devil and klamath weed. These generous displays of bright flowers prefer a sunny, moist position, may be easily grown, and have a rapid rate of growth by runners, which can quickly cover an area. *H. calycinum* (the rose of Sharon) is a low-growing evergreen shrub with ascending stems bearing very large, solitary, terminal yellow flowers with very numerous projecting stamens. This low-growing shrub spreads rapidly, suppressing weeds while providing a colourful floral display from June to autumn. It is useful for covering sunny banks and as a carpet beneath other shrubs and trees, and on dry banks.

H. patulum has slightly smaller, more cup-shaped flowers and is deciduous; and *H. moserianum* is spreading and good for the front of the border. They can also be propagated by seed, cuttings and rooted runners. The plant is native to South-East Europe, but naturalised elsewhere, particularly in the West.

PHLOX
Phlox paniculata (garden phlox, fall phlox, perennial phlox, tall phlox)

The Painting

A complex cluster of petals meant intense observation and a careful drawing in pencil before painting. Each petal was painted with a light pink and a thicker mix of the same pure colour added immediately in places so that the light and dark paint merged and did not form any hard edges. This same pink was painted around the edges of the petals, especially where one petal crossed another.

When the paint was dry a yellow-green was used for the leaves and a darker green added in the centre of the flower head, behind the petals and in the shadowed areas at the base of the clump. This dark gave the flower cluster depth.

The centres of each flower were dark, as were the veins in the petals. The leaves were pale, but I added more of the deeper colours so as to enhance the feeling of tone and depth.

The Gardener

Phlox is the name used by Theophrastus for a plant with flame-coloured flowers, which is one of the names given in the language of flowers. Other names are fire, and blaze. It is a North American native with fragrant clusters of magenta, white, pink, lavender, blue or bicolour flowers on tall spikes. There are three groups: the annual *Phlox drummondii*, the tall-growing border plants and the many dwarf plants suitable for the rock garden, dry wall or front of a mixed border. *P drummondii* gives a variety of good colours well into the autumn, tolerating a certain amount of autumn frost without suffering greatly. Seed should be sown in gentle heat in March or can be grown from cuttings in a sandy soil. They need good supplies of water. An occasional drenching in dry weather is beneficial, as is a mulch of manure. The tall-growing *P. paniculata* has been intercrossed to give a very large number of varieties varying in colour, size of flower and season of flowering.

Phlox is a moderately hardy upright or bushy biennial, bearing dense erect heads of flowers in most colours except blue. There are single or double flowers. The colours of the massive flower trusses are magnificent. They are most effective when planted en masse. A west-facing site is preferable as they need an amount of shade from hot sunshine as their need for water in a dry summer will be greater. Shade from overhanging trees is not, however, worth taking advantage of, as any drips from their leaves does more harm than good.

In the first season every shoot will be valuable, but in the following year they may need thinning, taking out the weakest with the object of leaving four or five of the strongest growths to develop. It is when this thinning-out process is neglected that clumps deteriorate, and instead of the bloom trusses becoming finer, they grow less as the clumps increase, which is just the reverse of what should happen. The best growths will always be found round the outsides of the clumps, and it is those in the centre that should be removed. They have shallow roots, so the top layer of soil, which dries out quickly, must be kept watered – not always possible in my dry garden. It is beneficial to give an occasional drenching in dry weather. In the spring it is important that the plant receives enough water during the first period of growth, or the flower set can be stunted. In the autumn the plants can be lifted and divided. The plants should not be allowed to remain more than three years in one spot, and the weak shoots in the clump should be removed annually early in the season to give the remainder more room and to economise on the water required.

The earliest varieties flower from mid to late summer and last for about four weeks. All phlox, which range in size, blooming time and colour, have five-petalled flowers which appear in clusters at the tip of the stems. The centres have a deeply contrasting shade. Phlox like a sunny position and look well with other perennials. A very large number of varieties have been raised varying in colour, in size of flower and in the season of flowering. By planting various varieties with different colours and flowering times a continually changing display can be ensured. They are among the indispensable plants for the herbaceous border, but need good moist soil.

Propagation is by division of the clumps, taking pieces from the outside for replanting and discarding the middle, but better still by cuttings, the young shoots being taken in early spring. These root readily at almost any season in a little warmth. The end of March is the best time to take them when there are many shoots at the base of the old plants, then plant them in sandy compost to root. Root cuttings can also be made by cutting short lengths and taking care that they do not dry out. Seeds may be gathered, but may not reproduce the same as the parent. They are best sown in warmth until germination in spring, then pricked out when large enough to handle, hardening off, and plant out in April.

In addition to the showy herbaceous phlox, there are some mat-forming kinds suitable for rock gardens or walls. *P. subulata*, the creeping phlox, is the most vigorous, making wide carpets of narrow leaves covered in flowers from rose pink, soft pink, light blue and light crimson.

P. douglasii is more compact, but otherwise similar in colours – white to mauve and soft rose.

P. divaricata laphamii is taller, like a miniature herbaceous phlox with lavender-blue flowers.

LAVENDER
Lavandula officinalis

Paintings 1 and 2

I like to use highly concentrated, brilliant colours, especially when portraying a beautiful flower such as lavender. Here the delicacy of the individual petals is made evident by the pure, rich dark of the blue interior, creating contrast and the appearance of depth. Watercolour is often thought of as big wet washes and atmospheric glazes, but often it is the small all-important details which create a beautiful image.

Brushstrokes should be direct and confident to keep colours fresh and lively. In small areas, washy paint flows, creating lost edges which are indefinite. Creating lost edges in watercolour requires some technical expertise and it is often vital to leave some areas to mingle so as to create an element of mystery. When dry, some areas can be built up to create sharp definition by applying more paint.

I use good-quality round sable brushes. but any brush with a fine point can be used for intricate shapes and detail. Sable brushes hold water better than any other.

Very few colours were used in this painting – Ultramarine Violet and green. The green was darkened with the violet where appropriate. The whole painting was wet with clear water, avoiding areas which would remain light – for example, the stalks and little leaves. Violet was dropped into the wet area at random and allowed to dry, then dark areas were drawn with the brush to express the shapes of leaves and flowers. The violet was placed quite thickly and then eased up to form the shape. The dark violet in the background helped to show the light in the foreground stalks.

When deciding upon a subject to draw or paint, it is essential to study and look beyond the initial attraction. There are usually certain aspects which attract, and perhaps the rest are ignored until study begins. It helps to understand before starting the drawing just what appeals most, so that the design can be implemented. It is useful to remember that not all the information needs to be recorded. A narrow depth of field will present surrounding objects out of focus. Alternatively, an artist may create something, using reality as a tool, which a photographer may never be able to do. An artist can create their own light, mix colours that may not really exist, or forms that would be difficult to find in the real world. A painting or drawing may be a product of an artist's fantasy or imagination. It is often practical to think of space, or air, as solid when drawing. If the space under a chair can be seen as positively as the parts of the chair, it is easier to make a good, solid drawing. Shadows are not necessarily empty holes to be filled with flat shading, but can be made interesting in themselves, contributing to the whole picture. In this painting I looked at the space surrounding the flower head as a positive element and studied the shadows so that they gave shape, texture and depth, taking careful note of the play of light on the petals.

Painting 3

This painting has a much looser appearance, suggesting more lavender flowers in the background. The main feature – the foreground lavender – was painted first; and when dry, the background was wetted with clear water avoiding the stalks, which I wanted to remain clear green. Violet was then dropped on to the wetted paper and allowed to disperse as it dried.

The Gardener

Lavender, seemingly the epitome of the English garden, is native to the sunny shores of the Mediterranean, especially the Greek islands. It grows among rocks in the driest, most inhospitable places, on free-draining scrubby mountain hillsides. Silver-leaved plants such as lavender are definitely the answer in dry sun-exposed areas.

> Lavander spike is called in Latine *'Lavendula'* and 'spica': in Spanish, 'spigo', and 'languda'. The first is the male, and the second the female.
>
> *Gerard*

The name lavender comes from the Latin *lavandus*, to be washed, indicating how it was used in the ancient world when sprigs were used to perfume baths, and its use in the preparation of lavender water. In the language of flowers it is 'tender respect'. It was the Romans who brought the lavender to Britain, where the plant settled like a native, responding to the moister climate, and developed as an English strain, which is the finest in the world. It has been valued since ancient times for its antibacterial properties and its perfume, which masked unpleasant odours. Lavender has been used for both culinary and medicinal purposes for centuries, long before it was marketed as a stress-relieving bath oil or for its antiseptic properties. It was used during the First World War to disinfect hospital wards.

Lavender is still used as a protection against moths and to perfume linen. At one time it was used in every laundry, and in the seventeenth century court ruffles were scented with it, and cushions were stuffed with it and hung over the backs of chairs. In the garden, primulas and yellow crocuses can remain untouched by birds if planted beside a lavender hedge. It could be that lavender planted in the soft fruit beds could act in the same way, though strawberries dislike the proximity of so strong a herb.

Europe's main lavender-growing regions are in the south, especially in France. A planted field stands for three or four years, and is then rested before replanting. The oil is used for medicines, soaps, lotions and perfumes. Some varieties yielded an oil that was used by artists for varnishing.

In the nineteenth century the lavender harvest was taken to a mobile still, which travelled from village to village. In England there were three main centres of cultivation: Mitcham in Surrey, the distillery founded by gardeners Potter and Moore in 1749; Ransom in Hertfordshire, where the best lavender water was produced; and in Norfolk. Yardley adopted it as their trademark for all lavender products in 1913. It was immortalised in one of the fourteen paintings representing lavender girls by Francis Wheatley, RA. This painting depicts a lavender seller and two children bearing their baskets of lavender spikes for sale. Porcelain figures were also produced based on the painting.

The best lavender water contained English oil of lavender, distilled spirit and rose water. Today, highly complicated formulas include other ingredients, such as attar of rose, musk, neroli and French rose absolute, an essential oil. Lavender is harvested before the flowers open, usually in July, which means that the bees are deprived of their precious harvest. I leave the flower heads for the bees and for decoration, but if they are to be dried they should be laid in boxes, spread on paper or hung in bunches in a dry place. Once dry, the flowers can be rubbed free of the stem. A mask should be worn as lavender is a strong sneeze inducer.

Today lavender is used in perfume, soaps, potpourri, etc., and its essential oils are used in aromatherapy products, such as candles and oils, and to soothe headaches or tension, used fresh or in sachets in baths or bouquets. Lavender has very fragrant leaves and flowers. The leaves are grey-green and the flowers blue to violet-blue and there are some pink-purple forms. Above all it is a well-loved garden plant, looking good in pots, as edgings, under roses and in the vegetable garden, and has a long period of flowering. It succeeds in open soil in full sunshine.

Lavandula spica and *L.* 'Vera' are highly valued for cuttings and drying for their exquisite fragrance. *L. spica* should be cut back in early spring, nearly back to the previous year's growth. Considerable variations occur in seedlings, the most marked differences being in flower colour and stature. Mauve is one of the more gentle colours in the garden – soft and misty.

Lavender will grow best in dry, dusty, exposed places. Poor soil produces more fragrant varieties. If planted in rich soil it will grow quickly, but will become straggly. Lavender is not long-lived and benefits from pruning after flowering so that it has time to make fresh growth before winter. This keeps the plant compact and avoids old, woody stems, which will not regrow. It can be easily propagated from cuttings – these should be taken with a heel and set in sandy compost at almost any time of year.

Varieties are 'Alba', with white flowers but less scented; 'Folgate', which has deeply coloured flowers; 'Twickel Purple', with bright deep-purple flowers; 'Gigantea', which is the most robust; 'Nana Compacta', a dwarf French; and 'Munstead Dwarf', with early, deep-purple flowers, best for hedges. 'Hidcote' has dark strongly scented flowers. 'Blue Rider' has showy blue flowers on compact plants and a good fragrance. 'Little Lady' is distinctive for its compact neat habit and relatively green foliage and will flower for a long time. It has a strong pleasant fragrance. 'Melissa Lilac' has pale-blue flowers opening from dark buds and is compact but spreading and makes a wonderful show. *L. stoechas*, commonly called French lavender, or Spanish lavender, is early to flower, but may not be hardy. It has deep-purple bracts at the top of the flower spikes and can have a second flowering.

There is no better hedge to border a cottage garden. Neat and grey at all times of the year, as long as they are clipped after flowering, and in the flowering season looking like long silvery pincushions headed with fragrant flowers. These are the flowers that memories are made of.

TRITELEIA
(triplet lilies, grassnut, Luthuriel's spear, pretty face or wild hyacinth)

The Painting

The blue background harmonised with the violet of the flowers. This same blue was used in mixing the green, which was darkened towards the base of the painting and behind the paler stalks by adding a touch of violet. The flowers were painted with a light pure violet, leaving white centres, and then a thicker, and consequently darker, violet was added to some petals in shadows and in the veins.

The Gardener

Tritelia is native to North America and Mexico and is a common wild flower in California. Tritelia is in the Asparagaceae family. It is edible and similar in taste to the potato. They are perennial plants growing from a fibrous corm with funnel-shaped purple, light-blue, lavender or white flowers in large, loose umbels rising from long, slender stalks. They flower in late spring or early summer, opening one at a time, which means that they last many weeks before becoming dormant, and then they rest in summer. They are best planted in groups in among low-growing plants. They will naturalise, returning year after year, and are virtually disease-free.

They are a good source of pollen for bees and butterflies.

GAILLARDIA
(blanket flower)

The Painting

The petals of flowers, buds and stems were masked and, once dried, the background was wet with clear water and various strengths of green dropped into the wet surface. When this had merged successfully and dried, the flowers were painted with Winsor Orange, and Quinacridone Red was added in the centre of the flower heads when the orange was still wet or damp in places. These colours were used, diluted and tinged with green, for the stems. The same green was used on the leaves, but with different amounts of pigment and water. The interior of the clumps was darkened by adding red to the green.

The Gardener

Gaillardia is named in honour of Gaillard de Marentonneau, a French patron of botany. It is a medium-sized genus of annuals and perennials, native of America, especially in the west, and is in the family of Asteraceae, related to *Helenium*. The leaves are alternate, toothed and rough, and the flowers of a few species are daisy-like, composed of many seed-producing flowers in the central disc surrounded by sterile flowers that look like petals. The ray florets are yellow and red with the disc florets purple and fertile.

The annuals can be sown in March where they are to flower, and can be raised from cuttings taken in autumn, making excellent plants if overwintered in a cold frame. *G. amblyodon* and *G. pulchella* are beautiful.

The perennial forms, *G. aristata,* are fine border plants forming a clump of brilliantly coloured, orange-, red- or bronze-petalled flowers. There are variants, some yellow-rayed, some with red, some with double flowers with a narrow disc or a yellow disc floret instead of purple. They should be planted in good light and well-drained soil in full sun, but are not reliably hardy in a wet and cold place. As they are not long-lived, they are best propagated by cuttings taken in August or September and wintered under glass, by root cuttings or divided in autumn. Gaillards have a long flowering period, beginning in early summer and continuing into late autumn, withstanding hot, dry weather better than most plants. They are good for nectar-seeking butterflies.

ESCALLONIA
(the Chilean gum box)

The Painting

The pretty petals were painted with Permanent Rose, darkened in the flower centre with violet, which was added to darken the green for shadows on the leaves. What inspires me to paint is the intense colour and the strong contrast between light and shadow. Light can transform and inspire passion for the subject. Preplanning starts with thumbnail sketches, colour studies, assessing different values between light and dark and their impact on the composition.

I paint alone with my faithful St Bernard by my side. The isolation can be difficult for others to understand, but is essential to me. When inspired, the interpretation of the subject is a reflection from the soul. What happens in the mind of an artist during drawing and painting is quite complex.

The Gardener

Escallonia, native to Chile and the Andes mountain range, is named after a Spanish traveller in South America. It is in the family of *Saxifragaceae,* of about forty, mostly evergreen, shrubs and small trees. It is an evergreen shrub of great beauty and the small pink, white or crimson honey-scented flowers are funnel-shaped borne on terminal panicles or racemes from June to October. The small, oval, glossy leaves have a pungent aroma. There is a beautiful gold-and-green variety which always looks bright and cheerful whatever time of year, but especially when in sunshine.

Escallonia loves warmth, sheltered from wind. Regular pruning will encourage denser foliage and increase blooming. The old flower growths should be cut back after flowering. Giving fertiliser in spring will increase blooming in summer. Those in pots require more-frequent watering as the soil dries off much faster.

Escallonia is widely used as a hedging plant as it is very tolerant, is evergreen and practically self-sufficient, needing little maintenance.

They are easily propagated from cuttings made of short side shoots, placed in gentle heat. Softwood cuttings can be made in late spring or early summer; semi-hardwood/semi-ripe in summer or early autumn; and hardwood in late autumn or winter. Softwood cuttings are full of growth hormones and root the most quickly. Stem cuttings should be made just below a leaf node and lower leaves stripped off. They are best taken in the early morning. They should be ready to pot on and hardened off within a month. Suckers can be taken and transplanted in April. They are best planted in a sheltered spot in full sun.

HEBE
Plantaginaceae – the plantain family (New Zealand hebe, showy hebe, showy speedwell, veronica)

The Painting and Drawing

I did an ink study on hot-pressed paper, which is smooth and robust, ideal for drawing as well as painting. The pretty flowers are numerous, but the detail of the flowers is balanced nicely with the plain, simple leaves. I had sorted out the design by arranging the leaves around the flowers, and as they grow outwards from the centre of the plant I decided to have an angle from right to left. The fine individual petals were established before painting the dark greens behind them. The veins of the leaves are yellow with the rest of the leaf a cool green. I used Prussian Green in the background and warmed it with yellow in the foreground. The masking fluid was then removed and the flowers painted with light violet with the new bud in yellow with added Burnt Sienna. After I had painted the shadows, I stepped back from the painting to assess the darks, adding more where needed.

The Gardener

Hebe or veronica is possibly named in honour of St Veronica or after the Greek goddess of youth, Hebe. Hebes are probably better considered a part of the veronica family than as generically distinct. *Hebe* was first published as a genus in 1789. It is a genus of 250 species of small trees, shrubs, and annual and perennial herbs, which includes plants diverse in size and habit of growth. The majority of hebes are native to New Zealand.

They are moderately hardy evergreen shrubs, grown both for foliage and flowers, which are normally small with fluffy stamens, borne in long tapering spikes in shades of mauve, purple-blue, reddish mauve, pink or white. Each flower has a short throat spreading into a four-lobed corolla. Two very long stamens protrude from the throat of each, giving a whiskery appearance. The fruit is a capsule containing flat, smooth seeds. They normally have a long flowering season, but in my garden it is brief as the garden is very free-draining and often there is no rain in summer, which is not what hebes require.

There are variegated plants with multicoloured foliage from purple to white, lilac, blues and pinks. *H. andersonii* has grey-green leaves with creamy-white mottled edging and flowers lavender blue fading to white, which will flower into autumn and give wonderful colour in winter. 'Alicia Amhurst' is a spectacular deep purple, 'Gloriosa' is bright pink and 'La Séduisante' is bright crimson. The small-leaved variegated plants make neat bushes. Colours can be enriched by the cold, but may be damaged by excessive cold. The larger the leaves and the more colourful, the more susceptible to cold they are – the less hardy – but they can thrive in warm, sheltered, sunny places, facing south or west, helping them to produce many flower spikes. Full sun is best in free-draining soil. Hebes are good plants for containers. After flowering, hebe plants can be pruned to promote bushier growth.

Hebes are propagated from June to September by taking cuttings of young wood from stems which have grown in the current year, where the base of the stem is slightly woody but the top is soft and green – generally from the top of the plant, where there aren't any flowers, I cut below a leaf node and insert the cutting in compost. Then I cover the pot with a plastic bag to protect it from falling leaves. After four weeks it should have rooted. The dwarf herbaceous kinds are propagated by division in August or March to April, or by cuttings from June to September. They can be propagated by seed. Young plants should be potted on in spring, adding compost to the soil during planting, which helps to promote healthy growth, though their nutrient requirements are low. In the autumn they can be planted in their proposed flowering positions.

They are easy to cultivate so long as the climate suits them. When grown in the open ground and in very dry conditions they need watering as they prefer cool summers and mild winters. In my garden we have long, hot and generally dry summers, so they are cosseted. When I tried growing them in shade they became leggy and did not flower. In a pot they need frequent watering.

HYDRANGEA
Hydrangea macrophyllia (hortensia)

The Painting

I kept the blues in the background as blue is the colour of distance. Yellow, used in the foreground, is the colour of light and the two together influence each other. The shadows were stronger in the foreground. In some background petals I used cool Alizarin Crimson as it makes a good transition into Ultramarine Blue. The hydrangea has numerous florets, which are all slightly different in colour. A general indication of some crisp blue florets superimposed on others gives the impression required.

The composition is created by careful selection of plants and definite intention. Attempting to capture the character is as important as capturing beauty, which is why I chose it in the first instance. The aesthetics of the subject will appear so long as close observation combines with personal expression and using colour rather than contour to determine geometric form.

The Gardener

In the language of flowers it is 'fantasy'. *Hydro* means water and *angeion* means vessel – an allusion to the cup-shaped fruit. The name 'hydrangea' means water vessel, but this is probably because of the 'urn' shape of the seed pod or the hollow pipe-like stems rather than referring to their need for water. However, they grow better if not short of water. The hydrangea was brought to Europe from China

173

towards the end of the eighteenth century. At first highly valued for its rosy tinge, it soon attracted the attention of floriculturists, who learned how to change the flowers into blue flowers by growing them in acidic soil. Hydrangeas are still sometimes used in medicines and eaten in salads, and are an important ingredient in Chartreuse. The petals contain low levels of cyanide, which Buddhists drink in a sweet tea as part of a cleansing ritual. The tea is said to help treat autoimmune disorders as well as malaria, kidney stones and enlarged prostate. North Americans used the root as a diuretic and the bark as pain relief, specifically for muscle pain and burns. Traditionally, in Japan hydrangeas are a polite way of telling a suitor that there is no interest, as they are a sign of apology or gratitude, but in Europe they were used to declare arrogance. They also became synonymous with frigidity in the medieval ages as it was believed that young women who grew them would never find husbands. Pink hydrangeas have a meaning of love and sincere emotions; blue hydrangeas mean forgiveness, regret and rejection; white hydrangeas mean purity, grace, abundance and bragging; and purple hydrangeas mean abundance, wealth and royalty.

Hydrangeas are deciduous, hardy, woody shrubs with delicate, lacy summer flowers of tight rounded clusters with a proportion of sterile florets having no stamens or pistil, but they have flat, spreading sepals and are very showy. They are good border plants, their foliage handsome and their mauve-blue, pink or white flowers fit well with other colours. The sterile showy flowers are pink when grown in limy soil and turn blue when sulphate of ammonia is added or when grown in acid soil. The large, round flower heads attract pollinating insects, but there are no fertile flowers in the ornamental cultivars.

Variation in the genus is not great as the species are mostly distinguished from each other by small differences in the flowers. The flower heads remain throughout the winter and are pruned back in spring by cutting back to the first pair of healthy buds. These buds will potentially produce flowers. Hydrangeas form their flowers on ripened shoots grown in the previous year. Any old or crowded, weak or damaged branches should be cut out at this time. Hortensia or mop-headed varieties produce flowers on quite young plants. They all need the same treatment, which is good damp soil and a mulch every year. They cope with shade and prefer shelter from cold winds. The ideal is dappled sunlight, morning sun and afternoon shade.

Hydrangea paniculata is a native of Eastern and Southern China, Japan and Russia in sparse forests, mountaintops and slopes by streams in climates ranging from cool to subtropical. In 1735 a North American variety was brought to England. It needs a sheltered place, protected from cold winds, spring frosts and early morning sun. The soil should be moisture-retentive and organic-rich and mulched in spring to conserve moisture and improve soil structure. This hydrangea has creamy-white conical heads and can be left to grow into a large bush with medium-sized flowers or pruned each spring to make huge flower trusses. It can grow bigger if the stems are shortened to half their length each March – unlike *H. macrophylla*, which should not be pruned as this checks the flowering.

Hydrangea quercifolia, the oak-leaved hydrangea, has trusses of creamy white flowers in late summer. The leaves turn red, orange and russet, brilliant in the autumn sunshine.

H. hortensis is the big mop-head form. It is easy to grow and enjoys a moisture-retentive soil slightly on the acid side and is fully hardy and will thrive in partial shade. The climbing hydrangea, *H. macrophylla*, clings like ivy by means of aerial roots. *H. petiolaris* has flat circular heads of little creamy-white flowers surrounded by a few large ones like a lacecap hydrangea. *Schizophragma hydrangeoides* is similar, but the flower heads are more showy. Both are deciduous, flowering in June and July. Another, *Pileostegia viburnoides*, is evergreen and flowers from August to October. It has fluffy heads of creamy-white flowers and prefers shade. All like good, rich moist soils and watering is important. Everything dries out faster in hot, dry weather, especially if there is a breeze and if plants are in pots. Watering in the evening is beneficial as plants have all night to soak up the moisture before the heat of the next day.

Hydrangeas are easily propagated by taking cuttings of half-ripened, non-flowering, leafy twigs placed in gentle heat or in spring from young growths that do not bear flower heads, grown on through the summer and well ripened in autumn by exposure outside.

HOSTA
(funkia or plantain lily)

The Painting

Watercolour is a versatile pigment which can be used with plenty of water to give a free-flowing, atmospheric mood, or can be applied almost neat to create dramatic hard edges. Being a transparent medium, the white of the paper glows through the pigment. Watercolour paints are made by combining finely ground pigments with gum arabic, a binder that dissolves when water is added. The pigment particles are carried in suspension as the paint is brushed on to the paper. The pigment doesn't dissolve in the water. When the paint dries the gum arabic causes the pigment to adhere to the paper, allowing subsequent layers of colours to be laid over without disturbing the colours underneath. Light shines through the pigment layers and is reflected back from the white of the paper, creating the unique radiance of watercolour. Pale washes in small areas unite the shapes and establish a base for subsequent applications. Mid tones are then added, all the time judging the tonal strength and allowing for the fact that it will be lighter as it dries. For crisp edges, wet paint is not merged with other colours and, when dry, dark shadows are added.

The Gardener

The hosta was named in honour of Australian botanist Nicolas Thomas Host (1761–1834) in 1812. Five years later the plant was also named funkia after Heinrich Christian Funck (1771–1839), a Bavarian who collected alpine ferns. However, they were first recorded by Englebert Kaempfer (1651–1716), who was stationed on a tiny Japanese island while working for the Dutch East India Company. He made drawings and sent them back to the Netherlands, but couldn't send any plant material because it was forbidden. In Japan the hosta was not regarded as an ornamental plant until recently as young leaves were traditionally eaten in spring.

Hostas are happy in good soil, where clumps can grow larger and denser in time. They are hardy, long-lived perennials with striking lush, broad lance-shaped foliage, often prominently blue-green variegated often with yellow, white or silvery markings and are sometimes heavily veined and crinkled and can have strokes of vibrant colour or be richly textured. Leaf colour can be affected by sunshine and shade; even glaucous hostas can tolerate more sun than the green varieties.

There are hundreds of species, variations and hybrids. Some are statuesque and some tiny, but it is this diversity of form and colour which makes them such popular plants for shady places. Apart from their remarkable leaf formations, some varieties have amazingly sweet-scented flowers. In summer the spikes of funnel-shaped flowers, in the shape of lilies, in nodding clusters rise from the rosettes of the leaves and hang from one side in mainly white and violet-purple. The flowers are short-lived, but are produced in succession.

Hosta albomarginata has leaves edged with white. *H. fortunei* has grey-blue leaves and lilac flowers. *H. lancifolia* has narrow green leaves, *H. sieboldiana* has grey-green leaves and white flowers. *H. undulata* 'Variegata' has silver variegated leaves. All thrive in partial shade, where the bright gold forms appear brightest in the shade. Blue-grey 'Halcyon' hostas are highly prized, but they can clash with rich greens. The blue sheen is produced by a waxy coating, which will rub off between finger and thumb. This waxy coating melts away in hot sunshine, so blue-leaved hostas need a cool position well away from midday sun. The most stunning is *H.* 'Buckshaw Blue'. *H. plantaginea* differs from the rest by its very long, more-upright, pure-white and fragrant flowers and double bracts.

Hostas need plenty of water in the growing season, appreciating summer rainfall, which encourages more sumptuous foliage, but they also need prolonged cold weather to encourage the necessary period of dormancy. They make excellent weed smotherers and are useful for covering the lower, more-sparse stalks of taller plants, such as delphiniums or lupins. They can be left alone for years. An elevated position helps to keep the slugs at bay and by spacing them far apart, rather than clumped together, their graceful form can be appreciated as well as giving access for slug control. Slugs begin to feed at dusk and do most damage when the leaves are emerging. By disturbing the soil between plants, the slug eggs are brought to the surface, where they will be eaten by birds or dehydrate. By collecting wilted foliage, slugs and snails cannot hide in the autumn. The leaves die down in the frost. I keep those in pots dry during winter to prevent freezing.

Propagation is by division of healthy clumps by cutting through with a sharp spade in winter or when growth begins in spring. These are then potted on prior to planting out. Growing from seed can be slow and plants can deviate from the mother plant as they hybridise. Some set seed regularly and are true to species while others are sterile.

The majority of hostas come from Japan, where they have been grown for centuries and from where a large collection was imported to Holland by von Siebold in 1829, but natural hybrids have occurred widely in woodlands and eventually into gardens. Natural mutations can occur in that a green-leafed form can become variegated one year and then have a completely different variation the next. With micropropagation there are now more than 8,000 named cultivars.

HIBISCUS
Althaea frutex; Hibiscus syriacus (rose mallow, hemp mallow)

Painting 1

In order to paint well one must have a good command of the medium. A large part of the appeal of watercolour lies in the freshness and spontaneity, but the interpretation is important. Choosing the most positive aspects and enhancing the attractive aspects are part of the design process.

The ratio of water to pigment is an important factor in keeping colour intensity and transparency. Plenty of water and pigment was used for the petals, with less water and more pigment when painting darker areas, such as the centre of the flowers and the shadows on the stems and leaves. Glazing can be used to build up these darker areas, modifying the value, hue or intensity. Value is the quality that distinguishes between light and dark shades of the same hue. Hue identifies colour on the colour wheel, such as red or blue. Intensity describes the strength of a colour in terms of purity. Colour at its most intense is pure, clean and bright, whereas less-intense colour is neutralised, dull or greyed. Generally as layers are added the colours become darker and duller. The original hue, value and intensity are altered by these layers, but transparent watercolour allows previously painted layers to show through. The beauty of watercolour rests in its simplicity and in the delightful transparency of washes of colour which allow the white paper to glow through.

I wet the paper, avoiding the stem and stamen, with clear water, and ran in Winsor Lemon in the still-wet areas, making it thicker in some areas than in others. I quickly added Winsor Orange into this in places and then Quinacridone Red and Permanent Rose, deepening the red into the centre of the flower, still avoiding the stamen. When dry, I used a much drier mix of red and rose to add to shadowed areas and veins in the petals.

When dry, I painted the stamens with Lemon Yellow, darkening with red and violet in the shadows. The background was wet all around the flower head and Permanent Sap Green was dropped into it and thickened in places. Leaf shapes were suggested. Immediately around the flower I added a thicker mix of green plus a little Ultramarine Violet. I used violet to darken without cooling the colour. More violet was used in the shadowed stem behind the flower.

Painting 2

Some flowers are very sculptural as in the double tree mallow. The different stages from bud to fully open flower are intriguing. The way the petals curve round gives soft and hard edges with delicate light and shade, giving form and shape as well as fabulous colour where the light catches. The crisp bright edges of the petals in sunshine contrast with the deeper, soft shadows of leaves. Shadows are also cast from one petal on to another, and this must be thought out. It is not a separate colour. The local colour must remain. It is important to judge when adding more detail no longer improves the painting. Assessing the colour comes with experience as watercolour dries lighter. It can appear too dark or too bright, but changes as it dries. If the painting is too pale, changes can be made by overlaying with another layer a tone darker than the previous. Watercolour is transparent, so glazing one colour over another can create amazing richness and luminosity.

The Gardener

Few flowers are as exotic-looking as hibiscus, with its glowing jewel-like colours and silky petals marked by deeper colour at the base. It is a long-lived, hardy, upright bush with saucer-shaped blooms from summer to autumn cultivated for over 400 years. The hibiscus flower is formed from five bright overlapping petals. The colour deepens at the point where they fuse and each has a prominent stamen which pokes, tongue-like, out of the flower funnel. It can be grown as a small tree, being a moderate grower, and reaches its final height in about five years. If let to grow freely it will have a more interesting appearance. Hibiscus flower well in a sunny position. It has flowers reminiscent of the hollyhock with some double, in white, pink, mauve or blue. I have violet-mauve and rose-pink, which grow in full sun. The Chinese hibiscus is the most common for the garden. It has brilliantly coloured flowers, white, pink, orange, purple, red or yellow.

Hibiscus is the ancient Greek name used by Dioscorides for the marsh mallow. It is a genus of about 150 species of herbs, shrubs or trees native to the tropics with a few in temperate regions. The hibiscus belongs to the mallow family; hollyhocks, lavatera and abutilon are all mallows and share the same flower shape. The violet-blue flowers of 'Blue Bird' flower from summer to autumn.

They are propagated by seed, layering and cuttings. Mature wood of the current season is taken in early autumn, potted into sandy soil, where they will root in about fourteen days. The cuttings need shade from sun on bright days.

H. militaris is perennial and has whitish or rose-coloured flowers and is hardy. *H. syriacus* (Syrian ketmia) is a much branched deciduous shrub with large, solitary, bluish-purple or white, open bell-shaped flowers. The leaves are three-lobed and deeply toothed and the fruit is oblong-ovoid. It is a native of Asia.

Painting 3

A gorgeous plant to paint. Double mallow has exquisite flowers, just accented by a few leaves. A composition made for a painting. I used Opera Rose and Rose Madder for the darker interior of the petals, and a little Winsor Yellow for the stamens. The yellow was mixed with Ultramarine Blue for the leaves.

The Gardener

Malva sylvestris (the common mallow) is a tall, bushy perennial plant with rose-purple flowers which have five heart-shaped petals with darker-purple stripes. The edible fruit is often called a 'cheese', giving the plant alternative names such as fairy cheese, lady's cheese or bread and cheese. The leaves can be cooked like spinach, but they are full of mucilage so are better

178

in soup. Mallow was formerly a valued medicinal plant, its juices being used in cough mixtures, soothing ointments and poultices. The flower is a valuable source of nectar and pollen for bees, and the leaves are food for the painted lady butterfly and various moths. Mallow is useful in my garden as it withstands dry conditions. It can be propagated by sowing seed or by taking cuttings in spring.

M. arborea is also known as *Lavatera arborea* or more recently *M. eriocalyx*. This genus is named after the Lavater brothers – seventeenth-century Swiss physicians and naturalists. Lavateras are native to the Mediterranean, Asia, California, Mexico and Australia. They are an attractive perennial tall plant with pink or purple hibiscus-like flowers appearing exotic, but they are surprisingly hardy and can survive outside in a warm, sheltered position. The flowers are in clusters of two or seven and bloom for months. Repetition of the same flower colour, though it be different plant species, leaves and shapes, keeps the eye moving around and gives a sense of rhythm to the border.

Mallow was once used as animal fodder and its seeds as food for humans. Mild-tasting, young mallow leaves can be a substitute for lettuce, whereas older leaves are better cooked as a leafy green vegetable. The buds and flowers can be used in salads. Malva leaves are a highly cherished vegetable dish in the North Indian state of Kashmir. It is called *soachal*.

Cultivation is by sowing the seeds directly outdoors in early spring. As the plant is large it is best to cut it back hard in autumn or spring.

FUCHSIA
(lady's drops, in honour of Leonhard Fuchs, Peruvian fuchsia, Peruvian berry bush, vine fuchsia)

The Study

Coloured pencils vary from soft to hard, giving delicate precision when wanted. The points are best sharpened with a blade rather than with a pencil sharpener so as to retain the point for intricate drawing. A fine point was needed for the delicate flowers and leaves and especially in the shadows on the stems. Several colours were used to build up the depth – for example, a yellow-green on the leaves was overlaid with a mid green, and in shadowed areas I used a blue-green. The flowers were drawn with pink, red and violet. This study helped me with the painting.

Painting 1

When painting with watercolours I do not use white paint, but reserve the white of the paper. The unpainted paper provides the highlights. I use high-quality air-dried paper made in a village in France. The paper holds the paint well, so it can be a challenge to lift colour once applied, but highlights and hard edges can be softened by using a damp brush or cotton bud. Once the initial colour is laid down it is easier to assess tones, and then darker colours can be laid over the original ones if needed. It is best to assess the depth of colour at the beginning as overlaying too many times can result in a loss of freshness.

Once the positions of the highlights were established in my mind, I painted the long, slender sepals with Bright Red and the four shorter, broader petals with violet and a little Magenta. The leaves were painted with Sap Green with a little blue in the ones in the background, contrasting with the yellow in the green in the foreground. There was a small amount of reflected Magenta on the leaves.

Painting 2

When a dark colour is painted next to the white, radiant, glowing light is created. When painting the subtle shadows on the petals, I let the pigment settle uninterrupted and, when dry, lay over other layers where needed. If paint is allowed to settle without interference, the pigment forms a transparent, radiant wash and sometimes a hard edge, which in some circumstances is wanted and gives a sense of clarity and crispness.

Tones and colours do not work in isolation as they are influenced by their surroundings. A tone which appears dark on its own will suddenly seem much lighter when surrounded by darker tones, and similarly a warm colour may appear quite cool when surrounded by warmer colours.

In my painting of the purple-and-white fuchsias, the darks behind the flower heads were green darkened with violet. Although the sepals were white, there is very little white paper as they are shadowed by using the other colours, warm yellow and violet, in the petals and stamens.

The Gardener

There is a story that James Lee, who in 1745 started a nursery called The Vineyard on the present site of Olympia, saw a plant on the window sill of a sailor's house. He was so struck with the flower that he went in and asked the woman to whom it belonged whether she would sell it to him. At first she refused to part with it, as it had been sent to her by her husband, who was a sailor, but was persuaded to let him have it when he offered her eight guineas and promised to give her two of the first plants he grew. He succeeded in getting some 300 cuttings to strike and presented the woman with her share. Perhaps this is where it acquired the term 'ardour of the heart'.

The first fuchsia to be illustrated and described, in 1703, was by Father Plumier, a missionary botanist who became the royal botanist to Louis XIV. Plumier first recorded finding the plant in 1643, which he called 'fuchsia' in memory of Leonhard Fuchs, a German botanist of the sixteenth century. Fuchs was a practitioner and teacher of medicine in the sixteenth century and was known as one of the three founders of botany.

The fuchsia is a native of Central and South America, and New Zealand, where bushes can grow up to two metres, completely laden and dripping with flowers. By the 1800s there were some 1,500 named sorts. In Victorian England, fuchsias were at their peak of popularity when pillars, standards and pyramids were grown to line driveways. Many were lost during the First World War, when greenhouses were taken over to produce food. After the war, interest in growing and breeding fuchsias was revived, producing a range of plants with bigger and better blooms.

The fuchsia is often seen as a Manx symbol, often on the reverse of the halfpenny in sets of commemorative coinage, for which the Isle of Man is known.

There are many varieties, some grown as bushes and some trained as standards. Bush fuchsias are best on their own in beds or pots, whereas standard fuchsias look good in beds among other lower-growing plants.

Other varieties: *Fuchsia hybrida* includes a profusion of showy large-flowered hybrids, some tender, others moderately hardy. Sepals and petals are frequently of contrasting colours, ranging from white, through pinks, reds, mauves and deep purple. Flowers are borne in succession throughout summer and early autumn. *F. arborescens* (the Mexican myrtle, lilac fuchsia or tree fuchsia) is a perennial from Mexico and Central America. The large clusters are made up of individual tiny rose-purple flowers throughout the year. It needs hard pruning after flowering; otherwise it can become straggly and woody over time. It can be trained as a spectacular standard. The small berry-like dark-purple fruits are edible with a mildly sweet flavour. After a few years it is best to take cuttings to replace the old plants which may have lost vigour. Cuttings should be taken in spring or autumn. It grows best in the shelter of trees and shrubs.

Fuchsias can be raised from seed, but the named varieties must be propagated by cuttings. Seeds usually ripen well in summer, then should be washed free of pulp surrounding them and afterwards dried. They may be sown at once or kept until early the following year. Cuttings are obtained from the points of young growing shoots that are free from flowers, and they root readily in any season. The best are from old plants started in early spring, and these may grow very rapidly in summer. If given plenty of root room they remain much longer in flower. During the growing period they enjoy a cool, moist atmosphere, and slight shade when the sun is bright.

Tender varieties should be lifted and stored in a frost-free, cool, dry place as soon as frost occurs, and hardy varieties should be covered with ashes, kept dry at the roots in winter and pruned back to two eyes at the base of each shoot.

Many fuchsias are tender and need winter protection, but *F. magellanica* is deciduous but quite hardy. It forms a large plant in our mild area and produces small flowers throughout summer and into autumn. The plants are special to me as my mother-in-law gave me the plants. I think of her every time I look at them. The flowers are small and narrow with bright-red sepals and violet-purple petals. Apart from this bush I have three other hardy *Fuchsia magellanica*, which are special as they were a gift from my parents. I particularly like this fuchsia as it withstands the cold as well as recalling the pleasure of thinking of the company of my parents. The calyxes of its pendulous flowers open to four wide-spreading red lobes, which surround the long, closed purple petals, from where styles and stamens emerge. The style is a narrow upward extension, generally tube-like, of the ovary, connecting it to the stigmatic papillae. The stigma forms the distal portion of the style where the pollen grains are trapped to provide a place for them to germinate and grow. In my garden in France I have planted one in full sun, one in shade and one in semi-shade, which seems to be the best location as flowering is prolonged and the flowers are highlighted against the darker background.

PENSTEMON
Penstemon isophyllus (beard tongue)

The Painting

Dark shading enhances the fragile quality of the petals and takes the eye into the depths of the complicated flower heads. I used red for the upper part of the flower and the buds and cerise for the flower petals. This keeps harmony within the different colours. Colours can be modified by laying one colour over another so small touches of colours used in the flowers were added into the green to darken the shadows. Sometimes if the green is too cool, meaning it is too blue, it can be adjusted to a warmer, richer green by overlaying with a wash of yellow.

Direct painting means drawing and painting simultaneously, giving a spontaneous effect. Soft flowing edges occur on damp or wet paper, but in this painting I wanted crisp edges so painted on dry paper. I first considered the drawing, then the values, the edges, then the light and finally the colour. I like to have a balance of shapes, horizontal and vertical, and a variety of shape sizes. This painting depended on shape, tone and colour.

The Gardener

Pente means five and *stemon* means stamen; a staminode, representing a fifth stamen, distinguishes this genus from others. It is a genus of about 150 species of often woody-based natives of North America and Mexico, with one species in Northern Asia. Stems are usually erect, with flowers red, violet, blue and white. This is a tall, gorgeous, elegant plant with vivid scarlet, purple, white and pink petals. The flowers are tubular and long-lasting, reminiscent of the snapdragon. It will repeat flowering if the plant is deadheaded. Most are perennial and these should be cut down to the ground after flowering; and moderately hardy types should be protected with cloches or mulches in severe weather. The hardiest is *Penstemon angustifolius*.

Cuttings must be used for the propagation of named forms, but seed of a good strain of these hybrids will give results though the colours will be mixed. Seeds should be sown in pans or shallow boxes of light soil in spring and placed in gentle heat. When large enough to handle, the seedlings should be potted off singly and gradually hardened off and put in a cold frame and planted out in May. Many will flower in the following autumn. An alternative method is to sow outdoors in early June and pot up the seedlings in August, wintering them in a cold frame for early flowering in the following year after planting. Cuttings may be struck at almost any season when possible, but the best time is August and September, when the numerous side shoots offer good opportunities for cuttings. They can be placed in a cold frame, without heat, or even outdoors in sandy soil under a bell glass in a sheltered place. The rooted plants should be wintered in a cold frame and planted out in spring or earlier if the weather is warm. Wet and frost is very destructive to penstemons and, although they need plenty of water, good drainage is essential.

CLEOME
Cleome spinosa (spider flower)

Painting 1

I often work from sketches in sketchbooks and compositional thumbnails to develop ideas. Sketchbooks are also a very personal record which is only for my eyes. Sometimes, when time is limited, risks are taken which can result in very direct and spontaneous impressions. This was a complicated subject which was drawn first and then painted with a fine brush. I used Quinacridone Magenta for the flowers, one application dilute and then another deeper application added later. I used Ultramarine Violet for the stamens and shadows. Dilute Magenta shaded the lower white petals, leaving unpainted white paper at the top of the flower heads. A yellowy green was used for the finery and background. I later considered the painting and decided to make the background behind the flowers darker so as to differentiate the cleome from its surroundings. This was tricky in that a fine brush had to be used to preserve the intricacy of the plant. A big mix was made up so I had sufficient paint to complete the background, and I then painted as quickly as possible, bearing in mind the accuracy demanded.

Painting 2

The wispy tendrils were masked out and then a washy background added. The flower petals were reserved white paper shaped by a pale violet on the shadowed side. The leaves are fascinating, with their long pointed shape radiating out from the stalk. They were drawn first and painted with different greens.

The Gardener

A tropical native of Central and South America, the curious spider-like flower has long stamens and delicate petals in rose, pink, lavender and white. Several varieties have been developed from *Cleome spinosa* 'Cherry Queen', which has carmine-pink flowers. 'Colour Fountain' has pink, rose, purple, lilac and white flowers and 'Helen Campbell' is a white variety. The fragrant flowers open from midsummer until autumn. In a tub the plants remain small, but in well-prepared ground in a border they will grow substantially.

The foliage is a cheerful green, but it is also armed with vicious hooked green spines, so needs careful handling. The flowers are fascinating, but so also are the seed pods, which are long and green held horizontally on even longer stalks.

It is good for bees. It grows best in light, rich soil, though it will tolerate poor soil and light shade in a dry, warm spot

183

where there is plenty of room to spread. It should be raised from seed in early spring with slight warmth, possibly in a propagator as the seed germinates best at around 22°–25°C. I sow thinly and cover with vermiculite or a fine layer of compost as light aids germination. It is best to let the night-time temperature fall to 18°C as this mimics natural conditions. When the seedlings are large enough they can be potted singly, hardened off and planted out in May.

RUSSIAN SAGE
Perovskia atriplicifolia (sauge d'Afghanistan, blue spire)

The Painting

The tiny delicate flowers are a delight, but need careful observation before committing the paint to paper. Good drawing is absolutely essential to work out the structure for the finished design. Without a strong design and composition the painting will not succeed. The complexity of the little flowers led me to a suggestion rather than concentrating on detail; even so the little drawing was my guide for the painting, reminding me of the flower shapes throughout the process. It took some time to suggest the intricate flowers before wetting the paper and dabbing in dilute Cobalt Blue, Ultramarine Blue and Quinacridone Violet to represent the flowers in the background. When dry, I added some pale green in places where there were stalks supporting the flowers. I let the whole painting dry completely before adding much stronger colour to the flowers. The green stems stood out too starkly against the violet-blue flowers so I added more blue.

When drawing or painting in the open air all the major senses come into play – hearing, smell, touch and sight. Excitement and passion bring a magical ingredient to the work.

The Gardener
Perovskia atriplicifolia was named in honour of V. A. Perovski, a provincial governor of Russia. It is an erect small deciduous, semi-woody and very hardy perennial of shrubby habit with downy white branching stems bearing grey-green sage-scented leaves and clouds of small tubular fiery violet-blue flowers in August and September. Perovskia is closely related to sage.

It is propagated by cuttings of softwood in late spring or hardwood in mid to late summer. If growing from seed, they need to be exposed to cold before sowing. To take cuttings I remove young side shoots with a heel from the parent plant in early May. These should flower in late summer or early autumn. Other early rooted shrubs are caryopteris, weigelas, deutzias, escallonias, forsythias and philadelphus. The earlier the cutting is taken the stronger the plant will be for overwintering. Perovskia likes well-drained soil and is best grown in peat or sand, but can thrive in well-drained clay. It has a deep-feeding taproot, which makes it especially drought-tolerant. Overwatering or overfeeding can damage its roots and cause decline.

It has beautiful blue-to-violet blossoms, in many-branched panicles. Each flower's calyx is densely covered with white or purple hairs. It is tube-shaped with four lobes. The lower lip is slightly shorter than the upper lip. Fruits develop about a month after flowering. Flowers bloom only on new growth, so plants are best trimmed in early spring.

Perovskia has a long history of use in traditional medicine as a treatment for a variety of ailments. The flowers can be eaten in salads, having a fragrance described as a blend of sage and lavender, adding a sweet flavour. It can be added to vodka-based cocktails. The leaves and flowers have been considered an anti-diabetic medication and a treatment for dysentery.

Perovskia was awarded Plant of the Year in 1995 by the Perennial Plant Association and received the Award of Garden Merit from the Royal Horticultural Society.

ZINNIA
Zinnia elegans (golden Cinderella)

The Painting

With a well-sharpened pencil, I suggested the main shapes of the flower heads and leaves, adding more intricate shapes where needed. Watercolour is not easily changed once painted on to absorbent paper, so it is wise to plan in advance with a drawing before adding the paint. The pencil lines should be light, as watercolour is transparent and the lines may show through. The paint was laid in with light washes, but in restricted areas, and when nearly dry, stronger colour was carefully painted in the shadow areas between and under the petals, always keeping in mind the delicacy of the plant. In places the sharpness of the outlines of the petals was needed and in other places a soft, light touch was sufficient.

To complement the yellow, I wet around the flower head, into which I dropped in tiny amounts of Cobalt Blue.

The Gardener

Zinnias are named after Johann Gottfried Zinn, 1727–1759, professor of botany at Gottingham.

Zinnias are half-hardy annuals, flowering in summer and best in an open, sunny situation. The varieties *Zinnia elegans* last long in flower if the weather is hot and dry. They are drought-tolerant and thrive in rich, well-drained soil. They do best in a rich, deep, loamy soil, and are particularly useful for hot-summers flowering. Seeds should be sown at the end of March, the seedlings pricked off into pots and planted out when the weather is warm enough.

If sown too early and starved, they never grow very well afterwards. Once grown in ancient Aztec gardens, zinnias remain one of the easiest flowers to grow, with long-lasting bright blooms. They are sturdy plants which thrive in heat, but grow spindly in shade.

The flowers of almost all the varieties are double and resemble dahlias in a wide range of colours – white, cream, yellow, orange, scarlet, crimson, purple and green. They flower from midsummer to early autumn and last for weeks as cut flowers. The more they are cut the more bountifully they bloom.

PETUNIA
Petunia × hybrida

The Painting
For impact I painted only the flower head with the leaves and other surrounding flowers incidentally. The flower was an uneven wash of Magenta with thicker paint into the centre. When dry, I added a little violet into the centre and drew the veins with a fine brush and slightly thicker paint, working outwards from the centre. In the background, Magenta and violet were dropped into wet green paint so that they diffused and became indistinct. I wanted the base to be a darker green to give the impression of light from above.

The Gardener
Petun is a Brazilian name for tobacco, to which it is related. It also has the name obstacle.

Petunias are showy, with much diversity in colouring and marking, with veining and striping, and have double flowers. They are profuse and extremely showy funnel-shaped flowers in a range of colours, including red, purple, blue, pink, salmon, yellow and white, also bicolours. There are numerous named varieties classified according to flower size and type. Grandiflora varieties have fewer, larger flowers, often frilled. Pendula varieties have a trailing habit, and are good for boxes and hanging baskets, grown best in warm, sunny places. Multiflora varieties grow into bushy plants bearing large numbers of small flowers and are tougher than the Grandiflora varieties.

Petunias were introduced into Europe in 1830. At one time many forms were selected, named and propagated, but for many years past this practice has fallen away in favour of good strains grown annually from seed. Petunia seed is small and should be very lightly covered when sown during March, in pans of light, fine soil and placed in gentle heat. The seeds usually germinate quickly and the seedlings should be pricked out before they become crowded. When large enough they should be potted singly, the tips pinched out to induce a bushy habit and kept growing steadily under cover, hardened off and planted out to flower in late spring. They need plenty of water during the summer. If ruthlessly cut back after the first flush they will flower again later in the season. If they are left to seed their flowering time is over. Cuttings can be taken in autumn. If propagated by cuttings, it is best to strike them in the autumn. These will provide young shoots for cuttings in February and March, which will root freely in a closed frame.

PELARGONIUM
Pelargonium hybridum (zonal geranium)

Painting 1

Regal and zonal pelargoniums. Plants can be painted on site or brought into the studio. It is useful to include leaves as this gives an indication of the shape and size of the plant. I usually sketch in the shapes in pencil and lightly add a single colour for the flower to establish the form and then add subsequent layers in certain areas, leaving some areas light. In the leaves a rich colour effect can be achieved by applying a wash of blue over a dry wash of yellow. This creates a transparent and luminous green – more so than if the two colours were mixed together in the palette. The darker rings on the leaves were added when the previous washes were dry.

Painting 2

Orange pelargonium. The stunning vibrant colour was achieved by running Winsor Orange, Winsor Lemon and Quinacridone Red into each other so that they merged and created luminous petals. The background was kept subdued and washy so as not to detract from the splendid flower.

The Gardener

Until 1789 pelargoniums were known as geraniums, because their seed capsules resemble those of the native cranesbill or hardy geranium, the garden bedding plants, and are still referred to as such by many people. The Greek name *pelargos* means stork, the name given to the ripe seed heads, which resemble the head and beak of a stork, and hence pelargoniums are sometimes called stork's bill. Both belong to the Geraniaceae family, but have now been separated.

Pelargoniums are a genus of about 230 species, sometimes succulent, erect or trailing or woody below and almost shrubby, though the number of varieties now available is far smaller than it was in the nineteenth century. They originate from South Africa and are tender so are usually grown as annuals or from overwintering cuttings in a frost-free place. These hybrids fall into several sections – 'zonal', 'show', 'decorative' and 'fancy' – and range from scarlet huge-headed types to small 'angel' pelargoniums, 'ivy-leaved' trailing and 'scented-leaf' varieties. They are the results of cross-breeding and the five-petalled flowers, or semi-double or double, come in rounded clusters in a vast range of colours, including white, red, pink, rose pink, salmon, orange and mauve.

Pelargoniums are easy to grow and like hot weather and are perfectly adapted to the heat. Essential oils, which give them their distinctive aroma, and down on their leaves diffuse air that would otherwise shrivel the leaves. They hate being wet, so a free-draining compost is essential. Most plants are started off in multipurpose compost, which is light enough to absorb moisture and perfect for young roots to penetrate but is not high in nutrients. Spring and summer are the best times to take stem and root cuttings at the node from firm shoots. When rooted they should be put into clay pots, which are porous and let excess water evaporate, and in a soil-based compost, which keeps them growing strongly. If they are potted on into progressively larger pots before they flower, they will grow vigorously until the roots become constricted, when they will flower profusely. The succulent stems become woody with age, but old plants may be cut back and will regrow vigorously.

They are best drenched once a week rather than a daily watering. In winter they need no water, and should be overwintered in an airy greenhouse. In spring they can be potted on and, when growing well, the tips should be pinched out once for early flowering and twice for later flowering. Care should be taken in forming good shapes with a properly balanced head and well-spaced branches. Full sun and good ventilation are necessary to ripen the growth. Pelargoniums are easily grown from seed and mostly bear seeds freely if allowed to do so. The seed is best sown in spring in a light sandy compost in a warm greenhouse with the resultant young plants grown to flowering size in a cool greenhouse. Most pelargoniums now grown in gardens are of hybrid origin.

Zonal pelargoniums *Pelargonium hortorum,* are commonly called geraniums. This confusion dates back to the time when pelargoniums were first bought back to Europe from South Africa, when it was thought that they were related to European geraniums. It was later found that the two species do share many similarities and also differ in many ways. Geraniums have five petals, all being the same size and shape as each other, and ten fertile stamens. Pelargoniums have two upper petals of a different shape and size from the lower three, giving a symmetrical appearance. Seven of the ten stamens are fertile. They have thick stems that hold moisture to enable them to withstand drought. Geraniums and pelargoniums differ in their seed dispersal. Pelargonium seeds have a 'feathered' end, enabling them to float away on the breeze, while geraniums disperse seeds by way of a beak popping open and fling their seeds away. The fruits should be collected just before they burst and put into paper bags to ripen, otherwise the seeds will be flung out and scattered. Geraniums are hardy perennials while pelargoniums cannot survive frost. Zonal pelargoniums are the most commonly grown variety and are rounded with pale to mid-green leaves, often with scalloped margins with sometimes a maroon zone. They have a mass of flowers with tight heads on long stalks in various colours and are best for containers and bedding. They can be raised from seed or from cuttings, which produce larger flowers and are perennial as long as they are protected from frost in winter.

Regal pelargoniums, or *P. domesticum,* are a hybrid race of erect, shrubby plants with light-green lobed, toothed and often fluted leaves and large often frilly flowers in rose pink, maroon, rose red or crimson. These flower early and are among the most colourful, with the best and richest tones. Regal pelargoniums need more watering than other types and a warmer winter temperature. The name regal refers to their development in 1800 in the royal greenhouses at Sandringham, England.

Ivy-leaved pelargoniums, *P. peltatum,* are trailing and scrambling and best in hanging baskets, troughs and planters. Some have interestingly marked leaves. They have masses of small flowers and range from pink to deep purple-red, some with small tricoloured dainty blooms, often blotched deep magenta and paler pink and variegated leaves, some with scented leaves.

Scented-leaf pelargoniums are frost-tender and grown for their scented foliage rather than their flowers. Scent varies as does the foliage in shape, size and colour. There are 200 evergreen perennial pelargonium species with about thirty having scented leaves. These drought-tolerant plants need full sun and an open position and a high potash tomato feed every two weeks. Scented pelargoniums tend to be hardier than the larger-flowered, highly bred pelargoniums. They were introduced into orangeries in the seventeenth century, but it was the Victorians who bred and collected them, loving the rose- and lemon-scented plants. *P. odoratissimum* and *P. fragrans* have a pine scent; *P. tomentosum* is peppermint; and 'Mabel Grey' is lemon-scented. All are best watered with rainwater rather than tap water. The only commercial use is in the extraction of geranium oil for perfumery and aromatherapy. All the named varieties are derived from species found naturally and have *P. tomentosum* in their breeding. These are soft-leaved and suffer in bright sun, so should be in dappled shade. Some are rose-scented, others citrus-, apple-, pine- or turpentine-scented.

All need regular propagation as they become leggy and wiry. Cuttings should be taken between June and late August. They should be trimmed below a node and placed into sand, where they will root quickly. I pot them on in spring, keeping the new plants in the greenhouse until late spring. Feeding every two weeks with potash hardens the foliage and stems and helps the plants to overwinter. Deadheading the spent flowers in summer encourages more flowers.

Hoverflies and bees adore them.

GERANIUM
Geranion is the old Greek name used by Dioscorides. *Geranos*, meaning crane, is an allusion to the long 'beak' of the carpels – hence cranesbill.

Paintings 1 and 2
When painting a group of flowers, composition must be considered. Should it be a landscape or portrait format or even a square format? The light and shade is important as they establish the tonal values. Each flower varied from the others as did the positions of the leaves and buds. This creates interest and excitement in the painting. I take delight in the play of light on a flower or the luminosity of a cast shadow. The shadows should be painted in the opposite temperature to the light. If the light source is warm, then a cool dark is in the shadows; and if the light source is cool, then the darks are warm. They should be relatively warmer or cooler.

The richer colours are in the foreground and also the darkest values.

The veins of the flower petals were first painted with violet, drawn out from the centre. When dry, a light Cobalt was washed over each petal. The leaves and buds were painted with Sap Green with added yellow in the foreground and a little blue in the background. The darks of the interior of the plant were a mix of the original green and violet.

The Gardener

Herbaceous geraniums are hardy, mostly perennial, and although related are quite different from pelargoniums, which are sometimes called geraniums. The great range of scarlet, fancy, scented and show geraniums belong to the *Pelargonium* genus. The diversity of the true geranium, of which there are about 300 species scattered over the temperate regions of the world, makes identification difficult. The leaf form varies, but is always elaborately and deeply indented and can last all winter. Some species are naturalised and others native.

In the past, some have been valued for their medicinal properties, particularly in stopping haemorrhages. The leaves have a strong disagreeable smell. The flowers are often in pairs with five overlapping petals. Vernacular names are bloodwort, dragon's blood, fox geranium, fox grass (on account of the foxy smell), robin flower and stinking Bob. Its meaning in the language of flowers is 'feeling of love'.

The name of erodium comes from *erodios*, which means heron or crane, whereas pelargonium comes from *pelargos,* meaning stork.

Painting 3

Geranium sanguineum, the native cranesbill, has soft, long-lasting flowers in magenta, light pink, white and rose pink. They are saucer-shaped and have five petals. I painted the flowers first followed by the leaves and stalks. The dark background was a mix of the rose used for the flowers and the green in the leaves. This created a suitable dark green, which contrasted tonally with the lighter colours.

The Gardener

G. ibericum is in fact a hybrid between *G. ibericum* and *G. platypetalum.* It has vivid violet-blue flowers and can stand hot sun and should really be called *G. × magnificum.* This hybrid forms a mound of deeply cut green foliage and cup-shaped violet-blue flowers. Plants should be cut back hard after blooming to encourage fresh new foliage. *G. subcaulescens* has profuse black-centred magenta flowers in late spring to mid autumn. *G. macrorrhizum*, like all hardy geraniums, is useful in the garden for its dense weed-smothering foliage and pretty flowers. This one is evergreen and survives drought. *G. grandiflorum* has round mid-green leaves and forms clumps of violet-blue, red-veined flowers.

Geraniums are invaluable for half-shaded positions, giving months of beauty. They are effective and quick in covering the ground and good for edging a border. The flowers are followed by huge heron's-bill seed heads. As it dries, one side of the beak, in the thinnest area near the seed, contracts more quickly than the other. The long tail is pulled to one side and then begins to revolve, while the thin part gradually twists into a spiral. The seed has a sharp point, which pierces the earth when it falls. The rest of the seed is covered with stiff hairs pointed backwards from the sharp tip, so that predators are deterred from withdrawing the seed from the hole. The seed reacts to sun and dew, rotating into the ground. Propagation is easy, by division or by seed.

SNAPDRAGON
Antirrhinum majus

The Painting

Red and yellow can be difficult when placed together, so here I used warm red and warm yellow to avoid discordance. Red needs a balancing colour such as grey and neutral hues. I used red in the green to darken it and create balance. The warm red and warm yellow were used in the centre of the flower as a focal point.

The Gardener
Anti means like and *rhin* means snout – an allusion to the shape of the corolla, which is cylindrical. The flowers have a closed mouth with a large tube. Native to the Mediterranean region, the antirrhinum has graceful erect spires of open-mouth flowers and comes in all colours except blue. Antirrhinums are short-lived bushy perennials, but I have one growing in a crack up against the house wall which blooms each year. The warm, dry position obviously suits the plant. I cut it back after flowering and it regrows and flowers. They can get straggly with age, which is why they are often treated as annuals. To encourage bushier growth, I pinch out the tops of seedlings and cut flowers from mature plants, and grow from seed each year. They can also be propagated by taking cuttings in September and rooting them in a cold frame or, in spring, rooting them in a propagator to benefit from gentle heat. Some are excellent rock-garden plants and often seed into paths and rock walls.

Antirrhinum majus maximum is a short-lived erect perennial, usually treated as an annual and either sown in July or August for flowering the following season, or March in a warm environment, to be pricked out into pots and planted out in May for flowering in the same season. They have large reddish-purple flowers with a yellow throat in dense elongated spikes. *A. majus maximum* is the tallest, and varieties such as *tetraploid*, meaning flowers of double size, or 'Tetra Snaps' have large ruffled flowers. *A. latifolium* is a large snapdragon with yellow flowers. Snapdragons are normally associated with garden borders, but can be outstanding and give colourful displays when grown in pots. A tall yellow antirrhinum contrasts well with the blue of *Eryngium oliverianum* or the blue of perovskia. They can also be used as cut flowers. They flower from April to November in dry places.

Ancient cultures made necklaces from snapdragon flowers and wore them as protection from evil spirits.

ANGELICA
Angelica archangelica

The Painting

In traditional watercolour painting, pigment is mixed with water and brushed on paper to form a wash of colour. This may be left as a flat wash or be manipulated to create the fluid changes of colour which are unique to the medium. Further wet colour may be floated into it so that different colours meld together, and thicker paint may be introduced to produce shadowed effects.

Wet-in-wet painting is a system whereby the paper is wetted and paint quickly dropped into it, so that the colours run together forming no hard or sharp edges. When dropping one colour into another, the first is dispersed, which causes another unpredictable effect.

When wanting to reserve the white paper, in this case for the flowers, planning is necessary. A light pencil sketch established where the white was to be reserved and then the wet-in-wet background was created by dropping blue and yellow into the wet paper. The water was brushed into the background, avoiding the areas reserved for the blossoms and stems, which remained dry, white paper. The paint will flow into the wet areas. When nearly dry, green was splashed around the background, still avoiding the blooms and stems. The adumbrated appearance was due to the first wash being still slightly moist, so absorbing some colour and leaving an obscure hint of leaves.

The tip of the brush was used to dab on the same green at the base of each cluster of flowers and along the stems. This green was darkened with a little violet and used to shade the main stem and the little stalks. I decided to fade out the bottom of the main stem and left the rest of the painting only indicated.

The Gardener

A wonderfully architectural plant, it is a tall, robust aromatic annual or perennial with hollow stalks and large segmental branches, and many-rayed compound umbels of small greenish, white or purplish flowers in July and August. Each tiny flower has five petals with tips curved inwards, five stamens and no bracts. The nectar attracts large numbers of pollinating flies, short-tongued bees and numerous beetles, especially the soldier beetle. Tortricoid moths' caterpillars feed on the leaves, while the seed heads are a food source for birds in late summer. The lower leaves are large, triangular and divided into sets of oval leaflets. The upper leaves are often only a minute leaf at the top of the swollen stem. It prefers full sun in deep soil.

Angelica was at one time grown for its medicinal value and is cultivated for its leaf stalks, which are candied and used for flavouring. It is also used in the preparation of liqueurs, such as Chartreuse. The roots are aromatic and edible, eaten like a vegetable, and produce an oil used in confectionery and perfumery.

The blanched midribs of the leaves have been used like celery, and the leaf-stalks are used for flavouring, especially with rhubarb.

Propagation is by seed sown as soon as it is ripe in August, and the seedlings are transplanted while still small. Old plants do not transplant well. *A. archangelica* usually dies after seeding, but if flowering is prevented it stays perennial.

CROCOSMIA
(montbretia, falling stars, valentine flower)

The Painting
Watercolour is very different from other forms of painting. It can be a stain and mostly transparent with some colours being opaque. Once the paper is painted it is coloured as if by a dye, and so to retain freshness the paint must be applied to white paper and preferably not corrected, as is possible with opaque paints. Because of its transparency any previous washes show through. Watercolour is all about fresh, sparkling permanent paint.

I was inspired by the effect of light and aimed for shapes and values and to capture the magic of the moment, the spirit and the energy. Apart from the strong colours, I kept the design simple combined with tonal contrast to give a strong visual impact.

The Gardener
The name of crocosmia comes from *crocus* (saffron) and *osme* (smell) as the dried flowers when immersed in warm water smell strongly of saffron. The name of montbretia is after Antoine François Ernest Conquebert de Montbret, born in Hamburg in 1780 and died in Cairo in 1801. He was botanist of the French expedition to Egypt.

The plants known as montbretias are the result of crossing *Crocosmia aurea*, which has golden-yellow flowers, with *C. pottsii*. The common montbretia has branched spikes of orange-red flowers on stiff slender stems. Improved varieties with larger flowers in various colours from yellow to coppery red are available, but are not so hardy or so vigorous.

C. masoniorum has large flowers set close together and handsome leaves. *Curtonus paniculatus* is a tall montbretia with smaller, almost scarlet flowers. *C. × crocosmiiflora* grows wild and has given crocosmia a bad name as it is regarded as a weed. They don't all increase rapidly. Some, such as 'Rowallane Yellow' and 'Zeal Giant' form enormous corms. They don't all suffer from diseases. Rabbits and deer don't like them, slugs rarely touch them, they are tolerant of wind and with a deep mulch are hardy. Some are upright, while others are arching and are best planted on a high bank. The foliage is varied with some having sword-shaped leaves and others flat or pleated, some blue-grey and some apple green, so are attractive even without flowers. The plants do best in a sunny place with some shade during the day. They are best planted deeply with plenty of compost and a thick mulch. The old corms persist and act as storage organs. Every three or four years the clumps should be dug up in autumn and divided. This will encourage the plants to produce flowers.

SALVIA
Salvia guaranitica purpurea (meadow sage)

Painting 1
Making departures from the more traditional approach to watercolour painting encourages creative ideas and involves planning the concept and the execution.

Some small areas of the main flower stalk were masked so that I could keep the intricacy of the many flowers and use a strong dark immediately behind. I wanted to use the wet-in-wet technique when the paper is flooded with water using a large mop brush. The whole painting was first wet with clear water and then violet was brushed into the wet so as to diffuse the colour. Any excess colour was picked up with a damp brush. While still wet, Sap Green was washed in at the base along with a little Ultramarine Blue. Once the wash started to dry, I made sure that the paper was not moved, as the still-wet areas could have run into areas which had begun to dry. When the painting was almost dry, more flower heads were added and then the principle flower head was painted with Ultramarine Violet and green. It is important to judge the timing because if painted at the wrong time, water marks can occur. There is no set time as atmospheric conditions vary.

When completely dry, the masking fluid was removed and colour added on to the resultant white paper. More darks were added to the main flower stalk.

Painting 2
I simplified the shapes so that the painting looks almost abstract. This is because the shapes are separated from each other even though they are shaded. I used violet in a light wash and then a drier mix to deepen and darken shadows.

The Gardener
A hardy salvia has sturdy self-supporting stems and serrated, fresh green ovate aromatic leaves with deep-purple-pink double-lipped flowers held on prominent green calyxes, each with a protruding snake's tongue of female parts. The male parts are hidden within the heeled lower labia of each flower. The flowers are held on long terminal spikes and bloom over a long period as the plant continues to flower on axillary side branches.

Salvia, or sage or clary, can be a spectacular sight if planted in a swathe at the front of a border. The lower third of the strong upright stems is covered in bushy leaves and the upper section carries dense, richly coloured spikes of flowers in purple and blue, red and pink. They flower in long succession.

Salvia fulgens (the cardinal sage) is a half-hardy to moderately hardy small shrubby perennial with vivid red flowers opening from purplish-red bud cases. The crowns and roots need a protective winter mulch. *S. haematodes* is short-lived and has purple flowers. *S. × superba* is a very hardy hybrid with spikes of violet-blue flowers with crimson-purple bracts in midsummer. These need dividing and replanting from early autumn. They can be raised from seed in a cold frame in spring or can be overwintered in a cold frame. *S.* 'Amistad' is one of my favourite plants. It has fabulous rich-purple flowers emerging from purple-black calyxes and dark stems. It flowers from May to November. It is tender in the border, so needs winter protection unless protected by other plants. Salvias can be increased by taking cuttings.

I wait in anticipation for their blooming. These are fabulous plants in their shape, but mostly for their beautiful flowers, purple being my favourite. As with all favoured plants, one is not enough, so the garden is endowed with purple beauty wherever possible, along with the other colours.

GOLDEN ROD
Solidago

The Painting and Drawing

The drawing of this elegant flower consists of many ink circles in a distinct conical style. The stem and leaves are part of the design and explain more about the plant. Light touches using the tip of the pen give an indication of the leaf shapes.

When moving on to the painting I decided to include blue behind the yellow flowers. There are fewer problems placing yellow in the spectrum than with pinks and reds, which can easily clash. To show up the yellow flowers, washy green and blue were splashed loosely behind them, along with more yellow to suggest more flower heads.

I used a small brush for the flower spikes using dabs of Lemon Yellow. When dry I changed back to a sable brush and used a warmer yellow for the shadowed areas. The background was wet with clear water carefully eased around the blooms and then blue was dropped into the water and allowed to spread. Blue was used as a complement to the yellow of the solidago.

The Gardener

Solidago comes from the Latin *solidare*, meaning to make whole, referring to the plant's use in centuries past as a wound healer. Solidago is in the aster family, Asteraceae. Most are native to America and temperate Europe, Asia and the Azores. Golden rod is the state flower of Kentucky, Alabama and Nebraska, the state wild flower of South Carolina and the state herb of Delaware. Solidago is easily grown in most soils and an open position. The perennial golden rod has numerous sprays of small golden-yellow flowers on straight, erect branches in summer and early autumn. There are numerous varieties differing in height and shades of yellow. Tall plants are placed at the back of the border and sometimes in the middle, adding depth as well as height. *Solidago canadensis* is the most common species and parent of many hybrids.

Golden rod produces abundant nectar in warm sunny weather and when moisture is plentiful, but does not cause seasonal allergies as it has virtually no pollen and is pollinated by insects, not by wind. They are scented and good for nectar-seeking bees, solitary wasps and short-tongued flies and beetles, which eat the pollen and drink the nectar. The leaves are eaten by caterpillars of the peppered moth and several species of pug moth. The seed heads are a food source for seed-eating birds. Solidago is important to wildlife as well as to those who make a herbal tea from young leaves, and is known for its healing properties and to gardeners and artists who welcome the splash of colour and beauty in the flower border.

Propagation is by wind-disseminated seeds and by rhizomes, which spread underground forming large clumps from a single plant. More plants can be easily propagated by division of the clumps in spring or autumn. As it seeds freely it can be invasive and in some places has become common in the wild, displacing native vegetation from its natural habitat. However, golden rod, in some areas, is considered a sign of good fortune.

TRANSVAAL DAISY
Gerbera (Gerber daisy, African daisy)

The Painting

After careful study of the very intricate flower head, I made a pencil sketch of the petals. Without this careful study and drawing, I could have found brushstrokes were misplaced and consequently confusing. I paid attention to the centre of the flower and used the tip of a small brush to indicate the shapes. I worked in the traditional way of building up colour, starting with light colour and, when dried, adding darker, richer colour in successive layers. Watercolours are transparent or semi-transparent so do not show against dark colours, so a painting starts with the lightest colours and builds to the darker ones. I wet all the petals with clear water and immediately applied Quinacridone Red. When this was dry I used the same red, but this time a less-wet mix to build up the intensity of tone. I then deepened the red between the petals. The stamens were painted with Winsor Orange, darkened in places with a touch of Winsor Red. I assessed the darks behind the petals and deepened the colour where needed.

The Gardener
Gerberas are in the family Asteraceae, the daisy family, native to tropical regions of South America, Asia and South Africa. The common name is in honour of the German botanist and medical doctor Traugott Gerber,

196

1710–1743, who travelled extensively in Russia and was a friend of Carolus Linnaeus.

Gerbera jamesonii was discovered in 1884 near Barberton, South Africa, by Scotsman Robert Jameson. It is also known as Transvaal daisy, Barberton daisy or African daisy. It has tapering bright-green leaves and brilliant two-lipped florets in red, pink, yellow, orange, salmon or cream flowers.

Blooming time can change according to the light, which affects flower formation. Too much light, and too little moisture, leads to shorter stalks with the flowers amid the leaves. Short days promote flowering and long days delay flowering. As *G. jamesonii* are tender they should have winter protection in a frost-free place. The domesticated cultivars are mostly a result of a cross between *G. jamesonii* and another South African species, *G. viridifolia.* This cross is known as *G. hybrida.* They vary in shape and size and can have petals of several different colours. The centre of the flower is sometimes black.

G. garvinea is a hardy variety which is best grown at the front of the border. It will flower from spring through summer, and as a perennial will become dormant in winter.

Propagation is from seed, seedlings or division. Seeds should be sown fresh as they lose viability quickly. Propagation by division ensures that the flower will be true to type. It is best to divide the old plants in early spring, replanting the most vigorous and healthy specimens immediately. If planted too deeply, the crown may rot. They should be planted in borders with the crowns set above the soil level to avoid the soil splashing on to the plant and increasing the risk of rotting, and allowed to dry out between each watering. Watering is best in the morning so that leaves can dry during the day. This lessens the risk of rot and fungal diseases. Gerberas thrive in full sun. Without direct sun they can become leggy and pale and do not bloom so well.

Gerberas are one of the most popular cut flowers. They are a classic symbol of beauty and cheerfulness, with their meaning of innocence and purity being attributed to the general daisy family. Their vivid, brilliant colours can lift spirits and with their bold and striking colours they have become the most highly prized daisy variety.

VERBENA
(vervain, purple-top vervain, cluster-top vervain, Argentinian vervain, tall verbena or pretty verbena)

Painting 1
Verbena bonariensis has delicate and complicated flower heads. After careful study of light, shade, shape and colour, I lightly drew in the flower heads and petals, which had to stay unpainted until the end. The interior of the head was dark, and this helped to show up the lighter petals. The flowers are, in fact, pinky purple, but as the light was bright they appeared a lot lighter. This was an advantage as it created tonal contrast. The tiny flowers were painted with Ultramarine Violet, with the centre of each flower cluster painted in dark purple, mixed

by adding a touch of green to purple, carefully avoiding the petals and flower stalk, which were painted when dry. The stalks were painted with a dilute purple, again being careful not to touch the petals. I then added purple to the centre of each flower and with a damp brush eased a little colour out on to the petals.

The background was made dark to show up the light petals. I mixed violet and two greens, one with added violet and the other with added yellow to give a brighter green. It was a very hot day and the paint dried fast. I had plenty of water ready and used it to carefully wash around the flower head and especially the petals. I then dropped in the colours, being careful so that they didn't merge too much and create grey. Where necessary, more water was added to avoid water marks. The greens, especially the yellow-greens, enhanced the violet colour, and the darks accentuated the feeling of light.

Painting 2

The stems were painted with Sap Green and then darkened with violet for the shadows. A pale background was washed in, again using violet and the green used for the stems.

A swallowtail butterfly landed on the flower head, but I was not quick enough to include this delight in the picture. Skipper butterflies flitted from flower to flower, and although small they can fly at great speed and manoeuvrability. A golden comma basked in the sunshine, absorbing warmth before sipping nectar from flowers. A fritillary flew swiftly from the meadow flowers seeking out scabious and knapweeds. A peacock butterfly patrolled its territory, and groups of purple hairstreaks fluttered high up in the oak trees then descended to the lower branches to bask in the sun before visiting the sweet chestnut. To encounter these beautiful butterflies and moths is a delight and I like to think that they were as happy in the garden.

The Gardener

There are about 250 species of annual and perennial herbaceous or semi-woody flowering verbena in the family Verbenaceae. They are drought-tolerant, will grow in full or partial sun and enjoy well-drained average soil. The majority of the species are native to the Americas and Asia. *V. bonariensis* is tall and slender with strong, hairy, branching stems set with rough-textured dark-green leaves and tight clusters of purple-lilac flowers on terminal and axillary stems, flowering from midsummer into late autumn. They are generally pest-free. At maturity they will develop woody bases. Verbena, or vervain, has been used as a herbal tonic. It is believed that it can increase mental, emotional and spiritual well-being. The essential oil of various species, mainly vervain, is traded as 'Spanish verbena oil', but is considered inferior to oil of lemon verbena in perfumery.

Verbena has long been associated with divine and supernatural forces. It was called tears of Isis in ancient Egypt, and later called Hera's tears. In the early Christian era, folk legend stated that *V. officinalis* was used to staunch Jesus's wounds after His removal from the Cross. It was consequently called holy herb or devil's bane. Vervain flowers are engraved on Italian charms.

Common names of verbena are often associated with iron. The Dutch name means 'iron-hard'; Danish, 'medical iron-wort'; German, 'true iron-herb'; Slovak, 'medical iron herb'; and Hungarian, 'iron grass'. In the Victorian language of flowers, verbena held the dual meaning of 'enchantment and sensibility'.

They are usually grown from seed sown in autumn or early spring and flower in the first year. The seed can be gathered in autumn and saved in paper bags, stored in a cool, dry place before sowing in the spring. The plants from saved seed may not be the same as the parent plant due to the possibility of cross-pollination. They self-seed liberally, with resulting seedlings being stronger and more drought-tolerant than those transplanted. Leaving the old stalks and seed heads until spring before cutting back gives some protection to the plant as well as distributing the seeds. A mulch of leaf mould or compost also helps. Plants are borderline hardy, so may be damaged in a hard winter. They can also be propagated from cuttings, cutting just above a node, dipping the cut end in rooting powder, then letting it dry for a few moments before placing it in water. Roots should appear within a week. Verbena will also root in compost. Cut above a leaf node, dip in rooting hormone powder and plant in small pots. The stem will grow roots and can be left in the pots over the winter before transplanting outdoors in spring. Sometimes the stems will form roots if they touch the ground. They can be covered with garden soil, and when a good root system has formed the stem can be cut away from the main plant and transplanted.

Verbena grows above surrounding plants, where butterflies can easily find it. I have seen comma, gatekeeper, painted lady, small copper, speckled wood, hummingbird hawk moth, swallowtail and others. Some butterflies, like commas, can spend all day sipping nectar from asters, buddleias and daisies as well as verbena. To have a good butterfly garden the secret is to have a wide mixture of plants, including herbs and wild flowers such as nettles as well as garden flowers rich in nectar. Pastel colours, purple, pink, lilac and white are most attractive to butterflies.

THE POND

The colour of water is largely created by its surroundings. In shallow water the colour is affected by the sun reflecting off the bottom and the intensity of the underlying colour is increased where the water is deeper. Colour does not exist without light, so natural light affects the perceived colours of the water. Dull light reduces a body of water to a dark mass, whereas bright light reveals variations in colour and tone with areas of pure colour caused by reflected light from the sky. When light rays angle towards the surface of still water, some of the rays bounce off the surface and reflect while some travel down into it. A perfect mirror image is only possible when looking straight across it at a very shallow angle. As the steepness of the angle of reflection increases, the percentage of light entering the water also increases. Looking steeply down on to the surface of the water, not much light from the sky will reflect back to the eye. Completely still water gives a mirror image of the sky and any other features around it. The tranquil, mirror-like surface of water on a still, calm day is seldom exactly the same colour and tone all over, because of its reflective surface mirroring the sky. These shifts in colour and tone, often very subtle, are also affected by the angle of viewing. Water usually looks darker in the foreground because it is closer and thus reflects less light. A pond surrounded by trees will reflect the colour of the trees and other areas will reflect the sky. If the water has movement, such as ripples, there will be reflected highlights. In the distance ripples will decrease in size as they recede. The water is greatly influenced by the weather conditions and the effects produced by wind and rain. The effects of light on water can be fleeting, as in a shaft of sunlight breaking through the cloud to spotlight an area on the water and as quickly disappear. Observation is the key point and, with fleeting sunlight, painting from memory.

Shapes and colours reflected in the water give a strong impression, but mirror images may not necessarily make a good painting subject because it loses much of its identity as water. If the reflection is painted like the sky, the eye is confused and jumps from the sky to the water, trying to work out what is happening. It is, therefore, best to make it obvious which is which and the best solution is to distort the reflection a little. Often the reflected shape gives the impression of doubling the growth and colour.

Colours are not always true to the object casting the reflection, but tend to be modified by the colour of the water, which is influenced by reflections, light and shade, as well as depth, clarity of the water and green patches of plants which interrupt the surface. Here again the artist has to be aware of this fact and may have to exaggerate the difference. Water contains a considerable amount of organic matter, which affects the colour and reflective quality as well as the light from the sky. Colours can become darker, brighter, greyer, warmer or cooler in relation to other surrounding colours. Every light source has its own colour and temperature, such as warm orange or cool blue-violet, and every object has its own colour, which is affected by the colour of the light source. A cool light intensifies cool objects and neutralises warm objects, whereas warm light will intensify warm objects. On dull days, when the light is weak, a cloudy sky will not dominate the water in the same way.

Water is no more difficult to paint than anything else, because reflections follow general principles. Dark objects reflect slightly lighter in water, while light objects reflect slightly darker. Shadows across the water offer a contrast to the brighter reflections. A multitude of colours applied in small strokes make the shadows shimmer. Smooth, glassy light reflecting off the surface of water is best expressed as simply as possible, observing the tonal values in all parts of the water, as it is the contrast between light and dark values which gives the impression of light in the painting. Putting down a dark shape against the white paper will make the dark seem darker, unless it is surrounded by other darker values. A value sketch helps to determine whether the shape will be correct at the completion of the painting. Working from the value sketch, it can translate value to colour. Generally the water reflection is darker than the sky. Where the lightest area of the water is surrounded by some strong darks it creates the impression that the water is the lightest light.

Points of light on the water surface can only be seen as such if they are contrasted with dark colours. Highlights are rarely pure white. Light nearly always leans towards a colour, usually with a little of the predominant light. Streaks of light can be removed by using a damp edge of card dragged across the surface before the original paint is dry. A dry brush can be dragged across the paper to suggest lines and patches of wind-ruffled water.

If the water is ruffled by a breeze, and the light is very bright, then the tips of the ruffles catch the light, and these fragments of light can appear across a whole stretch of water. If the light is from a single source, there is a sparkling, reflecting path across the water. Touches of reflected light can be used as a lead into the focal point. When trees, figures or buildings are reflected on a shiny surface, they often appear to be vertical. These can be painted vertically from top to bottom with transparent paint. When painting with oil paints, horizontal ripples in water can be overlaid using thicker, more opaque marks to create a sensation of depth and movement. If painting in oils, the ripples in the foreground can be applied with a palette knife. The most exciting effects can be when small movements across the water cause ripples that break the reflections into separate shapes. As night falls and the water becomes still, the reflections seem more pronounced.

Painting 1

With the different leaf shapes and flowers, I planned the painting carefully, drew the main features and masked out the areas to remain light against dark. The irises were painted with Lemon Yellow, adding Indian Yellow in their centres. The water lilies were Quinacridone Rose with darker centres, as were the sarracenia. The leaves of the sarracenia were slightly more orange, so the rose was adjusted with Indian Yellow. The greens were a mix of Ultramarine Blue, which was used for the water, and the different yellows, darkened with rose and in places with Ultramarine Violet, which was used in the darks between the water-lily leaves. The background was a simple expanse of lawn, providing a calm area amid the busy surrounds to the pond, with the far border being soft pinks and greens backed by a loose wash of various greens and blues. The suggestion of greens in the background can be achieved by wetting the whole area and then dropping the colour into it or by using very wet mixes of colour so that they run together.

I try to develop the whole of the painting and not linger in one area too long. This leads to a more cohesive understanding of the image, and working from reality is part of bringing the image to life. Details are remembered pieced together with memories of sounds, scents, weather, colour and the wildlife which comes and goes as I sit quietly by the side of the pond. Knowing the garden well is not as important as observation.

No amount of technical knowledge and expertise can be a substitute for observation, passion and determination. Technique is only a tool.

Painting 2

The appeal of water evokes responses and moods as the light changes and distorts, creating images which are enticing to the artist. It helps to understand why the light catches the water in certain ways. This means analysing colour, mood, depth, reflections and shadows. Capturing the quality of light is one of the most important elements in a painting. It creates atmosphere. A subject may be passed by many times without being noticed, then one day the light reveals the image in a different, inspiring way, highlighting and transforming, creating delicious colour and magical light.

The light was in the foreground centred around the main water lily, though subtle changes took place in the scene during painting. The sun moved constantly, changing shadows, lighting and the general atmosphere of the scene. One must work with verve and emotion to capture the essence of the subject. The different pinks of the water lilies were echoed in the other water lilies and in the arum lilies and various other plants around the pond edge. The eye then travels around the painting and back to the main water lilies.

The back of the pond was kept dark by overpainting with various layers of green paint ending in dark green and some semi-opaque Yellow Ochre, painted as a light reflection from the background rocks. Shadows on water appear as an absence of reflection rather than a lack of light, allowing the dark depths to be seen. The light around the water lilies is dry white paper, which is more luminous than white paint. The rocks are a mix of Yellow Ochre and Burnt Sienna and the darkest darks are from Burnt Sienna mixed with the same blue used in the water. All the greens are the same original mix varied by the addition of colours used in the painting.

A wet-in-wet technique is particularly effective when painting water, producing gentle gradations of tone that capture the ever changing effects of atmosphere and light. It is best for a soft, diffused impression and can convey a misty day when colours spread and merge softly together with no hard lines. The paint dries with a soft, hazy quality. The big shapes of leaves and the wonderful water-lily blooms and the reflections are really just shapes, colours and values which work together to make the picture. Foreground reflections could be emphasised by painting wet-on-dry, and for those in the background a more diffused, softer quality using wet-in-wet.

There is a subtle difference between reflections of the sky and reflections of direct light from the sun. The sun lights up the sky, which can be reflected on the surface of the water. If the water surface is broken the direct rays will create bright highlights so that reflections of a blue sky can be fragmented by light ripples catching brighter light from the sun.

WATER LILY
Nymphaea odorata. Nymphe means a water nymph.

The Painting

The play of light from the sky on the pond and the images of surrounding colours create a beautiful reflection. Objects absorb and reflect light. The local colour of an object is generally described as the natural colour of the object in white light unhindered by influences of other colours. As light is cast upon an object some areas are exposed to direct light while other areas are in shadows. This effect causes gradations of lightness, or values, as the light strikes the object at different angles. Everything we see is composed of light – direct light, reflected light, light diffused through different atmospheric conditions – or a cast shadow falling across a faceted surface. Each painting is a result of a direct experience with nature, and nothing substitutes for this experience.

On water which is flat and clear, like a mirror, the stronger the light, the brighter and more distinct the reflections. In poor light, the water appears dark and only bright tones will be reflected. If the water is ruffled, the pattern of reflected light will then depend on where the sun is positioned, either catching the angles of each ripple or highlighting them. The angle of the sun makes a difference – whether it is overhead, giving harsh, bright light, or at sunrise or sunset, when the light is softened; and winter sun is low in comparison with summer. When the sun is high in the sky, the whole sky is bright, and a lower sun means more mellow light with the tones deeper. The sun reflecting from the surface of water can create wonderful sparkling effects, but these need to be handled with care, by painting fewer, larger marks even if there appear to be thousands of facets of light sparkling on the surface. Reflections can produce a mirror image. Direct mirror images can look a little obvious and so subtlety must be used.

I am fascinated by water, so long as I'm not in it! I strived to express its diverse characteristics in this painting. The inspiration and challenge was to use the lily pads to suggest the water's surface.

Objects reflected in the water should be studied, as the reflection starts from the base of the object, not from the water's edge. So if a tree is set back from the edge, the base will not be reflected in the water. How much is included in the reflection is in direct relation to the distance the object reflected is set back. Even when water appears to be glass-like in its stillness, it is rarely so in actuality as there is always a slight movement in the water which will distort the reflection. Reflections are never quite the same colours as the objects being reflected. Objects and surfaces that create reflections generally have little colour of their own; they are mostly influenced by the colours of their surroundings. Colours are generally muted as if seen over a distance. Reflections of dark trees will be weaker in tone than the actual trees and the colour will be less saturated, while a white reflection will appear darker in tone. Any movement on the surface of the water will break up reflections to some degree, from slight distortion to the complete fragmentation of the image. Reflections are generally harder-edged where they are closer to the subject, the edges becoming more diffused and broken up as they get further away.

Drawing with colour requires a different kind of approach as the colour is a major compositional element both in choice of subject and in the arrangement into a pictorial image. Other important features should not be ignored – outline and contour, tone and values, composition and texture – while thinking about colour from the beginning. Colour relationships significantly affect the character of the composition.

Making preparatory sketches (thumbnail sketches) is important to painting in all mediums. A full-colour drawing will take as much time and effort as a painting, so it makes sense to work out potential problems in a thumbnail sketch beforehand. This preparatory work reduces the risk of making a major error of judgement that could spoil a painting.

In this painting I wanted the light to be an important element to portray the brightness and vitality of the sun reflecting on the water, so I used a lot of pure, bright colours and semi-neutral colour combinations. The brightest colours are best used in small amounts, while softer colours were used in larger areas with the darker colours used at the edges, hence accentuating the light.

When painting water, the artist is describing an effect, capturing a moment. The sparkle on the surface that is created when sunlight hits it can be achieved by using the dry-brush technique. This means dragging pigment in a not-too-wet brush across dry paper. By holding the brush at an angle the brush skirts over the paper surface leaving tiny unpainted areas which represent the light ripples. It helps to use fairly textured paper.

The Gardener

There is an evocative charm in a lily pond with arum lilies growing among irises and hostas, and water buttercups giving a splash of yellow. The water in the pond is clearest in winter and most opaque in spring, when the light is strong and the water warming rapidly, and conditions are ideal for developing algae. When water lilies expand their leaves over the surface, light is excluded and usually the algae disappears. Water lilies are a genus of about forty species of aquatics with a fleshy or tuberous rootstock, mostly natives of the northern hemisphere or the tropics, a few in South Africa and Australia. The leaves are large and deeply heart-shaped and the floating flowers are white, yellow, blue, red or pink. The hardy species may be grown in a basket or planted firmly directly into compost in the bottom of the pond.

The Ancient Egyptians dedicated the water lily to the sun, because the lily flower closes at sunset and sinks under the surface of the water, then rises again and opens at dawn.

The lovely luxuriant floating flowers of the water lilies provide a romantic and magical display. There are numerous varieties of water lilies, all flowering in summer, but differing in vigour as well as in the size and colour of their flowers. Full light is essential for free flowering. *Nymphaea alba*, the common white water lily, is scentless. *N. rubra* is rosy pink and is from Sweden. *N. fennica*, from Finland, is white with lobes tipped yellow or violet. *N. nitida*, from Siberia, is white and scentless. *N. pygmaea* 'Alba' has small white flowers and may be grown in a bowl. It is hardy and seeds freely with seedlings flowering in the first year. *N. tetragona* is dwarf and has dark-green mottled reddish-brown leaves when young, dull red beneath and the flowers small, white and sometimes scented. *N. tuberosa* has a creeping rootstock with oblong tubers, the flowers white and faintly scented. *N. rosea* has pale-rose flowers and is fragrant and is apt to spread very freely.

The water lily has creeping underwater rhizomes from which grow the circular leaves and flower stems. All have floating leaves which are dark, glossy green on the surface and often reddish underneath. The scented flowers open completely only in full sunlight, and as day draws on they close, dipping slightly below the surface of the water. Each bloom has four spear-shaped sepals, and between twenty and twenty-five spirally arranged oval petals. The flowers are fragrant when they first open and attract bees, flies and beetles to assist in pollination.

After flowering, the spongy, globular fruit capsule sinks to ripen underwater. The seeds have a spongy air-filled coating, and when the fruit rots they float to the surface, drifting away from the parent plant. It can also be propagated by dividing the thick rhizome in spring.

A glint of water evokes a touch of tranquillity and calm and provides unique possibilities in the garden. The sound of trickling water adds another dimension – a musical effect. A pond is the best way of introducing wildlife of every kind into the garden. We introduced an assortment of plants to attract different kinds of wildlife. Frogs, newts, insects, birds, bats, mammals and grass snakes contribute to the health and well-being of garden plants as well as creating interest. The softening of green plants enhances the appearance of the pond as well as being a magnet for wildlife and keeps the water healthy. Marginal plants provide for butterflies, damselflies, dragonflies and bees, and, with the right planting, for moths, hoverflies and wasps. With different depths, diving beetles enjoy more water whereas the edges are perfect for newts to sunbathe. Water lilies provide stems for dragonfly and damselfly nymphs to emerge and dry their wings. There are three key types of pond plants: those which oxygenate and are submerged, those which float and give shade below and provide sun-basking opportunities, and emerging plants on which creatures can climb. Plants like water iris need their roots submerged, while others, such as floating oxygenators, grow above water and are simply placed on the water surface. I keep the planting simple, with two kinds of water lilies and clumps of iris and on the damp edges I have water forget-me-nots, bog primulas, marginal kingcups, or marigolds, and other moisture-loving plants.

Primulas are plants which like to feel the influence of water without being overwhelmed by it, so are best grown in damp, marshy soil rather than in the pond. The candelabra types, like *Primula japonica* and *P. pulverulenta*, have flowers in whorls at intervals along the stems and come in oranges, yellows, soft pinks, rosy salmon and Crimson reds.

Falling leaves in autumn can be a trial and they need to be removed before they decay. Keeping the water transparent and clean is an essential part of water gardening as pollution from mineral salts released into the water from rotting vegetation encourages the rapid spread of algae, which feed upon the salts using natural light as a source of energy. Underwater oxygenating plants use soluble salts to promote growth, and photosynthesis discharges oxygen into the water. Their green leaves take in carbon dioxide through myriads of pores, use the carbon and combine it with water from the roots to make sugars and then return the unwanted oxygen to the atmosphere.

MARSH MARIGOLD
Caltha palustris (kingcup)

The Painting
Good tonal relationships are far more important than colour relationships. Almost all the old masters worked with limited colours and, in most cases, primarily earth tones. For this reason they had to manipulate the surrounding values to make a colour appear brighter.

The eye only sees part of the scene at one time with the focal point being the most important and the surrounding scene more generalised and on the edges of the peripheral vision. The focal point should have the most detail, with the surrounding areas becoming more blended and softer as they recede. This is very different from a photo, which captures everything with the same clarity and detail. By using the technique of lost edges, the artist learns to create the mystery of peripheral vision. The advantage of using photos as a reference is that they can capture fleeting effects of light. Squinting is a good way of evaluating a subject as it helps to block out detail and gives an overall sense of the colour and mood of the scene.

The interest in this painting was the flower colour and lacy detail on the leaves. I first masked out the stamens in the three main flowers and then washed in Lemon Yellow and Indian Yellow, then added to the centres and drew out across the petals with a darker centre. When dry, the masking fluid was removed and the stamens painted with Lemon Yellow.

206

The leaves were painted lightly with pale green, darkening in various places. Then, using a fine brush, the complicated veining was added and in places the darker paint was used to make lighter veins by incorporating round shapes and leaving the underpainting to show through. The lower leaf was partially below water, so was made indistinct but edged darker in the upper sections with dark water between the leaf highlights, the stalks, the middle leaf and the flower petals.

The Gardener

John Gerard speaks of the marsh marigold's 'gallant green' leaves and 'goodly yellow flowers, glittering like gold'.

The generic name *Caltha* is derived from the Ancient Greek, meaning goblet, referring to the shape of the flower. *Palustris* is Latin for 'of the marsh'. The common name marigold refers to its use in medieval churches at Easter as a tribute to the Virgin Mary, as in Mary gold. Other names are brave bassinets, crazy Beth, horse blob, May blob, boots, water boots, meadow bright, bull-flower, meadow buttercup, water buttercup, soldier's buttons, meadow cowslip, publican's cloak, crowfoot, water dragon, drunkards, water goggles, meadow gowan, yellow gowan, goldes, golds, goldings, gools, cow lily, marybuds, publicans and sinners.

C. palustris is in the buttercup family. It is often found in wet meadows, preferring an open site in muddy soil or in very shallow oxygen-rich water. It is probably one of the most ancient native plants in the regions of the northern hemisphere, surviving the glaciations and flourishing after the last retreat of the ice in a landscape inundated with glacial meltwaters. This creeping perennial has kidney-shaped, glossy dark-green leaves with toothed margins growing from the base on long stalks. Thick hollow stems carry the large waxy-looking bloom of yellow flowers, containing up to 100 stamens. Each flower produces up to ten pod-like follicles, which split open to release seed before they are dry. The plant is adapted to rain pollination. Up to 200 seeds may be produced by each flower. When the follicles open, they form a 'splash cup'. When raindrops hit one at the right angle, the walls are shaped so that the seeds are expelled. The seeds also have a spongy tissue that makes them float on water until they wash up in a suitable location where they can germinate. Ripe seed can be collected and sown into damp compost in a cool, shady place, or the plants can be propagated by division in autumn or early spring. In autumn the plant dies down and overwinters with buds near the water surface.

Very young flower buds were once used in cooking instead of capers and they were used as a spice. Early spring leaves can be cooked in boiling water until tender, served with butter and vinegar, and the bright flowers were woven into garlands to decorate houses and churches on May Day. Flowers produce both nectar and copious amounts of pollen, which attracts insects such as bumblebees, dragonflies and stoneflies.

C. palustris grows on the water margin and Farrer's kingcup, *C. polypetala,* the largest marsh marigold, lives in shallow water. Farrer gives an account of a romantic legend that the kingcup was only known in Europe in the ponds of the Vatican. The old Pope refused to let it go into a heretical world, but one day a hero hooked out some fragments with his umbrella and introduced it to the horticultural (if heretical) world. It does not form clumps, unlike *C. palustris,* but has a sprawling habit; and where the stems sprawl they root, setting up a colony in a short while. The first very large flowers come in April. *C. palustris* '*Flore Pleno*', the double marsh marigold, produces masses of pompom-like bright-yellow flowers in spring in neat mounds of shiny green heart-shaped leaves. They are clump-forming and very ornamental and easy to grow.

WATER IRIS
(flag iris, water iris, rabbit ear iris)

The Painting

Blues and yellows were the main feature of this painting. I used Cobalt Blue with Ultramarine in the background. Winsor Lemon was darkened with a little Indian Yellow and all colours were mixed together to form various greens for the leaves. *Iris sibirica* flowers in shades of blue from light to dark, tending towards a reddish purple. There is also a variegated form with cream-striped foliage, which adds interest to the surrounding green. Mine was given to me by a friend, so is a special reminder of her.

The Gardener

There are two distinct types of iris: one with rhizomes and one with bulb-like corms. The yellow iris (*I. pseudacorus*) is one of the most distinctive plants in marginal vegetation throughout Europe, covering watery meadows and banks of rivers and canals. In my garden I have them on the edge of the pond, but have to divide them every few years as they increase their rhizomes, spreading quickly. Their young foliage rising out of the water is very beautiful and the flowers last well. The seed pods need to be cut off so that they don't float across the water and eventually form another colony of seedlings. *I. pseudacorus* is often known as yellow flag or the fleur-de-lys of France. It has large yellow flowers in terminal and lateral clusters in summer. These grow on the edges of ponds. It will tolerate drier soil, but prefers a moist soil. It can be invasive. They were used medicinally in the past and are poisonous to livestock. *I. variegata* has broad, ridged grey-green leaves striped with yellow. It can have up to ten flowers that often have a dark central patch. *I. cristata* is the crested iris; *I. kaempferi*, the Japanese iris; and *I. pallida*, the sweet flag. *Iris sibirica,* the Siberian iris, flowers in shades of blue from light to dark, tending towards a reddish purple. There is also a variegated form with cream-striped foliage, which adds interest to the surrounding green. There is also pale yellow. A deep-blue iris *I. laevigata*, has a number of forms, with pink, white or bicoloured blue-and-white flowers. *I. versicolor* is semiaquatic. It has striking blue-violet flowers, yellow-blotched at the base, in late spring to early summer. Leaves are narrow, grey-green and sword-shaped. It enjoys full sun to partial shade, but needs more sun the deeper the water. This iris will tolerate fluctuating water levels in a natural pond and even survived a severe drought when its roots were out of water. It blooms in spring with showy violet-blue-striped petals with yellow bases. I remove spent blooms to encourage more flowers. It is an excellent plant for removing nitrates and phosphates from the water, keeping the pond healthy.

For hundreds of years the yellow iris has been used as a dye plant. The rhizomes produce a black dye and the flowers provide yellow, the commonest colour obtainable from vegetable material. The roots were also used to scent and starch laundry, and the powered root, orris root, was mixed with ordinary hair powder and sold as violet powder for the hair. It was suppose to cure toothache, suspended in beer casks to prevent the beer becoming stale, and in wine casks to give bouquet. The common blue flower was mixed with alum by the monks to produce a green pigment for the illuminations of manuscripts.

In the south of England it was called levers, from 'laefer', a flag, and sometimes flag-flower, dagger-flower and dragon-flower. In Scotland it might be luggs or waterskegs, or segg, a corruption of 'sedge', a small sword. Because of its sword-like leaves it is the Japanese emblem of a warrior.

In the past 'flags' along the riverbank indicated a ford, for the creeping roots or rhizomes, broken and torn by hooves and wheels, drifted downstream and established themselves in the shallows to root again. The yellow iris has the most interesting history of all the irises for in the sixth century Clovis, the first king of the Franks, discovered a ford on the Rhine indicated by yellow flag irises and bought his army to safety from the overpowering Goths, near Cologne. Quite naturally he adopted the flower as his emblem. Its three large petals symbolised faith, wisdom, and valour. In the twelfth century Louis V of France adopted the fleur-de-lys emblem during the Crusades. Thereafter it was emblazoned upon the escutcheons of the kings of France. When Edward of England claimed the crown of France, the fleur-de-lys was added to the English coat of arms and remained there until 1801 – nearly 250 years after Calais had been reclaimed by the French. The symbol was outlawed during the French Revolution, in 1792, and hundreds of men and women found wearing it were condemned to death. It was reinstated with Louis XVIII in 1814 and it was continued with Charles X and again outlawed in 1830, when Charles was dethroned.

In England, the Plantagent standard bearing the fleur-de-lys of France is the emblem on the arms of Eton College, founded by Henry VI. Edward III added it to the arms of England. It was not until 1800 that George III replaced the fleur-de-lys with the shamrock.

The name lily when applied to the iris is merely a confusion of common usage, dating back across the centuries to biblical times, referring to 'lilies of the field'. It seems to be a collective name for any showy flower, as was the name rose.

Shakespeare called the golden-yellow flower 'flower de luce'. Other English names are legion-flag, flagons, Jacob's sword, laister, levers, lug, maiken, yellow saggan, seggs, water seg, seggin, shaldon, skeg, sword lily, fliggers (referring to the movement of the sword-like leaves in the breeze) and cucumber (which is descriptive of the seed capsule).

SCHIZOSTYLIS

The Painting

These delicate flowers are a pale pink with bright-bluish-green leaves. I included a bit of background so as to show up the pale colour of the petals. There was a shadow underneath the flowers, so I added a little of the Permanent Rose, used to paint the flowers, with the Sap Green, which darkened it and provided a good dark. This gives a sense of depth. I was careful to leave white paper for the stamens, very gently darkening them in the centres so that they don't appear flat and lifeless. The centres of the flowers were also left as white paper, and then painted with Winsor Lemon.

The Gardener

The name Kaffir lily is an offensive term to black South Africans. In better use are the names crimson flag lily, crimson river lily, cape lily and scarlet river lily. The name Kaffir lily derives from its natural habitat along brooks and wet zones in a South African area formally called Kaffraria, the land of the Kaffirs.

Schizostylis is in the iris family, Iridaceae. The genus name comes from the Greek words *schizo*, meaning to divide, and *stylis*, meaning a column or style, as the style is divided into three parts. It forms a clump of narrow iris-like leaves bearing short spikes of star-shaped soft-pink, crimson, white or red flowers with a yellow centre, with darker streaks in the petals in autumn. Schizostylis has linear grass-green leaves throughout the year in its natural habitat, but in Europe it dies back and regrows in late spring. Once established, which may take some time, each stem can produce an abundance of flowers. In warm winter climates, blooms may continue into winter, with foliage staying evergreen. The plant needs moisture-retentive soil and a sunny position to perform well, but cannot survive being waterlogged, especially in winter. Adequate drainage is needed and in summer a mulch keeps the plant cool and damp.

Propagation is by rhizome division, which should be planted in a pot of soil and watered regularly. Once the root system has developed, it can be planted out. Schizostylis tends to propagate around the mother plant.

Hesperantha is almost identical to schizostylis, but grows from a corm, while schizostylis has short rhizomes. Most hesperanthas flower in spring and have attractive pink, yellow, purple or white flowers.

PURPLE LOOSESTRIFE
Lythrum salicaria (black blood, spiked loosestrife, purple lythrum). *Lythron* is Greek for blood; *salicaria* refers to the willow-like foliage.

Painting 1

I first washed over the background with Lemon Yellow, leaving some small areas for white flowers and the loosestrife. The flower heads were painted with Quinacridone Magenta when the initial wash was dry. The leaves of the plant were painted with the same yellow, darkened with Sap Green and a further dark green, mixed by adding a little Magenta, added in the shadowed areas. The water was a wash of Ultramarine, and when dry the colours of the plants were painted over the blue and allowed to merge in places, so as to give

210

the impression of reflections. In the foreground, small dabs of all the colours – Lemon Yellow, Ultramarine Blue, Sap Green and Quinacridone Magenta – were dotted on, with some marks left prominent while others were allowed to run together. The background was painted in a loose, washy style, over the original yellow with Ultramarine Blue and Sap Green, making sure that the darks were behind some of the flower heads. Further dark greens suggested shadows on the leaves, especially at the base of the loosestrife plants and in the leafy plant on the right.

Painting 2

This was a careful drawing, painted with a fine brush using Quinacridone Magenta for the flowers. The stalk and leaves were painted with Sap Green, which was darkened with Magenta for the shadows. More Magenta was added to the green mix for the dark stamens.

The Gardener

Purple loosestrife should not be confused with members of the family of Primulaceae, bearing the same name of loosestrife. This loosestrife grows in the shallow part of the wildlife pond.

The magenta-pink-purple flowers are held on tall reddish-purple stems through summer to September. They have attractive lance-shaped dark-green foliage, which turns bright red in early autumn.

The spires of flowers attract butterflies, moths, beetles and many other insects to the nectar. The structure of the stigma and stamen allows pollen to be transferred easily, encouraging genetic diversity and vigour. The fruit is a small capsule containing numerous minute seeds. A single plant may produce up to 2 million seeds annually. It is therefore important to cut away the spent flowers in autumn before the seeds scatter and the plant becomes invasive. The seed can be carried by wind and water and the plant can also sprout from pieces of root left in soil or water. It has been known to encroach into crops and pastureland. Once established it is difficult to remove, but some sterile plants have been developed. Some cultivars have different flower colours. *Atropurpureum* has dark-purple flowers, 'Brightness' has deep pink, and 'Happy' has red flowers with a short stem. 'Purple Spires' is purple on a tall stem, '*Roseum Superbum*' has large pink flowers, 'Blush' has pink and 'Feuerkerze' has rose-red flowers.

The plant has been used as an astringent medicinal herb to treat diarrhoea and dysentery, but in my garden it is strictly ornamental.

ARUM LILY
Zantedeschia aethiopica (richardia, calla lily, lords and ladies, cuckoo pint)

The Painting

White is the most important colour in watercolour. It makes all the other colours glow. This is why the white of the paper must be considered first. Also the contrast is the key to good design. The greater the contrast the more it attracts attention. Contrast can be dark values against light, hard edges against soft, round or sharp.

I begin the painting by thinking through how I will paint and which colours I will use, then I refine the drawing so as to isolate the white flowers, which will remain as white paper. The ability to interpret tone is one of the most exciting tools that an artist has. Through the use of tone the illusion of three-dimensionality on a two-dimensional surface is achieved. Tonal values are more important than colour, as demonstrated in the paintings of Rembrandt. Watercolour is the medium for the expression of light. The brilliant white of the paper and the transparency of the colour are the personification of light. At the same time, working with the white of the paper and maintaining transparency are the challenges of watercolour.

Arum lilies can look amazing when reflected in water. *Zantedeschia aethiopica* was a favourite subject of the artists Georgia O'Keeffe and Diego Rivera.

The Gardener

Arum lilies are striking architectural plants. They have large, glossy spear-like leaves with, in spring, large white-hooded flowers which grow at the pond margin and in the shallow waters of my pond. All parts of the plant are frost-sensitive, so if the plant is submerged in water the buds are protected. Here, in my garden, we rarely have severe weather so those in the water are in good health. Those in the ground fare better, growing continuously if fed and watered, and can survive periods of minor frosts.

Arums are amazingly resilient plants and they set good seed if allowed to do so. The seed can be germinated with plants large enough to flower in their second year. They also multiply by rhizome offsets.

Many Calla lilies are now available in a multitude of colours, including black, with some having attractive foliage. Breeding began around thirty years ago in New Zealand, producing plants with long stems and large blooms. Dutch growers have developed smaller plants for the indoor pot-plant market. Those like *Z.* × *rehmannii* are produced on a large scale and grown at a high temperature and kept moist to bring them into flower as quickly as possible. These are less hardy. Plants for the garden are grown more slowly at lower temperatures and kept drier, which produces sturdier plants better adapted for outdoor life. Dry rhizomes can be planted into multipurpose compost, kept moist in a cool greenhouse and brought into growth in spring.

In mild areas they can be planted directly into the ground once the risk of frost has passed. The main difference between hybrid callas and familiar Z. *aethiopica*, or arum lily, is that hybrids have a lower requirement for moisture and are not plants for pond margins. The initial flush of flowers will last up to six weeks with individual blooms long-lived. When the blooms finish flowering, they should be removed, taking care to pull the stem from the base to avoid rot damaging the plant. For those overwintering outdoors, apply a thick mulch of organic matter. Tender varieties should be lifted and the rhizomes stored frost-free in winter.

Flowers such as Z. × *rehmannii* 'Neon Amour' were a passionate and secret way of expressing feelings without the use of words. The calla lily, due to its physical resemblance to female genitalia, was a hidden sexual symbol. They have white-spotted leaves and flowers in many colours, such as yellow, orange, pink and purple. In the nineteenth century there were strict social codes as to how to express feelings.

I believe the elegant white lily blooms lend a coolly exotic, romantic yet dramatic air to the garden in the dimming evening light.

PITCHER PLANT
Sarracenia

The Drawing

Drawing in ink is a combination of lines expressing tone with fine lines giving depth and a suggestion of a three-dimensional plant. Forward planning is essential. I use the sketchbook to make thumbnail sketches as a plan for composition, tonal values and balance in design. In this arrangement I liked the way the light touched and bent around the curved tops and the shadowed underside. When working with an immediate medium, which cannot be changed once drawn, it is essential to plan. Thorough planning requires more thought than the actual drawing, and then the mind can take over, sometimes with unexpected beautiful results.

The Painting
Exotic blooms and showy flowers make interesting paintings and will inspire, but beauty can be found all around, be it in the garden or by the side of the pond where these sarracenias grow. In this painting the twists and turns of the petals and leaves catch the light and create interesting variations, and this is where careful observation is necessary. The foliage is just as important a factor as the flowers themselves and can often be a link between flower and leaves – as in this painting, where the same pink of the flower is tinged in the leaf tip and the same

green as in the leaf is in the centre of the flower bracts. Every painting presents a new challenge, stretching the artist's technical ability. The process of learning and experimenting continues every day.

The Gardener

Interestingly, sarracenia derives its nutriment from insects. It has very weak roots, so gains little from the soil – hence the modification of the leaves to entice insects as food. The pretty flowers come before the leaves, which are in the shape of pitchers, or a tubular shape, with a cap. The pitchers have a receptacle containing a viscid fluid in which flies and even small rodents become submerged and eventually dissolved. As a carnivorous plant, a sugary secretion near the mouth attracts the insects which enter the pitcher, the exit being obstructed by downward-pointing hairs. The captives fall into the liquid at the bottom of the pitcher, where they are digested and absorbed.

These are my husband's plants, which grow in leaf mould and sand on the edge of the pond and in the shade of the cherry tree. I include sarracenia in the spring flowers as it has unusual, beautiful flowers from late winter into spring. When the early morning sun catches on the flowers, they glow with a rich reddish colour.

Dr Sarrazin of Quebec first sent species from North America to Europe in the seventeenth century. Many names have been given to these curious plants – Indian cup, pitcher plant, side-saddle flower, and trumpet leaf. They are best grown in moist, boggy areas in good fibrous peat and sphagnum, which does not become sour as other composts are apt to. Large quantities of water are needed for its successful cultivation.

Close by, in the verges of the pond, are marsh marigolds in flower, and yellow iris rushing up from their watery bed and domes of frogspawn among the water-lily leaves.

BOGBEAN
Menyanthes trifoliata (boghop, marsh trefoil, bognut)

The Painting

This was a tricky subject, so masking fluid was used for the 'hairy' edges of the petals. When the fluid was dry, a mix of green was washed in and left to dry. The masking fluid was removed once the wash was dry. Masking fluid protects the paper from being painted and when removed leaves a hard edge. These edges can be painted or softened with a damp brush. Painting around, or negative painting, needs planning where the light is against the dark and dark against light. Negative painting can be hard to master as it is natural to see positive things rather than the space around objects. It is the opposite of the 'wiping out' method, when paint is applied and, while wet, the paint is wiped out, leaving soft edges and muted colour; but in watercolour the white of the paper cannot be retrieved, and white paint doesn't have that special sparkle.

214

A thin, washy purple was carefully painted in shadows on the buds and base of the white flowers. The stalk was darkened with a thicker mix of the same green used in the background, adding more in the shadowed areas. Winsor Red was dabbed into the tips of the buds and a warm yellow, Indian Yellow, was used for the stamens.

The Gardener
Bogbean is a rhizomatous perennial of shallow water with ovate leaflets and bean-like seeds, which resemble a broad-bean plant – hence the name. The seeds have been found deeply buried in bogs. Each leaf is divided into three leaflets, hence the Latin species name, *trifoliata*, meaning three leaves. The name menyanthes comes from the Greek word *menyein*, meaning disclosing, and *anthos*, meaning flower. The common name boghop arose from the use of the leaves as a flavouring in beer making, and boiled in honey to make mead. In the past the rootstock was fed to cattle and milled to stretch out flour, which produced a nutritious but bitter-tasting bread. Both the leaves and the root have a bitter taste, and were once used to treat jaundice and rheumatism.

Bogbean grows in shallow water on the edges of ponds, forming wide mats with leaves held just above the water. Pretty pink buds open to lovely little white star-shaped flowers flushed pink on the outside with long white hairs around the edges of the petals. It is believed that the hairs may protect the flower's store of nectar from small insects, including butterflies and honeybees, which are useless for pollination. Propagation is by dividing plants in spring. Each division should contain a growing tip.

It helps to remove nutrients from the water to aid in algae reduction.

The bogbean is found throughout Europe, North and Central Asia, Morocco, Greenland and North America. In some places it has disappeared due to drainage of its former habitats.

PICKERELWEED
Pontederia cordata

The Painting
The delicate petals and buds of the pickerelweed needed careful observation. I began with a light application of watery purple followed by a thicker mix for the darker stripes and buds in the centre. A light-green wash was only just suggested so as to show up the pale petals. Space is defined as the area around the object. The object is termed as a positive shape and the space around it is called the negative space, hence the term negative/positive painting. Once the background space was dry, a thicker, darker green was added for the stem and a darker green for the shadow under the flowers and along the stem.

The Gardener

Pickerelweed is a herbaceous perennial from marginal aquatic areas, forming clumps of erect lance-shaped leaves with two-lipped flowers in dense terminal spikes. It flowers in late summer to early autumn. The purple flowers have yellow markings, resembling an orchid. Once the plant begins to produce seeds the stems supporting the flower heads bend to submerge the fruits and seeds, which need stratification to be able to germinate. It can also reproduce asexually by branching rhizomes, which can be divided in spring. It can be invasive, so is best planted in baskets to prevent excessive spreading. It can tolerate fluctuating water levels.

LOBELIA
Lobelia cardinalis (bog sage)

The Painting

The foreground petals were painted and then a thicker mix of Winsor Red was added. The green background was washed in and, when dry, Rose Madder painted to simulate petals in shade. As the Rose Madder was painted over the green background, the green appeared darker and less brilliant.

The Gardener

Lobelia cardinalis is a beautiful plant with tall spikes of brilliant-scarlet-red flowers, which flower in mid to late summer. It grows on the margins of the pond or in shallow water. When the flowers are finished, the spikes can be trimmed to tidy, but the foliage should be left to die back naturally to encourage winter bud formation on basal rosettes close to the ground. In spring these send up one or more unbranched stems with smaller leaves that by midsummer develop the stunning flowers.

It is not long-lived, but will self-seed when happy. Little maintenance is required, but a mulch in late autumn or winter protects it from frost. The flowers drop seeds into the mulch after they mature. New plants can be propagated by bending a stem down into the mud and fastening it with a rock or stick. Clumps may be divided in early spring. The plant takes nutrients out of the water, which helps to keep the pond clean.

WATER HAWTHORN

Aponogeton distachyos (Cape pondweed, water hyacinth, water floret)

The Painting

This is a close view. The closer the plant is examined the more interesting it becomes. Even when painting unambitious subjects, concentration on the process of painting and controlling the paint is important. In this way, ordinary subjects can often be surprising, intriguing, mystifying or just beautiful.

I tried to capture a mixture of soft edges in the petals, and hard edges between the water and leaves. By varying these edges, interest is created by the gradual transition from one colour or tone to another.

The Gardener

Aponogeton distachyos (water hawthorn) is native to South Africa's Western Cape – hence the common name of Cape pondweed. It was introduced to ponds in warm, temperate to subtropical climates and has become naturalised in Australia and Europe. Plants have adapted to growing in ponds that dry out in the heat of summer, when they become dormant, coming back into growth when winter rains fill ponds, thriving in cool weather, and are hardy. The floating lance-shaped leaves provide an element of shade and water filtration in the pond. They make good companion plants to water lilies as they occupy the same area of water, but grow at different times of the year. Water hawthorn has small fragrant white flowers in forked racemes or panicles, with purple anthers, held just above the water surface from late winter to October. The flowers have a strong fragrance, resembling a wild hawthorn – hence the common name.

The stalks have medicinal properties. Their high juice content makes soothing treatments for burns and scrapes, and it takes the pain out of sunburn if the juice is applied every hour until redness fades. It is also considered a great delicacy. The flowering spike is pickled or used as spinach, and young shoots are used as an asparagus substitute. The flowers are used as a flavouring. It is widely cultivated in South Africa for its edible buds and flowers.

Propagation is by seed, best sown in a pot as soon as they are ripe and kept immersed in water. The seed can be stored in water and sown in spring, germinating after several months. When the seedlings are large enough to handle, they can be potted on into larger pots, covered with water and kept in the greenhouse for their first winter. They can be planted out in late spring or early summer. The submerged rhizomes can be divided during the growing season and planted immediately in their permanent positions.

WATER FORGET-ME-NOT
Myosotis scorpioides

The Painting

The little flowers were painted with a fine-pointed brush using Cerulean Blue, with thicker paint for darker areas in the petals. The centres were in Winsor Yellow, and these two colours were mixed together to create the green used for the stalks and leaves. These were darkened with thicker, drier paint in the shadows underneath the flowers, and the shadow side of the stalk.

The Gardener

The generic name *Myosotis* is Ancient Greek and means 'mouse ear', which the small, hairy, round-tipped leaves resemble. It is in the borage family. Water forget-me-not is known as scorpion grass due to the spiralling curve of the clusters of its buds and early blooms, resembling a coiled scorpion's tail. A legend about the origin of the name comes from a medieval knight and his lady-love, who were walking beside a river. The knight held a bouquet in his hands and, because of the weight of his armour, he fell into the water. He threw the bouquet at her, shouting, "Forget me not."

There is a Christian legend according to which Jesus Christ created forget-me-nots so that the generations to come would be able to see him and his Mother Mary, on whose lap he was sitting.

Unlike the garden forget-me-not, which is biennial, the water forget-me-not is a rhizomatous perennial with clusters of delicate sprays of sky-blue flowers with five petals and yellow centres and has white honey guides. The flowers are pink in bud, becoming blue when fully open. It blooms from mid spring to the first frosts. When the flowers fade, further flowering can be encouraged by cutting back. In warm climates, the plant may blacken during summer. Damaged growth can be pinched off and the plant will regrow in cooler weather. The leaves are alternate with pointed tips, 'mouse ears', and stems covered in closely pressed hairs.

It self-seeds and spreads by creeping rhizomes, without being invasive. It is best in the pond margins, in wet ground, and can survive being submerged in shallow water, often forming floating rafts. It is useful for covering the edges of the pond. Water forget-me-not can be grown in places too wet for other plants, but may seed into drier areas, where they need watering. It can also be propagated by division or stem cuttings.

Wildlife love this plant. Finches feed on the seeds, bees and butterflies are attracted by the nectar, and newts lay their eggs in the folded leaves.

WATER VIOLET
Hottonia palustris

The Painting

I considered that the white flowers would show better with a coloured background of washy blue-green. This meant a careful drawing of petals and buds, which remained white paper. A light violet-grey was painted delicately in shadows within the flowers. The flower centres were Winsor Yellow, which was used in the green mix for the stalks. I took time to be sure the composition was strong and carefully planned.

This is an ordinary subject, so I had to consider what would make it compelling and engaging. How can the ordinary be made extraordinary?

The Gardener

Despite its name, it is not a violet, but is in the primrose family. The water violet is a deciduous oxygenating perennial which forms spreading masses of light-green, deeply divided feathery foliage, held both below and above the water surface. The delicate flowers are white, mauve or pale lilac with a yellow centre, on spikes which emerge above the water in spring. The flowers are arranged in whorls around the stalk, opening at the same time, with more buds developing at the top of the stem.

It can survive summer droughts, but not permanent drainage.

It can be propagated by division or by seed. The flowers are hermaphrodite, having both male and female organs, and are pollinated by insects. The water violet provides shelter to all kinds of aquatic wildlife, including fish, larvae, dragonfly nymphs, tadpoles and water beetles.

FROGBIT
Hydrocharis morsus-ranae

The Painting

This was painted on cartridge paper in my sketchbook, and as the paper does not accept washes well, causing run-backs, unwanted water marks developed. Watercolour can dry quickly, but a good technique is to wash in colours while the paper is wet. When dry, darker tones can be added with a moistened brush. If hard edges do form, they can be softened with a damp brush or damp sponge, so long as the quality of the paper allows. In this case I overlaid the paint with coloured pencils. I used Ultramarine and dark violet over the painted water, May Green and Sap Green in the leaves, with a little light violet in the centre of the flowers. Because coloured pencils are translucent, they can create incredible colour quality and achieve dynamic value ranges.

Trial and error is an integral part of the process of creativity; defining and portraying nature's natural beauty is intriguing. It is the representational depiction which appeals to me, spending time developing the relationship between large masses, establishing a link from one passage to another. However, it is the shadows against the light that read as abstract. To be spontaneous, one needs to experiment and eventually understand techniques.

The Gardener

The generic name comes the Greek *hydro*, meaning water, and *charis*, meaning 'some sort of plant'. The specific name comes from the Latin *morsus*, meaning bite, and *rana*, meaning frog, referring to frogs biting at the leaves searching for caterpillars that make their protective envelopes from the plant. It was named by Linnaeus in 1753.

Frogbit is a small floating plant resembling a small water lily with three-petalled white flowers with a yellow centre. Each flower has nine to twelve stamens, the two outer whorls being fully fertile, and the inner whorls sterile or partly sterile. The male and female flowers are found on separate plants. The female flowers are borne singly, the male in clusters of three or four flowers. Seed production is low – instead it propagates by producing stolons, which form juvenile plants. In the autumn, the ends of the stolons produce buds that survive through the winter, break off the main plant, sink to the pond bottom and become dormant. In the spring they float to the surface and begin to grow into small floating rosettes. The floating leaves are kidney-shaped and grow in rosettes on the water surface, with the roots hanging down into the water, but not touching the bottom. It grows fast and spreads rapidly, and can be invasive.

Frogbit is an excellent surface cover for a wildlife pond as it prefers still shallow water, creating useful shelter for aquatic creatures, and is a food plant for a number of insects and water snails, waterbirds, rodents and fish.

MIMULUS
Mimulus guttatus (monkey flower or musk flower)

The Painting

Our eyes are attracted to contrast, essentially light against dark, hard edges and complementary colours. All three together give a strong focal point. Place too much of any of these in the less important areas, and competition is created, drawing attention away from the focal point. The closer you are to an object, the warmer and richer the colour will seem. Unlike a sunset, which is unique, the further away an object is, the weaker the colours appear.

With this in mind, I chose a blue-green next to the yellow flower, darkening around the hard edges of the petals.

Winsor Yellow was washed into the petal areas, and then darkened, in places, with Winsor Orange. A touch of very washy Ultramarine Violet darkened the interior of the main flower and Winsor Red was dotted into the centres of the flowers and lower lips. A blue-green was washed around the flowers and buds and, when dry, a thicker mix of green was added for stalks and buds, darkening with a drier, darker green.

The Gardener

Mimulus guttatus has cheerful yellow trumpet-shaped flowers with dark-red spots on the lower lips. It has leafy stems that grow upright or trail along the ground. It was introduced from North America and is widely established in marshes and by fresh water and in damp margins or shallow water of ponds. It forms a glorious floating carpet of flowers from early summer to mid autumn, but can be invasive. It can grow in full sun so long as the soil does not dry out; otherwise it is best in partial shade. It can become untidy in late summer. After flowering, it should be cut back, which promotes new growth. It can be divided in spring.

Mimulus is pollinated by bees and is a food source of the larvae of some moth species. It can regenerate from fragments of the plant and will self-seed, producing abundant amounts of vegetation. Self-seeding reduces flower quality and size, and pollen quality and quantity. If seed is collected, the seed heads need to dry on the plant, and then be removed. Plants are produced in only seven to eight weeks after sowing. Mimulus is a longer-day plant and responds to extra lighting. Flowering can be delayed if lighting is not supplied.

Mimulus is an astringent and a decoction of the leaves and stems has been used as a herbal steam bath for chest and back soreness. The crushed leaves have been used as a poultice, applied to wounds and burns. Raw or cooked leaves have a slightly bitter flavour, but can be used as a lettuce substitute.

There are several species having red, pink, purple and combinations of colours – for example, *M. cardinalis* (the scarlet monkey flower) is a branching perennial with sprays of bright-red snapdragon-like flowers. Some species produce copious amounts of aromatic compounds, giving them a musky odour, hence the common name of musk flower.

LILIES

DAY LILY
Hemerocallis liloasphodelus

Painting 1

Not every edge needs to be crisp; some can be muted, hard, textured, accentuated, straight, broken or even vanish. It is amazing how the eye fills in the rest. It is the start of the painting which is important. If this is correct, then adding the details will be easier. It is important to paint shapes of colours, not things. When painting brilliant, intense colours, such as lilies, it is best to lay them in first and paint around them with the darker coloured background. This keeps the brilliant colours clean and rich. The perfect background for hemerocallis is generally green. When combined with yellow, a component of green along with blue, the result is harmony.

The Gardener

Lilies are among the most beautiful, stately and fragrant of flowers. They are one of the oldest and most beautiful flowers on earth. They are believed to be a survival of the Ice Age. Greek *hemera* means day and *kallos* means beauty. The day lily is so called because each of their flowers lasts for one day; although fleeting, there is a succession of buds, which ensures a display for weeks.

Originating in Asia, day lilies were mentioned in Chinese literature as early as AD 656 as being used as food and in medicine. From early herbals, we know the plant had arrived in Europe by the mid sixteenth century. They are among the plants taken to America by European settlers and they escaped into the wild from domestic gardens. The original orange and yellow forms have been developed into a range of colours, from deep orange to creamy white, mahogany, deep-black-red to crimson flowers. There are over 400 listed by the RHS. Hemerocallis lilies are classified according to the shapes of their flowers and the way in which they are borne. There are two main groups – those which produce roots from the base and those which produce roots from the base of the bulb and later from the stem above the bulb. The basal-rooted species are best planted in open ground as they usually take a season to become established. The species most successful in pots are among the stem-rooted species, as they develop basal roots more readily than bulbs of the other kind. Tubs planted with several bulbs are very decorative. After planting they need little or no water until the roots are developed and shoots have begun to grow. Most flower six months after planting.

Day lilies normally open their flowers during the morning and each individual bloom fades by evening, though *Hemerocallis altissima* and spidery *H. citrina* are night-flowering, opening in the afternoon and closing by morning. The graceful flowers consist of five long petals, sometimes ruffled, in wide-open trumpet form, with yellow or red anthers at the centre.

Lilium 'Star Gazer', *lilium orientalis*, is a magnificent and fragrant lily, more fragrant, taller and blooming earlier than Asiatic lilies. They are true lilies, not day lilies, sending up a single unbranched flower stalk from the underground bulb. By contrast, day-lily flower stalks have no leaves and are multi-branched. Day lilies send up long leaves from a tuberous root system, not from a bulb. Lilies are suitable for a pot or they are good garden plants, and make good cut flowers. To prolong the flower's life, it is best to remove anthers from the stamens which protrude from the middle of the flower. Deadheading prevents the formation of seed pods, which would use energy that would otherwise go down to the bulb. After flowering, and when the foliage turns completely brown, they can be cut down to the ground. The bulbs can be divided in the autumn to make more plants.

The lily is regarded as deeply spiritual and philosophical. The lily family traditionally represents innocence and purity, with the white 'Star Gazer' lily characterising purity and often sympathy, with pink being a symbol of wealth and prosperity and a sign of aspiration. It is a hybrid lily, developed in the twentieth century by Leslie Woodriff, a lily breeder in California, to overcome the downward habit of other lilies. The new lily was called 'Star Gazer' because the blooms face towards the sky. Colours range from light pink to deep pink, and crimson with edges of white and dotted with prominent darker spots. Some people don't like the fragrance, reporting headaches, nausea, nasal congestion and breathing difficulties. Consequently, in the twenty-first century, a large commercial flower farm in California developed a pink lily similar to 'Star Gazer', but with no fragrance. It was discontinued due to lack of demand.

Hemerocallis are long-lived plants and will tolerate a wide range of soils, and once established make big clumps of narrow leaves and look magnificent planted en masse or among taller plants. They are hungry plants, so need plenty of home-made compost and leaf mould to retain moisture, with a feed of composted chicken manure to encourage growth and high-potash feed to ensure plenty of flowers. They like to grow with their roots in shade, but with their flowers in the sun, so are well suited to the back of a herbaceous border, throwing up a tall stem of narrow leaves before blooming and then disappearing.

In its natural state the lily is temperamental and demanding, but the new hybrids have a new vigour and ease of growth as well as blossoms of increased size. It is markedly less vulnerable to diseases. A choice of hybrids will provide lilies in flower from May to September. All need well-drained soil, cool roots and protection from strong winds and sun on their foliage. They require plenty of water during the growing season, deep cultivation and mulching in summer. Care is needed in handling the bulbs as their fleshy overlapping scales can be damaged and can suffer if left exposed to dry air for any length of time. Propagation can be by seed, offsets, bulbils and bulb scales. Each scale of the bulb will produce bulb-lcts along its broken edge. The scales are broken off from the bulb and placed upright in boxes of sandy soil and leaf mould, all but the tip of the scale being buried, and placed in the greenhouse. They can be potted on about four to eight weeks later. The bulbs will flower in one to three years. Many stem-rooted lilies will form aerial bulbils if the stem is severed below its roots and above the bulb, then potted and placed in a heated propagator and kept moist.

The lily beetle, *Crioceris lilii,* closely related to the asparagus beetle, is a bright-scarlet adult which has dirty-white, fleshy, short, humpbacked grubs, which can destroy the plant in summer and pupate in the earth beneath the plant. The best control is to squash them.

Painting 2

In this painting, the details were worked out first, bearing in mind that the details are just small shapes. My first approach is to look carefully at the subject and simplify, especially when there is a lot of detail. I take the key elements and enhance them using light and shade, shape and space, and colour. As the blooms of day lilies die at the end of the day, they shrivel and hang on the ends of the stems, so need to be removed – otherwise they could spoil the composition. I try not to spend too long on the painting, keeping it spontaneous, quick and loose and not too laboured. How many blooms to include is part of these decisions. A light drawing keeps the mind focused. Once the details, such as stamens and stalks as well as petals, are established and have dried, the darker background can be added. A blue-green was used as a complement to the yellows.

MADONNA LILY
Lilium candidum

The Painting

I've used broken colour in this painting. Broken colour refers to a method of building up an image with small strokes and dabs of pure colour which are not joined or blended together, but leave some of the toned underpainting showing through. The base colour could be a toned paper for pastel, a wash for watercolour, acrylic or oil painting. In this watercolour I've used various colours around the lilies, leaving the paper unpainted for the pure-white flowers. From a distance these splashes of colour appear to merge into one mass of colour which is more vibrant than a solid area of smoothly blended colour. This gives a luminous, shimmering effect. Using complementary colours has an even more pronounced effect. The orange stamens appear brighter against the violet used in the shadows, and the warm colour is enhanced by the surrounding cool colours. Primary colours seem more brilliant when they are in contrast with their complementary colours.

The Gardener

The Madonna lily has pure-white trumpet-shaped flowers with yellow pollen and has a wonderful fragrance. It is the flower of weddings and of funerals. Known until Tudor days simply as the lily, or the white lady, it was not called the Madonna lily until the late nineteenth century, and as the 'white lily' it came to share with the rose the honour of symbolising the Immaculate Conception. It also appears at the feast of the Visitation, 2 July, to commemorate the journey that Mary took to visit her cousin Elizabeth. In paintings of this event there is usually a vase of three white lilies standing at the Virgin's side. Cistercian monks adopted a single flower as an emblem of the Virgin in their churches. Dante Gabriel Rossetti's *Blessed Damozel* has three white lilies, and three symbolic lilies appear in the arms of the city of Winchester, as well as in those of the college.

To the Egyptians it was the emblem of fruitfulness. In ancient Greece it was the flower of Hera, the goddess of the moon. It was painted on the walls of the Cretan palace of Knossos, and found in Minoan and Assyrian art. In Rome it was the emblem of Juno and the pillars

225

of Solomon's temple were topped with sculptured lily forms. They were grown in monastery gardens both for the decoration of the church and for medicinal purposes.

The Madonna lily loves basking in the sun and heavy soil. It should be planted just below the surface and not be disturbed. The basal leaves appear in autumn and continue through the winter, from which the flower stems rise, often reaching two metres high.

LILIUM REGALE
(Chinese lily)

The Gardener

Lilium regale has clusters of fragrant white funnel-shaped flowers with yellow centres, and the petals are shaded rose-purple. There is also a pure-white variety, which has trumpet-shaped flowers with purple streaks outside and a golden throat and exquisite scent. It likes an open situation and prefers to have its roots in the shade, but it flowers in the sun or part shade, and is not too fussy about soil. Grown in groups it gradually increases the number of tall stems on which are borne as many as thirty large white funnel-shaped flowers with blushes of pink on the outside. 'Royal Gold' is a cool yellow and sweetly scented. They flower for a long time from midsummer. *L. regale* germinates in about three weeks and begins to flower in the second year. They are the most widely grown and are extremely hardy.

Lilium tigrinum (the tiger lily) has Turk's-cap flowers, bright-orange-red clusters of nodding brilliant flowers spotted with purple-black spots and prominent orange-brown anthers.

Asiatic hybrids have upright flowers, single or in clusters of flowers. Trumpet and Aurelian hybrids have large trumpet-shaped fragrant flowers. The white and yellow varieties grow in sun or partial shade, but the pink-flowered varieties must have shade or their colours fade. Oriental hybrids have large strikingly coloured flowers in crimson and pinks and are best in dappled shade. The most popular are the Asiatic hybrids with upward-facing scentless flowers in bright and pastel colours, some of which are pollen-free. Oriental hybrids have larger scented saucer-shaped flowers, 'Star Gazer' being the most popular. Pink, red and white blooms are often streaked with yellow. There are hybrids which are a mixture of Asiatic and white Easter lilies, combining large, bold flowers and fragrance.

Lilium martagon (the martagon or Turk's-cap lily) has rose-purple nodding flowers, but has an unpleasant smell. It has small dull-purple musky-scented flowers and will spread in quite dense shade. This lily thrives in shade, naturalising under trees or between shrubs in humus-rich soil.

Lilium speciosum has fragrant bowl-shaped white flowers, shaded and spotted with pink. Many lilies are fragrant. Oriental lilies have some of the finest scent. The large trumpet lilies have wonderful scent and the new hybrid lilies, which include the tall tree lilies, are easy to grow and have a strong scent. They should be planted deeply and left undisturbed. Lilies are increased by seed, bulbs, bulb-lets, scales and offsets. Whenever possible they should be increased by seed as there is less danger of transmitting disease, but lily hybrids do not come true to type and should be propagated vegetatively. When grown from seed they should be sown thinly in pans or boxes and placed in a cold frame or in outdoor beds. They should be pricked out as soon as they are large enough to handle and grown on until well established under glass. A mixture of peat, leaf soil and sandy loam is best. When well established, the young plants should be planted in a warm place outdoors, giving room between each plant. A deep, sloping, sheltered border suits them. The period of germination varies greatly. The seeds can take two years to germinate and five to six years to produce a flowering bulb. Some species germinate and form a small bulb underground, showing no sign of germination above ground until the second year, when the first true leaf appears.

L. giganteum is one of the most beautiful flowers. The bulbs are just under the surface and throw up the sharply pointed bottle-green tips, which expand into heart-shaped leaves, like arum foliage. It is remarkable for the rapidity and vigour of the four months' growth from bulb to giant flowering plant. The stem is a hollow fleshy tube and has large radiating roots, like those of a tree. Offsets can be carefully detached and replanted. They need good compost. The upper part of the flower stem bears gracefully drooping great white flowers, greenish when in bud, but changing to white when fully developed. Inside each petal is a purplish-red stripe. In the evening the almost overpowering scent pours out of the trumpets, but from a distance can seem delicate. The flowers last a day, but the plant remains beautiful since the handsome leaves remain into autumn and seed heads can be attractive.

L. formosanum, treated as a greenhouse annual, can be flowering in nine to twelve months from seed. Offsets can be slow. Bulb scales can produce bulb-lets along their broken edge. The scales are broken off from the bulb and placed upright in boxes of sandy soil or sand and leaf soil, all but the tip being buried, then stood in a frame or greenhouse and in about four to eight weeks the bulb-lets can be removed and grown on. Bulbils form in the axils of the upper leaves. These should be removed when ready to drop and planted immediately. Flowering bulbs will result in one to three years. They may also be increased by separating the clusters of roots into as many pieces as there are crowns, but this must be done carefully in autumn or spring. Most lily seedlings are frost-hardy, coming through the most severe winters undamaged, and thrive in sun or partial shade and in most soils although they do not like hot, dry areas. The species most suitable for pot cultivation are among the stem-rooting species, not only because the stem roots are easy, but they appear to develop a new set of basal roots more readily than do bulbs of the other kind. Tubs planted with several bulbs are very decorative. The infamous lily beetle, which I referred to before, can be a problem.

Lilium amabile has nodding bright-red-spotted black flowers. They are particularly hardy and thrive in light shade.

ALSTROEMARIA
(Peruvian lily or Inca lily)

Certain strong colours or combinations of colour cause different reactions and can influence the way of seeing colour. Some painters have a fairly consistent palette. Van Gogh preferred strong complementaries while Matisse favoured pink, purple and orange. It is an expression of personality. Colours can evoke mood. Blue can mean happiness; dark blue means success; red evokes love and passion; and yellow calls to mind sunshine.

Rich colour effects can be obtained by applying a wash of colour, allowing it to dry and then applying a second wash over the first so that the underlying colour shows through.

The simple trumpet resembles a cone, roughly elliptical when seen sideways, narrowing to a point. Winsor Lemon was painted over the whole petals and a darker, warmer yellow was used in the centres to give the illusion of depth. The stamens indicate the tubular nature of the flower, so I used dark tones to emphasise the areas between them. I used this same method when painting the raindrops, giving each drop a shadow. By using the complementary colour in the background, the yellow appears brighter.

Painting 1

When painting plants, I start by observing the growth pattern and the forms the leaves and blossoms take. Then I draw a simplified growth shape, noting the basic shape of the blossom and leaves before developing details like the main shapes of the petals and the individual differences. Lilies have petals which curl around and away from the stamens, giving the flower its characteristic appearance. The coloured speckles on the petals give a sense of the shape as they curve around. Lily buds are simple shapes as the petals hold together before opening, then they curve back with stamens protruding from the centre. When fully open the petals curl around the edges and press even further back from the stamens, giving their characteristic profile. It is helpful to have a darker background to show up the pale petals.

The Gardener

Alstroemerias are maned in honour of Baron Klas von Alstroemer, 1736–1796, friend of Linnaeus, who introduced seeds from South America. They are a symbol of devotion.

This is a genus of about fifty species, native to South America. These are versatile plants in a large range of colours, of yellow, pink, orange and white with multiple blooms per stem. Sizes are from tall plants to dwarf varieties. Old varieties, such as vivid-orange *Alstroemaria aurea* and yellow *A. lutea*, flower once in July and have a reputation for spreading. New varieties flower for a longer time. They are easy to grow, but their brittle tuberous roots don't move well once they are established, so they need a permanent site in free-draining soil in sun or shade. *L. longiflorum*, or the Easter lily, is half-hardy and has horizontal trumpet-shaped white flowers with golden anthers.

Painting 2

Relationships are everything in a painting. To paint well, one must look at the subject and the painting to make comparisons, compare values, the sizes and positions of shapes, the position of the light and colour harmony. Titian was the first person to explore this idea. Before him, it was popular to use 'local colour'. Everything was painted in a bright, pure colour, but Titian found it was more important to harmonise colours, with one influencing all the others and the colours working together. White lilies portray innocence and purity, as in the medieval paintings of the Virgin Mary.

Working outdoors can create a feeling of pleasure, and this pervades the painting. To capture the flower realistically, I prefer to paint from life and preferably in the garden. When painting from life, it is important not to work for too long as the quality and direction of the light changes. The colour of the light can affect the shadow colours. Contre-jour has the effect of throwing the intricate shapes of the shadows forward, while side lighting gives distinct light and dark, throwing shadows sideways. Front light can eliminate all shadows from the frontal view, but can give interesting back shadows. I try to look at the subject from various viewpoints, in different light, and, to help the design, I add or subtract some elements if needed. Changing or dappled light can be confusing, but it is not necessary to include everything. I look for shapes and patterns to help the design, and in this painting used complementary colours in the shadows to give impact as well as delineating the shapes of the flower.

It was important to distinguish between the white petals, so a washy light blue was used to shadow the inner petals and around the outside of all the blooms. The directions of the stamens help to explain the positions of the flowers, and their orange tips are ideal as a complement to the blues in the painting.

Painting 3

Watercolour is a subtle, complex and demanding medium and quite difficult to master, but fantastic if done properly. A watercolour painting is not easily changed and light colours cannot be painted over dark colours, and the luminosity is lost if too many washes are overlaid. This means that a lot of preplanning is required before painting, and an awareness of the consequences of every brushstroke. There are no short cuts in watercolour painting, and success can only come through dedication and sound observation from nature.

The nearest flower faced slightly to one side while the second faced upwards, both in sharp focus and contrasting with the bluer background. Keen observation was needed to understand the curling petals, anthers and stamens. Blue and yellow mixed together make green, but in this picture I wanted the blue to enhance the yellow. When looking at the background, we see predominantly blue, and there is also reflected a good deal of green, and in the shadows some violet, which is a mix of blue and red. Similarly the yellow reflects red in the shadows. Ultramarine Blue contains red so is not a good colour for mixing green, unless a subdued green is required. A cooler blue, such as Phthalocyanine Blue, is preferable because it does reflect a large proportion of green light in addition to predominantly reflecting blue light. The yellow used was a cool Lemon Yellow, used on the lighter outer petals, while a warmer yellow, with more red in it, was used for the inner sections. Mixing the cool yellow with the cool blue gives a bright cool green. If a warm and a cool of each of these colours is used then a medium green is achieved.

All surfaces, even those that are not highly reflective, will pick up some influences from the prevailing light and surrounding colours. Sometimes these are mere hints of colour, but all such accents serve to modify the appearance of local colours. For example, white petals may reflect traces of yellows or greens in the white, and blue or purple tinges in the shadows, and a hint of warmth where the outer edges of the petals catch the sunlight. This can be due to the texture and colour of the flower itself and to its surroundings. Close attention to detail is needed.

SUMMER

CLEMATIS
Clematis (traveller's joy, referred to as 'desire')

Painting 1

The inspiration to paint these flowers came from the beautiful flower and also from the light striking the petals. The opening buds gave a sense of promise and added to the magic. A painting should reflect an emotional reaction to the subject, the lighting, colours and shapes. Colour is a powerful tool for expression, but it is good practice to use a fairly limited palette. It is not necessary to have numerous tubes of different colours. A good basic few are more than enough to create interesting subtle colours. *Clematis* 'Blue Angel' is a fabulous purple-blue, so I used Ultramarine Violet and French Ultramarine Blue, and Winsor Lemon for the stamens.

Painting 2

'Diana's Delight' is a warm blue with pale centres. The sunlit highlights on the petals were almost white. In this oil painting, the aim was to capture the feel of light on the petals, and there is no hint of dark paint in the highlights. The lighter stamens were added last. The relationships between the different parts of the painting are very important. In general, the foreground is like the door to the composition, so it should have the biggest value and colour-temperature contrast and the highest intensities, with the middle distance more subtle. The warm yellow-greens of the leaves come forward while cool blue-greens recede.

The illusion of a third dimension on a two-dimensional surface is achieved with tone. This means judging how light or dark a tone appears relative to the tone beside it. By squinting the eyes, the detail and colour are simplified into shapes of tone.

231

Artists such as Rembrandt and Turner created paintings with both great depth and luminosity. They appreciated that thick opaque paint reflects light, and an impasto (thick paint) can create the illusion of light. This means reserving the impasto for the brightest areas and creating a contrast between thick and thin areas. So I avoid thick areas of dark paint in shadows, as thick paint appears brighter as it gets thicker. In oil painting transparent colours are best reserved for glazing.

Painting 3

'Pink Champagne' has deep-rose petals and yellow stamens. It looked especially stunning against the twining green foliage. Winsor Lemon was used to paint the stamens, and mixed with Ultramarine Blue for the foliage. The same blue created the shadows on flowers, stems and leaves, and a little orange was added in places to shade the stamens.

The Gardener

There are few plants that produce flowers every month of the year, but the clematis family does. The flowers are in fact large sepals and have been bred to give bigger blooms, which can be as large as dinner plates, some with single or semi-double flowers, and some have a central ruff of showy petals and stamens. It is a very versatile plant in that it will climb a trellis or weave through other plants, through fencing and up trees. There are about 200 species, many of which come from China. The European native is old man's beard (*C. vitalba*), whose silvery seed heads grow in hedgerows. The most well-known garden clematises are the large-flowered summer varieties – such as 'Nelly Moser', with mauve-pink flowers and wide carmine stripes which in full sun can fade, but the sepals last a long time. The fading flowers create a lovely mix of newly opened, brighter-striped flowers alongside the paler blooms. Some of my favourites are 'The President', deep violet; 'Ville de Lyon', which is bright carmine red; and 'Crystal Fountain' or 'Fairy blue', which has large double flowers in May from the previous year's growth, and then again in August from the current year's growth, though these tend to be slightly smaller. The petals are violet-blue with the centre a mass of narrow sepals, which begin white, changing colour to a lighter shade of the main sepal colour with narrow light-green sepals in the centre. It is sterile and needs a high-potash feed to produce the best flowers. 'Blue Angel' has ruffled petals, violet blue along the edges and lighter towards the centre. It has bright-yellow stamens and is a prolific bloomer. But there are many other kinds of clematis, including non-climbing herbaceous forms for the border.

Of the climbers, one of the first to flower is *C. armandii*, with glossy evergreen leaves and clusters of small white strongly scented flowers. It flowers in April and needs plenty of space, though no pruning is necessary. It is best planted in a sheltered position in well-drained soil, with its roots in shade and where the top growth can be in the sun. It is slightly tender.

C. Montana, which fills the air with perfume from its masses of pink or white flowers, is one of the most vigorous of all climbers, but can be kept in check by shortening side growths after flowering. In its native Himalayan mountains it will grow twelve metres through trees. It is ideal for a north-facing wall.

C. alpina and *C. macropetala* both have little nodding bell-shaped pale-lavender-blue or soft-mauve-pink downward-facing flowers in late spring and early summer. The flowers are followed by fluffy seed heads. *C. macropetala* 'Rosy O'Grady' is very hardy and vigorous, double-flowered with dainty mauve-pink and cream flowers. *C. alpina* 'Frances Rivis' is lavender blue and very hardy. *C. viticella* has medium-sized deep-purple-blue or red blossoms, which flower well in shade in summer. *C.* 'Alba Luxurians' grows on the walls of the white garden at Sissinghurst Garden in Kent, England, while 'Royal Velours' is port red and 'Blue Angel' is the pale violet blue. Also in summer is *C. flammula*, which comes from the Mediterranean and North Africa, a semi-evergreen vigorous climber with very fragrant, starry white flowers, good for poor, dry soils; and *C. terniflora* comes from China. Both need full sun and warmth, so a south-facing wall, shelter and free-draining soil is ideal. *C. orientalis* has nodding bell-shaped orange-yellow fragrant flowers followed by showy, silky seed heads in autumn. In autumn *C. tangutica* is similar with tiny butter-yellow lantern-shaped flowers followed by fluffy seed heads. Both have fern-like deciduous foliage. 'Bill Mackenzie' has single bell-shaped petals like lemon rind, flowering in July to October. In December or very early spring, the white petals of *C. cirrhosa* bloom. *C. cirrhosa* var. *balearica* has ferny evergreen foliage and pale-lemon/cream bell-like flowers speckled maroon inside. It needs sun and a sheltered site. *C. cirrhosa* 'Freckles' has small flowers heavily spotted red inside. It is frost-hardy, but needs shelter from cold winds. *C. florida* var. *sieboldiana* has large white flowers with a central double ruff of dark-purple petals. *C.* 'Hagley Hybrid' is a large-flowered pale-mauve-pink clematis with contrasting red anthers and is good for shade. *C. integrifolia* is a non-climbing, scrambling herbaceous clematis with small purple-blue, white or rose-pink flowers with twisted sepals. *C.* 'Niobe' has dark buds which open to ruby-red flowers with a central ruff of golden stamens. The flower colour is best when grown in shade. *C. recta* is a scrambling herbaceous clematis with bronze-tinted foliage and white heavily scented starry flowers. *C. repens* is evergreen with bell-shaped, drooping, scented, waxy yellow flowers with fleshy petals. This clematis is non-clinging. *C. texensis* 'Etoile Rose' has small trumpet-shaped deep-rose flowers with pale edges and upswept sepals. This is a good clematis for a container. It can be cut down in spring to flower later in the summer on new-season growth.

By growing clematis in pots, they can be moved to places where wanted, such as patios, and after flowering moved back again to make room for other flowering plants in pots. The best pots for clematis are terracotta or wooden containers so as to insulate the roots. They should be stood on stones to ensure good drainage, and it is best to provide shade by grouping other pots around them. Bamboo canes pushed around the pot rim and tied together with twine at the top, to form a 'wigwam', will give climbing supports. They will need watering and feeding. By adding fresh compost and trimming congested roots each year they can grow in the same pots for years.

C. alpina 'Constance' is shade-tolerant and is a vigorous climber with masses of deep-pink nodding flowers. *C. cartmanii* 'Avalanche' has large showy non-scented green-centred flowers with deeply cut leaves. As their roots are not so vigorous they can be grown in a container or a sheltered border.

C. koreana has pointed downward-facing early flowers in blue, rose or white. 'Rebecca' has dramatic scarlet flowers, which are offset by creamy-yellow anthers. 'Diana's Delight' is an unusual, free-flowering blue variety with light and dark tones and creamy-yellow anthers and sepals, which become paler towards the centre. 'Picardy' is a long-lasting variety, which has an abundance of dusky deep-purplish-red flowers with a brighter-red bar on the sepals and reddish-brown anthers.

Clematises like good well-cultivated and manured soil and grow best with their roots shaded but their stems in the sun, which can be done by planting them behind a low-growing shrub or leafy herbaceous plant. The less vigorous can be allowed to scramble through rambling roses or other plants trained on wires or a trellis. The vigorous kinds may be allowed to grow round trees, climb over sheds or cover walls and fences. Clematises flower at the ends of the stems, so to avoid having great lengths of growth, and to induce flowering lower down, it is best to prune after flowering, or the stems can be pegged down into the soil in winter to form new roots instead of pruning. Pruning can be confusing, but generally those which flower on the current year's growth, from June onwards, should be hard-pruned; but I don't prune those which flower on the previous year's growth, before June.

A large flowering clematis has more impact when allowed to scramble through the branches and foliage of other plants. The large blue and purple flowers enhance the charm of rambling and climbing roses, both in bud and in flower. The different shapes and textures are made more fascinating by the play of light and cast shadow.

Plants on walls require more discipline and care than those almost anywhere else. There is no alternative to providing proper anchorage. The trellis will become invisible behind the stems and foliage of the plants until pruning, which depends on the type.

Propagation can be by seeds and layering. Cuttings of half-ripe wood, internodal rather than the normal nodal cutting, taken in July or August and put into a warm sand frame, root fairly well.

By June, plants that originate closer to the equator, such as dahlias, agapanthus and cosmos start to flower.

AGAPANTHUS
Liliaceae (African lily or lily of the Nile)

The Painting

The agapanthus has a complicated head with many stems, which need careful observation. The white flowers are left as unpainted paper with darks behind them. Some of the colours in the background were mixed together and watered down and used as shadows on the flowers. Most shadows have a definite and quite surprising amount of colour in them. In general shadows are cooler in colour than the illuminated parts of the same subject, often containing blue, green or violet.

One of the ways to improve painting is to develop drawing skills. Good drawing is the foundation on which to build the painting, and the only way to improve is to practise constantly. It is important to analyse the drawing and develop a strongly critical approach.

234

The Gardener

The Greek *agape* means unconditional love, and *anthus* means flower.

Big, bold and beautiful, agapanthus can be a major feature in the garden. *Agapanthus* is a small genus of two main groups: the *praecox* and the *campanulatus*. A *praecox,* formally known as African or *umbellatus,* has thick fleshy roots and big, arching, strap-like leaves with substantial heads of large funnel-shaped flowers borne on tall erect stems in summer, and they are evergreen unless subjected to severe cold. They flower best when pot-bound, and in Europe need winter protection.

A. campanulatus needs no cosseting and makes a reliable garden plant. These agapanthuses come from the mountains of South Africa, which has cold winters, plenty of sunshine, copious moisture though good drainage, and acidic soils. In the open ground it is more difficult to restrict the roots, but competition from other plants should encourage flowering. Colours range from pale-blue to purple and white trumpet flowers in flat loose clusters borne on tall and sturdy stems above narrow strap-shaped deciduous leaves, which are shed in winter. They also do well when crowded in pots and containers.

A. 'Headbourne Hybrids' are hardier and can be grown in the open ground in mild areas, but need winter protection over the fleshy roots. The spheres of flowers are in colours of pale blue to deepest violet blue. Named hybrids, such as 'Bressingham White' have pure-white flowers. *A.* 'Charlotte' is a late-flowering agapanthus with relatively short, sturdy stems with deep-purple veins in the centre of the petals. Being low-growing it is good for the front of the border. 'Snowball' produces pure-white flowers later in the season. 'Baby Pete' is a miniature, thirty-five centimetres high. 'Regal Beauty' is dark blue, 'Silver Moon' has variegated leaves and 'Queen Mum' is bicolour with large white flowers with blue centres.

Although agapanthuses originate from South Africa, they look equally at home among alliums, foxgloves, lavender and hardy geraniums. They are synonymous with growing in pots as they respond well to having their roots restricted. In containers they can thrive. Lovers of sun, they enjoy being baked and grow well in dry conditions, but need water at least a couple of times a week through the summer if grown in pots. Where watering is not practicable, in dry spells in the open, the plants benefit by having flat stones placed around them to keep the moisture in the soil. Once a week, a high-potash liquid feed will promote flower development. In winter they should be kept as dry as possible. Sharp drainage is essential and any accumulation of water round their roots is apt to be fatal. They are not troubled by slugs and snails or vine weevil and are drought-tolerant. They are also very architectural as they can provide height to a border.

Very young plants, grown from seed, may take a year to become established before they flower, but I have had plants flower in the first year. The different species hybridise very freely with each other and therefore seeds can vary. This characteristic has caused confusion in the past and practically all plants now cultivated in gardens are of hybrid origin. Some differ in hardiness, flower colour and the character of the leaf. If seed is not required, the old flower stems can be cut back so as to prevent the plants wasting their energy by producing unwanted seeds. They also increase rapidly by offsets, and the parent plant can be divided in early spring to any extent desired.

ICE PLANT
Delosperma (former *Mesembryanthemum*) (trailing ice plant, pink carpet)

The Painting

Each painting is a learning opportunity, bringing more knowledge and more experience. Skills are improved with a good work ethic and an insatiable appetite for wanting to know more. The most important aspect of painting from life is observing the subtle colour changes. For a complicated accent colour to have the necessary impact, the painting should be from a group of adjacent colours in a small band of the colour wheel which is where the complementary colours are more vibrant.

Painting is a vehicle for self-expression, and flowers are just one of the many subjects which inspire and excite. The importance of skills and technique cannot be underestimated, and with experience the artist can express emotions and some deeper meanings. The brushstrokes can be delicate and transparent or bold and strident, which, twinned with control of colour and values, can determine the mood in the painting. Delosperma have glorious vibrant cerise-pink flowers offset by the cool greens of the foliage.

The Gardener

The earliest species known flowered at midday, hence the name mesembrianthemum – *mesembria* meaning midday – but when night-flowering species were discovered the name was changed to mesembryanthemum, with a 'y': a change of meaning without change of sound. *Mesos* means middle, *embryon* means fruit and *anthemon* means flower, the name no longer coming from *mesembria* (midday).

Delosperma is called ice plant because the leaves shimmer as if covered with frost or ice crystals. Delospermas are succulent perennials mainly from South Africa, preferring full sun, and thrive in dry, hot environments; they do not do well in damp or wet soil. They do best when the stems grow over the top of gravel, which keeps their roots moist and their leaves and stems dry. In autumn they need to shrink down and harden off for the cold winter ahead. They do not need fertiliser in the growing season as this encourages growth in the autumn and keeps them plump with water in their leaves, which means they could freeze and then die.

Propagation can be by division, cuttings or seeds. It is best to divide plants in spring. Cuttings can be taken in spring, summer or autumn, taken from stems with no flowers. The bottom leaves should be stripped off and the cutting inserted into similar soil to that in which the parent plant grew. They establish very quickly. Seeds should be scattered on the surface of the soil and, as they need light to germinate, should not be covered.

Delosperma cooperi is the most common variety. The daisy-like flowers are dazzlingly bright orange, apricot, pink, vermilion and carmine, often with contrasting zones, blooming from July – and I have had flowers in November. *D. brunnthaleri* has lovely yellow flowers. *D. floribundum* has pink flowers with a white centre. *D. herbeau* is an exceptionally beautiful white-flowered type. *D. nubiginum* has large pink flowers which fade to apricot. They need some afternoon shade to show off the pastel-coloured flowers. *D.* 'Alan's Apricot' is a new hybrid which is long-blooming and is cold-hardy. *D. dyeri* 'Red Mountain Flame' has scarlet-orange flowers in spring and has excellent heat-tolerance, so is good in hot, dry places. *D. ashtonii* 'Blut' has dark-magenta flowers with leaves which turn a plum colour in winter. *D.* 'Lavender Ice' has bright-green foliage and brilliant-pink flowers. It needs cooler summers, and water in summer heat. *D.* 'Fire Spinner' has a combination of purple and orange flowers in spring. It needs to be chilled in winter to flower.

Delosperma has been cultivated and hybridised so that there are new cultivars with single, semi-double and double flowers. They are very attractive to bees and so easily cross-pollinated, creating more hybrids. It has succulent leaves and is useful for covering rocks and banks. The spreading plants are ideal for edgings, but they demand full sun. They germinate, flower and set seed in a short time and are said to be short-lived and tender, but mine are several years old and grow among rocks, which must give some winter protection, and have self-seeded around the pond, obviously happy with the combination of sunshine, rock protection and the moisture from the pond edge.

If hard-pruned after flowering they may flower again in the autumn, but can look very attractive in the winter with their evergreen foliage. Delaspermas are beautiful and easily managed.

AUBRETIA
Aubretia (purple rock cress, rainbow rock cress, lilac bush)

Painting 1
Types of plants are identified by the shape of leaves, flowers and stature. When creating a painting it is easy to become sidetracked by all the confusing detail. It is important to concentrate on the main shapes and relate those shapes to those around it, analysing in depth. Pictorial interest in the visible world begins with an active mind assembling all the relative material with the application of technique, and with this information and accumulated experience comes understanding and the ability to portray the image required. When viewed close to, the plant appears quite open, but even so it needs to be examined so as to understand its character. This study is an enjoyable experience, a learning curve and almost a spiritual experience. The flowers are a beautiful shape and the leaves and stalks are delicate as they gracefully twist and turn.

Often a sketch is just a quick impression of an interesting subject, and in the process the mind is free to make a searching study of the detail. Sketches are invaluable as inspiration as well as reference. It is good practice to try new ways to portray the subject without the pressure to achieve a good finished painting. I feel that the drawing experience is more important than style or technique.

Painting 2

The simple study was made on hot-pressed paper, which gives a smooth finish. The flowers were painted in watercolour with Quinacridone Magenta, and the yellow centres in Winsor Lemon, and the leaves plainly painted in light green and then darkened in shadowed areas to give definition.

The Gardener

The aubretia plant was named in honour of Claude Aubriet, 1668–1743, the famous French botanical artist.

Aubretia is a genus of about a dozen species of evergreen trailing plants, natives of mountainous regions from Sicily to Iran. In the spring the flowers are usually a vibrant violet, lavender, pink, crimson or purple. It is related to *Alyssum* and *Arabis*. Aubretias have attractive leaves which are ovate or long. They make excellent and showy rock plants and will thrive in any deep rich loam and do well in a rockery or as edgings to sunny borders, banks and dry walls – anywhere except under the shade of trees. *Aubretia* is the spelling of the generic name, and has also become the common name. Aubretias are best cut back immediately after flowering, which encourages new shoots to grow from the base, or, alternatively, the long slender branches may be layered at any time after flowering. If covered with a mixture of sand and leaf soil they will root freely and may then be separated and planted for spring flowering. To propagate new plants the old plants may be divided after flowering. Cuttings struck, or seeds sown in April, generally make fine, dense cushion-like growths and can be transplanted when the plants are large enough.

LOBELIA

Rapuntium inflatum (pukeweed, Indian tobacco, gagroot, asthma weed, vomitweed, bladderpod, cardinal flower)

The Painting

The complexity of these tiny flowers meant keen observation and exact painting. The flower shapes were quite simple and came alive when shadows were added to the petals. Colours used were Ultramarine Violet, Quinacridone Magenta and dilute Cobalt Blue for the shadows on the white flowers. The leaves in the background were painted with a pale green and then the green was darkened with violet for the darks on the sides of the leaves. More violet was added for the darks behind the leaves.

The Gardener

The genus *Lobelia* was named after Matthias de Lobel, 1538–1616, a celebrated Flemish botanist, author, and physician to James I of England. Lobelias are native to the USA and Canada. In the sixteenth century the early settlers transplanted plants into their gardens and sent lobelias back to gardeners in France and England for their flower borders.

Mag loved the dwarf forms as bedding plants, with their blue and rich-crimson flowers being freely produced over a long period. She used them in hanging baskets and pots, where they produce masses of small tubular flowers in white, light blue, purple-blue and wine red.

Lobelia seed can be sown in March. The seed is very small and should be sown thinly, covered lightly and placed in a propagator. Seedlings should be pricked out and kept under glass until ready to plant out. The tall varieties can be raised from seed or cuttings of young shoots taken when overwintering plants, and in spring division can be effective.

The half-hardy perennial *L. erinus* is taller, and should be grown in deep, rich soil, in which it will grow much more vigorously than in poor, shallow soils. They need plenty of water and must be staked as a precaution against damage by wind. When frost cuts them down the roots should be lifted and stored in a cool frame for the winter, or they may be covered with ashes to a good depth and allowed to remain outside, but the former method is better so that the roots do not become too dry. They can be cut back in winter and stored in a cool frame until spring. Propagation is by seed, cuttings or division of plants, but seeds rarely come true to parental characters.

Some lobelias are annuals, but several more are herbaceous plants. The larger border perennial lobelias outshine other reds in the herbaceous border. Their vivid colours create a zing in the garden. All grow from rosettes, with the flowers opening all around the statuesque and mature clumps. The perennial lobelias have distinct tubular-lipped flowers and, once flowering has finished, it is best to cut off the flower spikes at the base so that plants put energy into building a strong root system and large basal rosettes, to provide a much more mature plant for the following year. Failure to do so could mean the plant produces seed, weakens and dies over the winter. It also comes in shades of blue and purple.

L. cardinalis is short-lived and not reliably hardy, but has brilliant-scarlet flowers. *L. fulgens* also has tall slender spikes of brilliant-scarlet flowers. However, *L. hybrida* is generally hardy, tall with reddish to coppery-tinted leaves. *L. vedrariensis* has dark-green leaves and spikes of purple trumpet-shaped flowers.

Moderately hardy lobelias need protection in winter. They can be propagated by seed in autumn, and this will produce secure stronger plants for the following year. Cuttings of young shoots taken from the old plants also root freely in spring, and division may also be carried out.

YARROW
Achillea (arrowroot, bloodwort, milfoil, nosebleed, snake's grass, devil's nettle, woundwort, sneezewort)

The Painting
These elegant, statuesque plants were sketched lightly in pencil so as to establish where the flower heads would be. These were painted using warm and cool yellows using a stiff brush. The stalks and leaves were painted in light green and afterwards the background was washed in. When this was dry the dark greens were added. I didn't worry about the water marks in the background as I felt the flower heads were most important.

The Gardener
Achillea is in the aster family with unusual fern-like foliage, which is pale to medium green. All parts of the plant exude a strong, sweet scent, similar to that of the chrysanthemums. Achillea is a creeping perennial with erect, downy, furrowed stems with flat-headed panicles of numerous ray and disc flowers. Its flowers are visited by a great number of insects, including ladybirds and hoverflies. Several birds, including the common starling, use yarrow to line their nests. It is believed that this deters insects. The dark-blue essential oil kills the larvae of the mosquito. It repels some pest insects and attracts beneficial insects. Predatory wasps drink the nectar and then use the insect pests as food for their larvae.

There are many types of achillea – some dwarf plants for the rock garden, some larger plants for herbaceous borders and beds. The larger varieties come in three main groups in regards to flower character. 'Gold Plate' has flat heads of yellow flowers on tall stems. 'Coronation Gold' is smaller. Red cultivars include 'Paprika', 'Red Beauty', 'Red Velvet', 'Saucy Seduction', 'Strawberry Seduction' and 'Cerise Queen', which has flat heads of carmine flowers. Pink cultivars are 'Island Pink', 'Kelway', and 'Lansdorferglut'. 'The Pearl', 'Calistoga', 'Sonoma Coast' and 'Perry's White' have sprays of little double white pompom flowers. *A. filipendulina* has a flat, wide head of compact clusters of lemon-yellow or pink flowers. The foliage is fern-like, aromatic grey-green. The perennial yarrows are very hardy and easily pleased. The grey-foliaged varieties like a soil that is well drained and sunny, whereas other forms will grow anywhere, tolerating dry or damp soil.

From Anglo-Saxon times it was held in high esteem as a medicinal plant, used to staunch wounds and ward off illness and bad luck. It was said to cause nosebleeds if a leaf was put into the nostril – hence it was known as nosebleed in some areas. The leaves and flowers have a bitter, astringent and pungent taste, hence the name old man's pepper. It is thought that the name achillea arose as Achilles used the herb to treat wounds of his soldiers, producing another name, herbal militaris. The name yarrow derives from the Anglo-Saxon name for the plant, *gearwe*. In America yarrow was used to cure toothache and earache and for other pain relief and to aid in restful sleep. In New Mexico and Southern Colorado it is called plumajillo – Spanish for little feather, from the leaf shape and texture. Other names are devil's nettle, sanguinary, soldier's woundwort, thousand-leaf, thousand seal, Goraldo and milfoil.

In the Middle Ages, yarrow was part of a herbal mixture known as 'gruit', used in flavouring beer prior to the use of hops. The flowers and leaves are used in making some liquors and bitters.

Achillea can spread by seed or creeping stems, known as stolons. For propagation, seeds require light for germination, and warmth of 18–24°C. Achillea has a relatively short life, but may be divided in spring. It can be invasive.

TOBACCO PLANT
Solanaceae, *Nicotiana tabacum* (sweet-scented or jasmine tobacco plant)

Painting 1

The dark background was used to show up the white flowers and stems of the nicotiana. Dilute blue was used to give shape and shadow to the petals, with Quinacridone Magenta in the flowers on the right and Quinacridone Violet for the shadows. These colours were mixed into the green for the darker areas behind the flowers and the shadowed areas on the stalks.

Painting 2

The flowers are white unpainted paper. The dark green behind them helps to promote their brightness. The various leaves surrounding the nicotiana are a complex mix of shapes, which makes the painting interesting. Here again the dark greens help to explain the shapes and pulls them forward. The background was kept simple with a wash of green and blue merged together. In the foreground the path is kept warm by using warm yellow and a touch of red. This red is echoed in the red nasturtium and the red markings on the leaves. Dots of subdued red are in the greens along the path, which was built up with different greens using only the point of the brush.

The Gardener

Tobacco was first introduced into Europe from America in the 1560s, when seeds were sent by Jean Nicot, a French consul in Portugal to Catherine de Medici, and in 1586 the practice of smoking the huge leaves began. Jean Nicot is commemorated in the generic name. It is generally believed that Sir Walter Raleigh and his seamen and returning settlers from Virginia introduced the smoking of tobacco into England.

Nicotiana is a genus of about forty-five species, one of which is *N. tabacum*, the common tobacco. The garden or ornamental nicotiana is a relative of the tobacco plant and is sweet-scented, most notably in the evening. They have long-tubed starry flowers in yellow, white, pink, scarlet to mauve or lime green, carried well above the foliage, and some varieties open in the evening with a wonderful fragrance, especially at dusk and during the night, when they attract nocturnal moths, which ensure fertilisation. Modern species flower during the daylight hours rather than, as previously, in the evening. They have a long flowering period in colours of white. There are dwarf varieties and hybrids which bear flowers which open in the daytime and are good for pots and containers. The fruit capsules split, to cast out numerous tiny seeds. They grow best in deep, rich, moist soil in full sun, though if in shade the flowers open all day rather than in the evening. They should be sown in February in gentle heat and the young plants pricked out when large enough, into boxes and planted out in spring – ideally near paths or seating areas, where their fragrance can be appreciated. If planted near the house on warm summer nights, the delightful perfume of these old-fashioned plants can waft through open windows. Nicotiana is closely related to the petunia.

MONARDA
(bee balm, wild bergamot, Oswego tea, horsemint, sweet bergamot and bergamot)

The Painting
An extraordinary abstract-looking flower head, the spikes and protrusions making for an unusual design. The reds and pinks were made even more dramatic with the addition of green in the background.

The spontaneity of a sketch often holds a vivacity which is not easy to recreate in the studio. Working in the studio there is more time for careful planning, for using the imagination and for reflection, but the best method is to use the sketch made outdoors as a base for a painting.

Painting is about understanding and communicating the best response to a subject. I chose not to change my interpretation of the plant as it was so stunning. Whether painted in a conventional or experimental way, this subject was an adventure.

The Gardener
Monarda is named in honour of Nicolas Monardes, 1493–1588, physician and botanist of Seville, who wrote in 1571 a book on American products, afterwards translated into English as *Joyful News out of the New Found World*.

243

Close up, the flower head looks abstract, almost alien, unlike a plant. Monardas are easily grown in ordinary soil, provided it is not too dry as they need moisture and plenty of light. They are readily increased by division in autumn or, better, in warmer weather in spring. Named varieties are *Monarda didyma* and *M. fistulosa*, which can only be increased true to type by division. Seed is usually formed freely. They are best planted en masse rather than in small clumps. They are hardy and perennial. *M. didyma*, or Oswego tea or bee balm, has bright-scarlet solitary or twin terminal whorls with bracts tinged red from June to September. *M. fistulosa,* wild bergamot, has bracts tinged purple. *M. purpurea* has deep-purplish crimson, *M. media* is deep purple and *M. rubra* is crimson. *M. Violacea superba* is deep violet-purple and succeeds better in drier situations.

JASMINE
Jasminum officinale (poet's jasmine, hardy jasmine, white jasmine, jessamine)

Painting 1
White is the most assertive colour among flowers. One of the best ways to achieve drama is to have the shapes of similar value, linking them together to form patterns that move the eye through the composition. High contrast can give a painting strength. Shadows provide contrasting dark next to sunlit areas. As watercolour dries lighter than when wet, so washes should be full strength to make sure they will not become anaemic when dry. Phthalo Blue and Winsor Green stay transparent and dark, which I prefer to opaque colours, and were used in background leaves.

Painting 2
A close-up view revealed the delicate nature of the flowers. Each flower appeared to be a different shape as they turned and caught the light in a differing manner. I kept the colours limited and simple using only green, tempered by added yellow or blue where needed and hints of colour in the shade on the flowers.

244

The Gardener

Jasmine is one of the sweetest and most delicious-scented flowers, far more heavily perfumed when planted in a warm place, such as against the south-facing wall of a house. It is the ultimate plant for a summer's evening in the garden, when the flowers exude their intoxicating fragrance for which jasmine is famous. The white, starry jasmine flowers on the young wood, and so it must be pruned in the autumn after flowering; otherwise the whole growth will become a tangled mass. It is, however, a delight trained over an arbour or sitting area, where it makes a scented place to sit. It was used in making bridal headdresses combined with orange blossom and was said to assure the bride of constancy and love. According to legend, jasmine was introduced by the Duke of Tuscany, who jealously guarded it as a treasure, wishing to preserve it solely for his own plant collection, but the wonderful fragrance tempted the gardener to take a sprig for his sweetheart on her birthday. The sweetheart planted the spray, which rooted and flourished, bringing her much wealth from the sale of its precious blossoms – wealth she took with her in marriage to the dismissed gardener.

The fragrance of the jasmine is emitted slowly as long as the petals are fresh. As a perfume it is particularly difficult to capture, but is a constituent of 'eau de Chypre'; and although synthetic perfumes are available, the true 'eau de jasmine' is much prized.

The name is derived from the Persian *yasmin. Jasminum officinale,* the garden jasmine, is a species native to Persia and Northern India. In ancient Persia (today's Iran) gardens were designed to be beautiful by night as well as day. It was often too hot outside in daylight, so white flowers were chosen to glow in the moonlight. It was introduced into Europe in the mid sixteenth century and grafted stock from Spanish or Catalonian *Jasmine grandiflorum.* It is grown extensively in Grasse and Cannes in France, centre of the perfume industry. Perfumers prize this scent – hence the name 'voluptuous love'.

Jasmine belongs to the olive family (Oleaceae). It was brought to Europe by the Moors, who grew it in Andalucia. The majority are climbers with fragrant flowers, but a few are shrubs and a few are unscented. They are able to cope with drought and all sorts of soil, but can be very vigorous and rampant – a small price to pay for the romantic intoxicating scent.

ERYNGIUM
(eryngo, Miss Wilmott's ghost, sea holly)

The Painting

A group of densely clustered blossoms with no green at all will have a dramatic effect. To create tonal contrast in order to describe the light, the first principle is to exaggerate the lightness of colour of the sunlit surfaces and the darkness of those surfaces in shadow. To darken a shadow requires careful judgement and practice, and to keep the painting fresh and transparent it is best done in one sweep. This gives a sense of movement and drama, with the dark purple accentuating the yellow and enhancing the feel of light. The greatest tonal contrast occurs when the sun is on the petals, highlighting them against a darker background. As with all paintings, getting the tone right is absolutely crucial.

The Gardener

Eryngiums are perennial spiny plants native to temperate and subtropical regions, especially in South America. They are monocarpic, taking two or three years to reach flowering size depending on how crowded are its growing conditions, but after flowering it dies. A mass of seed is set, but they do not germinate until the spring eighteen months later. Once established, a colony of this wonderful plant, popularly known as Miss Wilmott's ghost, does the sowing and growing by itself and only needs a little thinning out. Eryngiums are metallic blue with glaucous foliage and stem and branching heads of startlingly beautiful amethyst-blue flowers, but are spiny and prickly. The teasel-like heads retain their colour even on drying, so make excellent winter flower arrangements. Sea-holly plants look like small thistles and are similar to the globe thistle, echinops, but sea hollies have a distinctive collar. The colours look almost metallic and change in the sunlight. They are strongest and give the most blooms when grown in full sun. The giant sea holly, *Eryngeum giganteum* (common name Miss Wilmott's Ghost) has shadowy colouring and is named after the English gardener Miss Ellen Wilmott. They flower from midsummer into autumn. Frequent deadheading prolongs bloom time. They have a long taproot, which makes them drought-tolerant as it finds water deep in the soil.

They were much prized for their bitter roots, which when candied with sugar were one of the valued tonics of the time, having strong restorative properties for nervous disorders, and were sold for a considerable price. Today the young shoots of *E. maritimum* are eaten in Sweden like asparagus shoots and were formerly used this way by fishermen in the West Country of England. Propagation is by seed sown uncovered, with germination up to ninety days, or careful division of root cuttings.

E. oliverianum is a strong-growing plant with several forms all carrying good teasel-like heads, with a dark-blue metallic finish. These are very good plants

246

to introduce variety of form and colour in the flower borders. Too many yellow-leaved plants can be dazzling, exciting and cheerful, but many colours will appear to fade when planted close by. Pink looks dreadful as it clashes and is incompatible with the yellow, though blue and purple look stunning. The purple leaves and flowers of eryngium make a much better background for flowers. Reds and pinks are enhanced, whites are emphasised, yellows glow and blues and mauves harmonise.

ECHINOPS
Echinops (globe thistle, steel thistle)

The Painting

Before I start painting, I have in my mind a clear image of how the finished painting should be. This is a guide, and sometimes other creative ideas occur. Careful drawing is needed to establish the fine points of the flower head, though often some parts are left out as the drawing is only a guide. Drawing with the brush takes over.

Because the petals of the globe thistle are so fine and twisted, the thread-like shapes were masked out. Once dry, I wet the whole painting and washed in Cobalt Blue and Lemon Yellow in different places. I chose the blue to harmonise with the metallic Ultramarine Violet of the flowers, and the yellow as a complementary to the blue and violet. It is interesting to compare the effects of the globe head against the blue in one area and the yellow in another. I chose the complementary colour yellow against the globe head to make the area more interesting and more prominent.

When the paint was dry, I dropped pure Ultramarine Violet into the centres and a more washy violet around the edges. I let this dry completely before removing the masking fluid. A very washy violet was painted over the petals, with the top of the head paler and the base darker. The stalks were pale in colour, but with the light above the plants the shadows were underneath the heads and along the stems. There were also shadows on the lower parts of the heads.

The yellow and purple (complementary colours) when mixed together make a neutral. Mixing complementary colours can provide an infinity of greys. Mixed in equal ratios they cancel each other out and become a neutral, but in places I used unequal mixes, creating an interesting and varied grey. Adding complementary colours to shaded areas provides the necessary depth to the picture, so a knowledge of the colour wheel becomes important. I added blue into the mix in places. Darker colours were used behind the spikes, which are metallic blue when in bud.

247

The eye receives a wonderful surprise when colours jump from warm to cool. It is part of the experience of getting to know how to use colour to achieve the best effects.

Painting is a labour of love and, combined with passion for the subject, experience gives confidence to try new ideas. This may lead to risk and failure, but, hopefully, may create something extraordinary.

The Gardener

Echinops has globular heads of bright blue, deeply pinnately cut into narrow, very shiny subtending umbels with white woolly stems. This is a beautifully striking, architectural, prickly, deep-mauve to blue-green perennial with heads above jagged metallic, deeply cut thistle-like leaves. *Echinops ritro* is more compact. The flower heads are composed of numerous scales or tiny flowers, forming a globe. It flowers from July to September.

'Veitch's Blue' has richer-blue flowers. It tolerates poor soil and drought and can be easily grown by seed sown in April or by division. By day echinops is attractive for bees, and to moths by night.

Deadheading the spent flowers can prevent seeding and enhance longevity. To shape the plants they can be cut hard back to the main trunk. New growth sprouts near the cut ends. The flowers are hermaphrodite, having both male and female organs. The flowers produce nectar all the time they are open and, if not visited by pollinating insects, the sweetness increases the longer the flower is open. They have no scent.

The well-planned border has ever changing flowers, which eventually fade but are succeeded by a succession of other developing blooms. They can be chosen for the beauty of their colours, shapes or scent. Beauty is fragile, transitory and vulnerable, so the moment must be cherished.

COSMOS

Kosmos means beautiful. (Mexican aster)

Painting 1

When planning a painting, careful consideration of the qualities of the flower is essential: the colour, texture and whether the petals are smooth, velvety, curved or frilled and if the veins are raised or indented. Careful thought and drawing with the tip of the brush is vital as it is complicated. The feathery leaves were hinted at with quick brushstrokes, but shadows on the leaves are also important as this gives depth and places them behind the flowers. The same applies to the flowers, where the darker pink is shadowed into the centre, where two different yellows were used.

248

There is such enjoyment when excited by the subject, and what better medium to express the intrigues of light and the delicacy of the flowers than watercolour with its transparency and intense colour!

Painting 2
Different colours meant using Winsor Red, Quinacridone Magenta and a washy Magenta for the slightly pink flower and light blue for the shadowed side of the white flower. The feathery green foliage contrasted well with the flower colours.

Painting 3

The flowers were painted with two reds and two yellows. The initial red was Permanent Rose with Quinacridone Magenta in the base of the petals. Lemon Yellow was painted into the centres of the flowers and then overpainted with dabs of Yellow Ochre. The background, Cobalt Blue, was washed between the flowers with a touch of Ultramarine Violet lower down. The blue was mixed with the yellow for the leaves, darkened with a little violet for the shaded parts of the foliage.

The Gardener
Cosmos has an abundance of delicate richly coloured dahlia-like flowers. It is a tender annual famed for its long-stemmed colourful pink, red, rose, purple, yellow and white flowers with yellow central discs filled with nectar – a magnet for bees and other insects – which makes it an excellent plant for attracting butterflies. Its feathery foliage makes it ideal for a background to medium companion plants. Cosmos plants, annual and perennial, are native to Mexico. They are easily grown from seed in gentle heat in early spring. It seems the simplest idea to sow direct into borders where they are to flower, but even when the soil is perfect for them it is also ideal for weed seedlings and may need protection from birds and slugs. They are best sown under controlled conditions in pots or trays, and seedlings should be pricked out as soon as they are large enough to handle – and the earlier the better, as the roots are less damaged. Hold each seedling gently by one leaf, being careful not to bruise the stem or roots when dibbing in. They should then be hardened off and planted out in a south-facing border with a poor, light, well-drained soil in a hot, dry place. If the soil is too rich, they send up lots of attractive feathery foliage. If spent flowers are removed they will flower for four months, from summer into autumn.

Cosmos bipinnatus has fine feathery leaves, similar to ferns. The flowers are airy, delicate, white, dark rose and many luscious shades of pink. *C. sulphureus* 'Polidor' has semi-double blooms in hot yellow, reds and orange. *C. atrosanguineus* gets its name from the Latin word for the colour of dried blood. Its popular name, chocolate cosmos, comes from its wonderful chocolate fragrance. It is tender, so needs to overwinter in a frost-free place. 'Picotee' is essentially white with pink edges to the petals.

Because the flowers have evenly spaced petals, Spanish missionaries who grew them named them *cosmos*, a Greek word for harmony or 'ordered universe'.

GEUM
(avens, herb bennet, wood avens)

The Painting

I tried to create a dramatic impression along with the natural appearance of the flowers and their surroundings. Winsor Lemon was used in the flower petals with a touch Winsor Orange and dropped into the inner part of the petals, leaving the outer petals yellow. The same yellow was used in mixing the green. Both the centres of the flower petals and the green were darkened with red. It is quite useful to have yellow against the green so that it becomes a highlight and gives an element of sparkle. This gives a bit of drama and impact to the colour of the flowers.

The Gardener

Geums are sun-loving perennials, flowering from June to September. There are fifty species of geum, which grow wild in the meadows and woods of Europe, Asia, Africa and the Americas. They belong to the Rosaceae family, which also includes potentillas, hawthorn, apples and roses. Most grow in fertile, moist soil in meadow or woodlands, but some prefer poorer soil in more-open sunny areas, with others preferring shade. The bright long-lasting flowers are single or double blooms in brilliant shades of yellow, red or orange. There is a purple avens with yellow-pink flowers veined with red-purple sepals. It thrives in wet soil, and its roots can be used to make a chocolate-flavoured drink. The semi-double orange variety flowers in my garden from June to October. It has two or three times the normal number of petals, and appears fuller and more lush, giving pollen and nectar to butterflies and bees. Full-double flowers have many more petals, but are of no value to insects. The seeds are hooked to help dispersal. These varieties will self-seed. Plants can be lifted and divided in spring or autumn.

As a general rule, geums prefer cool semi-shade and dislike dry soil, preferring moist but well-drained soil, and do well on riverbanks. Most will live a long time if they are divided every few years in spring or autumn; otherwise they become bare in the centre. The majority of flowers are yellow, orange, pink and red, which glow in dappled light. These small stunningly bright flowers stand aloft on long stems, perfecting a summer's evening.

Water avens, *Geum rivale*, has orange-pink to purple-pink drooping flowers under a reddish-brown calyx bonnet. The one-seeded fruits cluster like a raspberry, each fruit being hooked at the top. Water avens grows in damp earth by the pond in semi-shade. Propagation is by division in spring or autumn or from seed sown in spring. Honeybees and bumblebees are the main pollinators.

OSTEOSPERMUM
(daisy bush, African daisy, Cape daisy, blue-eyed daisy)

The Drawing

The hand acquires precision, especially when working with permanent ink. Ruskin wrote, 'Work with the hand, the mind and heart.'

The value of observation is important as every line in a drawing should carry meaning and nothing should be left vague. Here the lines are precise but even; though the subject is complicated, I tried to keep the lines simple. Intricate line work can be appreciated better against a simple background, directing attention to the main feature. Drawing evokes a quiet contemplation, concentration and a level of meditation. Drawing, as well as a pleasure, heightens visual awareness.

Rembrandt made his drawings with a quill pen, achieving a rugged line. He diluted the ink to create a fainter line, which he used most effectively to simulate the effect of atmosphere and distance. I didn't use a quill pen, but an old-fashioned dip pen, which gave me a particular effect. The drawing was an enormous aid to understanding the structure of the plant before starting the painting.

The Painting

Depicting the light and shade, however subtle, can evoke a sense of the time of day. By studying the effects the changes in light will have on the subject, one can capture the feel of light with only an approximation, as the light changes constantly. With practice, the eyes not only see, but investigate, analyse and perceive and can produce vitality, vibration and freshness.

Sometimes a petal has one colour in the centre and another at its tip. First dip the brush into one colour. Then, holding

the brush level, dry the tip on a tissue and dip into another colour. Stroke the brush on the petal shape, pushing out the colours. Another way is to wet the petal shape and drop colour into the wet shape.

The temperamental behaviour of watercolour is an exciting process regardless of whether the results are intentionally or accidentally caused. What matters most is the way the pigments interact, creating exciting runs. The amount of water in the brush, the wetness of the paper and the pressure from the brush all have an effect. If I want strong colour, I use little water and a lot of pigment in the brush. As the paper dries, losing moisture, when it is between the very wet and the very dry stage, is when it is most vulnerable. This is when happy accidents can happen and can be exciting. Once dry,

the sharp-edged shapes and details can be added, but being careful to preserve the initial softness of the first washes.

The Gardener

Osteospermums belong to the Calenduleae family, like Shasta daisies and zinnias. They are annual and perennial plants, closely related to the chrysanthemum and are similar to marguerites, flowering from May to October.

The scientific name is derived from the Greek *osteon*, meaning bone, and the Latin *spermum*, meaning seed. In the language of flowers osteospermum is 'valued and confidence'.

Osteospermums come in blue, yellow and purple. The hardy types show a dark-blue centre in the disc until the pollen is shed. Cultivars with dark-blue centres will tolerate some frost. These flower profusely in spring, but do not have a second flush, while other species flower a second time in late summer, stimulated by the cooler night temperatures. Yellow hybrids have a yellow centre. Modern cultivars will flower continuously when watered and fertilised and sheltered from rain.

The petals vary from smooth and regular to dipped and spoon-shaped. The flowers open fully in direct sun, and close every evening. They bloom best when the nights are cool.

Osteospermums prefer a warm fully sunny position in rich soil and will tolerate drought, though if they dry out completely may stop flowering and drop any flower buds and not easily come back into flower. They do not set seed easily, but non-perennial varieties can be sown in a permanent position in spring and thinned out. Osteospermums are hybrids, so saving seed results in seedlings which will not resemble the parent plant. They need light and cool temperatures to germinate.

Propagation from cuttings can be taken in spring and early summer, which means they have a long time in which to establish as young plants before the onset of winter. Cuttings can be taken by carefully removing the lower leaves and cutting the stem below a leaf node with a sharp knife, dipping into rooting hormone to promote the growth of new roots, which helps prevent rotting, and then inserting into sterile seedling mixture. The cuttings should form roots in three to four weeks and when they start to put out new growth they can be planted in the garden. By pinching them back the cuttings will branch out and form side shoots.

Perennials are above ground for little more than half the year, whereas a shrub is there all the time; the glorious show of colour is worth the wait.

OX-EYE DAISY

Leucanthemum vulgare (moon daisy, moon flower, moon penny, herb marguerite, oxey daisy, dog daisy, dun daisy, horse daisy, horse gowan, large white gowan, love-me, love-me-not, mathes, maudlinwort, midsummer daisy, poor-land daisy, pretty maids, sheriff pink, white cap, white daisy, white goldes, white man's weed, white ox-eye, big daisy, bull daisy, espibawn, field daisy)

The Painting

Painting en plein air is one of the greatest pleasures. The connection with the garden, the plants, colours and forms is deepest when painting outside. The resulting paintings are fresher and more spontaneous than those produced in the studio. Before I start, I visualise how the painting will look and make a quick sketch, always keeping in mind that initial attraction and I try to keep this image right up to the last brushstroke.

Most paintings start with drawing or sketching to develop the idea, but it is important that the idea is not exhausted by overstating the detail. Shapes are important and sometimes need to be introduced or omitted according to the design. Learning to use shapes effectively is essential, being the foundation of the painting or drawing. Strong statements can build passages through the painting with contrast of value complementing the shapes. Planning the shapes takes time, and when satisfied with the composition I sketch in the main features, especially when the subject is complicated and, as in the daisy painting, the white of the paper needs to be preserved. White petals are not painted, but suggested by putting colour around them, then toning with some shadow colour. Tonal contrast is best portrayed when the sunlit petals stand out against the shadows behind, creating an illusion of the flowers coming forward while the background recedes. This tonal contrast is important in creating an illusion of three dimensions of depth, space and light. The arrangement of lights and darks is vital to the success of the finished piece.

The Gardener

These daisies have hundreds of flowers, tall and graceful with large heads of white petals around a golden centre. The ox-eye daisy is more delicate than the Shasta daisy. They consist of two types of flowers. Those with a yellow centre are densely packed with tiny disc florets and petal-like white ray florets at the periphery, but they can give the impression of being a single flower. The nectar is at the bottom of the tubular corolla and available to insects with a proboscis. The pollen is higher up in the corolla mouth and is available to non-specialised insects, such as beetles, butterflies and hoverflies. They enjoy the sun and will flower from spring to summer. The ox-eye daisy has a rhizome, which spreads as it ages but is not invasive. Sometimes the rhizomes survive earth-moving operations, thereby establishing colonies of plants in new areas.

It is a hardy perennial and easy to maintain. Its white petals mix well with other flowers. The simple daisy is one of the most beautiful flowers. It belongs to the Asterceae family, which includes asters and sunflowers, and is native to North and Central Europe. It is believed to be a flower of innocence, purity and new beginnings. The Shasta daisy was developed by Luther Burbank from Eurasian species. Its flower heads tend to be larger than those of the ox-eye daisy and its leaves are less likely to be pinnatifid.

Some daisies have a pink or rose colour. Gerbera daisies have a wide range of colours, including pink, red, orange, yellow, blue and white. Some daisies of this species have multiple-coloured petals, black centres and brightly coloured markings on the tips of the florets. For this reason, gerbera daisies are especially attractive to bees and butterflies.

W. H. Hudson wrote of 'cycling over the high down country' near Dorchester, Dorset, England. He caught sight of what looked like a broad band of snow lying across the green hills. As he approached he found the old Roman road, which normally is very distinct as it has shorter turf and a brighter green than the downs it lies across. It was so thickly overgrown with daisies that the crowded flowers touched and obliterated the green beneath them – a wonderful sight as these millions of small blossoms occupied the road only and there was not a single daisy on either side. He found it such a lovely sight – a beauty almost supernatural – he could not bear to walk or ride on it. It was like a road leading to some earthly brighter place – some paradise of flowers.

Ox-eye daisy meadows have decreased with the increase of agriculture, but they thrive on sunny banks and in gardens. It is the national flower of Latvia.

Young leaves can be added to salads, but have a strong taste. Extracts were once used to treat a variety of ailments, from chest diseases to watery eyes. Daisy roots were frequently boiled in milk and given to puppies to keep them small, which was why it was known as the dog daisy. Another explanation was that it is a common flower, just like the dog rose and dog violet.

SWEET PEA
Lathyrus odoratus

Painting 1

Watercolour is the ideal medium for painting the softness and transparency of sweet peas. I deepened the pure red in the centre to help to give shape, with small patches of light indicated by the white of the paper. The green of the leaves accentuates the red, as it is the complementary colour.

Painting is a process of seeing and feeling. The great challenge is how to integrate vision and reality along with understanding the qualities of the medium, of temperature and moisture and how each of these affects the outcome. Watercolour allows a certain freedom of expression not always possible with other mediums.

Painting 2

The fragrant purple-maroon sweet peas are my favourite and while painting them I appreciate their fabulous perfume. I wet each petal and ran Quinacridone Purple, or violet, together with the Quinacridone Magenta, adding a little Ultramarine in places where they were shadowed.

The Gardener

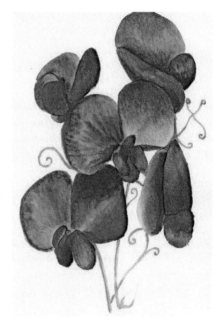

Lathyros odoratus was introduced to England in 1699 when Father Cupani sent seeds from Italy to Dr Uvedale at Enfield. The plant is a native of South Italy and Sicily and was well known to botanists before 1700, but there is no evidence that it was grown in gardens until then. The flowers of these early plants were purple, pale purple and red, or white and red with hooded standards and closed wings, graceful and with wonderful perfume. There was comparatively little change in type or range of colour until 1865, when 'Scarlet Invincible' was given an award by the Royal Horticultural Society. In 1870 Henry Eckford began to cross sweet peas. Thirty-one awards were given between 1870 and 1900, with most going to Eckford. There was a greater range of colours with larger flowers and they retained their fragrance. These were known as Giant or Grandiflora varieties and they became generally and widely grown for both garden decoration and cutting. It was during this period that bunches of flowers in distinct colours – white, pink, carmine, mauve and purple – first appeared in Covent Garden Market. Before 1880 bunches of mixed colours were the vogue and sweet peas were generally grown as mixtures. The year 1900 saw a new form of sweet pea introduced, with standards so ample that, instead of being flat as in the Grandiflora types, they were waved and frilled at the edges. This was the shell-pink variety 'Countess Spencer', raised and shown by Silas Cole, and in the same year the smaller and paler 'Gladys Unwin' was developed by W. J. Unwin. From these, a whole range of colour varieties were raised. The years 1901 to 1920 saw ninety-two new varieties receive awards, and new varieties ran into thousands.

There are several different types of sweet pea. The most commonly grown are modern Spencer types with large frilly flowers, which carry four large blooms on each long stem. They were bred by Charlie Hammer in the mid 1980s and later introduced by Unwins. This was the first Spencer sweet pea to receive an Award of Garden Merit by the Royal Horticultural Society. Charlie Hammer was a retired mining engineer and widower who spent his time growing and showing sweet peas. At each show he had a team of ladies who looked after his every need and they became known as 'Charlie's Angels', and so he named his seedlings. They have large frilly florets and superb perfume.

Grandiflora sweet peas are often referred to as heirloom varieties because of their Victorian origins. They have smaller flowers than the Spencer types but are highly scented, having the strongest fragrance and colour. They flower for weeks, as long as flowers are picked and no seed pods form. Once pods form and seed production is under way the plant stops producing flowers. By harvesting the flowers every day or two days the plant will continue to produce more flowers. When cutting, the buds need to be open, as the buds will not develop and open once cut. Sweet peas look best massed together, gathered into a bouquet. Once cut they fade quickly.

There are bicolour sweet peas where the upper petals and the lower petals are different colours. This colour pattern is striking in 'Painted Lady', which is a bold red and white. Breeders continue to make subtle changes in the colours of sweet peas and in the shape of the petals from single to furled and doubles, curled and crimped, often with coloured edgings or mottling on the petals. Flaked sweet peas are always showy with ruffled blooms and a dazzling combination of reddish purple and white.

The 'Solway' series are perfect for pots as they are bushy, grow to a metre, and have lots of slender stems and small leaves. For baskets there is a lower-growing sweet pea, 'Villa Roma', with short flower stems, too short for cutting; and they do not have tendrils, so need no support, and are tolerant of heat. Sweet peas are a pure delight in a window box with the scent of these cascading flowers wafting through an open window.

Sweet peas are hardy and can be sown in autumn or spring. For the earliest flowers, autumn sowing is preferable, but early flowers can be obtained from a January sowing. Those sown in spring are not as vigorous as those sown in autumn. They should be sown in ordinary compost mixed with leaf mould and sand and placed in a cold frame covered with cardboard, which avoids them drying out. Germination takes between ten and fifteen days. Ventilation is important, as is protection from frost. When the seedlings have made their first true leaves they can be potted on and grown on in a cold frame using the same soil mix. They must never dry out or be encouraged to make fast growth by feeding or by keeping them warmer. When they have several sets of leaves they are ready to be planted out in spring in a prepared trench filled with well-rotted compost, when they are ready to climb the support poles. Finer flowers with better stems for cutting are obtained by growing on a single stem. My grandfather used to pinch out the tip of each seedling and kept the best subsequent shoot on each plant and removed all others, removing all side shoots and tendrils, so restricting each plant to a single stem. Pinching out the tips encourages side shoots, eventually producing multi-stemmed plants with more flowers. They require deep, rich soil and need to be well fed and watered, and grow best in well-drained slightly alkaline soil in an open site in full sun, though they will tolerate some shade. Watering is very important and it may be necessary to give water at least once a week in dry weather conditions. The tendrils of the plant will attach to any support, creating an elegant covering for fences and trellises. Tendrils are tiny curling stems by which the plant clings to supports; the tendrils help it to climb. Cane tripods should be in position prior to planting. I wind strings around the canes so that the plant's tendrils attach themselves.

One of my favourites is 'Windsor', which has dark-maroon flowers and straight stems and is good for cutting. Continual pickings provide a fabulous show in the house and encourage more flowers to form on the plant, which prolongs the life of the plant. If the plants show signs of exhaustion, they can be cut back so as to promote fresh growth.

Sweet peas are pollinated before the flowers open, and therefore any cross-pollination must be done by hand before the flower opens. By breeding from a selected individual, collecting and keeping and sowing seed from each plant raised from that individual, a pure breeding strain can usually be had and is unlikely to vary. The seed is usually set free in dry weather when the seed pod dries out and curls back.

It is a relative of the edible pea, but probably acquired the name sweet pea in recognition of its delicious scent. Blue and mauve sweet peas are heavily scented, while creams, pinks and oranges have less perfume. Sweet aromas tend to have a soothing effect and can link to our other senses and evoke sensual or romantic moods. The important aim is to attract pollinating insects, which accounts for some less attractive plants being powerfully fragrant. I grow these fragrant flowers in the most frequented places of the garden, near windows, seating areas and paths, so that the scent can be appreciated to the full.

The best time of day to cut sweet peas for the house is first thing in the morning or in the evening. It is best to avoid cutting at midday, when they will potentially be stressed and dehydrated and this will reduce their life. The perfect stage of plant growth is when the lower flowers are fully open but the top flower is only just unfurling. They should be picked regularly, perhaps every second day, and all spent flowers should be removed before they form seed. The more the flowers are picked the more new flowers are produced.

EVERLASTING SWEET PEA
Lathyrus latifolius

The Painting

Thin transparent washes are essential when depicting delicate petals. Glazing and soft washes allow light to reflect off the white paper and through the colours. The pure translucency of watercolour makes it an ideal medium for capturing the delicate quality of the petals.

The Gardener

The everlasting or perennial sweet pea resembles old-fashioned varieties of sweet pea, but with large flowers. It is hardy with rose to purple or white flowers through summer. It is easily grown from seed and will flower in the first year. It is a true herbaceous perennial. It makes new vigorous shoots, which grow two metres from the base each year and die back in autumn, regrowing again in spring. Unlike *Lathyrus odoratus,* the flowers are unscented. The sweet pea uses its tendrils to scramble up trellises, fences or other plants. They appear different from sweet peas as the flowers are not ruffled and have a narrow colour range of pink or white. The most common is deep mauve-pink, which takes on a bluish tint when the flowers fade. It is best to deadhead when the flowers fade, unless seed is required.

DELPHINIUM
(larkspur)

Painting 1

When painting flowers it is important to keep colour as pure as possible, avoiding any unnecessary fussing and then losing freshness. Variations in tone add life to the painting, and by keeping the value changes small it is more effective without becoming chaotic. The edges of the background petals were kept soft to create distance, while harder edges were near the foreground.

I try to paint each shape as carefully as I can from start to finish while bearing in mind the whole painting. Each shape leads on to another and then the next. The importance of light and capturing fleeting moments of sun and shadow can be very dramatic – as in this painting, with sunlight in the foreground and shadow behind. I plan a composition of plant shapes and colours, but nature has the upper hand and dictates her beautiful arrangements into something more exciting. My aim is to capture the same exhilarating visual experience of when I first saw the scene, capturing the colours, the light, the shapes and a magical illusion of perfume. The challenge is to translate these feelings into a painted image. I usually work hard at design, trying to portray a specific emotional response, but sometimes the design is right in front of me and a painting takes a direction of its own, as in nature when the unexpected happens.

Painting 2

I wanted to use complementary colours, and these flowers – delphinium and rudbeckia – are ideal. For colour contrast I chose yellow flowers against the blue.

I painted the delphiniums first as I wanted to preserve the pale centres of each flower. I used Cobalt Blue for the pale petals and then a richer, darker Ultramarine Blue where needed. I painted the rudbeckias using Raw Sienna and Indian Yellow with touches of red in the yellow to warm some areas. I used Raw Sienna as it is transparent. Some colours block the light of the paper, which in turn creates a stronger transparency in adjacent colours. Yellow Ochre is opaque, so blocks light, while Raw Sienna is transparent, and when they are placed side by side the Raw Sienna seems brighter.

The whole of the background area was wetted, being careful not to wet the flower spikes. Blue and yellow were floated in so that they merged and created an even flow. When almost dry, a hint of blue was added behind the delphiniums, and, when a little drier, suggested yellow flower spikes were dotted in on the right-hand side

The blues and yellows were mixed together for the greens, with more yellow added to the greens on the bottom left to balance the yellow in the background, top right. More blue was added to the bottom-right area to echo the blue in the top-left area.

The Gardener

Both larkspur and delphinium share the same botanical classification of delphinium, but the older annual larkspur was likened to a bird – hence lark's head, lark's toes, lark's claw and larkspur – and in France *pied-d'alouette*. This was named delphinium as the bud resembles a dolphin. The modern varieties of larkspur owe their origin to two species – *Delphinium ajacis* (rocket larkspur) and *D. consolida*. The former has showy spikes of flowers varying from white through rose to purple, and has been developed to produce mixtures of tall and dwarf forms and also a double-flowered strain known as Hyacinth-flowered. The wild larkspur, which is related to both buttercup and columbine, was a weed of cornfields, where it escaped from gardens. It is said to have been brought from Siberia in the sixteenth century, and single larkspurs were certainly cultivated in Elizabethan gardens. In the seventeenth century the Dutch greatly improved the larkspur with doubling of the flowers, and the delphinium evolved – taller, with thicker heads of blossom, a wider leaf and more-branching stems. The larkspur has also improved in size and colour. There is a red from California and a Siberian larkspur with a metallic lustre.

D. ajacis (rocket larkspur) has sparsely branching stems bearing spires of loosely arranged flowers in blues, purples, pinks and whites. *D. consolida* is a taller species, reaching 1.2 metres high, with a more-branching habit. The flowers are more densely packed in blue, red, purple, pink and white. *D. belladonna* has mainly white to dark-blue flowers on slender branching stems. White provides the buffer between strident colours. A succession of blooms can be achieved with planning, so white delphiniums give way to phlox, so continuing the season of white blooms. *D. elatum* is tall and has sturdy stems with dense spikes of flattish flowers in colours ranging from white, rose and blue to violet. They all have different-coloured eyes. Some flowers are white with an attractive black eye. The pale-blue form has dark-brown eyes; the creamy-white has yellow eyes. There are semi-double flowers and some have side spikes. D. *grandiflorum* has violet-blue flowers on branching stems.

The seeds of larkspurs were used by Ancient Egyptians to ward off scorpions. When introduced into Britain in the 1500s, the plants were used as insecticides. These plants can be dried for flower arrangements. The stalks should be cut, stripped of the leaves, placed in a jug three-quarters full of water and left until the water has been absorbed. Then dry them in a clean vase, where they will keep their colour for several years. Larkspur was the common name for all delphiniums.

Delphiniums are wonderful statuesque herbaceous plants with tall spikes of flowers. They are a good choice as a theme plant at the back of a herbaceous border along with *Lychnis chalcedonica,* regal lilies and interplanting of rudbeckia, achillea, helianthus, heliopsis and white, yellow, apricot and orange dahlias to coincide with the second flowering of the delphinium. Sometimes in the middle of the border they add to the depth of field. Strong-blue flowers are best next to deep pink and cerise. The flower colours are repeated throughout the border, giving a rhythm. Delphiniums enjoy a sunny position and benefit greatly from good, rich soil that is moisture-retentive.

There are two types – the large-flowered, or Elatum, which is up to two metres high with long spikes of blooms, and the Belladona, about one metre high with smaller spikes or sprays of blooms. There are many varieties of the Elatum type – single-flowered, semi-double and fully double in colours from white, pale blue and lilac to bright blue and deep purple. There are fewer Belladonna varieties, though the colour range is similar. There was an introduction into Western Europe of the wild Scarlet and orange-red-flowered *D. cardinale,* and *D. nudicaule* has orange-red cup-shaped flowers on airy spikes, which grow in sun or shade but benefit from afternoon shade in areas of high heat, and should be well watered for best growth.

The annuals developed into perennials, and simple colours improved yearly. Records of the exact crosses made do not appear to have been kept, but the first hybrids had small single flowers on spikes with a semi-branching habit, and the first developments consisted of the selection of varieties with much longer and less-branching spikes. Later breeding turned to selection for semi-double and double flowers. In the latter half of the nineteenth century English nurserymen began crossing the current English hybrids, which had the stronger constitutions, with imported French varieties, whose chief characteristics were their increased range of colour coupled with semi-double though small flowers. The first white delphiniums appeared in 1890. Delphiniums are predominantly blue, almost midnight-blue, white and some shades of pink, lavender and mauve. Some have splashes of black or brown with fern-like foliage. Blues mix well with most other colours. Light-blue flowers surrounded by grey or silver foliage appear more luminous, making them ideal in beds near the house, where they can be appreciated during the evening. Warm blues, with a tendency towards red, will be less luminous but add warmth to groups of cooler blues. Blues can give the impression of depth, so if grown at the end of the border can make the garden appear longer. Colour harmony is part of good garden design, so placing delphiniums with complementary colours, such as orange marigolds and yellow lilies, makes for perfect companions.

Delphiniums are best grown in the herbaceous borders where there is plenty of space. The dazzling-coloured flowers are densely packed on the spikes. The Egyptians believed that a pale blue meant happiness and a dark blue meant success. This could be why blue paintings appear so attractive, while red evokes love, passion and tenderness.

An arrangement of colour harmony in the garden in a gradual progression from red to yellow works well, but I sometimes use complementary colours with the blues; so deep-blue delphiniums and yellow or orange companions look fantastic. When complementary-coloured plants – those which are diametrically opposite on the colour wheel – grow together, they each will appear more brilliant than when on their own. A blue next to an orange will appear far brighter, as will the orange. A border with blues, mauves, violet, lilac and lavender becomes dramatic with a dash of yellow among them. Few combinations are as powerful as the complementary colours of blue and yellow. To avoid glaring contrasts, the brilliance can be toned down by using a lighter tint of one colour with a darker shade of the other.

They are short-lived and need care, and slugs and snails may eat the emerging shoots.

Propagation by cuttings taken in early spring is much preferable to division. The young shoots should be severed close to the main stool and have a solid base, which should be white in colour. Root them in sand or sandy soil and place in a cold frame, shaded from the sun. Rooting takes approximately five weeks, when white hair roots have formed. The plants can be transplanted into their flowering position in early June. They can also be grown from seed. The seed can be harvested in July and will quickly lose its viability. It should be sown in fine soil in shallow boxes, covered with a thin layer of soil and stood in a cool frame. Germination should take place in about fourteen days. If buying seed, germination can be increased if the seed packet is placed in the freezer for a week before sowing outdoors in April or under glass in February. If sown in the autumn, the young seedlings will die down and lose all foliage during the winter months and should be protected from slugs; and in spring, whether spring- or autumn-sown, the plants should be transplanted and finally planted out in their flowering positions when large enough.

Delphiniums do best in heavy soils, and a soaking before flowering time is particularly appreciated, especially if a mulch can be applied to assist in retaining the water and preventing the soil cracking. The first year after planting, the number of shoots per plant should be restricted to two. Thinning of the weakest growths should be done at the same time as stacking. The spikes grow quickly and can be bent or broken by the wind, so often need support. Staking is best done with canes placed triangularly around each plant, adding strings at intervals during the season as the plant grows. This allows the flower spikes to sway within the confines of the ties. After flowering it is best to cut down the spikes to just above the foliage to prevent weakening by seed formation and to enable the plant to build up resources for the winter. In the autumn, when the leaves have withered, the stems should be cut down. Having said all that, I was delighted that my flowering and budding delphinium survived a very heavy frost and days of -6°C.

HOLLYHOCK
Althaea or *Alcea rosea*

The Painting

Each painting begins with hope and with a fabulous result in mind. Often it starts well, but there may be questions about whether it is working. A painting may have complications to endure and solve, resulting in ecstatic moments along with moments of doubt, but with experience comes the ability to resolve and overcome. Painting is the result of experience and cumulative knowledge. It is good mental practice to sharpen the powers of observation, even when not in the process of painting or drawing. This mental exercise of observing shapes, colours, textures, light and dark, and hard and soft edges, helps in the practice of seeing.

In this painting the blooms were close together, with the red flowers stronger in colour than the more gentle pink, which made a difference in the composition. I used a little Ultramarine Violet in the central flower, and this same colour was washed over the background greens with added Cobalt Blue to give a sense of perspective. All the blooms had yellow in the centres, and this was washed over the foreground green leaves, giving them a more prominent appearance and linking the colours throughout the painting.

The Gardener

Hollyhocks give a blaze of colour and are one of the old-fashioned country-garden flowers cultivated in gardens since the fifteenth century, in Asia probably as early as the Crusades. The hollyhock was at one time a florist's flower and had its own special class at exhibitions. It was one of the favourite plants in the nineteenth century until a plague of rust wiped out interest. Hollyhock rust is more likely to damage old plants than young seedlings. Rust is difficult to control as it overwinters in the crown of the plant. It is best to remove the first early leaves from the main stalk, as they can harbour fungal spores. Water well and apply a thick mulch to prevent spores in the soil spreading. It is best to raise fresh seedlings each year. Rust can be treated with a garlic spray in late spring through summer. Rust also attacks mallow and lavatera.

Seeds should be saved from the finest plants and sown when ripe, in pots in gentle heat, or in the open in June or July, and transplanted into pots to be overwintered in a cold frame. Propagation by cuttings gives better plants than division of the old root at almost any time, planting them singly in pots of light soil, and keeping them shaded until roots form. Side shoots can be taken as cuttings when they are firming up in summer, and rooted under glass. The young plants, if overwintered under glass, must be given plenty of light and air, but little water. They should be hardened off in early spring and planted out where they are to flower. They need plenty of water in summer. A top dressing of compost is beneficial when the flower spikes appear. The flower spikes should be staked before there is danger of damage from strong winds, and after flowering the spikes should be cut down. Many varieties have been raised by crossing and selection, including the double forms. The clumps of stately spires blossom in single or double, pink, red, yellow, white, black or striped forms. Hollyhocks lend an air of antiquity in borders, against walls or in wild areas in sun and sheltered from wind. Both the flowers and seeds are so abundant that it is a natural symbol of fruitfulness.

CENTRANTHUS

Centranthus ruber; Valeriana officinalis (all-heal, amantilla, baldrian, common valerian, English valerian, fragrant valerian, garden heliotrope, garden valerian, set well, St George's herb, vandal root, red valerian, kiss-me-quick, fox's bush, Jupiter's beard)

Painting 1

This beautiful plant has many flower heads of intricate tiny flowers. An ink drawing was made on hot-pressed paper, and doing the drawing helped in understanding the nature of the plant and so helped in planning the composition.

Red is a powerful colour and, when planning, should be placed with care as too much red tires the eyes. Red is invariably best among green or grey foliage. In a mixed border one way of overcoming what might be a visual problem is to include other flowers with a hint of red in them. Red against yellow clashes as the two colours annihilate one another unless an intermediate orange is added. Also blue and red when side by side can appear too intense. Better to have reds, oranges, crimson and violets together, perhaps then leading into violet blues. Red is more intense on a white surface than when placed near a higher-intensity colour. Colours can appear to have a higher intensity when surrounded by colours of lower intensity. To lower the intensity the complementary colour, or the two adjacent colours on the colour wheel, can be added. These will cause the least shift of colour and value, while retaining some of the pigment's luminosity.

Painting 2

As a painter of flowers I like harmonious combinations, so selecting a specific group of colours means considering the mood of the painting. There is no formula for painting intuitively but it is a blend of spontaneity and control, a structured approach, but requiring a bold, creative spirit.

I started with washes of pale red and green in various places. When dry, a pale washy red was dotted in clusters and left to dry. A slightly thicker red was dotted in and around the main clustered flowers and more added to the underside. The red was added to the green to create the dark stems. The flower contains red, but green in the stems. There may be traces of green in the red which, when added to the red, darken, and if the red is added to the green the resulting green becomes a red brown depending on the ratio of each.

Painting is a fascinating process of finding techniques which express the subject, but technique should not take over. The technique should be adapted to express and excite. It is a process of exploration.

It is only necessary to have passion for the paintings to have life.

The Gardener

Centranthus ruber has distinctive long-lasting, small, red-pink, star-shaped flower heads. It often grows in crevices in rock and walls, where its powerful woody roots can penetrate.

It is an erect robust perennial with upright stems carrying opposite pairs of long leaves divided into pairs of narrowly branched flower heads of masses of distinctively scented tiny pink tubular blooms, numerous red and sometimes white flowers in a pyramidal cluster from April to October. The white variety is *C. ruber* 'Albus'. The small, dry, ribbed fruit has a feathery parachute at the top similar to dandelions, which aids dispersal of the seed by the wind and so plants can self-seed and become invasive. Because it tolerates lime it often grows in old walls.

Both leaves and roots can be eaten in salads or soups. Since Roman times it has been used to treat a number of ailments, and extracts from the roots make sedatives used for headaches and insomnia. The genus name *Valerian* comes from the Latin *valeo,* meaning to be well.

Valerian attracts many insects – butterflies, moths, bees, sawflies, wasps and other short-tongued insects. Purple nectar guides on the petals lead the insects to a small pouch of nectar at the base of the flower. The leaves may be eaten by caterpillars of the valerian pug moth.

Valerian will grow in sun or light shade and will flourish in a wide range of soils. Propagation is by division in spring or autumn, or by sowing seed in spring in a sunny position.

The red valerian (*C. ruber*) is a robust, fleshy perennial plant with dark-pink to red flowers, occasionally white. It is best combined with other white or mauve flowers rather than near-yellow or blue flowers. Valerian has a single stamen, which ripens before the ovary, which develops ewer-shaped seed pods that are wind-distributed by a pappus – part of the flower's structure. It has been grown as a garden plant from 1590 onwards and has been a naturalised escapee since the 1760s. It can grow on walls, where it looks wonderful but can cause a great deal of damage. It will grow in any place that is neither shady nor wet, and properly handled it will flower for months on end. It makes rounded clumps which need no staking.

V. officinalis has been used as a medical herb for centuries, but its most distinctive feature is its scent, which is a cherry-like vanilla. The roots smell unpleasant and it is the root which is most often dried, powdered and used in herbal preparations. It is a premier sleep aid and a useful tranquilliser and antidepressant. When brewing valerian tea, passion flower and hop leaves can be added, both being sleep aids. Propagation can be by seed, root division or root runners. Seeds should be planted when fresh in rich, loose soil. Seeds germinate close to the surface and need light, so are apt to be taken by birds. Kept moist they should germinate in seven to ten days.

265

EVENING PRIMROSE
Scrophulariaceae, *Oenothera fruticosa* (evening primrose, suncaps, sundrops); *Verbascum thapsus* (Aaron's rod, mullein)

Painting 1

Each petal is round, but seen from the side it sometimes appears as an oval. To make the petals show better, the background is darker and in a complementary colour. Part of the planning is deciding which highlights need to be reserved and then working from the palest to the darkest tones. Delicate washes can produce the effects of light shining through the petals. Fresh, clear colours are essential in flower painting, so the choice of transparent colours is important. Observation has to be a major consideration as there is not one single device which will symbolise the character of any one plant.

I started with a light detailed pencil drawing, to which I added watercolour. The main petals were painted with a wash of Winsor Lemon, fairly thinly in some petals and overpainted with Raw Sienna in the shadowed central areas. As it was an extremely hot day and the sun was overhead, the paint dried very quickly, causing hard lines and making the shadows quite marked. Quinacridone Red was used for the stamens and added to green for shadows on the stem. The background behind the flowers was wet with water and then small amounts of Ultramarine Blue and Quinacridone Red were dropped into it. I chose blue to complement the yellow.

Painting 2
I enjoyed painting this pretty plant with its lemon-yellow flowers and magenta stamens against the green of the sturdy stem. The petals of the flowers were painted first with Lemon Yellow and, when dry, a touch of Yellow Ochre was applied around the edges where they were shadowed. The dark shadows behind the yellow petals helped to give the painting a three-dimensional effect. The stamens were added using a fine pointed brush with Magenta. Sap Green was used for the stem and the shadow on the side and underneath the flowers was a mix of green and Magenta. Building up the painting in a series of small brushstrokes, waiting for each application to dry before applying another, produces crispness and clarity.

Working from life, outdoors, can present challenges of changing light as the sun moves across the sky and the colours and tones can change dramatically. A solution is to work in separate sessions at the same time of day or to use quick studies and sketches.

The Gardener

This is a striking ornamental flower from North America and has been introduced to most of Europe. It is so named as it opens its sulphur-yellow flowers in the evening. Flowers of the *Oenothera* genus are not primroses and only some of them open in the evening, but they all have similar and recognisable features. The evening primrose is an erect, robust biennial with immense broad multi-branched spikes of yellow flowers, which keep their depth of colour as the flowers mature.

A remarkable technique is employed to open them. The petals are held together by hooks at the end of the flower cup and their segments separate at the lower part, so that the corolla, the inner whorl, can be seen for some time before the force of expansion is strong enough to unhook the flower cup at the top. When unhooked, the corolla opens out instantaneously and then halts as it takes time to spread out flat. The interval taken from the first exposure of the corolla at the bottom to its full expansion is about half an hour. Naturally this remarkable operation is a source of wonder.

They are a varied group of biennials, long-lived perennials and short lived perennials producing insect-friendly spikes of flowers. There are 250 species, mostly native to Europe and Turkey, all found on poorer disturbed soil, in sunny open sites with good drainage, and they are excellent for dry gardens like mine. They have deep taproots, which allow them to suck up water in drought conditions. Verbascum often sets copious amounts of seed, and saved seed should be kept until spring and sown in warm conditions by pressing into damp compost, keeping in the shade and avoiding hot conditions, as high temperatures impede germination and halt growth. The seedlings should be pricked out and kept in cool conditions until the roots reach the bottom of the pot, and then planted out before the taproot develops. If the strong taproot on a verbascum is disturbed the plant fails.

O. biennis is a biennial, making a rosette of narrow leaves in its first year, and in the second it puts up a slender stem carrying a daily succession of one or two yellow blooms from early evening until morning. Another biennial is *O. erythrosepala*, which is much stronger-growing with broader leaves. It is pleasantly scented and once established in the garden is unlikely to fail. *O. missouriensis* is a prostrate, sprawling herbaceous perennial and is hardy if not waterlogged. It is excellent as a front-line plant with yellow flowers opening in early evening and lasting for about a day. These are scentless. In winter it disappears, so the area needs careful observation when weeding. *O. macrocarpa* has enormous seed pods with flanges like wings. *O. tetragona riparia* is a hardy perennial which makes dense basal rosettes of narrow foliage in winter. In early summer the flowering stems are small but numerous, expanding in the day and shutting at night. The flowers come in subtle and unusual shades of white, citrus lemon, caramel, strawberry pink and violet-purple and often have dark-purple-with-pink centres.

Aaron's rod is one of the common names for great mullein and is a magnificent upright architectural-looking plant which self-seeds. *V. bombyciferum*, the statuesque mullein, has numerous silver stems of yellow flowers enclosed in a woolly down. The furry leaves resist water loss. They are reputed to have been used as insoles for children's shoes as they are soft to the touch. *V. phoeniceum* has violet flowers. *V.* 'Helen Johnson' was a seedling that occurred at Kew Gardens in 1990. It has strawberry-pink flowers with brown overtones and gave rise to *V.* 'Cherry Helen', a cherry-red to pink, and *V.* 'Megan's Mauve'. Several strains have been bred by Patricia Cooper in Norfolk, England, and Vic Johnstone and Claire Wilson from Whitchurch. Their introductions include the pale-pink *V.* 'Merlin', with finely rimmed pink petals, and *V.* 'Clementine', a radiant sunset orange with purple stamens. Also available are bright-yellow *V.* 'Tropic Sun' and orange-brown *V.* 'Tropic Spice', and, from Thompson and Morgan, *V.* 'Blue Lagoon', the bluest verbascum so far. These hybrids are short in stature and are sterile, so never set seed. They have to be propagated by root cuttings from dormant plants. However, being sterile means that they have prolonged flowering, giving months of colour.

Root cuttings should be taken from strong, healthy roots, divided into lengths, remembering which is top and bottom, and buried vertically in gritty compost so that the top part is just at soil level. Choose vigorous plants with pencil-thick roots, cutting at the crown. They succeed better with warmth from below rather than in the sun, and should be kept moist. When healthy new growth appears it means the cutting has taken. Pot them on individually in potting compost. When the roots fill the pot they can be planted out in the garden. Some other plants which can be propagated from root cuttings are acanthus, campanula, Japanese anemone, mint, oriental poppy and *Primula denticulata*.

Verbascum has strong branching flower spikes, which open from waxy buds and are set flat against the stem so that the flowers face outwards. It is a majestic feature for the back of the border or in semi-wild settings.

V. × hybrida is a group of summer-flowering hybrids with flower spikes in chrome yellow, deep yellow with a magenta eye at the top to pale yellow and lilac lower down. There are also terracotta and yellow, amber and buff, primrose yellow, yellow and pink, white and deep rose. *V. longifolia* has hairy leaves and bright-yellow flowers in dense spikes. *V. olympicum* is long-lived and suitable for wild gardens and has tall stems of bright-yellow flowers in widely branched spikes. *V. thapsiforme* is rosette-forming, with felted, crinkly, mid-green oblong leaves densely covered with yellow hairs and tapering spikes of yellow flowers. The perfume is wonderful and it sets copious amounts of seed and, like most species of mulleins, is biennial, dying once they have flowered, but life can be prolonged by cutting the flower spike. They originate from Turkey, the Middle East and the Mediterranean.

These architectural plants are often found as seeding plants in the road verges. The common mullein has spires of yellow flowers, each with clear-orange stamens. The modern cultivars are in pink, rose and salmon.

The mullein is a native of Southern Europe, but now ranges over all Europe and North Africa. *Verbascum thapsus* takes its name first from Pliny, as a corruption of *barbascum*, meaning with beards, and *thapsus* comes from the Sicilian town where it grew. It is thought that the seed was brought in sailing ships among ballast to colonise the New World. It is mucilaginous and has been used since ancient times in the treatment of pulmonary congestion, even for cattle, and is still considered an effective remedy for coughs and colds. In the second season, the pale rigid stalk rises from the centre – hence the names Jacob's staff, Jupiter's staff, Peter's staff and shepherd's staff. At this time the stalks were dipped in suet or wax and used for torchlight. It was also known as candlewick plant, for the silky down of its leaves was used to form wicks and tinder before lamps were in general use. The vernacular name hag-taper is from the Anglo-Saxon *hege* or *haga*, a hedge, denoting the usual habitat of the plant, where its tapering growth looked like candles or torches as they stood in the hedge to light the harvest-home procession. Its thick felt-like foliage, which forms a stout-based rosette and then sends up sturdy stems, gives it the vernacular names of blanket weed, beggar's blanket, blanket leaf, velvet dock, feltwort, flannel weed, Our Lord's flannel, fluffweed, hare's bear, old man's flannel and rag paper. In France, its local name is *bouillon blanc* (white soup) and also *herbe de St Fiacre*, who is the patron saint of gardeners and whose saint's day is 30 August. It has an impressive, tall, tapering spire of light-yellow flowers with soft-green-silver foliage covered in woolly hairs. The egg-shaped capsules split lengthwise to release many tiny pitted seeds. The dried tops of the plant were once used as flares – hence other common names such as torch-blade and hedge-taper. A distillation of the flowers was formerly used to treat gout, and an infusion made a remedy for coughs and colds even though the plant is poisonous. The nectar and pollen of the flowers is easily accessible to both honeybees and bumblebees as well as sawflies, and the mullein moth eats the leaves. In the garden it is most effective at the back of the border and in full sun. As it is a biennial it should be raised from seed annually.

V. nigrum (dark mullein) is distinguished by its stamens with dense purple hairs on the filaments and its kidney-shaped anthers. Flowers are on a long, slender spike, yellow with purple spots at the base.

V. creticum is a robust greyish-hairy biennial with a slender spike of large yellow and strongly toothed or lobed leaves.

Mulleins are poisonous to livestock and are avoided by them.

HEUCHERA
(coral bells, coral flower, alum root)

The Painting
At the start of a painting I have a goal which determines everything that I want to portray. This includes the image, the size, the colours and the composition, all of which are carefully chosen and assembled to create the atmosphere I want to capture.

Shapes of individual plants are not as important as how they are placed in relation to each other. A disjointed composition can result when shapes are placed aimlessly rather than combining them into interesting groups. Visually I want a beautifully balanced pattern of attractive shapes working within the scene to support the original idea. The colours must relate to each other, so a little of each colour placed in adjoining shapes helps to create colour harmony. Each colour influences its surrounding colour – for example, orange surrounded by reds will appear more yellow, but if surrounded by yellow it will appear more red. Green in a field of yellow appears more blue, but in a field of blue appears more yellow. Violet will appear more red when surrounded by blue, but in among shades of red becomes indigo.

Tone is a measure of the lightness and darkness of a colour. Light and dark tones are also referred to as high and low tones. Yellow is the lightest-toned of the hues; violet is the darkest. Tonal order is important when placing colours. A pale orange is good next to a deep blue and a dark orange with light blue. Warm colours such as hues in the yellow/orange/red part of the spectrum, tend to stand out and appear closer than cool colours – the blues, blue-greens and violets.

269

The heuchera leaves and flower stalks were carefully painted before adding the background using yellow-greens to complement the dominant Quinacridone Violet.

The Gardener
The plant is named after Johann Heinrich von Heucher 1677–1747, professor of medicine at Wittenberg.

Heucheras are one of the few perennials with intense, lasting and vibrant leaf colour. The heart-shaped leaves range from green to pink and purple, spangled with various colours, and some have contrastingly coloured veins. The bell-shaped flowers are borne in elegant sprays on long reddish stems, in shades of pink, red, white or greenish yellow. The leaves are attractive in themselves. Purple-leaved plants can have their colour enhanced by sunshine and can fade to dirty-green tints in shade. Yellow leaves enjoy full sunshine and are restful to the eye without detracting from other elements in the scene. Yellow foliage can have a similar effect to that of yellow flowers and provides a welcome splash of colour throughout the year. However, some plants which grew happily in my garden in Devon were not happy in dry free-draining soil here in the Pays de la Loire, so had to be moved to shade and in some cases from a sunny border into the shade.

Heucheras are woodland plants from North America to Mexico and almost to the Arctic, and so can tolerate shade. In the late 1980s in an Oregon garden a plant was found with white-mottled leaves, and at Kew Gardens a spotted deep-purple-leaved plant was found among a batch of seedlings. It was called 'Palace Purple' after the royal residence in the gardens and inspired a breeding programme that resulted in a wealth of leaf colours. Since 2010, fifty-seven new varieties have been launched, with breeders producing plants with larger leaves and trailing stems. They are readily divided in spring; but where more than one species is grown, crossing is apt to occur, so that seed cannot be relied upon to be true to the parent.

Heucheras sanguinea 'Ruby bells' has crossed with other species to give wonderful varieties. Most of the improvements in recent years have come from crosses between *H. brizoides* and *H. sanguinea*. The former species has small flowers carried gracefully on wiry stems, more freely produced than those of the larger, brighter-flowered *H. sanguinea*. The result has been to induce free-flowering varieties with a wider colour range that greatly enhances the border from May to July or even longer.

Heucheras need good drainage. They form compact evergreen clumps suitable either for the front of the border or around the base of shrubs. Planting is safe at any time between September and April, and when dividing old clumps only the most vigorous shoots are used and set in a deep hole with added compost and leaf mould.

SUMMER HYACINTH

Galtonia candicans (jacinthe du cap, spire lily). Galtonia is in the family of Hyacinthaceae and Asparagaceae.

The Painting

I did a detailed drawing and because I wanted a washy background I masked out the white flowers and buds so as to retain the white of the paper. I laid in a wash of differing amounts of Sap Green, let it dry and then removed the mask. I then painted the leaves and stalks, darkening the green in the shadow areas. I used a dilute blue to indicate shadows on the flowers and buds to give an idea of shape and shadow. Then the painting was assessed and more darks were added where needed.

The Gardener

Candicans means becoming pure white. Galtonias were discovered by Thomas Cooper at the side of a stream in the foothills of the De Beers Pass in South Africa. It was described by Baker in 1870 as *Hyacinthus candicans*, but was transferred shortly afterwards to the genus *Galtonia* by the French botanist Decaisne. The genus is named after Sir Francis Galton, 1822–1911, who published a book on his travels in South Africa. A recent study of the hyacinth family in sub-Saharan Africa proposes to include galtonias in the large genus *Ornithogalum*.

These bulbous perennials have erect strap-shaped leaves with tall stems of dainty nodding, pendulous, bell-shaped, waxy, luminous white flowers, which have a light but heady scent. *G. viridiflora* has green flowers. They sometimes have pale green on the outside with a very pale-green median band running up the back of each lobe. They are one of the latest bulbous flowering plants, giving a fabulous late-summer show when many other plants are past their best. The flowers are long-lasting (up to six weeks), so are ideal for cut-flower arrangements.

Galtonias look wonderful massed together or in borders and superb if planted in containers or as a centrepiece. They should be planted from late winter to early spring and placed in full sun, but in moist conditions, and the bulbs set just below the soil surface. If planted later in May the flowers last longer in the slightly cooler autumn than those flowering in the summer heat. I water the plants regularly in spring and summer, but keep them dry in winter. They are reasonably hardy, but benefit from a winter mulch as they are dormant from autumn to spring.

They can be propagated from collected seed as soon as they are ripe and sown into seed compost and protected in a cold greenhouse or cold frame for two years. It is easier to take offsets during the dormant season in early spring and grow them on in containers for the first year, planting out in the following spring.

BELLFLOWER
Campanulaceae, *Campanula lactiflora* (Canterbury bell). The campanula represents gratitude, or faith and constancy, or coquetry.

Painting 1

Canterbury bells are beautifully shaped. This was a simple study using only violet for the flowers, a mixed green for the foliage and a little yellow for the stamens. The shapes of the flowers are intriguing in that they are fat, rounded and yet at the same time delicate, and each forms a beautiful arrangement on the plant. Quinacridone Violet was used for the main body of the flowers with a touch of Quinacridone Magenta added into the violet for the outer petals and prominent veins. The leaves and stalks were mixed with the same yellow used for the stamens, plus Cobalt Blue and a little violet added to darken shadows on the leaves and stem. The flowers make quite a statement on their own. I decided against adding a background.

The Gardener

Campanula medium originates in Southern Europe and is naturalised in mostly European countries. Canterbury bells carry their large bell-shaped flowers in broad spikes in summer. The cup-and-saucer varieties have an extra ring and flat petals behind each bell, and the double varieties have several bells, one inside the other. They grow well in my flower border in full sun or part shade, lasting longer in dappled shade. They reach 1.2 metres when in flower and will self-seed, flowering in the following year. The seeds ripen from August to September and are dispersed by gravity alone.

They are either self-fertilised or pollinated by bees and butterflies. They are a good source of food for bees and other insects as the bell-shaped flowers are easy to enter.

Painting 2
The linking of positive and negative spaces forces the mind to be creative and form an implied space around the image. The reduction of shape and value to a limited scale focuses the mind on detail. What is studied can be magically transformed into a visual statement of images, colours and lines all based on the original

study. The better the observation the more is understood, and these details can be incorporated into the painting. Working from direct observation, recording light and its transitory nature means that planning is crucial. The period available before the light and shadows change is about three hours on a sunny day and perhaps four under an overcast sky. The time may be drastically reduced if painting in the early or late hours of the day. The changing light can alter the scene dramatically, so time management is important. There are no hard rules when working from nature, due to the possibilities and challenges presented.

The Gardener

After the richly scented wallflowers, the brilliance of sweet williams and the fabulous sweet rocket come foxgloves, delphiniums and Canterbury bells. All these plants are biennial and should be sown so that they have a year to mature before flowering in the following year. Biennials produce vegetative growth, roots and foliage, and then rest over winter before long-lasting violet, blue, pink or white blooms appear from May to July, and eventually set seed. Campanula is associated with the cottage garden and often is planted alongside hollyhocks, foxgloves, roses and ox-eye daisies, giving grace and elegance to the flower border.

My favourite campanula is a showy, vigorous spreader which looks beautiful growing over a wall. It has violet-blue bellflowers which bloom for a long period in sheltered areas, from February. The pretty leaves are small and toothed and are attractive even without the flowers.

This genus has over 500 species of mostly perennial herbs with a few annuals or biennials and some low-growing alpines widely dispersed over the northern hemisphere, especially the Mediterranean region. Campanulas have bell-shaped flowers which vary from open saucer to tubular shapes. It is a diverse group, varying from invasive creepers to tall perennials. They grow in a range of wild habitats, from rocky mountains to damp woodland, hence there is a campanula for each situation in a garden. Generally doubles last longer than singles, but these must be cut down after flowering to prevent inferior seedlings germinating. Some self-seed aggressively. The majority are hardy, needing good drainage but plenty of moisture in the growing season. The annuals are sown in April, the biennials in June, the perennials in April or May in the open or in a cold frame. The perennials are mostly propagated by division or by seed or – the preferred method – by young cuttings in spring. The name is from the Latin *campana,* a bell, an allusion to the starry bell shape of the flower. In the wild they are known as harebells. The dainty harebell grows on free-draining banks or the sides of ditches along the lanes. In the garden they do best in a sunny position and in good soil.

C. rapunculoides (creeping bellflower) is a perennial with blue drooping flowers borne in slender one-sided spike-like leafless clusters. It must be planted with discretion as it spreads freely with running rhizomes. *C. bonariensis* is similar to *C. rapunculoides*, but with smaller blue-lilac flowers and without 'creeping buds'. *C. crustalocalyx* is easily grown in ordinary soil. *C.* 'Alba Coronata' is a semi-double, white, and *C.* 'Alba Flore Pleno' double, white and good for cutting. *C.* 'Coerulea Coronata' and *C.* 'Coerulea Flore Pleno' are semi-double and blue. *C. moerheimii* is white, semi-double on slender stems. *C. maxima* is about twice as large as type. The elegant *C.* 'Hampstead White' has white flowers and cool green buds on strong stems, and flowers for many weeks. 'La Belle' is a newer deep-blue double. *C. lactiflora* has panicles of white flowers similar to phlox and, like all campanulas, turns brown as it fades, but by cutting off the upper spent flowers, more will appear lower down, giving many more weeks of blooms. All *lactiflora*s fade after three or four years as the woody roots become gnarled and rise above the soil. It is best to take cuttings every spring. *C. garganica* has star-shaped blue or white flowers and a trailing habit, so is ideal for a drystone wall or a rock garden. They need no fertiliser – especially the taller-growing varieties – as this will make them grow even taller and then they will need staking. They are very happy in my free-draining soil in between rocks and in full sun. They are a good source of food for insects as the flower is easy for them to access. *C.*

trachelium, or bats in the belfry, is an erect rough-stemmed perennial with large bell-shaped blue flowers in a long leafy cluster. *C. latiloba* 'Hidcote Amethyst' has pretty lilac-pink flowers and is a favourite, as is *C. latifolia* 'Eriocarpa', with elegant spires of purple flowers. It prefers good soil.

FOXGLOVE

Digitalis purpurea (common foxglove, goblin gloves). *Digitus* means finger, with reference to the flower shape.
Their likeness to thimbles gives the species the Latin name *Digitalis*, which means thimble.

The Painting and Drawing

French apothecaries took the foxglove for their symbol and ornamented their doorposts and the piers between their windows with paintings of the flowers. When drawing the flowers I analysed the shape. This flower is seen as a cylinder within which are the individual florets. I looked closely at the form and detail. The stem is important to the drawing, with leaves in rosettes and also on the stems. I noted how the buds and stem decrease in size at the tip. Drawing is the foundation of all visual art forms and essential to creating a good painting, so a range of tones is important and observation must be paramount.

This study made the painting easier and I really enjoyed this painting as the shapes of the flowers and the pyramid shape of the plant are so elegant. I used only a few colours. Quinacridone Magenta in varying shades was used for the flowers. It was important to use a dilute Magenta for the light areas, and the darks had to be very dark, so a little violet was added. Quinacridone Violet was used for the interior spots of the flower and the shaded parts of the stalks. For the leaves the green was a mix of Ultramarine Blue and Indian Yellow, and this same yellow was lightly brushed on to the buds at the top of the plant.

It is fascinating to watch the bees climbing into the foxglove tubes and emerging laden with pollen.

The Gardener

Leonhard Fuchs, whose own name was given to the fuchsia, was the first writer to call this plant by the name of digitalis, because of the flowers resembling finger stalls. According to the naturalist Sowerby, foxglove means 'Fuchs' glove', but only in so far as 'Fuchs' is German for fox. Other authorities suggest that the name is a corruption of 'fairy folks' gloves', and in various country districts it has various names of fairy bells, fairy petticoats, fairy thimbles, fairy fingers, red fingers and Our Lady's glove. The slight tendency of the stem to arch, allowing the bell-shaped flowers to fall, earns the plant its English name, from the Anglo-Saxon *foxes-gleow*. A *gleow* being a musical instrument in the form of an arch hung with graduated bells. There is a host of local names – flowater-leaves, fox-fingers, lady's thimble, pop-glove (because the unopened flowers will pop when pressure is exerted by the finger and thumb, opening to make a finger stall), witches' fingers and witches' bells. In Devon it was called flop-top, flappy-dock and flop-a-dock, and on the borders of Dartmoor the children played a game in which they puffed the bells full of wind to make them go off with a bang when struck with the hand. In literature it had a sinister role when Gideon Sarn in *Precious Bane* poisoned his old mother with foxglove tea. The Scots called it dead man's bells and bloody fingers. In the precincts of Edinburgh Castle there is a drinking fountain designed by John Duncan to mark the spot where the last of the witches were burned. Two female heads – one full of hate and venom, and the other serene and beautiful – a serpent, standing for both evil and wisdom, and a foxglove flower, for its dual nature of poisoning and healing, commemorate the martyrdom of the wise women, or witches of the superstitious past.

When I moved to France, I collected as many plants as I was able, and in doing so gained knowledge about what would grow in my garden and what conditions are best for them. I have never before had such a variety of garden plants, including exotic species from overseas and new hybrids as well as wild flowers that have strayed from fields and woods. The foxglove is a beautiful wild flower. It was brought to the herbalists' gardens, and thence to the cottage garden, when its medicinal properties were discovered. It was a remedy for the healing of wounds and the cure of diseases of the heart. There was nothing that the foxglove was not expected to do, and it is still used in medicine today.

The magnificent perennial foxglove (its common name) has tapering columns of hanging bell-shaped yellow or pink flowers, some spotted pinky purple, and soft downy leaves. In the ordinary varieties the flowers droop on one side of the spike, but in 'Excelsior' they are held outwards all round the spike. Colours range from white and cream to pink and rose red.

The foxglove has given medicine one of its most useful drugs – digitalin – which is used in the treatment of disease. It was William Withering who first recorded the use of digitalin in the treatment of dropsy and years later published his own theories. His studies were of necessity slow, because his patients were also his human guinea pigs. Unfortunately, his partner, Erasmus Darwin, being more eminent at the time, was credited with much of the work and accepted the credit. Withering wrote his thesis and was able to report his case histories in considerable detail, with the result that he was highly regarded for this work and received recognition by being elected a Fellow of the Royal Society. So closely identified was Withering with the plant that his memorial in Edgbaston old church in Birmingham, England, is embellished with the foxglove. In the National Museum, Stockholm, his portrait shows him holding the plant with which his name is associated. He died in 1799 – the year when it was established that the primary action of digitalin is upon the heart, as a reducer of the pulse rate. The drug digitalin is obtained from the dark-green leaves of the common foxglove – one of the few British native plants to be included in the British Pharmacopoeia.

The foxglove is a hardy biennial which thrives in partial shade, flowering in its second year. Biennials will die after they set seed, but may take longer to pass through the various stages of their growth. The name suggests that biennials survive for two years, but in practice it is nearer eighteen months.

Foxgloves make excellent plants, valued in the garden for their spire form, which is so useful at the back of lightly shaded borders, woodlands or wild gardens in a humus-rich soil. The purple spikes of the foxglove give drama as well as height to the borders and can self-seed in the most unexpected places. Cultivation is simple. The plants grow from seed, and once the plant has flowered will self-seed for many years. The egg-shaped seed capsule ripens and turns black, splitting to release small dark seeds, and once established will seed freely, but can smother other plants and seedlings. Spring-sown plants can be planted out in their final flowering positions during September and October and will flower the following year. They grow naturally in woodland edges and glades, so they like their roots in cool shade, while the flowers are happy in heavy shade or bright sunshine. The middle of a well-stocked sunny border is perfect for them. They need loose, well-drained soil to encourage their roots to settle. They also like moisture, so I add plenty of organic compost before planting and keep them well watered while they grow. Foxgloves can be invasive, spreading by seeding, and can damage other plants by smothering them, so need plenty of space. Foxgloves produce a growth stimulant that gives nearby plants increased vigour.

The foxglove is native to Europe, but new plants have been bred from *Digitalis purpurea* – pink and white, some splattered with chocolate spots. *D. purpurea* is a tall, erect biennial with large tubular bright-pinkish-purple flowers with purple spots on a white background on the lower side of the corolla tube within. Several varieties have been developed from the wild *D. purpurea*. 'Alba' has white flowers; others have tall spikes of white, cream, pink and Carmine flowers spotted with maroon. *D.* 'Excelsior' bears flowers that are held almost horizontally, allowing a glimpse of the spotted throats. *D. grandiflora* is a long-lived and reliable species. It has soft, hairy leaves and arching stems of soft-yellow flowers loved by bees. The flowers have a network of brown veins within, hairy outside and are very poisonous. *D.* × *mertonensis* comes true from seed, and its colour has been described as 'squashed strawberries'. It is not quite as tall as other foxgloves and is a short-lived hybrid between *D. grandiflora* and the common biennial foxglove. It has tapering spikes of densely packed strawberry-pink flowers.

Steeped in mythology, the bell-shaped blooms attract birds, bees and gardeners alike. The nectar attracts bees, which pollinate the flowers as they work their way up into the throat of the flower. The leaves are food for the caterpillars of fritillary butterflies.

BEGONIA
Begoniaceae (angel-wing, cordiality)

Painting 1

Observation is important, but knowing, not just seeing, and exaggerating the positive and eliminating the negative, comes into the composition. Stalks and leaves will pass either behind or in front of the flowers, while between them are shapes of empty space. In reality, these shapes are various greens and are an important part of the painting. Every painting must have a design, a structure, a foundation of lines and shapes on which to build. Used carefully they provide balance in colour, shape and tone, offsetting the flowers to great effect.

The power of red is enhanced when surrounded by greys and neutrals. If another colour is introduced then the power of the red is diminished. For this reason I decided not to include a background. The most important shapes are those between the flower heads. These are called negative spaces and are important as they highlight the positive shapes. Unequal proportions and dark and light areas are part of the design.

276

The Gardener

The begonia is named after Michel Bégon, 1638–1710, a French patron of botany, Governor of Canada. *Begonia* is a genus of 350 species of succulent herbs or sub-shrubs, with a few climbers and some tuberous rhizomes and in others a distinct tuber. The forms of the tuberous-rooted begonias include a very wide range of colours and fimbriated, frilled and crested varieties as well as pendulous ones ideal for hanging baskets. Pendula varieties, or cascading begonias, are shade-loving and have a slender trailing habit suitable for hanging baskets. They prefer low light or partial shade with no more than several hours of sunshine. Too much light will cause the foliage to become dull and the flower colour to fade. These begonias are planted in the spring and bloom from midsummer until frosts begin. They should not be allowed to dry out or, conversely, to sit in excess moisture as this may cause rot. Extra-long stems should be picked off to encourage blooming, and by pinching out the primary growing tip to create lots of branches. Deadheading will encourage repeat flowering.

Painting 2

The orange of the flowers is picked up by the yellow used in mixing the green, hinting at a touch of orange in the tips of the leaves and accentuated by the cool blue-green in the background. The coiled shapes of the flowers was complicated, but, with attention to the tones, can be explained so the light and dark areas are evident. The petals were painted with Indian Orange, with red used to shadow the inner part of each petal, leaving the outer rims paler where they caught the light.

The Gardener

There is no week throughout the year when the rich colours and beautiful form of the flowers are not on display either in the cool or the warm greenhouse, while the many tuberous- or fibrous-rooted varieties bloom in summer bedding. The tuberous-rooted varieties are descended from several species introduced by Messrs James Veitch & Sons of Chelsea between 1865 and 1868. *B. boliviensis* and *B. cinnabarina* were introduced by E. G. Henderson of Pineapple Place Nursery. The first hybrid tuberous-rooted begonia raised in England was *B.* × *sedenii* in 1870, the result of crossing *B. boliviensis* with an unknown Andean species. Many different forms and colours were introduced at Chelsea – the progenitors of the present-day begonias.

Begonia semperflorens has fleshy stems with vibrant-coloured blooms in scarlet, orange, yellow, white, pink and red, and flowers in full sun or partial shade. The leaves are shiny and succulent and either green, variegated or bronze-coloured. As they are not frost-hardy, they need to be potted up and brought into the house so as to continue flowering. It is regarded as the queen of bedding plants, hanging baskets and window boxes and thrives in sun or shade. *B. semperflorens* and its many beautiful variations are, like the tuberous-rooted varieties, easily raised from seed or from cuttings. These must be grown from shoots springing from the base of the old flowering stems and started in warmth early in the year. Some varieties come true from seed raised in the autumn or early in the year, grown on steadily and gradually hardened off until ready for planting out when all danger of frost is past. They flower with great profusion all season and appear indifferent to the weather, doing equally well in hot, dry or wet spells.

The half-hardy *B. tuberhybrida*, will grow outdoors in summer, but needs storing in dry compost in a frost-free environment in winter. Multiflora non-stop varieties have clusters of small bright flowers carried above the foliage and are useful for summer bedding as the plants are dwarf and compact, They are double or semi-double. Where large numbers are required, they are propagated by cutting up the tubers. They should be started in gentle heat early in the year, and then shoots can be taken and potted into a propagator to root. Large camellia-flowered double varieties are vigorous and weather-resistant, have double flowers with frilled petals, are drought-tolerant and have scented flowers which open at dusk through to dawn. Begonia seeds are extremely small and should be sown on pans or pots of well-drained, light, sandy soil which has been well watered before the seed is sown. They should not be covered in soil. A pane of glass should be put over the pans and they should be placed in warmth, shaded from sunshine. As soon as seedlings are big enough to handle safely, they should be pricked out into leaf mould until large enough to pot on. Stem cuttings root freely in pots of sand and leaf mould in heat, as do leaf cuttings, cut across the main veins and held down with rock. Male and female flowers are borne separately on the same plant, but the latter are insignificant compared with the showy, generally double, male flowers.

B. semperflorens-cultorum, or wax begonias, come in shades of red, pink or white in summer to autumn. *Begonia* 'Lucerna' is a vigorous hybrid capable of growing into a massive ornamental plant.

Painting 3

I was attracted to this subject because of the many types of bright light on the petals against darker leaves. My paintings are almost always a visual response to the light and how it changes the simplest subjects into fascinating forms. The movement of light moves the interest around the painting.

I started with a positive image of what to emphasise and what to convey and an idea of the composition of colours and the balance of light and shade. I began with a precise drawing, thinking about the shapes and considering the colour combinations. I wanted to paint as if seeing for the first time and to be faithful to nature – not simply to copy, but to recreate nature and life through understanding what is seen. Accidents and the unexpected are part of the risk-taking and often produce interesting results, creating a unique experience. Going beyond the superficial appearance of things forces an artist into the realm of exploration.

278

The dark leaves gave the white petals a dramatic feel. Contrast creates drama. For these dark areas I used dilute Permanent Rose and green, which was mixed from Ultramarine Blue and Winsor Yellow. Both the rose and green were used in painting the leaves. These same colours were used in a suggestion of the background, and dilute touches of blue were used in the shadows on the petals and yellow for the stamens.

KNIPHOFIA

(tritona, red-hot poker plant or torch lily)

Johann Hieronymus Kniphof, 1704–1763, professor of medicine at Erfut, Germany, was the author of *Botanica in Originali*, a folio of coloured illustrations of plants, in 1747.

Painting 1

Sometimes too much in a scene will be confusing. It is better to exaggerate the object or focal point and create a definite eye path around the painting. An interesting tonal plan includes very dark and very light areas, and these should be grouped. Lots of contrast suggests a sunny bright day, and colours close in tone create a moody, misty, mysterious effect.

The real beauty of watercolour is its brilliance of colour and ability to dry quickly. I strive to give the shadows the right colour and to keep them transparent so that they shine out, giving the painting a lively feel, emanating light as if the shadows glow with an inner light. Here I painted an initial wet wash over the background, hopefully to suggest the roses on the wall and the slate path. When dry, darker, but still subtle, colour was added. Care was taken to reserve the white of the paper for the flowers and spiky leaves, and then these were worked up when the initial painting was dry. Sunlit flowers projecting forward from the darker background give the subject contrast with interplay of light against dark, one intensifying the other. Once the correct balance of mood, atmosphere, lighting, soft and hard edges, colour and tonal contrast has been achieved, the painting is put to one side for later assessment. The importance is not what is painted, but how it is painted, and to stop painting once the statement has been made.

279

Painting 2

I chose a blue wash for the background as a complementary to the yellow flowers of the kniphofia. The main flower petals were painted with Winsor Yellow and the shadowed centres with Indian Yellow. These two yellows were mixed with the Ultramarine used in the background.

Painting 3

Flowers are inspirational, as are the arrangements of shapes, forms, colours and groupings. The garden is an amazing subject and a great source of inspiration. The sunlight creates wonderful lights and shadows that filter through fragile petals. There are endless fascinating ways in which the light interacts in surprising and beautiful ways to compose rich darks and sparkling highlights. It is always the narrative of light which is important; light can change even the most mundane and everyday scene into a source of inspiration.

I often place a dark value on the paper to provide a level from which to gauge the other values. When using watercolour it is easy to paint too light; so by placing the dark early on, the other values can be more easily assessed. It is interesting to compare the flower heads against the dark greens and those against the pale green.

The Gardener

Comprising a genus of about twenty-four species, red-hot pokers are natives of Southern and Eastern Africa and Madagascar – hence they like full sun and well-drained soil. The common names refer to the close heads of typically scarlet flowers surmounting a stout stem. There are many varieties, differing in colour. 'Maid of Orleans' is ivory, 'Royal Standard' is scarlet and yellow, and *Kniphofia uvaria* 'Grandiflora' is coral and yellow. 'Goldelse' is a soft golden yellow and 'Atlanta' is evergreen with red-and-yellow flowers early to midsummer. They are perennials with lower spikes and narrow strappy leaves, from which grow a thick stalk with flower spikes in yellow with hot-red or orange tips. They are outstanding as a focal point in a border, especially when planted in bold groups and clumps, which should remain undisturbed. Most have a specific flowering time and none will flower all summer. There are also mid- to late-season kniphofias.

Deadheading after flowering will not induce more flowers, but will stop the plants wasting energy in producing seed pods and improves the look of the plant. A good mulch around the crowns in spring will feed them and help retain moisture and encourage flowering. Even the more hardy species benefit from some protection in severe weather.

Propagation is by division of old plants in early spring by easing them apart underwater so as to limit root damage. Care should be taken that the divisions do not become dry before or after planting. They need plenty of water in spring and summer. Kniphofias can also be raised from seed.

Amazingly, I have some self-seeded kniphofia growing in shaded areas and blooming well.

MARIGOLD
Tagetes (Mexican tarragon, French marigold, African marigold)

The Painting

The marigold has bright-orange flowers and leaves of green; but if viewed in sunshine, the intensity of the orange distorts the perception of the colour of the leaves so that they appear to be bright blue. However, in marigold plants that contain brilliant reds the cold-toned foliage acts as a foil.

Marigold blooms are complicated to paint, so I drew the shapes in light pencil. I used Winsor Lemon for the petals, using a fairly small brush for the detail and used Indian Yellow – a warmer, more orange yellow – to darken around the petals.

The green was mixed using the Winsor Yellow with Cobalt Blue for some leaves and the orange, Indian Yellow, with Ultramarine Blue for shaded areas, with shadowed areas darkened with Quinacridone Red. When dry, a larger brush loaded with water was used to wash around the flowers, as I wanted the background to be indistinct. Cobalt and Ultramarine Blue and green were dropped on to the wet paper, so as to enhance the contrast of cool colours against the yellow, and then I painted carefully up to and in between each outer petal. The washy green at the base gives the appearance of coolness. As it was a hot day I had to work quickly before the water evaporated, drying the paint, creating lines and unwanted marks, and the flowers drooped.

The Gardener

Marigolds are uniform in their height and compact habit. Their brilliant cheerfully coloured flowers bloom in succession through every sort of weather. By observation and experimentation one can learn to use plant characteristics to create pleasing effects, and gradually by experience build up a useful storehouse of plant knowledge. An understanding of how combinations of colour, form and texture work happily and productively together, together with knowledge of times of flowering, speeds of growth, and each plant's preferred growing conditions, and remembering to place scented plants near seating areas, are all part of the planning. I grow *Calendula officinalis* in the vegetable garden. It is not a true marigold, but is called pot or English marigold as its outer flower petals were used as flavouring in soups, stews and cheeses. The flowers may bloom all year long if the conditions are suitable. *C. officinalis* is widely cultivated and can be grown easily in sunny locations in most kinds of soil. Although perennial, it is commonly treated as an annual. Leaves are spirally arranged, simple and slightly hairy. The flower heads range from pastel yellow to deep orange, with both ray florets and disc florets. Most cultivars have a spicy aroma. It is recommended to remove dying flower heads so that plants maintain blossom production.

Seeds can be sown in March or April and pricked out as soon as seedlings are large enough to handle, and planted out when all chance of frost is past. They can be sown in open ground in May with the flowering display later, and can keep flowering into winter.

Marigold extract is an extremely effective herb for the treatment of skin problems and can be used wherever there is inflammation of the skin, whether due to infection or physical damage. As an ointment, marigold is an excellent cosmetic remedy for repairing minor damage to the skin, such as sub-dermal broken capillaries or sunburn. The sap from the stem is reputed to remove warts, corns and calluses.

African or American marigolds, *Tagetes erecta,* are tall, upright-growing plants with large flowers. African Marigolds are very good bedding plants. These flowers are yellow to orange and do not include red marigolds. The African marigold takes longer to reach its flowering stage than the French type.

The French marigold, *Tagetes patula,* has flowers of red, orange and yellow, also with red-and-orange bicolour. French marigolds are ideal for edging flower beds and in mass plantings. They also do well in containers and window boxes. The signet marigolds, *T. signata pumila,* produce compact plants with finely divided lacy foliage and clusters of small single flowers. They have yellow-to-orange edible flowers. The flowers of signet marigolds have a spicy tarragon flavour. The foliage has a pleasant lemon fragrance. Signet marigolds are excellent plants for edging beds and in window boxes.

MORNING GLORY
Convolvulus; Ipomoea (moonflower, bindweed)

Painting 1

I paint many different subjects because my passion for painting is endless; and I am inspired by flowers – an amazing subject, with their many varied forms and settings. Using a fine brush, I painted the flower with several blues – Cobalt and Ultramarine – and light Magenta for the buds. I then changed to a larger brush and thicker paint for the edges of the petals, keeping the central area light by adding more water, before adding in the stamens with Lemon Yellow. I painted the background freely with a mixture of greens, darkened in areas with a little Quinacridone Magenta. When this was dry, I painted leaves and tendrils using the same colours, darkening shadowed stems.

Painting 2
These stunningly beautiful flowers are a delight to paint as they twine and twist, making ready-made patterns and reflecting the light in their perfect blue.

The Gardener
Morning glory is in the family Convolvulaceae, with the generic name originating from the Greek *ipos* meaning worm or bindweed, and *homoios* meaning resembling, referring to their twining habit. In the language of flowers it is 'devoted friendship'. They are related to sweet potato, bindweed and moonflower. Morning glory has flowers shaped like trumpets in shades of blue or red with varieties in violet, white and yellow with white centres. I sometimes plant them among climbing roses or in among wisteria as they need support on which to twine. They can also be planted in hanging baskets and left to spill over the sides, creating a stunning display. The flowers come singly or in multiples in the axils of the upper leaves, closing by midday. The leaves are heart-shaped, long and pointed.

The seeds of morning glory are relatively hard and can be filed or nicked or soaked in water overnight prior to sowing in early spring. They prefer full sun and need little attention once established, except to water them now and then.

From midsummer onwards the profuse, transient trumpet-shaped flowers smother arches and trellises on which they climb with their twining habit.

Morning glory was first known in China for its medicinal uses due to the laxative properties of its seeds. It was introduced into Japan in the ninth century, where it was cultivated as an ornamental flower. The Japanese have developed hundreds of varieties, and it has come to symbolise summer in Japanese horticulture and art. Some varieties have evocative names, such as 'Heavenly Blue', which is a rich azure blue with a white throat, 'Brocade at Dawn', 'Wisteria Girl' and 'The Moon in the Dusk', a nocturnal bloomer which opens its flowers in the evening and closes them the next morning. It is very attractive to moths.

Ipomoea alba has white flowers. *I. nil* has violet, rose or blue flowers. 'Scarlett O'Hara' was named because of its larger stunningly red flowers and has a white throat. It is fast growing. *I. purpurea* (common morning glory) is more vigorous, with white, red or purple flowers; and *I. tricolor* has reddish-purple or blue yellow-throated long flowers.

LUPIN
Lupinus polyphyllus (lupine)

Painting 1

It is a pleasure to paint outside, interpreting all the elements – wind, clouds, heat, cold and rain – and developing a knowledge of what happens in nature. This was a complicated subject, so needed careful observation. Painting is all about being seduced by light and atmosphere and expressing one's emotional response and experiencing the mood, colours and dramatic shapes. Watercolour allows me to express my passions and, as I love lupins, what better subject?

Drawing is the foundation of paintings, just as a house must have foundations. By drawing before painting many problems can be faced and solved before starting to paint. I look at placing the shapes in the design, hoping the eye follows from one to another, but this flow can be made even more interesting when a profile is made prominent. The profile of the lupins takes centre stage, with the surrounding back border hinted at rather than described and the foreground more detailed. The most prominent flower spike was painted with Phthalo Blue in the centre and Ultramarine in the lower petals of each flower head, and in places it was overpainted with Winsor Violet. A very light, dilute violet was used for the shadowed parts of the white blooms. The adjacent flowers were less prominent, so the contrast was less marked. The bases of the foreground blooms were painted with Ultramarine Blue and violet, with a touch of pink in the shadowed white petals. I used Permanent

284

Rose in different strengths on the pink flower head, with a mix of light and dark green for the shoots, leaves and stalks, darkened in places with violet and blue.

Some brushstrokes were very carefully executed, while those in the background were loose to suggest rather than explain the detail.

The Gardener

Lupinus is the Latin name used by Virgil and Pliny, said to be from *lupus*, meaning wolf, as it was believed that lupins destroyed the fertility of the soil.

The stout spikes of the lupins are among the prettiest flowers, with their pea-like blooms packed densely on strong upright stems in pink, rich blues, deep purples, gold, orange, red, white and bright yellow. They can be in one colour, or the lower petals and upper may contrast in colour. If the spent blooms are cut back, a second flush of flowers may come later. It is best to remove the spent blooms as they can look untidy, and seed production weakens the plant. The lupin has handsome leaves.

Lupins are often classed as biennial – propagated one year to flower in the next. Seed can be sown in spring or autumn to germinate when placed in a cold frame. Home-raised plants and cuttings from friends are always more special. My dear friend Alison has given me a red lupin plant which will flower next year. Home propagation is a good way of obtaining plants which are not otherwise easily available for replacing short-lived plants. Carnations, pinks, delphiniums, aquilegias and strawberries are other short-lived plants.

The perennial lupins may be increased by commercially produced seed sown in spring, the seedlings planted in their permanent positions as soon as possible since they do not like being transplanted. Seed saved from the plant may be disappointing. They may successfully be increased by division or by basal cuttings in spring, when the shoots appear. These will root in water. Most species are hardy and are easily grown in moderately good soil, although some are intolerant of lime.

Tree lupins, *Lupinus arboreus*, flower in their second year from seed, and make very handsome fragrant bushes with masses of flowers in yellow or white or blue, on short racemes. *L. polyphyllus* crossed with *L. arboreus* has provided a range of colours and varied habits from careful selection, culminating in the Russel lupins.

Annual lupins – especially the yellow- or mauve-flowered *L. luteus* – have been used to increase the fertility of sandy soil as they have to take nitrogen from the air and, when they die, leave the soil richer in combined nitrogen than when they were sown. Lupins produce the best-quality protein of virtually any crop – even superior to that of soya, peas, beans and clover. They are then ploughed in as a green manure. These should be sown where they are to flower in April or May.

Lupins sit well with other summer flowers, such as hollyhocks, delphiniums and mallow. One group follows the other in rapid succession. The whole effect is of natural abundance, but, in fact, needs planning of shape and colour.

AMARANTHUS

Amaranthus caudatus (love-lies-bleeding); *Amaranthus hypochonriacus* (prince's feather)

The Painting

The perfect background for flower colours is green. Foliage is the most important element in the garden. With careful planning it gives a structure and creates atmosphere.

A blue-green will be cool, while a yellow-green stands out. I initially painted the background with a cool green, but there was too much contrast against the maroon of the flower tassels. When dry I washed pale yellow over the cool green, which solved the problem.

The shadows on the twisted flower stems were important in understanding the shape and pattern, but I used a harmonious violet against the pink. The cool shadow washes were painted over the dried warm pinks, allowing some of the warmth to glow through. The result is a luminous shadow that seems to vibrate with light.

The Gardener

Amaranthus is named after the Greek word *amarantos*, which means everlasting, or one that does not wither. It was cultivated by the Aztecs in Peru 8,000 years ago. It is thought to have been eighty per cent of their calorific consumption. The Aztec people celebrated with a festival involving amaranth and honey made into a statue of a god. They decorated their homes with flags, and there were dances, processions, songs, prayers and, finally, human sacrifices. At the end of the festivities the statue was cut into small pieces so everybody could eat a little piece of the god. After the Spanish conquest cultivation of amaranth was outlawed.

Today the grains are toasted and mixed with honey, molasses or chocolate to make a treat called *alegria*, meaning joy in Spanish. It is now grown in Africa, India, China, Russia, South America, North America and Europe.

The amaranthus, collectively known as amaranth, is upright, is moderately tall and is broad-leaved. Its flowers can be huge tassels or tiny globes, red, pink, yellow, cream or gold, and it is an annual plant. There are a number of different species of amaranthus and a huge number of varieties within those species. Amaranth is related to a common weed – pigweed. The wild amaranth types are also edible and taste similar to the cultivated varieties. They don't grow as large and leafy, or produce as many grains, or look as good in the garden.

Amaranthus leaves can be round or lance-shaped, five to fifteen centimetres long or more, light green, dark green, reddish or variegated. Seeds may be white, yellow, pink or black and appear similar to minuscule grains, but it is not a grain as in oats, wheat or rice. It is sometimes referred to as a 'pseudo-cereal' because its nutritional profile is very similar. It is gluten-free, and when ground is a pale-ivory shade, but as it is dense is best used with other grains for a lighter texture. Cooking the seeds is similar to rice. It is higher in minerals, such as calcium, iron, phosphorous, magnesium and potassium, carotenoids and vitamin C than most vegetables, yet contains few carbohydrates. Amaranthus leaves can be harvested at any time before it flowers. The buds are edible as well. The youngest leaves have a milder flavour and are good to use in salads; the mature leaves are better cooked like spinach. Amaranthus leaves contain three times more calcium and three times more niacin (vitamin B3) than spinach leaves, or twenty times more calcium and seven times more iron than lettuce. The leaves have a slightly sweet flavour.

My amaranthus loves the heat and can cope with dry conditions better than other leafy vegetables. It can grow to two metres high if given the right location. When I cut back the stem it reshoots and another harvest is produced. I leave some plants to mature so that the seed can be collected. The colourful flowers stay vibrant even after drying, when the seed can be shaken into a paper bag. There will be thousands of seeds for the next plantings. Seeds should be sown in April by thinly sprinkling them on the ground and raking them in, then thinning them out and transplanting them into permanent places in May. They are easily and best grown in rich loam. Like all fast-growing leafy greens, amaranth loves rich soil with steady moisture and a good supply of nutrients, especially nitrogen. Amaranth is easier than spinach or silver beet and is much hardier.

Some species are well-known garden plants, such as *A. caudatus* (love-lies-bleeding). It is a vigorous hardy annual with dark-purplish flowers on drooping spikes. *A. hypochondriacus* (prince's feather) has deeply veined lance-shaped leaves, purple on the under face, and deep-crimson flowers densely packed on erect spikes.

THUNBERGIA
Thunbergia alata (black-eyed Susan, blue trumpet, skyflower, or clock vine)

The Painting
This was a tangle of stems, leaves, buds and flowers, so close observation was needed. Two yellows were used for the flowers – Winsor Lemon and Indian Yellow – and these with Ultramarine Blue were mixed together for the greens in the leaves and stalks. Ultramarine Violet was added into the green making a suitable dark for the flower centres, and this was used behind the stalks and leaves. These darks, mostly in the centre of the study, helped to intensify the yellow of the petals.

The Gardener
The genus *Thunbergia* is named after Carl Peter Thunberg, a Swedish doctor who studied under Carolus Linnaeus. Thunbergias are herbaceous perennial climbing plants native to Eastern Africa and have naturalised in other parts of the

world. They have broad-mouthed trumpet flowers in summer. They are ornamental, perfect for hanging baskets or in the flower borders, where they will flow easily over walls and will grow up supports, spilling over edges. As they grow quickly they need a light feed with a complete fertiliser to keep them growing strongly. Mulching around the base of the plant helps keep the roots cool and moist. They can look stunning when grown with morning glory. They are tender to half tender, although often treated as hardy annuals, but can be overwintered under cover. I intend to buy *T. grandiflorum*, which is a more vigorous climber, reaching six metres, which may be perennial in milder climates. It has heart-shaped leaves and light-violet trumpet-shaped flowers with a yellow throat. *T. gregorii*, or orange clock vine, has brilliant golden-orange trumpet-shaped flowers. I also have a *T. alata*, or black-eyed Susan, which has orange flowers with dark brown-eyed centres. Thunbergia flowers have five warm-orange petals with a characteristic dark spot in the centre, although different varieties can be red, orange, red-orange, white, pale yellow or bright yellow, with or without a chocolate-purple centre. Flowers occur singly in the leaf axils. The flowers reflect ultraviolet light in a pattern that helps pollinating insects find the centre of the flower. A light trimming encourages more blossoms.

The name black-eyed Susan is thought to have come from a character that figures in many traditional ballads and songs. In the 'Ballad of Black-Eyed Susan' by John Gay, Susan goes aboard a ship in dock to ask the sailors where her lover 'sweet William' has gone. Black-eyed Susan is also a name given to other species of flowers in the genus *Rudbeckia*.

Propagation is easy if the seed is first soaked in warm water for a few days and then sown in loam-based compost under glass in bright light. Softwood cuttings can be taken in summer.

CARNATION AND PINK
Dianthus

The Greek name was given by Theophrastus in reference to the flower's fragrance and brilliance. *Dios* means divine and *anthos* means flower. In the language of flowers it is 'flower of love' or 'flower of the gods' and 'ardour.'

Painting 1
There is an intense sensual pleasure when sunlight bounces off leaves and through delicate petals. The intention was to portray this pleasure in the painting.

In watercolour, the highlights, the lightest values, must be left as unpainted white paper. These can be reserved by painting around, but the highlights should not be too numerous; otherwise the effect is ruined. Edges are important in that lost edges can be produced with very wet washes and the found edges with dry brushstrokes. This range of brushstrokes can be exhilarating – soft, subtle and transparent to dark and

288

dramatic. Every brushstroke subtracts from the total amount of light or white paper, which means that planning before starting the painting is essential. The 'saved whites' become the source of light for the entire painting.

To know and appreciate a plant, its height, size, spread, flowering time and other requirements, one has to grow it. Petals may twist and turn, be tightly packed, be crinkly, as in carnations, and spiral out from the centre. As the petals rotate outwards from the centre, they increase in size and become softer and more delicate in colour. Because flowers are so intricate and complex, there is always a temptation to describe every single petal, but too much detail can look overstated. In some paintings it is better to simplify and establish tone, shape and colour.

Lost and found edges help to create atmosphere and achieve depth and the illusion of objects disappearing into the background or coming forward. The eye may pass over the muted edge while hard edges call attention to the focal point. The colour pink may be named after the flower, coming from the frilled edges of the flowers.

Painting 2

Here I kept the details simple, which include the colour mixing, which was just a few colours tinting the white paper with blue in the background flowers and a mix of blue and pink in the foreground. The green was a mix of Indian Yellow and Ultramarine Blue for the leaves, with a touch of Alizarin Crimson in the green for shadows.

Diaz once advised Renoir and Pissarro advised Cezanne, 'Paint only with the three primary colours and their derivatives.'

The Gardener

Carnations are one of the most popular flowers in the world, surpassing even the popularity of the rose. Carnations symbolise love and fascination. A light-red carnation conveys admiration; dark red expresses deeper sentiments of love and affection. White expresses purity and luck, and pink is a sign of gratitude. In the early part of the twentieth century, the carnation became the official flower of Mother's Day. Carnations and pinks are perennial, annual and biennial cottage-garden plants, many with charming fragrance and delicate or brightly coloured flowers in shades of pink, red, mauve and white.

The pink is a grey-leaved perennial which sometimes naturalises in the stonework of rocky walls, looking beautiful tumbling in a natural way rather than being staked in a border. They are generally smaller than carnations and scented. They have dainty stems and fine slightly overlapping petals. Flowers like carnations, dahlias and chrysanthemums tend to spiral out from the centre. The petals are small, tight and crisply defined in the middle, and as they rotate outwards the petals increase in size and become softer and more delicate in colour. The true pinks have been derived from *Dianthus plumarius*, a native of the Mediterranean shores of Southern Europe and North Africa. It was introduced about 1629, since when numerous varieties have been bred, especially in the double forms. *D. caryophyllus* also seems to have played a part, with the latter species giving rise to the border carnation, and in European languages the same word is applied for both. In Britain pinks have been further developed so that pinks can be distinguished by their more compact growth and generally less heavy stems and flowers. Also when pinks have two or more colours in the flower they have a darker colour as a zone or 'eye', circular in shape, in the centre of the flower. In the nineteenth century exhibitors of pinks used to grow their plants in beds or pots of highly nitrogenous soil, rich in organic matter, and this led to plants which were unsuitable for ordinary garden use. These exhibition pinks have died out completely and only a few hybrid plants suitable for gardens have survived. These have retained the perfection of form and colouring and have been greatly extended.

Pinks can be propagated by seed, but the named varieties only by vegetative means – by layers or cuttings. The best cuttings should be taken after flowering and should have three or four pairs of fully developed leaves. They can be secured by a sharp pull, separating the piping (the cutting) from the parent plant. The lower leaves should be removed, taking care to preserve the buds, and if necessary trimming the base by a cut just below a joint using a sharp knife. The pipings should be inserted into sandy soil and kept under glass, shaded from bright sunshine until roots are formed. Then air can be gradually admitted and the plants hardened off before planting out in a well-drained flower border. Hardy varieties can be planted in permanent positions in September so that they have well-developed roots before winter. Planting must be firm, but not deep and as little as possible of the stem buried. They like a rich loamy soil, leaf mould, well-decomposed compost and some grit to ensure good drainage. A top dressing of compost should be given in March and again in May, and a thorough watering on hot, dry days in summer. A spring application of potash fertiliser is beneficial, but should not be given in the autumn. Where large flowers are wanted, the side shoots should be removed at an early stage, but this is not necessary if they are for border decoration.

The Study
This study is from my sketchbook. Being lightweight paper, the watery paint in the background created water marks as it sat on the surface. The painting of the flower was with thicker paint – hence the difference between the two.

The Gardener
The clove pink, so called for its aroma, is a parent of the cultivated carnations. The clove gilliflower, or carnation, comes from the Old French *clou de girofle* and Middle English *clowe gilofre* or, as Chaucer used it, *clovegilofre*, both being a corruption of the Arabic *clove*, relating to the perfume. The original flower is

bright pink-purple. The generic name of the carnation, *Dianthus*, comes from the Greek for heavenly flower or the flower of Jove. Carnations were mentioned in Greek literature 2,000 years ago. The dianthus was named by the Greek botanist Theophrastus, and comes from *dios,* meaning a god, and *anthos*, meaning a flower: flower of the gods.

The clove gilliflower is also catalogued as *Caryophyllus hortensis*, but the name gilliflower applies to many other plants: wallflower is winter gilliflower; sweet rocket or dame's violet (*Hesperis matronalis*) was queen's gilliflower. There is gilliapple, a variety of apple; stock gilliflower, *Matthiola incana*; mock gilliflower, *Saponaria officinalis*; and water gilliflower, *Cardamine pratensis*. Its other name – carnation, or coronation – came from its use at festivals in wreaths and garlands. Stocks, wallflowers and carnations are all heavily scented, and the gilliapple may have been a particularly aromatic variety.

The carnation's history dates back to Ancient Greek and Roman times, when it was used in art and decoration. Christians believe that the first carnation bloomed on earth when Mary wept for Jesus as he carried His cross. The first pink worthy of notice was raised in the year 1772 by Mr James Major, who was then gardener to the Duchess of Lancaster. Having saved seed, he reared several plants, one of which proved to be a double flower with laced petals. In Chaucer's day, the clove gilliflower was one of the herbs imported into English gardens and grown for its flavour and scent. It became a favourite garden flower of the sixteenth and seventeenth centuries, rivalled only by the rose and the lily. The flower petals were used in Tudor and Stuart days to flavour wine possets, and from this practice comes the popular name of 'sops in wine'. Conserves, candies and dragées were flavoured with the spicy taste. In the seventeenth century the gilliflower was the most popular flower. In 1629, John Parkinson, perhaps the earliest writer on garden plants, describes no less than fifty kinds, a few of which are still to be recognised, though many are lost. He wrote, 'Bravery, variety and sweet smell joyned together, tyeth everyone's affection with great earnestness both to like and to have them.' William Coles, a contemporary of Culpeper and a physician, writing in 1657, describes a clove vinegar, which was used in the manner that smelling salts were used 200 years later. The petals of scented pinks and carnations can be candied – a process of painting each one with stiffened egg white, dredging with powdered sugar, turning and dredging again, then drying quickly. The flowers may be floated in fruit cups and wine punches or used to garnish summer salads and desserts. The popularity of the carnation reached its height in the reign of Charles I, but during the Civil War it was almost lost to our gardens. In Charles II's reign they were brought back from Holland and restarted, although they were not as hardy as before. There are also border carnations, picotees, marguerite carnations, Malmaison carnations, perpetual Malmaisons and perpetual flowering carnations, all of them in many varieties.

The carnation probably arrived in England during the Norman Conquest with stones imported for building work. The wild plant from which the garden varieties were developed naturalised on Norman castles, such as Rochester, Dover, Ludlow and Deal. Many well-known varieties in Europe and America can trace their ancestry back to older English varieties, like 'Pride of the Market' and 'Winter Cheer'. Tall-growing or remontant carnations had been grown in France as Mayonnais carnations as early as 1750. They differed from the border carnations in requiring no period of rest. Like other varieties of this class, they were not allowed to flower in the first year and sometimes not in the second, but were grown into large bushes and trained up the roof of the house in which they were grown, but they found less favour than the very popular border carnations.

In France and parts of Italy, 29 June is called Carnation Day, and it is dedicated to St Peter and St Paul; and the carnation has become the emblem of Mother's Day in America in May. It was cultivated by country people as well as kings and princes. Henry IV of Provence first brought it to the gardens of France, and the Prince de Condé, Louis II of Bourbon, known as the Great Condé when imprisoned at Vincennes, cheered his long hours of captivity with their cultivation, after being condemned as a traitor by the Parliament of Paris, until he was finally pardoned in 1659.

Like most other flowers the carnation has had its ups and downs in fashion. A hundred and twenty years ago the border carnation stood very high in the estimation of flower growers and had many local shows dedicated to it. It declined in favour of the bedding plants, but was again popular in 1880. In 1895, Mr Peter Fisher of Ellis, Massachusetts, raised the deep-rose-pink variety 'Mrs T. W. Lawson' by crossing 'Daybreak' and 'Van Leeuwen'. The 'Mrs T. W. Lawson' plant had strong stems, strong calyces, lasting petals and a free-flowering habit extending over the winter, which the best of the tree carnations, such as 'William Robinson', lacked. Every following year more varieties were developed. A sensation was caused by the purchase of the stock by the copper magnate Mr Lawson for a great sum. It was the forerunner of the perpetual-flowering varieties, which are now grown in huge quantities.

Border carnations, or picotees, are perennial and do well planted out in the open border, but also do well in pots. The situation must be open and away from the shade of trees. To obtain fine flowers they must be disbudded and given support as the heavy buds are apt to be borne down to the soil and may be ruined in mud. Plants wintered in pots in a cold frame may be planted out in favourable weather in spring. Border carnations need to be propagated frequently, with layering the side shoots in July or August, and after flowering, being the best way. The compost for layering should be a light sandy mix of loam, peat and leaf soil. This should be placed around the parent plant, the lower leaves removed and a slit made in the stem, then pegged down and covered with compost. They should be kept moist and in four to six weeks can be severed from the parent and potted up. The pipings should be inserted into sandy soil and kept under glass, but out of bright sunlight, until the roots are formed, when they can be hardened off and planted in the border.

'Mrs Sinkins' is a gloriously scented white beauty that flops all over the garden path. Garden pinks are all hybrids, having a longer flowering period than the old-fashioned pinks, but the perennials are short-lived.

D. sylvestris grows in stony, rocky places, so is ideal in the rockery. It is sun-loving and rock-clinging, with glorious bouquets of rosy-pink flowers. They have stout taproots which hold them in their situation, while their very narrow glaucous leaves, mostly in a basal tuft, keep evaporation of water to a minimum. Each flower has a long corolla tube which divides into five delicately fringed petals. There are ten stamens and three styles, which protrude when the stigmas mature. It is possible that the thick calyx tube, fortified by the scales, helps to prevent rogue insects from stealing nectar, by making it difficult for them to bite through the flower tube.

D. allwoodii is the result of crossing a perpetual-flowering carnation with an old-fashioned pink. They are fast-growing. *D. deltoides* (the maiden pink) is a mat-forming perennial in various shades of pink, red and white. It forms neat hummocks and will thrive in containers or on rockeries. They need baking sun and good drainage.

Malmaison carnations are massive in habit with broad leaves and large double flowers, mainly pink with well-filled centres. The buds are rounded and the calyx, compared with that of the perpetual-flowering carnations, short and apt to burst. They need greenhouse treatment except in summer, and even then a sheltered position is preferable. They call for more skill in growing than do the perpetuals. New varieties are continually being raised.

Marguerite carnations are annuals with single or double flowers freely produced over a long period. They come true from seed sown in January and grown on in pots in a cool, well-ventilated place indoors, when they will flower from July to Christmas, or outdoors in summer, and then in autumn carefully lifted and potted to continue flowering in a cool greenhouse. Seed sown in August in a cold house and planted out in May will give flowering plants from early summer onwards. The pink or carnation held in the hand of a young man or woman in many old portraits is a sign of their recent betrothal. 'Pretty as a pink' still remains as a compliment to a young girl. The verb 'to pink' dates from the fourteenth century, meaning to decorate with a perforated or punched pattern, as is also demonstrated by the name of pinking shears – special scissors for cloth that create a zigzag or decorative edge that discourages fraying.

The Greeks called it 'divine flower'. Many of the large species have been favoured for centuries, enjoyed for their spicy scent and easy growing habits. They add charm to borders and pathways, rock gardens and stone walls. Dianthuses have long been grown for their hardiness, their diversity in flower colours, their long season of flowering and the sweetness of their fragrance. They are native to Southern Europe and were introduced into English gardens in 1575, possibly earlier. The wild flower has light or dark-red flowers, often striped and with white spots, but in cultivation there is much variation of colouring, being white, light and dark violet, light and dark red, from pink to blackish red, and they may be striped, red, pink and white, and variegated flowers. There are advances in the pink and scarlet strains, with double forms, but these cannot be relied upon to come true to seed and are best propagated by cuttings or layers in the same way as carnations. Raising from seed is the best way for singles, though a perennial is best treated as a biennial as it produces seed freely in the open and is hardy. The best way is to sow seed in boxes in a cold frame in late spring, pricking out the seedlings into pots as soon as they are large enough and planting them out in autumn. They grow in almost any soil, but live longest in a rich, well-drained and sunny place. Dianthus varieties are short-lived and should be propagated by division, tip cuttings or layering.

D. barbatus, the annual sweet williams, are also known as velvet williams, bloomydowns and London tuftes, and in Wales they are known as sweet evanses. They flower in the same year as sown. They have hybridised in gardens and in nature, with several other species of dianthus. Sweet williams are hardy, sweetly scented biennials with flattened or domed wide clusters of variously coloured or bicoloured flowers in white, pink and red, borne on sturdy erect stems like a miniature bouquet of pinks. They are grown for their beauty and sweet scent. They need to be deadheaded regularly. The flower was probably raised from the small red pink found wild near Rochester, originally called St Sweet William and dedicated to St William of Rochester. The word 'St' was dropped after the demolition of St William's shrine in the cathedral. There are other St Williams, including St William of York, St William of Norwich, St William of Montpelier and St William of Aquitaine, and any of these could have claimed the flower as their own. There is also *D. plumarius*, the cottage pink.

Dianthus species are food plants of the various butterfly larvae.

SWEET WILLIAM
Dianthus barbatus

Painting 1

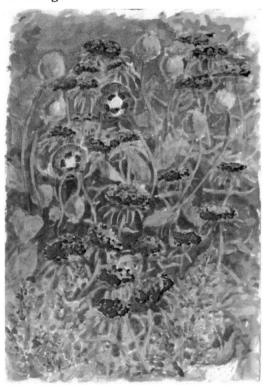

Considering colour in flowers and leaves is important as too much of the same can be monotonous. Contrast in form, texture, colour and size creates interest. The poppy seed heads provides a feeling of movement through the painting, and the blue flowers in the foreground harmonise with the blue in the poppy leaves, and the magenta of the poppy flowers echoes the colour of the sweet williams. Some of the most effective combinations can be the simplest.

Painting 2

The flowers are areas of unpainted paper coloured with touches of Cerulean and violet. This indicates shadows and gives an appearance of three dimensions. The feathery leaves were masked and, when dry, painted with green, but not uniformly so as to give a sense of depth.

The Gardener

Dianthuses have long been grown for their hardiness, their diversity in flower colours, their long season of flowering and the sweetness of their fragrance. They are native to Southern Europe and were introduced into English gardens in 1575 and probably earlier. The wild flower has light- or dark-red flowers, often striped and with white spots, but in cultivation there is much variation of colouring, being white, light and dark violet, light and dark red, from pink to blackish red, and they may be striped, red, pink and white, and variegated flowers. There are advances in the pink

and scarlet strains, with double forms, but these cannot be relied upon to come true to seed and are best propagated by cuttings or layers in the same way as carnations. Raising from seed is the best way for singles, though a perennial is best treated as a biennial as it produces seed freely in the open and is hardy. The best way is to sow seed in boxes in a cold frame in late spring, pricking out the seedlings into pots as soon as they are large enough and planting them out in autumn. They grow in almost any soil, but live longest in a rich, well-drained and sunny place. Annual sweet williams flower in the same year as sown.

Dianthus barbatus has hybridised in gardens and in nature with several other species of dianthus.

TEASEL
Dipsacus fullonum (wild teasel, Fuller's teasel)

The Painting

Various effects of broken colour can be made by regulating the amount of water in the brush and then skipping over the surface of the dry rough paper with quick movements. This produces a speckled effect as the paint lies on the surface and does not penetrate the paper.

This painting started as a watercolour and, when dry, I used coloured pencils for the intricate details and pastel pencils in some of the background. Usually I choose coloured pencils to benefit the subject by letting some of the paper colour show through lightly applied pastel. Colours are scumbled over in soft layers using very light pressure. The tips of the pastel pencils darkened the stems underneath the flower heads, and on the leaves, but a much broader approach was used for the base, merging the plant into the dark green.

Working with pastel pencils is a combination of painting and drawing, except the pastel colours are opaque rather than the transparent colours of watercolour. Pastels can enhance an effect by laying layer upon layer or hatching, scumbling and allowing underlying layers to shimmer through, becoming part of the whole.

Drawing with the Brush

The seed heads of the teasel are fascinating. The intricate patterning of the head was made possible by using a fine brush and concentrating on the tones.

The Gardener

The teasel is a tall structural biennial plant with masses of rosy-purple four-lobed tubular flowers on an egg-shaped flower head on long stalks which have spiny bracts. The flowers begin to bloom in a central ring around the flower head and continue upwards and downwards until it is covered. The flowers are short-lived and may die off leaving two rings, one growing towards the top and the other towards the bottom. Each flower develops into a ribbed fruit topped by a hairy calyx. Bees, butterflies and other long-tongued insects visit the flowers to collect the nectar. The ripe seed is food for birds like goldfinches.

295

The teasel is a good plant for the back of the border, or, in my garden, in the centre as there are walkways on either side of the borders. Teasels will grow in full sun or part shade. They will set seed, sometimes taking two years to germinate. In the first year the plant has shiny green rosettes of leaves with scalloped edges. The teasel does not grow in height until the second year.

Dipsacus fullonum, or *D. sylvestris*, is known by the common names wild teasel or Fuller's teasel, although the latter name is usually applied to the cultivated form. The genus name is derived from the word for thirst and refers to the cup-like formation made where sessile leaves merge at the stem. Rainwater can collect in this receptacle and prevents sap-sucking insects, such as aphids, from climbing the stem.

HELIOTROPE
Heliotropium arborescens (cherry-pie plant, Mary Fox, white queen)

The Painting

In ancient times it was believed that they owed the first light in the darkness at the beginning of the day to a female spider, who sat in the Milky Way and wove a great web to catch the light hiding in the darkness and forced it to shine so that people on earth could see their way. Colours Mars (iron) Cyan (almost turquoise blue), Turquoise Blue (greenish light blue) and Magenta (pure pink) are most beautiful in Quinacridone. I used Ultramarine (deep, warm blue), violet and Lemon Yellow, but none of these colours are exciting without light. I mixed two or three colours together to give the base colour of the flower head, but it is not one flat colour. There will be changes in tonal value as light moves over and through and beyond the plant. The shadow areas have more purple, more red, with the more distant flowers being more blue. There is a warm and cool version of each colour. Every pigment will lean towards some other colour.

Taking mental notes about the way colours affect each other helps in achieving certain value changes.

The Gardener

The eighteenth-century French botanist Jussieu was exploring the Andes when he became aware of an overpowering fresh scent. He thought that he must be on the verge of discovering some startlingly brilliant flower, but all he found was a clump of pretty herbaceous plants from which spikes of pale-blue blossoms hung loosely. He noticed that all the flowers were turned towards the sun and promptly labelled this new find the heliotrope – the Greek words being *helios*, meaning the sun, and *tropos*, meaning turn. He sent some seeds of this Peruvian plant to the Jardin du Roi, and the heliotrope was grown for the first time in Paris in 1740. This humble bloom with its high fragrance became very popular.

Varieties are white, pale lavender and (the hardiest, most fragrant and my favourite) the deep-purple 'Midnight Sky'. The fabulous scent is most noticeable at sunrise and sunset. They bloom in summer through to the first frost. Heliotrope grows one-sided as the sprays of flowers follow the sun. They need at least six hours of sun and prefer morning sun. The hotter the weather, the more afternoon shade they need.

Propagation is by cuttings taken in late summer. This is the preferred method as the cuttings will be true to the parent plant and make sturdy plants. Seedlings need warm temperatures to germinate. They can be planted outdoors once the ground has started to warm and there is no chance of frost. Heliotrope can become leggy and benefits from pinching out, which makes a bushier plant. Pinching out young plants encourages bushiness. This will delay the first flowers, but later blooms will be larger, and there will be a more constant supply of blossoms. The trimmings can be used as cuttings. Plants can be overwintered indoors on a sunny window sill. The branches need to be cut back and the plant repotted in rich compost and watered sparingly. They make good houseplants. They are a good choice for containers as they are not invasive or susceptible to insects or diseases. They are heavy feeders and need a feed of liquid fertiliser every two weeks.

KOLKWITZIA
(beauty bush)

The Drawing

Coloured pencils are versatile and can be used in various ways, including using solvents or mixed with their media, which can speed the process. However, I prefer the traditional layering, which retains the translucency when each layer shows through the next layer, similar to glazing. Many layers with a well-sharpened pencil will build up the pigment on to the paper's surface. A moderately toothed paper is best, avoiding very smooth and very rough papers. If the surface is too rough, the pencil will coat only the top of the paper's grain, whereas with a medium-toothed surface the pencil will cover most of the surface in a thin muted colour. A rougher surface gives a richer, denser colour with more sharpness and clarity.

Coloured pencils consist of clay coloured with pigment, and wax. The amount of wax in the pencils governs the degree of softness. They cannot be mixed as with paints, but there is a large range of different colours, shades and tints. Coloured pencils can be overlaid to create blended colours.

The Gardener
The plants are named after R. Kolkwitz, professor of botany, Berlin.

The beauty bush is an easy-to-grow shrub with arching stems festooned with pretty bell-shaped flowers in spring, similar to weigela. The flowers are pink, foxglove-like with yellow markings at the throat. The plant can grow very big if not pruned after flowering. This Chinese deciduous erect shrub is related to abelia, but with ovoid fruit, brown and bristly. It thrives in all types of soil – an excellent plant for the shrub border in a sunny spot. Propagate by rooting pieces from the parent bush, or take cuttings in summer.

ROSES

ROSE
Rosa (queen of flowers)

Painting 1

A pergola can be a pleasing garden feature, adding an inviting shady or flower-covered walkway leading to different areas of the garden. There is nothing more pleasant than a stroll through the garden on a warm evening, drinking in the fragrance of scented flowers. A pergola covered with roses can make a very pleasing background and pyramids can give a change of height to a flower bed. Humble plants and structures can have the most stunning effects. Gnarled wisteria, grapevines, honeysuckle and roses can complement lawns and borders in a three-dimensional way.

Light is seen through the atmosphere, which contains and breaks up colours. An object close by appears sharper and darker than it would when seen from a distance, no matter what light is there. When in the distance, that same object appears lighter and less distinct and its colour bluer than its true hue. It is important to study the real colour of a distant object and the influence of atmosphere in every painting.

To capture the velvety texture of the petals, a whole range of pinks and purples was used. In real life the rose is three-dimensional. In a two-dimensional painting, the roses appear as a complex mosaic of different tones and transparent shadows, which need to be thought out and interpreted. The importance of tone cannot be overestimated. The saturation and hue of the colour must be consistent with the light that the tone is representing. In nature, plants tend to grow in an ordered way and obtain the maximum benefit from the light. The form, colour and surface texture of an object are defined by light and also by the shadows cast on its surface. This means that the light source is one of the most important aspects of any painting, regardless of subject.

In nature there are limited colours in the plants themselves. A rose may contain red in the flower, and that red may be found in the leaves. A little green may also be found in the dark red of the flower petals. By using a limited number of colours, harmony will be easier to achieve. By using complementary colours – for example, blues and yellows to mix greens – a harmonious range of colours will enhance each other, resulting in a harmonious painting. When colours are chosen with care it is possible to create a range of the hues required. With too large a choice of colours, colour harmony may be lost.

Painting 2

This is a view of the pergola when the orange roses were in bloom. The soft background was painted first with light yellow, and when almost dry I used light green to suggest trees. Delphiniums and forget-me-nots in the mid distance helped to complement the warm colours of the foreground. The roses were painted first with yellow and then strengthened with orange, and in places a little red. The rose leaves were dabs of green built up from yellow-green to dark green. The wood supports were painted with Burnt Sienna, darkened on the shadow side with violet, and, finally, violet shadows were added. The violet painted over the yellow base appears grey, which is ideal.

Spending hours observing and appreciating a plant in all aspects of its growing cycle and habit leads to understanding form, character, tone and colour.

Memento

The scent of roses takes me back to my grandparents' garden, where roses scrambled around the bedroom windows, their wonderful fragrance wafting in along with the lyrical song of the blackbird sitting in the branches. These connections lend substance to the sensation of perfume, and plants with outstanding scent can be appreciated most when planted by a window or a door. Remembered scents of flowers through the year include jonquils, narcissi, hyacinths and lilies, wallflowers, sweet peas, petunias, sweet rocket, stocks and nicotianas, viburnums and daphnes and the wonderful rose.

The Gardener

The rose has developed many ways to ensure its survival, having spines and hooks with which to haul itself up into the canopy of other shrubs and trees. These hooks, or thorns, are a collection of hairs grouped together. Whereas many flowers produce both pollen and nectar, the wild rose devotes most of its energy to pollen production, which is easily accessible for insect pollination with its open upward-facing flowers.

Pliny, the Roman botanist, recorded at least ten varieties of roses already in cultivation. Some had occurred naturally as a result of random cross-pollination and had been brought into gardens. Some had extra petals – the result of genetic mutation in which stamens changed into petals. This initial variation and the subsequent breeding of roses can be attributed to their genetic make-up. Whereas most naturally occurring plants have two pairs of chromosomes, roses are able to produce multiple sets, resulting in larger plants and more mixing of genetic information.

In the language of flowers the rose is 'love'.

No other plant in cultivation is of such mixed parentage as the rose and none has such a long horticultural history. Roses are one of the oldest cultivated plants and the most popular of all flowers, although the modern roses of today were unknown to the early civilisations. The first trace of a rose has been found in a fossil at Colorado's Florissant Fossil Beds, dating back 40 million years, with some discovered in Montana and Oregon dating back 35 million years. Rose fossils have also been found in Yugoslavia and Germany, and wild roses in Norway and Alaska. The earliest record of a rose is thought to be a Damascene rose – a natural hybrid between *Rosa gallica* and *R. phoenicia*, found in frescoes at Knossos, a ruined city on the island of Crete and at one time capital of the Minoan civilisation from about 3000 to 1100 BC. Ancient Greeks wrote poetry about 'The Queen of Roses' in 600 BC. Also depicted on frescoes, this time in Pompeii, and subsequently mentioned by the Greek historian Herodotus (484–425 BC), later known as the 'father of history', is the autumn damask rose. The pink damask rose, 'Omar Khayyám', was raised by seeds collected from the bush growing over his grave in Nashapur, Iran.

These charming fragrant old roses flourish in full sun, have great vigour, resistance to disease, hardiness and tolerance to various growing and weather conditions. Often all that is needed is to prune out old unproductive and dead wood.

A Damascene rose was taken by early Christians to Abyssinia and planted in the province of Tigre, where it was known as the holy rose – *Rosa sancta*. It spread, and forms were introduced into Europe by returning Crusaders. The famous French poem *Le Roman de la Rose* (The Romance of the Rose), an elaborate allegory on love and secular life begun in the latter half of the thirteenth century, later translated and completed by Geoffrey Chaucer, tells of roses being introduced into France from the lands of the Saracens. The French poet and songwriter Thibault (sometimes Theobald) IV, Count of Champagne and Brie, and King of Navarre, returned to Provins in 1240 after two years in Palestine, taking roses with him. From the thirteenth century to the nineteenth century, Provins was famous for medicinal roses. Many of these roses became known as Gallicas because of their assumed derivation in France, but were really forms of the damask rose. Since the seventeenth century this rose has had various names in England, but was mostly referred to as the damask rose, probably because it was believed, quite rightly, to have originated in Damascus. The true apothecary's rose also reached Europe from Damascus, believed to have been introduced by Thibault IV, King of Navarre, in the thirteenth century, and to have provided the very beginning of the great rose perfumery and confection industry which was to flourish for the following six centuries.

In the thirteenth century the town of Provins, south of Paris, became the centre of rose growing for the production of petals. The industry prospered, reaching its height in the seventeenth century, when perfumes, conserves, confections, candies, syrups, sweet waters, wines, vinegars and powders were produced in profusion. The trade had begun with the discovery that a certain variety of the red rose had the miraculous property of retaining its perfume upon drying, even when reduced to a powder. This resulted in a flourishing industry – a virtual monopoly – with the main street of Provins famous for its apothecaries' establishments. The variety of rose used became known as the apothecary's rose – *R. gallica officinalis*. Graham Thomas, in his book *The Old Shrub Roses*, records that in Provins, the town was able to offer presents of conserves and dried roses to many visiting dignitaries, including the Archbishop of Sens, Joan of Arc in 1429, Kings Charles VII, Henry II in 1556, Louis XV in 1725, and the Emperor Napoleon I in 1814. By the middle of the nineteenth century, France had exported 36,000 kilos of Provins rose petals to America.

Cottage gardens were the first gardens where flowers were included for their beauty. Josephine Bonaparte, wife of Napoleon, was the most influential figure in the history of old roses, creating a 'rose renaissance' by growing 250 varieties in her garden at Malmaison. So great was her passion that even the English, who were at war with the French, allowed roses to cross borders to reach Josephine. The celebrated gardens at Malmaison proved to be beneficial for France, emerging as a leading rose-growing country cultivating 2,000 different varieties, which increased to 5,000 in only a decade. Pierre-Joseph Redouté illustrated 116 of Josephine Bonarparte 's roses in a three-volume work, *The Roses*, published from 1817 to 1824. 'Souvenir de la Malmaison' was bred in 1843 and named after Empress Josephine's rose garden at Malmaison. It is said that when Marie Antoinette entered France to be married to the Dauphin, maidens strewing rose petals preceded her. She was never seen without a rose, and held the bloom towards her face as she spoke, supposedly to cover certain dental deficiencies. Madame de Pompadour was frequently painted holding roses, especially the fragrant 'Belle de Crécy'.

The rose belongs to Venus, the goddess of love and beauty. According to myths, roses were originally white, until dyed by the blood of Venus or Adonis, or by a bowl of nectar that careless Cupid upset when leading a dance on Mount Olympus. Cleopatra covered her palace floors knee-deep in rose petals before Mark Antony arrived because she believed in the romantic powers of the perfume. In the twelfth century, the fair Rosamond was the mistress of Henry II, King of England. Legend has it that Henry's wife, Queen Eleanor of Aquitaine, on pretence of offering silken thread, poisoned her. The sixteenth-century poet Samuel Daniel wrote a poem on the sorrows of Rosamond called 'The Complaint of Rosamond', and it is said that *Rosa mundi, Rosa gallica* 'Versicolor', with Crimson flowers striped white, was named after her.

Throughout the world the rose is the flower of both love and war. Always loved for its beauty and fragrant scent, historically in war it represented a royal house – for example, the red rose of Lancaster and the white rose of York. Roses assumed a special significance in the fifteenth century, when there was a fierce struggle for the throne of England between the Houses of York and Lancaster during the Wars of the Roses. *R. damascena* is said to have been brought from Damascus by a Crusader and gave rise to the York and Lancaster roses. In 1455, a quarrel between the Dukes of York and Lancaster in the rose gardens of the Temple, in London, initiated the war. The protagonists are said to have each plucked a rose as their emblem. The red rose of Lancaster is thought to have been first cultivated in 3000 BC. Both these families of York and Lancaster were associated with roses. On the Yorkists' side, a white rose was the emblem of Eleanor of Provence, who in 1235 married Henry III, her emblem descending to her son, Edward I. The red rose was the emblem of Edmond, the second son of Henry III through his marriage in 1275 to Blanche, widow of Henry I of France. These emblems were worn throughout the thirty years of the civil war which became known as the War(s) of the Roses. The brutal conflict was settled by the marriage of Henry Tudor with Elizabeth Plantagenet, daughter of Edward, and the red and white *R. damascena versicolor*, Tudor rose, was named in 1551 to commemorate the English Wars of the Roses. The Tudor rose was chosen by Henry's son, Henry VIII, as his emblem.

Rose plants were a source of food, medicine, household supplies, protection and charms. Rose conserve was consumed as a remedy for colds and coughs. In Tudor England, rosewater or fresh roses were kept next to the bed to promote sleep and fortify the memory. In Renaissance Europe rose petals were burned with spices and odoriferous resins to ward off the plague. Attar of roses came from the East, and in the sixteenth century, when the first attempts to make medicines palatable were undertaken, among the primary substances to be used was oil of rose. It was included in the *Pharmacopoeia Collegii Regalis Londinium Medicorum* of 1720, and the 1746 edition insists that '*R. damascenarum*' be used – a practice still in use today. King Midas, the legendary King of Phrygia, a former kingdom in Western and Central Asia Minor, is said to have grown an autumn damask rose and introduced it into gardens in a district of Macedonia, where much later a form of it was used to produce rose water and attar of roses in the Kazanlik region of Bulgaria. In England, the main cultivation of the rose for cosmetic purposes, such as rose water, was in the hands of Potter and Moore of Mitcham, Surrey, though rosaries, or rose gardens, are known to have existed in London in the early seventeenth century, very probably for the production of dried rose petals. Rose water was distilled by various tedious distillation processes. Culpeper wrote, 'Red rose water is well known and of a similar use on all occasions and better than damask rose water; being cooling and cordial, refreshing, quickening the weak and faint spirits, used either in meats and broths, to wash the temples, to smell at the nose, or to smell the sweet vapours out of a perfume pot, or cast into a hot fire shovel.'

In Central Europe roses were used for carminative effect, and rose petals and rose hips in the treatment of pulmonary disorders, and white roses were used for the preparation of eyewashes. In modern China, rose-hip tea is used to treat diarrhoea. In modern times the value of the hips of some kinds of roses has been widely recognised and exploited as a source of vitamins. Rose hips are a rich source of vitamin C and may help prevent the common cold. Rose water, a cleansing astringent, promotes healthy skin. In colonial America, Native Americans combined rose petals with bear grease to cure mouth sores, and applied powdered petals to fever blisters.

The very best scented roses are classified as old roses, which are mostly crimson to violet, pink tones and white and have varied flower shapes. Old-fashioned roses, some hundreds of years old, show remarkable stamina and have flower shapes and colours not commonly found in modern roses. However, few of these old-fashioned roses have as long a flowering season as the new roses.

The first roses with double blooms date to Roman times and originated when unusual hybrids of wild species were preserved and subsequently cultivated. The wild dog rose plays an important part in commercial rose growing, providing the root stocks on to which exotic blooming varieties are grafted. The name dog rose originates from Roman times, when a mad dog bit a soldier and he applied the roots of a wild rose to heal the wound. The old 'species' roses mostly are single-flowered; they have wonderful scent, foliage and hips. They require little pruning, except removal of dead wood and old shoots so as to encourage new growth. Flowers and fruit are produced on the previous year's wood.

In spite of many attempts and much cross-breeding, there are no blue roses. Even the hybrid tea rose 'Blue Moon' is not true blue.

Roses have been widely used as emblems by many states in North America. The white Cherokee rose, *R. laevigata*, is claimed by Georgia, though it is not native to America, but to China. It was naturalised in the Southern States as early as 1780. In legend, it is associated with an Indian girl who was magically turned into a flower when captured by a hostile tribe. The District of Columbia has adopted the 'American Beauty' rose, while the wild prairie rose, *R. setigera*, is the emblem of North Dakota. The state also has *R. arkansana*, also known as *R. pratincola* or *R. suffulta*, which is a native rose and at one time was a persistent weed of prairie wheat fields. The pasture rose, *R. carolina,* is the state flower of Iowa. Wild roses greeted the Pilgrim Fathers at their Plymouth Rock landing in America. The blood-red Grant rose is said to have sprung from the blood of Mrs Grant, an early settler in Florida, killed by a Seminole, a Native American.

Garden roses have a complex ancestry because there has been much cross-breeding between the different species. It is debatable if many forms of rose were grown in private gardens before Elizabethan days. Gerard listed only fourteen kinds, and, as a collector of plants, he must have been familiar with the genus. Prior to Gerard's lifetime, roses had been used for strewing and are certainly depicted in numerous illustrations of medieval gardens, obviously included for their astonishing beauty. Parkinson, a few years later, added ten more varieties to Gerard's list, and as both men were connoisseurs of plants, one can conclude with certainty that far fewer roses were known generally in the Europe of the day.

The single rose was brought in from the wild into Far Eastern gardens and developed by budding, grafting and layering in the skilful hands of nurserymen, to form double scented roses. With the perfume of the double roses came trade, and in Alexandria, Tunis, Constantinople and many parts of Persia roses were grown for the making of perfume. No more than one ounce of attar could be made from 300 pounds of petals, and so it was a common sight to see petals piled into stacks like haystacks, ready to be taken away for distilling.

Fragrance is the strongest and most mysterious of the sensual pleasures, and each of us has our own remembered memories of certain scents. Roses, along with sweet peas and other scented flowers, conjure happy childhood memories of my grandfather tending the arbours and presenting bouquets to my grandmother. Fragrance is a powerful way to make our gardens memorable. A scented rose planted near the house can be enjoyed as the fragrance drifts through open doors and windows.

Many of the 'old' roses came into Western culture as a result of military campaigns, political upheavals and trading partnerships. The Gallica rose, often called the apothecary's rose because of its use in medicine, was known to many cultures. It was possibly brought to England by the Crusaders. In its plain colour this is the red rose of Lancaster, and a form of it, the pink-and-white-striped *R. mundi*, was named after the mistress of Henry II in the twelfth century. Alba roses are believed to have resulted from crosses between the Gallica rose and two of the wild roses, *R. arvensis* and *R. canina*. During the Middle Ages, roses were mainly grown in monasteries, often for religious and medicinal uses. Native species hybridised with each other and created natural seedlings of new varieties, while others produced mutations – a process which took thousands of years.

In 1954, the dog rose, *R. canina* by chance produced the beautiful 'Abbotswood'. The Albas, Centifolia, Damask, Gallica and musk roses were supreme until the introduction into Europe of Chinese hybrids between 1792 and 1824. These roses helped to create a wider colour range, as well as having the ability to flower repeatedly throughout the summer. Before this, most roses flowered once and were devoid of bloom for the rest of the year. Many roses have been introduced and cross-bred, resulting in 'noisettes', Bourbons, tea roses, hybrid 'chine' and hybrid 'perpetuals'. For many years roses were known as hybrid teas and floribundas, but should now be called 'large-flowered bush roses'. Cluster-flowered bush roses bear flowers in large trusses, with repeat flowering from midsummer to late autumn. Miniature roses have enabled roses to flourish in small gardens. Patio roses are bush-shaped. There are cabbage roses, dwarf roses, roses that closely carpet the ground, roses that droop like fountains, roses in clusters and roses blooming singly. Walls, fences, arbours and pergolas can be colourfully covered with climbers and ramblers.

Some tea roses are scented, but do not have the lasting fragrance of the old roses – Gallicas, Damasks, Centifolias, Bourbons, moss roses and Albas. They grow in a variety of shapes, colours and perfumes. The density of the rose colour, year after year, produces roses which are marginally different and can make fortunes on the open market. In response to this, the old-fashioned roses have become popular again. They may only flower once a year, but it is worth the wait for the exquisite scent.

Old-fashioned roses are similar to shrub roses in many ways, requiring little pruning and often looking their best when grown as specimens on their own. In the nineteenth century hundreds of moss hybrids were bred from a single Centifolia moss rose. The name Centifolia was derived directly from the physical character of the plant, which has 100 petals and the appearance of a cabbage. The flowers are opulent in petal and fragrance, having great ruffles of petals that hold their perfume; and, although small, they have a delicious scent.

Moss roses are related to Centifolias. They are mutations of normal roses – the name moss coming from the soft fur-like spines that grow from the surface and buds. A full moss rose is the rose without a thorn, a fine bloom surrounded by very soft green leaves. 'Chapeau de Napoléon' gets its name from the sprouting whiskers like a tricorn hat. The Burgundy roses are smaller with double flowers. The double form of *R. gallica*, from Southern Europe, is sometimes called *R. provincialis*, *R. foetida*, from the Orient, introduced deep yellow into garden roses, and *R. moschata*, another Eastern rose with fragrant flowers, also reached Europe in the sixteenth century. All have been successfully crossed to produce a great variety of roses, widely cultivated ever since.

Most old-fashioned roses are highly scented. China rose, *R. chinensis*, was the first rose to reach the West with 'Old Blush' in Sweden in 1752, arriving in other European regions in 1793. The tea rose was introduced to the West in 1808 or 1809. The tea rose, *R. odorata,* derived its name from the aroma of its foliage, which is similar to that of tea plants. The Chinese had grown roses for centuries before they were introduced into the West with phenomenal impact – an instant sensation. They flower repeatedly in one season. Hybrid teas and floribundas are especially noted for their scent. Most noted are 'Alec's Red', a crimson rose; 'Bonsoir', a peach pink; 'Duke of Windsor', a vermilion rose; 'Eden Rose', a deep pink; 'Ernest H. Morse', a red; 'Fragrant Cloud', coral flame; 'Arthur Bell', a yellow rose; and 'Dearest', a salmon pink. European rose breeders crossed the Chinese roses with existing roses to develop new varieties, possessing the best features of each parent plant. Tea roses derived from *R. odorata* were produced in France. A hardier strain appeared in 1853 in 'Gloire de Dijon', which proved excellent growing against a wall with its perfect form, delicate colouring and delightful scent, but in rain the buds suffer and fail to expand properly. Hybrid tea roses have large shapely flowers produced singly or in small clusters from June to October, with peak flowering in June, July and September. Some will carry more blooms in autumn than in summer. China and hybrid china roses were derived from crossing *R. chinensis* and *R.* 'Semperflorens'. Varieties with a stronger influence of *R. chinensis* make big bushes with white to deep-pink flowers, while those with more *R.* 'Semperflorens' are dwarf and mostly Crimson. Their long flowering period and hardy nature were a distinct advance on earlier roses.

The 'Queen Elizabeth' rose, 'Queen of England', was the first hybrid member of the Grandiflora class, a cross of *R.* 'Charlotte Armstrong' and *R.* 'Floradora'. It is hardy and as it can grow tall can be planted at the back of the border. The double flowers are silver pink in clusters on vigorous long stems from spring to autumn. Their blossoms do not have a strong fragrance and have few stems. It is best to remove faded blooms to stimulate growth of new flowers. To retain taller plants with early roses, cut back lightly, or for more compact shrub-like plants prune back more severely. It can be raised as a single plant or grouped to make a hedge. Mulch around the base of the plant to keep weeds at bay and improve moisture retention.

Noisette roses are the result of crossing *R. moschata* and *R. chinensis*, obtaining a hardy, vigorous rose with clusters of perfumed flowers. Later they were crossed with the tea-scented roses and gained in size, while the number of flowers decreased, making it difficult to distinguish between the noisettes and the tea-scented roses except by scent. 'Maréchal Niel' and the white, almost evergreen 'Aimée Vibert', introduced in 1828, are among the few survivors of many noisette roses once grown.

Damask roses are a variety which was in flower in every season of the year and known in France as *rose de quatre saisons*. They came from the Middle East and are related to Centiflora or cabbage roses, which featured in Dutch flower painting. They are crimson, red, pink or white and have short flowering periods. The breakthrough came on Réunion Island in the Indian Ocean, where traders and merchants from China and France had settled, bringing their roses with them. They created natural hybrids, inheriting repeat flowering from their Eastern antecedents and the beautiful blooms and fragrance from their other parent. The result was the exquisitely shaped Bourbon rose, *R. bourboniana,* which became one of the most popular roses because it produced intermittent blooms. The Bourbon rose, with its bright-pink flowers, is now lost, but several hybrids have been developed, being a major source of reds in most modern roses.

From this melting pot of roses from East and West, including yellow roses from China and Persia, new hybrids started to occur, but none of these crosses was planned, though thousands of rose bushes were grown from hips that were the random results of chance pollination. In the nineteenth century, a new scientific approach was developed by Henry Bennett, a cattle breeder who was also interested in roses and who developed controlled pollination. Having successfully bred prize cattle by selecting parents with the desired attributes, Bennett replicated the principle to roses, transferring the pollen from one to another, keeping records of his crosses and growing on the resulting seedlings in an organised fashion. Selection was the other important part of the process, discarding the second-rate blooms and keeping only the exceptional. Eventually, Bennett's efforts led to the development of the hybrid tea, which was to become the most sought-after rose, having perfectly scrolled buds in a classical shape. There are now roses for different situations and soils, for growing in beds and borders, up walls and pergolas and in pots.

The hybrid perpetuals continued to be one of the popular roses until the end of the nineteenth century, and after this they were overshadowed by hybrid tea roses, which were of a superior variety. Sadly the majority of these roses do not exist any more as, of the 3,000 different varieties of roses that were hybridised throughout this 'golden era', ranging from Empress Josephine's garden to the Orient, only about fifty are still in existence.

In the 1940s a copy of George Bunyard's book on old roses gave David Austin the idea of crossing the old-fashioned-style roses with all their qualities together with the repeat flowering and colours of the modern forms. From a hobby breeder as a young teenager, David Austin has gone on to breed a collection of roses renowned across the world. In the early 1950s David Austin set out to create a more beautiful rose. His objective was to create new roses in the style of old roses. The two roses were married together, producing reliability, aesthetic appeal and the character and fragrance of old roses such as Gallicas, Damasks and Albas, plus the repeat-flowering ability and wide colour range of modern roses. David Austin's first commercially available rose, 'Constance Spry', was introduced in 1961. In 1967 and 1968 he introduced 'Chianti' and 'Shropshire Lass' respectively. Although these first roses bloomed only once, in spring or early summer, they led, in 1969, to a series of repeat-flowering varieties, including 'Wife of Bath' and 'Canterbury' – both in honour of the English author Geoffrey Chaucer. David Austin's roses soon became the most successful group of new roses in the twentieth century. Since its founding in 1969, he and his firm, David Austin Roses, have introduced over 190 rose cultivars. Cultivars have been named in honour of his family, well-known rosarians, geographical landmarks in Britain, historical events and British writers, particularly Shakespeare and Chaucer, and their works or characters. For instance, roses have honoured such diverse entities as the rosarian and artist Graham Thomas and King Henry VIII's flagship, the *Mary Rose*.

David Austin separated his roses into four groups as a guide to further developments – the Old Rose Hybrids (roses with the appearance of the old roses but recurrent, healthy and with a wide range of colours), the Leander group, often with *R. wichurana* in their breeding (roses with larger bushes and arching growth, tending to make them pillar or low-climbing roses), the English Musk Roses, based on 'Iceberg' and the noisette roses (roses with pale-green, slender and airy growth; the musk-rose scent is missing from most, though other scents are present in many) and the English Alba Hybrids (roses with tall, rather blue-leaved bushes like the old Alba roses). In 2003, David Austin was awarded the Victoria Medal of Honour by the Royal Horticultural Society for his services to horticulture and the Dean Hole Medal from the Royal National Rose Society. He has received an honorary MSc from the University of East London for his work on rose breeding. He received the lifetime achievement award from the Garden Centre Association in 2004 and was awarded an OBE in 2007. In 2010, he was named a 'Great Rosarian of the World'. Rose breeding is often described as being as much an art as a science. English roses are now a booming international business. David Austin Roses remains a family business and he has been joined by his son David and his grandson, Richard. All David Austin roses have a collective style and reflect one man's vision. All have beautiful blooms and in most cases wonderful fragrance held on graceful attractive shrubs. A garden of these outstanding roses is hard to beat for sheer exuberance of flower and fragrance. Colours range from rich yellow to peach, apricot, white and crimson, and each has a distinctive perfume. These roses are best planted as individuals so as to appreciate their characteristics, but, because of their long flowering season, are equally beautiful in a mixed border. Today the rose continues to be the national flower of England.

Peter Beales was the first president of the Royal National Rose Society and was awarded nineteen gold medals at Chelsea. He broke away from the traditional glass bowls of cut flowers, creating romantic arches of roses and re-establishing the garden as a showcase for roses of every kind. He loved all roses, whether ancient or modern, but loved old roses including Gallicas, Damasks, Portlands and unfashionable historic cultivars that other nurserymen had forgotten. His daughter Amanda developed new roses, selecting them for health, scent and vigour, but, like her father, did not have a defined type of rose as her ideal.

Floribudas have smaller flowers in large clusters produced over the same period. These flower from June to October, opening about the same time so that the colour effect is better than hybrid teas. They make a fabulous display, but the individual flowers are not so beautiful, though now they have been bred to look more like those of the hybrid tea rose (although they are still in clusters), with the result that the two groups are no longer as distinct as they were. The first floribundas were produced from dwarf polyanthus roses with small rosette flowers in large clusters. Floribunda roses should be pruned to invigorate the plant, but stems should be left longer than those of hybrid roses so as to form clusters of flowers.

Roses need help to climb as they have thorns, not tendrils as vines do. However, unlike tendrils, thorns won't tear into the structure's woodwork or mortar, but will help them to grow successfully into trees and over walls. Roses that climb, ramble or stand upright need help to achieve their potential height, so the addition of supports in the form of pergolas or arches can bring a stunning vertical dimension to the garden, setting a style. Also, the raised blooms release scents at a more enjoyable level. Climbers have long, fairly stiff stems and medium to large flowers, singly or in clusters, and can reach six metres, and look good covering a wall or trellis.

My favourite rambler is 'Albertine', which is an old rambler rose with coppery-pink buds that open to pale pink, and is sweetly scented, sending delicious perfume into the house. It looks wonderful with blue clematis clambering through its branches. Being a rambler the display is spectacular, but brief. It can be prone to mildew, especially when grown in a hot, sunny spot in dry soil, as in its situation against our south-facing house wall. I also plant them on opposite sides of a path on strong uprights and train each plant across a beam or wire between the poles so that they are clad in creamy-pink flowers. I have also covered archways with the same roses. Autumn-flowering ramblers, such as 'Dorothy Perkins', 'Excelsa' and 'Turner's Crimson Rambler', do not get under way until late summer. There is a very special quality with autumn-flowering roses. October's blooms have a lushness unknown in summer. Roses in autumn tend to be darker in colour. If left to grow without any control, they may become a tangle of branches, which, considering the vicious thorns, can be a dangerous task to unravel; and also, left unpruned there are very few flowers. Regular pruning helps to keep the roses healthy, so they grow stronger, live longer and produce more flowers. The aim is to encourage the formation of flower-producing stems. Old shoots should be cut to the base and the top one-third of the plant cut back. This encourages branching and more flowers. Ramblers are vigorous and will regrow from the base.

Painting 3

The fabulous oranges and reds of these climbing roses teamed well with the warm shadows cast on to the sunlit wall. The warm yellow in the centres of the roses was also used on the wall, stronger on one side and more washy. Once the yellow was dry, I painted the shadows in violet, which was toned down by the yellow underpainting. Violet was a link to the red and was mixed into the green, where darks were needed. The greens acted as an intermediate between the various colours.

The Gardener

Climbing roses need to be limited in their height because they have to be pruned annually, and those that are repeat-flowering terminate in flower buds, which do not continue to grow upwards. Ramblers grow vigorously from the base and need careful pruning as soon as they finish blooming to keep them under control. By twisting and coaxing long canes of roses to intermingle, they can form natural arches. Climbers and ramblers flower most fully when they are bent horizontal before being tied into more upright positions. If canes go straight up there are only blooms at the top. Stems which have borne flowers need to be cut out and the new ones tied in every year. It may take two or three years to get the required result. Repeat-flowering climbers, which flower over a much longer period, are now available. *R. filipes* 'Kiftsgate' can grow to fifteen metres high and across. There is nothing to compare with it when in full flower. 'Kiftsgate' has masses of powerfully fragrant single white flowers while the double white *R. banksia* has a fragrance similar to the violet, and 'Omar Khayyám' has a rich damask scent. Another old-fashioned rambling rose with an enticing fragrance is 'Madame Alfred Carrière'. Several climbers do well on north-facing walls.

Painting 4

This rose contained yellow in the flower with mainly green in the leaves. The blue in the background is a complementary colour to yellow, meaning the two hues are opposite each other on the colour wheel. When these two complementary colours are mixed together they neutralise each other and produce green; but when placed next to each other, the individual colours are intensified, appear brighter and have a luminous effect, almost like an optical vibration.

Complementary colours are very effective when used in shadows, adding interest and excitement, but equal proportions of colour could appear brash and harsh. It is better to let one colour dominate. Only a few colours were used, some pure and others mixed together.

The Gardener

Tree or standard roses can look very effective planted among bush roses, giving a second tier of blooms. They are grafted to a base plant that has a strong trunk, so that they appear like miniature trees. The canes either cascade or form a lollipop shape. Rose cuttings should be taken before any of the eyes make new shoots, but usually they are all dormant at or just after flowering time. Cuttings taken from flowering or just-flowered shoots should have a bit of the older wood from which the shoot arises. All the thorns should be removed and all leaves bar the top two, cutting the top of the stem just above a leaf. The base of the cutting should be trimmed with secateurs at the juncture of the young wood with the old. The cuttings should be planted around the edge of a pot filled with two parts loam, three parts sand, watered and placed in a cold frame where the atmosphere is humid and the cuttings do not scorch. The foliage will gradually turn yellow and drop off naturally and new shoots will form, with roots developing in three to four weeks. The new plant should be cosseted for two years, grown on in larger pots before being planted into flower borders, where they will have to compete with established plants.

Species roses are wild roses, some of which have been used as parents of the garden hybrids. Most have single flowers which bloom once a year, and some have very handsome hips which follow the flowering. These grow in our hedge among hawthorn, lilac, holly and spindle – a beautiful sight.

Roses of all types look beautiful with delphiniums, lavender, alliums and violet-blue geraniums and climbing roses with clematis.

Painting 5

The delicate tightly curled petals are a delight to paint, capturing the deep-pink dark centres and the merest hint of colour in the light tips of the petals. The linear effect of the curled rose petals tightly spiralling around the centre is very characteristic of the rose. The areas I concentrate on are the darkest, the lightest and the richest. In watercolour it is the white of the paper which is the source of light and makes the colours glow. Throughout the painting the original idea must be in mind, but the painting evolves as if on its own.

Painting 6

An arrangement of light and dark creates a pleasing, and hopefully dramatic, impression regardless of either colour or subject. The most successful paintings are those that have an interesting and harmonious structure.

Chiaroscuro means light and shade. *Chiar*, from the Italian language, means light, and *scuro* means dark. Many powerful master artists, such as Leonardo da Vinci, Caravaggio and Rembrandt, used the technique to create dramatic contrasts. It is usually used when the artist wants to promote a certain feature of the painting with very simple value structures using only two or three or four value structures. To be effective it is necessary to have understanding of dominant values and a narrowing of minor values into a narrow value range. Value is one of the most important and powerful elements of a painting. A limited range of values helps promote harmony, and it is easier to maintain consistency with a limited value range. This is why many oil painters start with an underpainting of grey tones before adding colour.

In this oil painting I have used very little colour, concentrating on the values, making the background dark and the upper surfaces of the rose petals light, portraying full light. The human eye is immediately drawn to a light element against a dark element. I started the painting with a light drawing in charcoal, which takes away the complexity of colour and forces thinking in terms of light and dark, which gives a three-dimensional illusion. Then thin paint with a little medium was painted in, followed by thicker paint with more medium content in subsequent layers. This ensures that the first, thinner layers dry before the thicker, more oily layers, avoiding cracking of the paint. It is worth noting that different pigments and oils have different drying times.

Manufacturers add beeswax to help the pigment stick to the drying oil and also to help prevent the pigment from sinking to the bottom of the tube. Alkyd resin is sometimes added to add lustre and speed drying of the paint. A drying oil is a natural oil that oxidises when exposed to air, causing it to contract and harden into a solid layer.

Linseed oil is the most popular. It dries very thoroughly and creates very stable paint. Both refined linseed oil and cold-pressed linseed oil are used in paint manufacture. Cold-pressed linseed oil has not undergone any chemical treatment and is considered stable, while refined linseed oil has less impurities and will have less tendency to yellow over time. Stand oil is linseed oil that has been thickened through heating. It is good for glazing.

Poppy oil is very pale, more transparent and is less likely to yellow, but is slower-drying than linseed oil. This makes it ideal for working wet-into-wet.

Walnut oil has a long history. It yellows less than linseed oil, resulting in paler and cooler colours, suffering less change as they dry. It is a good oil to use in the initial layers of paint and for painting detail. It has a similar drying time to linseed oil.

Safflower oil is slower-drying and therefore best used in the final layers of a painting.

Turpentine dilutes the paint. I use it for cleaning brushes, before washing them in soap and water. Household white spirit is too abrasive and can kill vibrancy of paint. Not recommended.

Painting 7
There are no surrounding lines. We see objects because they are lighter or darker than the background. The time of day often brings rapid changes to the subject. In this painting, the roses were in shade. I could have chosen to highlight some petals catching the sunlight, but wanted an air of mystery. Sometimes I like to exaggerate or play down areas relative to the idea, giving an impression and seeing beyond the obvious. The longer a viewer is drawn to looking at a painting, the more interesting that painting is to them. The eye should move from one area to another and back again. The painting needs to have some more detail in one area while other areas are less detailed.

Painting harmonious colours next to each other lets the viewer's eye blend the colours. The Impressionists used this technique. The closer the colours are in tone or value, the more easily they will mix optically to create a third colour. The red in the inner petals of the rose mix with the blue of the outer petals to create an illusion of violet or purple. If the two colours were further apart they would remain distinct.

The Gardener

A bed of roses is not only a metaphor for a life of luxury, but the petals were made into mattresses for those of high rank because they could afford the high price. After a long flowering period, scent is perhaps the most important feature. With its evocative sweet scent and perfect form, the rose is a symbol of loveliness, epitomising summer and all its pleasures. *R. eglanteria* has a scent reminiscent of fresh green apples.

Some plants are related to roses only by name. The guelder rose (*Viburnum opulus*) can scent the whole garden in summer – hence its reference to roses. This large deciduous shrub obtained its name from the part of the Netherlands where it was supposed to have originated. Its large white-scented flowers have also earned it the name of snowball tree. These shrubs can eventually form small trees and have brilliant-red autumn colour.

A rosebud stripped of its thorns indicates 'there is everything to hope for'; if stripped of leaves 'there is everything to fear'. Sending messages through flowers was known in Turkey in the 1600s, but did not spread to Europe until 1716, when the celebrated letter writer and society poet Lady Mary Worley Montagu accompanied her husband to the Turkish court in Constantinople. She learned how messages of love could be passed without recourse to letter writing or talking. Returning to England in 1718, she immediately told friends of the meanings of flowers, but after quarrelling with the poet and satirist Alexander Pope, went to live abroad. The French were enthused by the romanticism of flowers and quickly took to using flowers to send quite complex messages, returning the idea to Britain during the reign of Queen Victoria through a book by Madame de la Tour, called *Le Langage des Fleurs*. Some of its sentiments and messages were too lusty for the Victorians and needed to be tempered.

Apart from beauty and intoxicating fragrance, the rose symbolises love and appreciation, but each rose has its own special significance. The red rose signifies romance. Robert Burns compared his love to a red rose in his poem 'Red, Red Rose'. It became the ultimate symbol of passionate affection. A bright-red rose implies romance, while burgundy means a love that has yet to be realised. In Greek and Roman iconography, it was tied to Aphrodite, or Venus, the goddess of love. In early Christian times it was associated with the virtue of the Virgin Mary.

Pink roses are a classic symbol of grace and elegance and are often given as a token of thoughtfulness, passion or sentiment. Pink roses are one of the most popular flowers sent on Valentine's Day. Dark-pink roses express appreciation or gratitude, and are used to say thank you. Medium-pink roses express congratulations or cheer a friend. Light-pink roses show gentleness and admiration. The first trace of the pink rose was found in fossils dating back 40 million years. Pink roses were grown in China's imperial rose gardens about 5,000 years ago. They were the first rose cultivated. Pink roses are the most common in the wild. During the Victorian era, the pink rose was used to decorate everything from wallpaper to greeting cards.

White roses have historically symbolised innocence and purity. In the fourteenth century, in England, the white rose was the heraldic sign of the Duke of York, with the red rose that of the Lancaster family – hence the Wars of the Roses. The yellow rose is the traditional symbol of friendship. Their warm, sunny colour evokes optimistic feelings. In Eastern cultures, yellow represents joy, wisdom and power. A yellow rose was discovered growing wild in the Middle East, but it lacked the sweet fragrance of other roses. Cultivation methods developed and refined and produced a sweet, spicy yellow rose. An orange rose is the combination of yellow and red roses, resulting in orange, which signifies passion, love, friendship and congratulations.

Purple roses symbolise majesty and royalty and enchantment, such as love at first sight. A lavender-coloured rose means majesty, opulence, enthralment and love at first sight, while blue roses are often portrayed in literature and art as symbols of love, prosperity or immortality. They can also symbolise the impossible or the unattainable, since, for centuries, the quest for the blue rose represents something too difficult to be achieved. Genetic engineering may produce a blue rose, but it cannot exist in nature as roses lack the specific gene or pigmentation needed to produce a true blue. A black rose means rebirth, new beginnings, death and farewell. The black rose does not exist in nature, although there are roses called 'Black Jade' and Black Prince', but they are primarily very deep, dark red in colour.

Planting an entire garden with a single type of rose presents an invitation to disease and pests. Instead I combine different types and varieties and mix them with plants which complement one another. Combinations need to be complementary in colour and share the same cultural requirements, such as light, moisture and fertility. In mixed borders roses add height, fragrance and seasonal long blooming, with perhaps low-growing plants such as lavender, sage and santolina covering trunks. Honeysuckle or clematis could be intertwined through climbers, giving textural difference and adding to the fragrance.

When garlic is grown next to roses, it is said that aphids are deterred and alliums, fennel, parsley or lemon balm attract beneficial insects which feed on the aphids. Other companion plants can be spring bulbs, daffodils, tulips and cottage-garden flowers such as violas and columbine. These all bloom before the roses, and as they fade the roses flower and conceal the fading foliage of other plants.

In the Pays de la Loire, mild winters and generally hot summers aid rose growing, even though they may suffer in frequent summer droughts. Each winter and spring a mulch in the form of compost is added, which helps to retain moisture.

There are two sun-loving plants that have delicate papery flowers reminiscent of the wild dog rose. The sun rose (helianthemum) and the rock rose (cistus). Both belong to the same plant family and enjoy the same poor soils and sunny positions. They come from the Mediterranean and need sharp drainage to thrive. They are evergreen and flower from spring through summer. Tuberose (*Polianthes tuberosa*) is a sun-lover from Mexico. This bulb is related to the agave, but has none of the spikiness. The tall stems can be a metre high and are interspersed with sweet-smelling single or double trumpet flowers with delicate scent.

In 1597, noted English herbalist John Gerard wrote about fourteen types of roses in his book *Herball*. In 1629, the pharmacist to James I, John Parkinson, noted twenty-four different types growing in his garden, called 'Paradisus'. In the 1700s artist Mary Lawrence illustrated ninety different roses in her book entitled *A Collection of Roses from Nature*.

Sending cards anonymously became popular – perhaps a legacy of the uncertainty and anticipation when a young man selected the name of a girl out of a Roman urn. Little is known about St Valentine other than that there were at least two martyrs of that name, both dying for their religion on 14 February. St Julius I, Pope from 337 to 352, allotted a saint's day to St Valentine and when Christianity reached Britain, the feast of Lupercalia (a very ancient possibly pre-Roman pastoral festival to avert evil spirits and purify the city by releasing health and fertility) was moved back one day and merged with St Valentine's Day. At one time it was commonly believed that all birds chose their mates on this day. This fertility festival gained popularity and gifts of roses were given.

THE ARBOUR

The Painting

Often in a corner of the garden an arrangement of pots and ornaments is all that is needed to create an interesting composition. It is exciting to see an arrangement before me and sometimes I enjoy rearranging to suit the idea. The crucial part of the painting is developing the concept and planning the composition, giving a vision of the finished painting before the start. Composition and values are the basics that provide the foundation, the strength of the painting. Selecting the time of day can be important as the changing light and cast shadows can be dramatic at certain times, but not interesting at others. Value, or tone, is the amount of light and dark in a colour and can directly affect composition. Tone affects the appearance of the subject by defining its form. Simple colour harmonies are usually more effective than garish multicolour arrangements.

I wanted to create a sense of mystery and romance with an air of enticement from glimpses of delights beyond the archway. Borders and frames create containment in the painting. The romantic idea was to draw the eye through the painting, retaining a sense of seclusion and the suggestion of a fabulous place to sit and relax, paint or just enjoy the view of the garden. I wanted to portray a feeling of being able to see through the arbour, with the colours warm in the foreground and paler and cooler in the distance, looking for interesting light patterns and experiencing the different tones and textures. Normally I would place all the pinks and reds in the foreground and the blues and violets in the background, giving a sense of perspective, but the blue-violet of the geranium, the clematis and the blue furniture carried the cool feel through to the second archway and beyond. The leaning tree helped to guide the eye into the centre of the painting. Good composition is a powerful way of controlling colour, perspective, form and tone and eliminating, or changing, anything unwanted.

One of the most rewarding advantages of painting in my own garden is being able to return to the same place and being able to choose the time of day and the weather conditions. I may choose a certain light effect which is fleeting and be able to catch that same atmosphere in the following days. An extra bonus is being surrounded by flowers and birdsong and having my St Bernard at my side.

The Gardener

Growing climbing plants on vertical structures can add interest, giving a new and different perspective. Arches and pergolas, obelisks, fences and trellises can support exciting plants, such as clematis, roses, glory vine, honeysuckle, wisteria, akebia and jasmine. Around the border edges are rock plants, geraniums, aubretia, campanula and spring bulbs. In pots are hydrangea, pelargonium and lobelia. It is exciting when planning plant-colour combinations, considering complementary or contrasting combinations. Also the flowering times should be considered as to whether the plants flower at the same time or follow one after the other. Another consideration is if the plants are near sitting areas, where their scent and colour could be important. Yellow flowers give a feeling of warmth and light, and this can be exaggerated by surrounding cool greens of shrubs and trees. Greenery can soothe the nerves more than the impact of a riot of colour. Pale colours reflect light, so in the evening whites, creams and pale yellows have a luminous glow long after darker colours are no longer visible.

It is important to plant away from walls or trees so that water can reach the roots of plants. The walnut tree on the left was originally a sapling hidden within a scrubby hedge, only discovered when we cleared the area. It has now grown and produces nuts, which the red squirrels love!

SUNFLOWERS

SUNFLOWER
Compositae, *Helianthus annuus* (sunbright)

Painting 1

Sunflowers are wonderfully architectural subjects to paint and seem to have their own natural light, full of life and vitality, and are a good excuse to use pure yellows. The colour yellow attracts the eye like a magnet and can be said to be uplifting. The centre of the sunflower was painted with just enough tone to give it texture. Sunflowers are a very bright yellow, which can be exaggerated by adding a dark tone behind the petals, and there is a strong contrast between the bright-yellow petals and the dark, rich Burnt Sienna in the centre of the flower. This makes them look brighter and more delicate. Yellow can be difficult to use. It traps pencil lines, making them impossible to erase. It is best to start painting the bright petals and stamens with Lemon Yellow or Aurelian, leaving the white paper in the lightest areas. Washes of Gamboge were added to the warmer areas and to build up shadows around the stamens and where the petals were shadowed, mostly in the centre of the flower. For intense colour I used transparent paint straight from the tube, adding a touch of red in the centre of the flower to suggest shadow. The warm and cool yellows need variety, so warmth was added using Vermilion. A hint of complementary blue behind the yellow petals heightened their brightness.

It is essential to keep the colours transparent and clean. The colour density depends on the amount of pigment in the water. If the pigment is strong, an intense colour will result. If there is more water in the mix, the colour intensity will be weakened and it may mean that another application is needed which may diminish the colour's vibrancy. It is important to thoroughly dissolve the pigments in water so that they do not accumulate in the paper's pores and lessen transparency.

Painting 2

The stunning, brilliant colours of sunflowers are a constant draw for artists. Sunflowers have a soft centre which develops into complex seeds, which capture the light, so accurate observation is needed. The centres were painted loosely with browns and reds over the yellow base once the initial yellow was dry. The canna leaves, in front of the sunflowers, were painted with the same range of colours – a yellow-green and, when dry, a darker green.

Watercolour demands a strong sense of control, so planning is important. Creating fascinating paintings means using some essential elements, which includes unusual positioning of the focal point and using a whole range of values around the bright colours. A combination of grouping, lighting and colour creates a beautiful picture with an exciting effect. Primarily it is the quality of the light and colour, the interaction of sunlight, patterns, contrasts and the shadows which create the vibrancy and brilliance of the colours.

Painting 3

For the best effect of sunlight, the light areas should be defined by distinctive shadows. The tonal value of the dark areas depends on the intensity of the brightness, and the brightest area should be enhanced by the darkest area of the painting. Darkening the background can throw the lighter areas into relief. I begin by sketching out ideas and organising thoughts

and composing the objects. The really creative thinking is in the design, sketched out before the painting starts. Strong patterns of light and colour will draw the attention to the centre of interest. I sometimes change colours to create a different feeling, so introduced warm colours into the foreground to give a sense of depth.

317

The use of strong contrast, where dark and light tonal values are positioned side by side, draws the eye more than if the areas are close in tonal value.

In this painting I used both watercolour and pastel to create a special effect in texture, also highlighting the form of the subject. A wash of watercolour over the paper can be very effective as an underpainting, with pastel added when completely dry. The fluid, translucent quality of watercolour combines well with the soft, powdery nature of pastel. This creates vibrant colours, brighter lights and darker darks. When choosing the ground I usually choose the complements to the main colours of the most important aspect of the painting. An underpainting that is complementary to colours placed over them, will add vibrancy. Using a soft underpainting adds depth, richness and complexity to the final painting. Pastels have the advantage that there is no premixing and no drying times. It is a very direct way to paint.

Pastel is the purest form of painting material, being made from powdered pigment – the same pigment from which all other artists' paints are made. It is a pure form of pigment. A weak gum is added to the pigment to form a dough-like consistency. This holds the pigment in shape and is the only addition. Then it is rolled on a flat surface, cut to the desired lengths and left to dry, allowing the water to evaporate. Pastels cannot be mixed with other colours to form new colours unless mixed when wet, during manufacture. A lighter or darker shade cannot be mixed as in oils or acrylic. In the manufacture of pastels, white can be added to lighten or black to darken. Pastel is the one medium where the quality of colour remains constant and in which tone is easily controlled. However, pastel is more dependent than other media on its support. Surfaces with tooth or texture are needed to hold the pastel particles in place. Various pastel papers, rough watercolour paper and canvas are suitable surfaces. Fine-grade glasspaper is a greedy consumer, but holds heavy applications of pastel securely. Soft pastels, used in this painting, contain more pigment and less binder than hard pastels and produce a velvety bloom, which can be blended or the colours left rich and vibrant. I avoid too much blending so as to keep the colours fresh and vital, though in some paintings skies and backgrounds need softening. Blending colours can define objects by the use of gradation from light to dark, softening and smoothing surfaces. The mark must be made lightly so that it creates an even tone. If too much pressure is used, the mark will be too ingrained and difficult to blend smoothly. Two adjoining colours can be blended together where they meet to achieve a graduated colour transition, or the colours can be applied one over the other and then blended to create a solid third colour. The side of the pastel can be used as well as the finger, tissues, rags and brushes. Over-blending can rob colours of their freshness, so should not be overdone. A light unblended application of one colour over another is more vibrant and exciting than a flat area of colour. It is best to retain textural qualities of the drawing as much as possible and to use blending in combination with other, more linear strokes.

The wipe method consists of sketching the composition, loosely blocking in shapes and masses of colour, and then lightly wiping out the colour with a cloth before building up with more pastel.

'Scumbling' is a technique in which pastel is dragged across the surface to create a variety of textural effects. The paper or underpainting can be left to show through, to create fresh and interesting textures.

Broken colour is a method of building up an image with small strokes and dabs of pure colour which are not joined, but have some of the paper showing through as we see in the background, where the green watercolour shows through the blue pastel.

Seen from a distance these strokes appear to merge into one mass of colour, but are very different from blended colour. The small, separate flecks of colour vibrate and appear to shimmer and sparkle, giving a more luminous effect than an area of flat colour. If complementary colours are juxtaposed the effect is even more pronounced. When dabs, dots or strokes of red and green or yellow and violet are intermixed, the colours are mutually enhanced by contrast and the effect is striking. It is best to keep to a fairly limited range of colours to achieve an overall harmony rather than a discordant mix of colours. It is also wise to keep the colours close in tone; otherwise the effect of light is lost. The aim of this technique is to achieve a sense of immediacy. The colours should be applied rapidly and confidently, then left with no attempt to blend them together. Altering the pressure on the pastel, varying the size, shape and density of the marks, avoids monotony.

Layering gives a very rich depth of colour. The base colour is the darkest, with blues, greens and violet added giving a rich dark. The highlights are built up over underlying layers, with the lightest last. The point created as the pastel wears down on one side can be used for fine details, as can the sharpened edge of a hard pastel, although they do not break or crumble as easily as the soft, because they contain more binder and are therefore less brilliant. Pastel pencils could be another option. These are pastel sticks encased in wood. They are clean, easy to use, do not break and give greater control, so are good for line drawings and adding detail. They are water-soluble, so can be used as an underpainting which, when washed over and dry, can be reworked with further layers of pastel. They can be used with conventional pastels.

Value is a good tool for contrast, so light and shadow play a big part in the planning as do warm colours against cool. I kept the intense colour limited so as to be more dramatic and powerful. This was supported by the muted surrounding colour. Too much colour everywhere could destroy the impact of colour, which is more effective when surrounded by neutral or subdued colour. I avoid using fixative as I find it can darken the colours. Tonal contrast is one of the easiest ways to dramatise the composition and make the painting bold, powerful and strong. Contrast happens naturally in nature when the sun casts contrasting dark shadows, particularly early or late in the day when the sun is low and the shadows are long. This lighting effect is called contre-jour. In this painting the shadows were cast from the side with the sunlight catching on the petals and leaves.

Colour can often convey the feelings which attracted me to the subject, and in this painting I used a limited selection of bright and subdued colours to intensify the sensation of my initial inspiration.

Painting 4
A garden scene with one predominant flower among others in the background. Complementary colours of blue-greens, and a touch of Ultramarine Violet, around the flower enhance the brightness of the sunflower. The violet was used in other areas to bring unity to the whole painting.

The Gardener

The giant annual sunflower is native to North America, from Minnesota, North Dakota and Idaho to Missouri, Texas and California. Under cultivation, the sunflower produces plants of gigantic dimensions.

The sunflower, with its exotic character, was used in the religious ceremonies of the Incas, who worshipped the god of day. The Inca civilisation immortalised the sunflower in their traditional designs. When the Spaniards, led by Pizarro, conquered Peru in 1532 they were astonished to see fields of giant gold sunflowers. Their seeds were some of the first to arrive in Europe from Peru, and those who raised them must have been astonished to see a vast stalk and enormous golden flower.

The Indians on the eastern shores of Lake Huron cultivated the sunflower when settlers in Canada realised the plants' economic value. The stalks provided the North American Indians and early settlers with fibres for rough textiles and leaves for fodder, and the flowers yielded a yellow dye. The seeds are rich in oil, which is used in soap-making, paints and lubricants as well as food. The seed is good for poultry, swine and cattle and for human consumption, and can be added to home-baked bread, scattered on salads and breakfast cereals, used medicinally or nibbled with drinks. The seeds may be ground into meal and made into cakes or roasted and used as coffee, and the seeds are eaten as nuts. Each flower head produces up to 2,000 seeds. Oil, extracted from the seed, has been cultivated in Russia, East Africa, Australia, China, America and Europe.

The Romanies gather the flower buds just before they break and boil them in salted water for use as a vegetable served with butter. Gerard must have known of this practice, for he calls them 'exceeding pleasant meate'. Sunflower tea, infused from the freshly picked leaves and flowers, acts as a febrifuge (medicine to reduce fever). It is a cooling drink and can be used instead of quinine – another Gypsy practice.

In recent times, three-quarters of the hashish fields of the Lebanon have been turned over to the cultivation of sunflowers for oil and cattle food. After extraction, the oilcake that remains may be fed to sheep, pigs, poultry, pigeons and rabbits. It is an excellent flower for bees, from which they extract large quantities of honey and wax.

The name helianthus is from the Greek *helios*, meaning sun, and *anthus* meaning flower. It became a favourite flower as a symbol for artists, depicted in flowing bold lines in metal, wood, textiles and pottery. It has been known by many names – flower of the sun, the marigold of Peru, the Indian sun and the golden flower of Peru. Because of its vital uses to the early pioneers, it was selected as the state flower of Kansas, and in the military cemeteries of Poland a sunflower grows on every grave. In France, sunflowers are grown as a crop, so their nutritional value is more important than their attractive blooms. Truly an international flower.

> The flour of the sun is called in Latin 'Flos solis' for that some have reported it to turn with the sun, which I could never observe, although I have indeavored to finde out the truth of it: but I rather thinke it was so called because it resembles the radiant beams of the sunne, whereupon some have called it 'corona solis', and 'sol Indianus', the Indian sunne-floure: others 'chrysanthemum Peruvianum' or the 'Golden floure of Peru': in English, the floure of the sun, or the sun-floure.
>
> *Gerard*

There are red and partially red and nearly black varieties. The red sunflower originates in a red wild plant found in 1910 by Mrs T. D. A. Cockerell at Boulder,

Colorado. *Helianthus annuus* is self-fertile, and the red form was therefore crossed with the common yellow and with the wild yellow, eventually producing the red, sometimes chestnut red, some with ends of the rays yellow, some with a ring of red. Natural hybridisation occurs between species, so consequently the exact colour of saved seed cannot be guaranteed.

The spectacular red, bronze and burnt-orange sunflowers complement the perennial borders of rudbeckias and heleniums. There are also dwarf varieties, which can be used in pots or at the front of the border. Flowers range from pale yellow to orange and maroon with each zoned with a darker band, and the seed discs are purple-blue to black. To encourage a second blooming from the side shoots, the main flower should be cut off when it fades. They are hardy annuals and can be sown in spring in sheltered positions. They need a rich and fertile soil, as they are hungry plants, and because of their size can easily overpower other plants. However, I have grown them in the vegetable garden, where they attract bees and butterflies and look wonderful. Sunflowers are easily grown in most soils in sunny places and do not thrive in shade. They may be sown where they are to flower or in pots in March and planted out when ready. *H. annuus* is grown for its rich oily seeds and does best in rich soil. Where seed is to be saved the heads should be cut off as they mature and laid in an airy, dry place. Mice and rats are very fond of the seeds as they make a tasty snack.

Seed must be set or sowne in the beginning of April, if the weather be temperat, in the most fertill ground that may be, and where the sun hath most power the whole day.

Gerard

Sunflowers are the symbol of adoration, loyalty and longevity.

Painting 5
This is a pastel painting with a watercolour underpainting. The two flower heads on the left were made warm and darker with the light catching on the main bloom. Colours were chosen to give the most impact, with a cool blue against the bright yellow. Red pastel used in the centres of the flowers was repeated subtly in the shadowed side of the petals. The last touches were a very pale-yellow pastel, giving a greater sense of light on the petals.

The Gardener
A relative to the sunflower, *H. tuberosus* is the Jerusalem artichoke, a wild sunflower native to North America and there known as Canada potato, earth apple, giasole (Italian for sunflower) or sunchokes. They are used as food, as the carbohydrates consist of inulin instead of starch, which is converted to fructose after several frosts, when it becomes more easily digestible and safer for diabetics. The name has evolved over the years to Jerusalem artichoke. I grow them in the flower

321

border as they can grow tall so that their yellow blooms are above other plants, making them useful at the back of the border. Jerusalem artichoke is a different species from globe artichoke, *Cynara scolymus,* which is in the thistle family. Globe artichokes are usually grown for their edible flower buds, but I adore the silvered leaves and the huge purple flower heads. I prefer to enjoy the flowers rather than to decapitate the buds for food.

EVERLASTING SUNFLOWER
Inula magnifica (fleabane)

The Painting

I wanted the flower to look delicate and lifelike, but observation and truthfulness is paramount. Here the concept is very simply capturing the beautiful image without complication. The 'petals' were drawn carefully as they twisted and turned in a complicated pattern. Then I painted in cool and warm yellows. The leaves helped to add power to the design and were painted in two strengths of green so that the veins showed lightly against the darker green.

The Gardener
The perennial sunflower has smaller yellow daisy-like flowers than the annual sunflower and has a very spreading nature. There is also a double form. As they grow tall they are best at the back of the border or in wild places. They can spread widely, becoming invasive, and are gross feeders. It is best to lift them every second or third year and give them fresh quarters; otherwise they deteriorate and the double forms can revert to the single form. Inula is distinguished by clumps of large round-toothed bright-green leaves with bright-yellow flowers on thick stems with many branches. They enjoy sun and rich soil. They are from Central and Southern Europe.

SEEDS

It is satisfying to gather seed from favourite plants following the cycle of life of the flower. The resultant plants from saved seed may be unique and may have exciting new features, such as unusual flower colours. It is also a thrifty way to proceed as one plant may produce hundreds of new plants from its own seed. Seeds collected from plants have proved able to cope with particular conditions, meaning that the new seedlings will have a better survival rate as they will have adapted to their environment.

The seeds must be mature to be able to germinate properly. If the seeds are collected too early they may not be viable, and by waiting too long may have dispersed. The dry pods should be gathered once they have turned from green to brown, but before they split open and fall or are taken by the birds. Seeds must be collected on a dry day when there is no moisture or dew. They should be dried and stored in paper bags or named envelopes in a dry, cool place, avoiding heat or moisture, which can induce premature germination and encourage harmful fungal growth.

The seed is a living matter which contains the characteristics of its parents. For the seed to germinate it needs warmth, water and oxygen. If the seed is sown into cold soil it will rot; and if sown too deeply or in waterlogged soil, it will die from lack of air. If the germinating seed is allowed to dry out, the cells cannot survive without water.

The root and shoot emerge from the seed shell and grow in opposite directions, reacting in different ways to the force of gravity. The root extends downwards, seeking moisture and the chemicals in the soil, while the shoot pushes up towards the light, where seed leaves expand and gather food from the air. Once the seed has exhausted the food reserves it must become self-supportive. If the soil structure is good, the seed can expand roots to take advantage of it, widening the system to sustain the food-gathering leaves above. The roots must keep the leaves supplied with water, and the greater the leaf area the harder the roots must work. From pores in the leaf surface, the plant transpires moisture, and this process becomes faster in hot weather. When plants droop, even though the ground may be moist, it means that the roots cannot take up enough water to replace that being transpired.

Some seed is best sown straight away while others need exposure to cold in winter in order to germinate. These should be placed in a cold frame or unheated greenhouse, where winter frosts will break down the germinator inhibitors that can be found in the seeds of many trees, shrubs and climbers that originate from temperate zones. Other seeds can be sown in spring. When plants are ready to plant out in the ground they should have short stems, spreading healthy green leaves and plenty of fibrous roots. The planting holes should be deep enough for the plants' lower leaves to be just clear of the soil. They should be firmed in and watered well and when the water has sunk in, more earth added. The plants may droop in hot sun for some days after planting, so watering in the evening is beneficial. Many tender plants may be planted outdoors when there is no risk of frost, but they must be properly hardened off. Cloches or some other covering are a good idea for the first few weeks.

Almost all self-sown plants like sun and reasonably good drainage. A self-sown seed is generally a survivor and often appears in unexpected places, creating various combinations. As some seedlings do not look like the parent plant it is important to recognise seedlings at an early stage.

There are seeds that will only germinate in autumn, when they are most viable. Some autumn-sown seeds, such as cornflowers, larkspur, phacelia, forget-me-nots, hollyhocks, foxgloves, mallow, rudbeckia and echinacea, will take a little longer to germinate. Sweet-pea seeds can be sown in pots and overwintered in a cold frame. I use toilet-roll tubes, which can be planted directly into the ground so avoiding disturbing the roots. These will flower weeks earlier than those sown in spring. Primrose seeds should be sown into pots, placed in a cold frame and covered with a fine sprinkling of grit and pricked out when they have four leaves. Seeds from marigolds will germinate at any time of year and can be sown in a sunny area, where they are to grow, or in shallow drill and then thinned in spring. Autumn-sown seeds need to be fresh for greater success and kept damp once sown. If the soil is too sandy they may dry out, and if too heavy may rot.

Self-sown seeds establish better than pot-raised plants as they are not damaged by transplanting. I find some real treasures in among the flower borders – allium, aquilegia, marigold, foxglove, viola and nasturtium and often squashes and tomatoes which have overwintered in the compost. There are also wild flowers, which are airborne from the fields around the garden, including beautiful wild garlic and poppies. Seeds are like a heavenly gift. I am always thankful for the miracle of seeds.

LATE SUMMER

ACANTHUS

Acanthus mollis (bear's breeches, sea dock, bear's foot, oyster plant, sea holly). *Mollis* means soft or smooth, referring to the smooth texture of the leaves. The origin of the term bear's breeches is unknown.

The Painting

Watercolour can be a difficult medium, but understanding its characteristics and how to manipulate it to best advantage is a constant joy. Clear, defined detail in the focal area suggests the detail elsewhere. Sometimes the most subtle hint is all that is necessary to help to describe what is suggested. In this painting I worked with a limited palette, using the same colours throughout the painting.

On a soft, sunny day the light enhanced the stunning flowers, giving a glow where the light shone through the delicate petals – I could not ignore this wonderful flower. I had to paint it! The background was painted in a wash of colours, but reserving the white of the paper for the petals, which, when the wash was dry, were painted in individual washes with the tips strengthened and then the darks in the stems and between the leaves added.

The Gardener

Sculptural plants have impact, and acanthus has dramatic glossy leaves and is one of my favourite plants. It is native to the Mediterranean region, and the name derives from the Greek term for the *Acanthus mollis*, a plant that was originally the inspiration for the Greek sculptor Callimachus to model the scrolls on the crown of Corinthian columns. It has since been used extensively in Greco-Roman architecture. Virgil describes Helen of Troy as wearing a dress embroidered with acanthus leaves.

It is a stately, ornamental, vigorous perennial with beautiful, lush, broad, shiny, sculptural divided foliage. The two-lipped flowers are dull white to rose and purple, densely clustered snap-dragon-shaped hooded flowers enclosed by spiny reddish-purple bracts on tall spikes rising well above the foliage, blooming from spring to summer. They look glorious in isolated groups, in borders or even rocky banks. They prefer full sun, but will grow in ordinary soil in partial shade and have good drought-tolerance. Its hairy leaves indicate a minimal need for water. Its propagation is by seed in autumn or early spring. Once established it can spread by creeping rootstock, particularly in loose soils, and can grow from small sections of root. If happy it can be invasive.

SENECIO
Senecio (cineraria, silver-leaved cineraria, dusty miller, groundsel, old-man-in-the-spring)

The Drawing

Coloured pencils are a transparent medium, so layering and mixing colours on the paper is much the same as using paint. Layering also creates strong light and shadow contrasts, giving a more three-dimensional appearance. I preserve the white of the paper for the highlights, building up to the dark.

Coloured pencils are particularly suited to the use of broken-colour techniques. In this drawing all the flowers were facing the sun and were virtually identical, but the leaves caught the light in a different way. Blues, greys and greens were intermingled, with the darks leading the eye into the centre of the plant. The focal point is in the most interesting, active part, where there is the highest contrast of values, colours and edges. This means that nothing detracts from the focal point, even with this being a tiny drawing. The viewer's eye should to be led around the painting and back to the central focal point.

The Gardener

It is probably due to the beard-like feature which is common to the species that the first Roman naturalist, Pliny the Elder, gave the plants the generic name of *Senecio* from the Latin *senex*, meaning old man.

Senecio is a very decorative semi-hardy small shrubby perennial with rich-green, irregularly toothed or dissected silver, woolly leaves, which are roughly triangular, and bright-yellow flowers carried on purple-brown spikes in June. The 'rocket' has bright-yellow flowers on black stems and toothed foliage. Propagation is by cuttings taken in summer and placed in a cold frame.

It can be cut back in April, which means it will not flower that season but will be more attractive when young shoots grow. It can be cut back after flowering, pruning thick wood behind the flower trusses.

Silver foliage brings light into the garden. Silver reflects more light so that it is seen as bright and is particularly effective in contrast with green evergreens. Silver and grey foliage usually have microscopic hairs on the leaf surface, which can make the leaf unattractive to predators. They have evolved to reduce water loss from the leaf in dry, sunny climates and reflect sunlight. They must have full sun to produce their palest leaf colouring, and have a compact habit.

CAMPSIS

Campsis radicans; Bignonia radicans (American trumpet creeper, trumpet vine)

The Painting

I love the brilliant colours of these exotic-looking flowers. I used pure Permanent Rose for the flower heads plus a little Quinacridone Magenta and then Ultramarine Violet for the interior darks. Yellow was painted over the flower tubes and buds, which, when mixed with rose, created a lively orange glow. This same yellow was mixed with blue for the green, and this in turn was darkened in places by violet to give depth and to enhance the stunning colour of the flowers.

The Gardener

Kampe means a bending, the stems being curved. *Bignonia* – trumpet climbers – is a genus of handsome deciduous woody climbers. *Campsis chinensis* from East Asia and *C. radicans* from North America are related to bignonia, but with opposite pinnate leaves and no tendrils.

Bignonia is generally hardy, a deciduous vigorous woody climber which is best grown against a warm sheltered wall in full sun. In midsummer and autumn it bears clusters of large orange-red long trumpet-shaped flowers, scarlet-tinged with yellow inside the throat, gathered into showy pendulous clusters on the current year's branches. *C. radicans* is hardier and clings by means of aerial roots, much like ivy, but is better with support. It can be grown on a pergola or archway, losing only its weaker lateral shoots in severe winters. In early spring I prune old stems which have flowered back to a few buds. Propagation is by root cuttings, suckers, woody cuttings,

327

layering in summer and seeds, which ripen in hot summers. The fruit is a long capsule with flattened seeds with transparent silvery wings. *C. radicans flava* has yellow flowers and *C.* 'Atropurpurea' is deep scarlet.

LOVE-IN-A-MIST
Nigella (devil in a bush)

Painting 1

All colours are affected by the light conditions in which they are seen, and the intensity of light varies with the time of day, season and situation. The stunning blue flower of nigella is intense in the morning when the light is crisp blue, but will appear paler in the softer, more yellow light of late afternoon and evening. This is a good reason to paint blue flowers in the morning and perhaps yellow later in the day. Shadows are useful in indicating the time of day and the type of weather conditions, and can therefore add to the mood and atmosphere of a painting. It was an overcast day when these nigella flowers were painted, as can be seen from the low light level, but there was still some shadow.

I love painting natural things, and these beautiful plants grace my garden every year. They self-seed in the borders, creating combinations of colour and shapes in among lilies, lychnis and roses. The difference in the lightness and darkness of the flower centres gave a contrast in value. There was a tonal difference in the strength of the paint used for the wonderfully blue petals, but, at the time, elusive and ever changing and moving light meant looking very hard at the shapes and colours with the aim of interpreting and expressing the beauty of the flowers. Fleeting light is elusive, changing continually. Capturing the atmosphere in a painting means portraying some of the spirit of the light, much more than recording an effect.

I drew the complicated shapes with a pencil as I needed a guide through the intricate flower heads and fine leaves. I used Ultramarine Blue on the petals starting with a thin wash and building up to a darker mix in shadowed places. Quinacridone Magenta was used for the stamens, with a much deeper Quinacridone Violet and a touch of green for the central stamens. The fine leaves were a wash of pale green, which was then deepened behind the stems.

328

Painting 2

A little later in the morning the light had changed and was clear and bright. The flower head was painted with several blues and violet, with the same green of the background used in the centre of the flower. As well as the fabulous colour, I loved the intricate shapes, twists and turns of the stamens.

The background was wet with clear water and Sap Green and a mix of green and violet dropped in to disperse, and then more colour was added as it dried. The stamens were also green, darkened on the sides. The petals were started with a wash of Cerulean Blue and then Ultramarine Blue was added while still wet. When dry, the veins of the petals were added with Ultramarine Blue, with some violet used on the stamens.

The Gardener
The name nigella comes from *niger*, meaning black, the colour of the handsome seed pods. It has common names such as devil in a bush and love-in-a-mist, which has blue flowers amid feathery leaves. 'Alba' is white, 'Flore Pléno' is double-flowered and 'Miss Jekyll' is bright cornflower blue. The flower season lasts for about eight weeks and is prolonged by deadheading. It is native to the Mediterranean and West Asia, but will grow well in good garden soil. Seeds should be sown where the plants are to flower in early September or in March, but autumn is best. Seedlings may be transplanted.

Nigella is easy to grow and is one of my favourite annual flowers, with its intriguing shapes and fabulous colours.

RUDBECKIA

(coneflower, black-eyed Susan, brown-eyed Susan, brown Betty, gloriosa daisy, golden Jerusalem, English bull's eye, poor-land daisy, yellow daisy and yellow ox-eye daisy)

Painting 1

This initial study was made in ink. Studying closely these rudbeckia flowers helps with understanding their shapes and how they relate to one another. I especially like the way they twist one behind the other.

The greatest tonal contrast occurs when looking into the light. Contre-jour, meaning against the light, gives a greater sense of brilliance than in any other light direction. In this case the sides of the flowers and the leaves were shaded, giving depth and substance to the drawing. Close study helped in understanding the complexity of the centres and how the light and shade explains their texture.

In the painting the petals were a mix of Lemon Yellow, Indian Yellow, Quinacridone Red and Winsor Orange. The centres were painted with little dots of various mid to dark colours with a little green in the shadow areas. The brightness of the flowers is accentuated where I have darkened the background. The furthest blossoms were toned down so as to accent the importance of the main flowers.

No matter how passionately one wishes to express oneself, a cool and profound understanding of the different elements in a painting is required.

Painting 2

In the process of creating the textures, the result is almost abstract – a characteristic of the flowers. Each individual petal was wet with clear water and Lemon Yellow, Indian Yellow, Winsor Orange and Quinacridone Red were dropped on to the wet paper. When the foreground petals had dried, then the background petals and the central core were added using the same colours with the addition of Burnt Sienna.

Painting 3

This painting isn't necessarily about the plants, but is about colour in an emotional and expressive interpretation. The colours need to be finely pitched so as not to compete, but rather to relate to each other. Too many opposing and unrelated colours in a confined space can create a visual din – a clamouring for attention.

What inspires me to paint is a mixture of passion for a beautiful subject, the painting process, colour combinations, unique textures and strong light effects. Light can transform objects into dramatic subjects. Here the strong backlighting, with complementary colours, creates powerful values throughout the painting. The vibrant Ultramarine Purple is reflected in the name *Rudbeckia purpurea*, and accented by the surrounding greenery and the flower's yellow central cone.

The Gardener

Rudbeckia is named after Olaf Rudbeck, 1660–1740, and his son, both professors of botany at Uppsala, Sweden. Famous for their brilliant golden-yellow blooms with black centres, rudbeckias are excellent long-lasting perennials both for the garden and as cut flowers. Their tall, strong, upright habit is good for the back of the border. In rich soils they often spread to wide clumps. They have numerous daisy-like flowers with a prominent central brown or greenish cone. Rudbeckias come as both annuals and perennials. They vary from short annuals, such as 'Becky' and 'Toto', to giants that tower more than two metres high. The annuals are easily grown from seed and have a great variety of flower shape and colour, from yellow to dark bronze and red shades. The perennial 'Goldsturm' is reliably tough and flowers profusely. The perennial types only come in variants of yellow, with no zones or bands of other colours. *R. fulgida* is up to ninety centimetres high with yellow to orange flowers and purple-brown cones. *R. laciniata* is two metres high and has yellow flowers with a greenish cone. *R. maxima* is ninety centimetres high and is moderately hardy with yellow blooms. *R. subtomentosa* is ninety centimetres high with yellow flowers and a button-shaped central disc.

This is a plant which copes well with changeable weather as it has thick fleshy roots which hold on to moisture when conditions above ground are hot and dry. They are sun-lovers, but also withstand wet and bitter winters. The stiff, wiry stems will weather storms intact, while the flower heads shrug off heavy rain showers.

They have a raised central domed cone of stamens and have a delicious honey fragrance. They are closely related to sunflowers. They get their name of coneflowers because in some kinds the central disc is raised into a cone. The yellow-flowered varieties are all rudbeckias, but the purple coneflowers are varieties of *Echinacea purpurea*. 'Autumn Sun' is one of the tallest. They will last for years, but can be divided when dormant. Propagation is by seed or by division. *R. maxima* has bright-yellow flowers and a green central cone. For the best effect I plant it en masse at the back of the border, giving a strong vertical statement. Small birds feed on the seeds and, despite its swampy origins, it is drought-resistant. It has several names: giant coneflower, great coneflower, great brown-eyed Susan and cabbage-leaf coneflower.

    R. sullivantii Goldsturm is self-supporting. In August and September my sunny south border is filled with its orange-yellow flowers. The dramatic black centres enhance the bright petals. *R. speciosa* is similar, but not so showy. 'Goldquelle' has double deep-yellow flowers. The purple coneflowers have rosy-purple flowers. They are related to echinacea and lapachys.

NASTURTIUM
Tropaeolum majus (garden nasturtium, Indian cress, monk's cress)

The Painting
This drawing was fun, as the twists and turns of the stalks gave a lively feel to the plant. The flower heads were all different as they faced forwards, upwards and outwards, making for an interesting composition. The leaves were mostly the same shape but gave a balance to the design.

    In the watercolour painting, the flower heads were the most important feature, and this was made more so by the strong orange against the green. The veins in the leaves were fine and delicate, so here I used masking fluid and, when dry, painted over the leaves. Once the fluid was removed, the veins were toned down with a washy hint of green and the shadows were added. The dark background and the shadows on the leaves helped to give depth to the study.

The Gardener
Nasturtiums are easily grown hardy annuals which are not too fussy about soil or position, but are killed by frost. They are mostly trailing or climbing plants with brightly coloured, spurred, and trumpet-shaped flowers on long stalks, in shades of red, orange or yellow in summer and autumn. All flower freely in poor soils and warm, sunny places. The nasturtium *Tropaeolum majus* originates from Peru and the

West Indies. The seed was introduced to England in 1597, when it was sent to John Gerard. Its ease of cultivation coupled with its exotic appearance ensured immediate popularity. Parkinson called it 'Yellow larked spurr'.

In the sixteenth century it was known as Indian cress, which suggests that it was eaten as a salad food. It bears the Latin generic name for watercress, *Nasturtium officinale*. The nutritive value is especially useful in diets devoid of salt and other seasoning, which benefit from its pleasant hot, spicy flavour. The vitamin-C content is high, as in watercress, and both have anti-scorbutic properties. The nasturtium was used in treatment for general debility following influenza. In addition the seeds can be used as a substitute for capers in caper sauce, particularly appetising when served with beetroot as a winter vegetable. The seeds can be dried and ground in a pepper mill. The leaves should be added to a salad with discretion, or may be crushed and rubbed around the inside of the bowl. Chopped leaves can be mixed into cream cheese, like chives, or can be sprinkled on a tomato salad. The flowers have a velvety finish and a peppery taste.

The double-flowered form first came from Italy in the mid-eighteenth century and, with the plethora of new plants arriving, not very much attention seems to have been paid to it. It was not until the Gleam Hybrids of the mid twentieth century that the nasturtium reached a new height of popularity, when double flowers were combined with scent. The scent of the flower was inbred from plants found in a garden in California. Since then, work has progressed on both sides of the Atlantic to produce a race of garden nasturtiums that hold their helmet-like flowers of glowing orange or yellow or apricot above ground, masking smooth green leaves. There are new strains with smaller leaves, non-trailing and many semi-double in colours ranging from apricot to dark cherry red.

T. peregrinum, or canary creeper, is a climbing annual with blue-green five-lobed leaves and bright-yellow-fringed flowers. *T. speciosum*, or flame creeper, is a moderately hardly perennial creeper with scarlet flowers and does best in a cool, moist climate.

Nasturtiums flower on and on and have a habit of sending out shoots through other plants in an unexpected way. They must be managed, otherwise they can become rampant and take over.

FOXTAIL LILY
Eremurus (desert candles)

The Painting

One of the best times to paint flowers is later in the day, when the light is warm and the lilies look stunning standing out from other colours in the evening.

Here I have painted *Eremurus elwesii*, which is pale peach pink and the most imposing species, growing to 1.8 metres. It has narrow bright-green leaves that die down before the flowers open in early summer, but, even so, I made a green background to emphasise the flowers of peach pink and their intricate stamens. These I masked out along with the stalks of the unopened flower buds. This allowed me to paint the green background without too much worry. The dramatic contrast of light and shade emphasised the light in the foreground. The flowers were painted with a dilute cerise with a stronger Magenta in places, including the buds and stripes on the flowers and for the main stem, adding a little green into the mix for the slightly darker shaded areas. Once the fluid was removed, the stamens were painted with Indian Yellow.

The Gardener

These striking flowers draw gasps of admiration wherever they are seen. Eremuruses are herbaceous perennials and generally hardy, best in sunny borders, where their tightly packed star-shaped blossoms add seasonal drama to the border. There are more than forty species, but only a handful are grown in gardens. I have several varieties, including *E.* 'Pinocchio', which has orange buds opening to deep-yellow flowers with bright-orange stamens. Other fabulous plants in this family are *E. stenophyllus*, which has small yellow and orange star-shaped flowers and is long-flowering; *E.* 'Romance', which has salmon-orange-pink flowers; *E.* × *isabellinus* 'Cleopatra', which is orange with a red-stripe on the petal; *E.* × *isabellinus* 'Obelisk', which has white and green stripes on the petal; and *E. himalaicus*, which has white and orange anthers, flowering in May. *E. elwesii* has elegant, fragrant soft-pink or pure-white flowers.

Foxtail lilies were introduced from Central Asia in the nineteenth century. They need to be planted in well-drained soil in full sun with no other plants to shade them or be in competition with their roots. Plantswoman Beth Chatto uses them in her dry garden. They grow from a tuber composed of a large central bud around which radiate a number of thick fleshy roots, rather like the arms of a starfish. A sheaf of fleshy red-hot-poker leaves grows in spring, followed by the flower spikes. They benefit from a feed of potash and water when in leaf. After they flower the leaves die back, becoming dormant for the remainder of the year. Foxtail lilies look fabulous wafting above other low-growing plants, but they are likely to fail if not given enough space and good drainage. They are best used in drifts or as accent planting. Each flower spike has hundreds of flowers, which open from the bottom upwards. They are a magnet to pollinating insects. As they need a cold, dry winter and spring moisture they benefit from an open sunny and sheltered position. Extra grit will help drainage, which is the key to success with eremurus.

Propagation is by fresh seed sown in autumn, taking three to five years to flower. Clumps may be divided, but great care must be taken so as not to damage the fleshy roots.

COLUMBINE
Aquilegia (grannys' bonnet)

The Painting
The complementary colours of violet and yellow bring a bright, lively feel to this painting. I drew the flower heads lightly in pencil, then, using Lemon Yellow, painted the inner petals and some stamens. Once dry, I added a warmer Indian Yellow for the smaller petals in the centre. I then painted the outer petals with violet and, when dry, added a thicker, slightly drier mix for the darker areas of the petals. The calyx – the five points which protrude at the base of the flower – were painted with a washy pink and, when dry, the green was painted around them so that they contrasted against the dark. This same pink was added to the green in areas where the green leaves were in shadow.

The background was a washy green, giving an illusion of green in the distance. The stems were first painted in light green and then a darker version was added to indicate shadow.

The Gardener
The names aquilegia and columbine come from two birds, the eagle (*aquila*) and the dove. It is called columbine from its fanciful likeness to the shape of doves, with beaks that meet in the centre and tails outspread. The genus was given its Latin name, *Aquilegia*, because the inverted tubes at the base of the flower are like the curved talons of an eagle. It was formally called herba lionis, because it was thought to be the favourite plant of the lion. To country children it was known as granny's bonnets in England and granny's mutch in Scotland. It was also called cocksfoot. The short-spurred variety grows in the wild, but the flowers were gathered to adorn houses, which led to its decline.

Aquilegia is a genus of about seventy species of perennial herbs with fibrous roots. These are short-lived perennials with dainty flowers on long stalks with five concave, spurred petals with some forming a tube, often curved at the end and in a wide colour range in bright or pastel colours, but especially pink and blue, with attractive foliage. The long spurs contain nectar. They grow in temperate and mountain regions of the northern hemisphere, with two or three species in Southern Africa. They do well in ordinary garden soil, preferring a moist but not wet soil and a sunny exposure. They are good in informal cottage-garden settings. Most bloom in spring to early summer, when the garden is at its loveliest. They self-seed prolifically, but are best in their first year. Most need a cold winter to stimulate flowering. The flowers are in red, yellow or soft shades of purple, rose, blue and white and hang gracefully on tall stems. I have a beautiful *A. vulgaris atrata*, which is dark violet. Aquiliega thrives in partial shade, but it can cross and dominate other species, impressing its character on its hybrid seedlings.

Variations are *A. alba* a white form; *A. atrata*, which is dark violet; *A.* 'Flore Pleno', which has various colours and is double-flowered; 'Nivea', which is robust, tall and pure white; *A. olympica*, which is large, pale lilac or bright purple; and *A. verbaeneana*, which is variegated yellow. Although not long-lived, they will often maintain themselves by self-sown seedlings.

They can be grown in varying heights, from miniature rock plants to long-spurred giants, with shorter hybrids in pink, crimson, blue, yellow and white.

FOUR O'CLOCK PLANT
Mirabilis (marvel of Peru, four o'clock plant, wonderful)

The Painting

Looking directly at the flowers, they appeared almost flat. The leaves were painted loosely and merely suggested with touches of rose here and there in buds and a little on the stems.

The veins on the leaves and the stamens of the flower were masked out to preserve the white of the paper while the rest of the flower was painted. The main flower was painted with brilliant Permanent Rose, with yellow stamens which sang out against the pink. When dry, I used a thicker, deeper application of rose in areas where petals turned or changed direction. The same principle was applied to the buds. Once the fluid was removed the stamens and veins on the leaves were painted.

336

The Gardener

Mirabilis is Latin for amazing, wonderful or remarkable. It is a genus of plants in the family Nyctaginaceae, and is known as the four o'clock plant or marvel of Peru. In China it is called shower flower, in Hong Kong purple jasmine, in Turkey evening pleasure and in France *belle de nuit*, meaning beauty of the night. The best-known species is *M. jalapa*. The tuberous roots enable them to penetrate through dry and cool seasons. They have small fragrant, trumpet-shaped, deep-throated cerise, rose-pink or white flowers, which open in the afternoon and stay open through the night, attracting many moths and closing in the morning. On warm nights the perfume is intoxicating. It has naturalised throughout tropical and warm temperate regions. It is a perennial plant in my garden, growing in a sunny, protected area and dies back in late autumn, regrowing in the spring and flowering in summer. The original seed was sent to me by a friend in Canada, so it is very special to me. I have it at the front of our south-facing house so that it enjoys the heat and the fragrance wafts in through the windows on warm summer nights. The single-sided fruits are spherical, wrinkled and black when mature and self-seed and spread rapidly where they find suitable homes.

NICANDRA
Nicandra physalodes (shoo-fly plant, apple of Peru, apple of Sodom, Peruvian bluebell)

The Painting

I did a careful drawing before adding any paint. I first painted the flower, wet the edges of the petals and ran in two blues – Cobalt Blue for the inner side of the petals and Ultramarine Blue with a touch of Quinacridone Violet for the outer – leaving white unpainted paper for the stamens. The leaves and pods were painted with Sap Green, and then I darkened the green with a little Burnt Umber, which was also dabbed on to the pods and a more washy mix was used for the veins. A thicker mix of green and Umber was painted on to parts of the stems. Ultramarine was used to paint the dark veins on the flower petals.

The Gardener

Nicandra is in the nightshade family, the same family as the potato. All parts of the plant are poisonous. It is a native of Peru, growing in bare, waste and cultivated ground and often germinates around bird feeders as it is often included in commercial birdseed mixes. It can become a weed nuisance, but is easily controlled by hoeing or hand weeding.

The bell-shaped flowers are short-lived, opening for only a few hours each day. The flower becomes lantern-shaped towards the end of its bloom. After pollination, cherry-shaped green-brown berries are encased in green or black mottled calyxes. The plants do not tolerate hot afternoon heat very well and will wilt in full sun, so are best in partial shade. They are best propagated from seed, which germinates in seven to fourteen days at 20–21°C in a mix of soil and sand.

I grow it because it repels aphids, gnats and whiteflies and I am intrigued by the plant's unusual ovate mid-green toothed and waved leaves and the flowers, which are pale violet with white throats, and its green lanterns.

GLADIOLUS

The name is originally from the Latin *gladius*, meaning a sword, and it is sometimes called sword lily. Gladiolus is the correct term for an individual bulb whereas gladioli is the plural. In the language of flowers it is 'appointment'.

The Painting

In the painting of these garden gladioli (which differ from the more hybridised commercial species) two yellows were used – a Lemon Yellow for the initial wash over the petals and then a warmer Indian Yellow for the centres of the flowers, the veins and shadows. At the root of good design are the light and dark elements. Here I decided on a purple background as a strong complement to the yellow, to enforce the importance of the yellow flowers and give depth to the darks and ultimately enrich the light areas. With a very fine brush, I used the same background colour, purple, in the centre of the flowers.

The Gardener

Prior to being given their Latin name, the gladiolus was called xiphium, which comes from the Greek word for sword. The gladiolus was seen as a sign of luck and protection during the time of the gladiators. This link led to current association with strength of character. The gladiolus has the meaning of strength, honour and infatuation.

In the 1740s, South African gladioli were brought to Europe by Dutch and English merchants following the Indian trade route. Several English horticulturists began hybridising them in the early nineteenth century, with James Colville producing fertile hybrids.

Gladioli have an extraordinarily wide colour range, and there is a very great variation in their form.

The beautifully coloured modern flowers are descendants of African species and not the European horticulturists, who developed high bud counts and multiple florets. The spectacular giant flower spikes are the products of centuries of hybridisation and selection.

Gladiolus is a genus of perennial corms in the iris family, originating mainly from Africa, and they are half-hardy in temperate climates. They have an ease of culture and adaptability with respect to varying soils and situations. Brilliant colours range from pink to red, light purple to white, white to cream and orange to red, and they are more effective when in clumps throughout the mixed herbaceous border. If clumps are confined to single varieties and those varieties are chosen with regard to height, colour and time of flowering, the effect is more pleasing. They can form a dramatic backdrop to flower borders or along fences, which help keep the spires upright. If planted in windy places some of the taller species need support, and timely staking is essential. Stakes need to be inserted away from the base of the stem, thus avoiding damage

Gladioli are food plants of the larvae of some Lepidoptera moths and can be pollinated by hawk moths and long-tongued insects. They need plenty of air at the root, so need to be planted close to the surface. Thereafter they need little attention other than shallow hoeing to aerate the soil and keep down weeds. The period of growth during which the gladiolus needs most water is when the flower spike is forming, and a good soaking is more beneficial than frequent sprinklings. Feeding should begin when the plants are growing freely, when there are plenty of roots to take up the food.

Gladiolus seed collected in the previous autumn can be sown in spring, covered with polythene and placed in an unheated greenhouse or polytunnel. Seeds will germinate after about three weeks, and by May the young seedlings have mature larger leaves. In summer the plants can be hardened off and transplanted into sunny, well-drained borders, and the first flower spikes will appear in July, sixteen weeks after sowing. These blooms may not be representative of the flowers produced by the original parent corm. The plant remains an annual unless the first flower spikes in bud are removed, as the development of the flower so early in the plant's life cycle weakens the formation of a good corm. The flowers in the second year will be typical of those produced in following years. If these form seed it can be collected once ripened and stored in a cool, dry place until the following spring.

Gladioli are traditionally given as a fortieth-anniversary gift and represent the birth flower of August. Victorian romantics suggested gladiolus flowers were capable of piercing someone's heart with their beauty, causing infatuation. Gladioli are referred to as a ladder to heaven, with their tall spires and blooms that grow from the bottom up. In China it is believed the gladiolus can help the deceased find heaven. Many believe the biblical reference to 'lilies of the field' was the first written reference to the gladiolus.

Modern African herbalists use the gladiolus to treat many illnesses, including treating colds, dysentery, diarrhoea and constipation. In the Congo it is a food, giving a good source of carbohydrates to help balance the diet.

GAURA
Gaura lindheimeri, recently renamed *Oenothera lindheimeri* (whirling butterflies, bee-blossom, wand-flower)

The Painting

The beautiful white flowers are contrasted against Ultramarine Blue, and lower down the painting by dark green. The stalks are a yellow-green darkened on the shadowed side by the same green with the addition of Ultramarine Blue and Permanent Rose. At the base of each bud, the colour rose has been run into yellow-green. The shadows on the flowers are a mix of rose, blue and green, and this is because of the light – the short blue wavelengths which reach our eyes from the surface, creating the most exciting, deeper, richer values of the local colour. 'Local colour' refers to the actual colour of the flowers. The shadow area can offer a wide range of values, from light-middle, middle, middle-dark to dark. The middle values can be vivid colours using strong pigments, reserving the strongest darks for exciting accents placed after the majority of middle-value shadows.

The use of lights and darks for high tonal contrast can create a strong visual impact. The high contrast in values causes the outlines of the petals to become important. Nature's ability to constantly surprise and delight produces the most exciting effects, which can never be planned.

The Gardener

Gaura lindheimeri has been developed from a North American wild flower with several hybrids which keep the cultivar under control and make it suitable for the flower bed. Gaura is closely related to the evening primrose.

Gaura is a bushy, graceful plant with long erect stems studded with delicate star-shaped flowers that open white from rose-pink buds and lance-shaped foliage, often tinged with pink, cream or gold, depending on the variety. In the breeze the sprays of white flowers, tinged pink, move constantly, suggesting clouds of butterflies.

Gaura is hardy, but sometimes short-lived. It has a long flowering season from mid spring until frost causes dieback. If the faded flowering stems are removed, further blooms are encouraged. I cut all stems back to ground level in late autumn. If competition is limited it will self-seed in a well-drained sunny or partly shaded spot. They thrive in dry, rich and deeply drained soil, which encourages development of the taproot. It is the long taproot which makes Gaura so drought-tolerant and also makes it difficult to transplant. Too much manure or fertiliser can make the plant floppy. Water and fertilisation needs are minimal once the plant is established. Poor and yellowish growth indicates that the soil and site are too cold and wet. It can survive lengthy periods of drought so is ideal for my garden, which is very well drained.

Gauras are best planted in groups of three or more in spring in light well-drained soil in full sun, and need little maintenance. They can be grown from seed in spring where the plants are to flower, and then the seedlings should be thinned out or started indoors in pots in early spring or autumn. New seedlings often emerge as they self-seed. They can be propagated by basal cuttings or softwood cuttings in spring or semi-hardwood cuttings in summer.

CANNA
Canna × *generalis* (Indian shot)

The Painting

The glorious vibrant colour of these canna flowers was an inspiration to use brilliant pure Quinacridone Red and Winsor Orange. The shapes were kept simple, as was the application of paint – red into orange while still wet. Pure Quinacridone Red was used for all the flower petals, applied in differing strengths to give a sense of depth and shape. When dry, green was used for the leaves with a little Ultramarine Violet in the stem and buds.

The Gardener

Cannas are native to tropical America and Asia. The flaring tubular flowers are best used as 'dot plants' for tropical elegance in a bedding scheme. The broad leaves are bright green, or bronze to purple on many red-flowering varieties. The flowers have three, usually green, sepals and three long, narrow coloured petals in red, pink, orange or white. Cannas are propagated by seed or by division of the rhizomes, the latter being essential for named varieties. The rootstock should be cut into pieces of suitable sizes and laid out in a bed or boxes in leafy soil or fibrous peat, kept warm and watered sparingly until they start into growth. Seed should be sown in February in a warm house in pans or boxes in light rich compost, but as the roots are very brittle it is a good idea to sow seeds singly in pots so that the seedlings can be potted on without injury to the roots. The seeds are very hard and germinate slowly, if at all, unless they are previously soaked for twenty-four hours in warm water or have the testa filed through. Cannas can be kept growing in warmth in a moist atmosphere and should be covered and moved outdoors after danger of frost has passed. The soil must be fertile – the richer the better – and the plants fed during the growing season. Cannas should be mulched and never allowed to dry out if they are to flower well. Individual flowers last only a day, but more are produced from the buds. When the flower fades the stem should be cut back to the next side shoot, where a second spike will appear. Most produce about three or four spikes.

At the end of the flowering season they should be lifted and the rhizomes dried and overwintered in a frost-free place, keeping them barely moist. The roots are fleshy and store enough food to take the plant through its dormancy in winter.

SPIRAEA
Caryopteris (blue spiraea, blue mist, blue beard)

The Painting

A painting can work on different levels, be it the subject, the concept, or the materials used. It is so important to observe closely rather than paint what is thought to be there. There is no formula when learning to see properly – it is a matter for the individual. Painting what is actually there means careful observation. With this in mind it is exciting to try new subjects and new ways of handling light and colour, which results in a convincing painting.

It was quite a challenge to suggest the delicate blooms of caryopteris. The flowers are closely packed together and it is difficult to distinguish one from another as the buds merge into the soft blue. The surrounding caryopteris flowers were indicated by dabs of Cobalt Blue – the same colour as was used for the main blossoms – with just a hint of green to suggest the leaves.

The Gardener

Caryopteris is a small, deciduous, sun-loving shrub, flowering from summer to autumn. If planted in partial shade it will not flower as freely and may bloom later. It is of the verbena family, needing sun and a free-draining situation. Its toothed leaves and shoots are clothed in a fine grey down with serrated edges. There are dense clusters of small, fuzzy violet-blue and deep-lavender-blue flowers with narrow petals and pin-like stamens on the upper leaf axils. They attract many insects, such as bees and butterflies.

Caryopteris is native over a wide territory, from China to Japan. Most common in gardens is *Caryopteris* × *clandonensis*, which has resulted from crosses between *C. incana* and *C. mongoholica*. 'First Choice' is a compact, erect shrub with dark-reddish stems, green toothy leaves and flowers of a richer, darker blue, and with a longer flowering season. Caryopteris is short-lived, but can be propagated by taking cuttings in June, and will root in days and bloom in September. It is easy from seed and will produce thousands of seedlings around the mother plant. These may vary, but will make good plants. Caryopteris is best pruned immediately after flowering and then pruned again to within a few buds of the base in spring. As they age, dead wood may appear in the centre. This should be pruned out. Once established they don't need any supplementary watering, and too much fertiliser makes for a leafy plant with fewer blooms. They are excellent in tubs and containers as they are heat-tolerant.

SEDUM

Hylotelephium telephium (stonecrop, life-everlasting, live-forever, livelong, orphan John, frog's-stomach, harping Johnny, witch's moneybags, midsummer men)

The Painting

Portraying the texture of the flower heads was tricky, as I had to portray individual buds within each bloom. Tiny blooms require close observation, and the light and shade are equally important. To start the painting I dipped the brush in dilute Quinacridone Magenta, and when this was dry added thicker paint in some areas. The shaded blooms were painted with dilute Ultramarine Violet, which appeared more pink because of the underlying Magenta.

The shade on the stems and stalk helped to pull the plant forward. The leaves were indicated rather than meticulously explained with a blue-green, with a slightly more yellow-green in places. Blue was added in the back area and a touch of violet in darker, shaded parts.

The Gardener

Sedums are drought-resistant succulent rock plants. *Sedo*, meaning to sit, is in reference to the manner in which some species attach themselves to rocks and walls. *Sedum acre*, or stonecrop, forms mats of rounded yellow-green and overlapping leaves and yellow flowers. *S. dasyphyllum* is even smaller, with carpeting mats of tiny fleshy blue-green leaves and white flowers. The larger *S. spectabile*, the ice plant or butterfly plant, is a perennial with fleshy grey-green leaves and flat heads of pink or red flowers in August. The hybrid 'Autumn Joy' is similar in habit, but flowers in September and October, and is reddish pink deepening to russet red. *S. maximum* 'Atropurpureum' has fleshy beetroot-purple leaves and creamy flowers in August. They are propagated by cuttings or by division or seed and will form new plants. Sedum provides nectar for butterflies and bees.

EARLY AUTUMN

EUCOMIS
(autumn pineapple flower, autumn pineapple lily, bear's ears)

Painting 1

As this was seen from a distance, the flowers were masked as it would have been too fiddly to paint around them. I could have used gouache, acrylic or Chinese White paint, but I prefer to retain the transparency of watercolour. Various greens were used, one with more yellow for the top leaves, stalks and veins in the lower leaves, and then the same blend had a little blue added for some areas while others had a touch of violet. The background was wetted, and blue and violet were washed in with a touch of green at the base. When dry, the masking fluid was rubbed off and a little pink added to the upper section of the flower heads.

Painting 2

The edges of the flowers and leaves were painted in pink before anything else. The top knot of leaves was painted carefully around the pink edges and then the unopened buds. A dilute green was used on the inner flower stems and then the green was darkened with the pink and used for the interior, the stalk and the shadow on the leaves. Once all was dry, the background was wet and the pale and dark greens were washed in with Ultramarine Blue at the top. These darks gave a contrast to the paler petals.

The Gardener

Eucomis is a lily in the Asparagaceae family, native to South Africa, first described in 1878 by John Gilbert Baker. It is a summer-flowering deciduous, bulbous perennial. Eucomis has a beautiful crown of leaves on the flower spike, looking like a pineapple top – hence the name. The botanical name comes from the Greek words *eu*, meaning good, and *kome*, meaning hair – *eucomis* meaning lovely-haired.

The flower spike rises from a basal rosette of broad waxy leaves with as many as 100 tiny greenish-white flowers, which open slowly from the bottom up over a period of three weeks or more. When fertilised they turn to green, and when the fruit ripens produce shiny black seeds. Eucomis is best planted in groups, either in the flower border, in large pots or in rockeries. Rock gardens are ideal for eucomis because the plants prefer the sharply drained soil. They should be planted with their tops at ground level, in full sun, in rich compost, adding more well-rotted compost every spring and lots of water during the growing season. This will promote good flowering. They are dormant in winter and frost-hardy to -7°C. Mulch will protect the bulbs from freezing. If planted in containers, they should be placed in a frost-free place in October. The compost should be allowed to dry, and all dry and yellowed foliage removed. In spring they can be watered when regrowth starts.

To propagate, the seed should be sown in spring, with seedlings appearing after four to six weeks. The seedlings should be protected for the first few years and planted in the garden in their third year. They may take five years to flower. The bulb may produce offsets, which can be removed while the plant is dormant, potted up and planted in the spring. Bulblets will flower in two to five years. They are fast-growing, so will need regular repotting. Leaf cuttings can be taken while the plant is in active growth. Sections planted in sterilised well-drained soil, and kept humid, should produce tiny bulbs within a few months.

Eucomis is pollinated almost exclusively by flies attracted to the floral scent, which resembles sulphur compounds attractive to carrion flies. The bulbs are used in Africa as medicine. Bulb and root shavings are boiled in water or milk and used as an ingredient in infusions to treat pain and fever. Extracts from *Eucomis bicolor* are also used to treat colic and as a purgative. Scientific research has found bulb and root extracts have anti-inflammatory properties.

E. autumnalis has pale-green flowers. *E. bicolor* has pale-green flowers with purple margins. *E. comosa* has white flowers with purple tepals. *E. comosa* 'Sparkling Burgundy' has reddish-purple foliage and purple-tinted flowers, and *E. pallidiflora* has greenish-white flowers.

JAPANESE ANEMONE
Anemone × *hybrida* (windflower)

Painting 1
Every painting begins with an idea, and this can be the most important stage as the outcome can never be completely certain. I drew the lovely shapes of the Japanese anemone in pencil to be accurate when painting the dark background around the flowers and stalks. The purple-greys of the background, and shadows cast by the morning sun, emphasised the soft curves of the petals. Colours for the background were Ultramarine Violet and Cobalt Blue and a green mixed from Cobalt Blue and Winsor Orange. The orange was used in the central stamens and helped to enliven the image. Violet and blue were used in the shadows on the flower petals.

Painting 2

The anemones looked wonderful clustered together, making a stunning composition. I used Opera Rose and for the shadows a little Quinacridone Magenta, with yellow for the centres. To suggest the stems, detailed lights and darks meant it was dependent on close observation. It helped to have darks around the flowers.

Painting 3

This painting was much less controlled in that the flowers were suggested and the leaves only indicated. I wanted to give a sense of movement as they moved in the breeze, and leaving a lot of white paper gave a sense of bright, shining light on the petals before adding dilute pink to them.

A careful drawing was made as I wanted to capture the complication of stalks, leaves and buds as well as the glorious flowers. Magenta was used for the flower petals and, in shadowed areas, touches of Cobalt Blue, which changed the Magenta to a light violet. The stamens were a mix of warm and cool yellow, both of which were used in the mix for the greens along with the blue. Quite a lot of blue was included in the greens for the background.

The Gardener

The name Japanese anemone is misleading as it is native to Eastern China, but it was grown in Japanese gardens for centuries – hence the confusion. Robert Fortune, 1812–1880, introduced anemones into Europe in 1844, having apparently discovered them growing between the tombstones in a Shanghai graveyard, where they were planted as a long-lived 'ethereal' plant, used to commemorate the dead.

Anemones flower in late summer, continuing well into October, being one of the longest-blooming flowers. The flowers are white, shades of rose pink, and mauve with yellow stamens. Both doubles and singles open out flat when mature and are held on loose open clusters on slender, graceful stems and sway delicately in the breeze. The attractive foliage, dense at the bottom of the plant, becomes lighter and smaller-leaved further above. They grow tall behind other flowers.

Anemone × *hybrida* has many quilled, uneven petals while *A.* × *hybrida* 'Honorine Jobert' has white flowers with a boss of golden-yellow stamens set around a green pin-eyed centre. 'Alba' has large white flowers and grows to ninety centimetres. These white flowers light up a shady area. *A. tomentosa* is similar to *A.* × *hybrida*, but with vine-like leaves and single pale-pink flowers. *A. hupehensis var. japonica* 'Bressingham Glow', bred by Alan Bloom in 1968, is shorter than most with deep-pink flowers. In my dry garden it is not especially happy, but it is still a delight. 'Prinz Heinrich', bred by Wilhelm Pfitzer in 1902, has deep-pink semi-double flowers and quilled petals. 'Camina' has purple-pink semi-double flowers.

Anemones grow in sun or shade and should be left undisturbed, and will then slowly spread outwards to form large clumps. They dislike disturbance, but to propagate them it is best to lift offshoots from the main plant as they emerge in late spring and pot them into soil-based compost. These can be planted out in midsummer. Root cuttings can also be taken in early winter.

Japanese anemones are resistant to pests and diseases, attract butterflies, are happy in sun or light shade. They are not fussy about soil, but are best in rich organic matter, moist but well drained.

PHYGELIUS
(Cape fuchsia, Cape figwort)

Painting 1

Red flowers form a stunning, vivid border. Vulgarity is avoided when cushioned by green foliage separating the colours. Green is the backdrop against which other colours are measured; and although a bright red draws attention, the eye has a chance to look away to calming green. This means that bright colours can be appreciated individually. Flowers are brightly coloured specifically to attract pollinators, not to gladden our hearts, although they do. Many plants have flowers which are not attractive to us, but are enticing to an insect with ultraviolet sight, but most pollinators are attracted to the same colours that we can see. What we perceive as beautiful are the colours, shapes and styles. This is determined by two separate parts of our brains. The fundamental ancient instincts have been modified by reflection and modern-day influences. Fashion may influence thinking. Perhaps pastels are in vogue whereas another school of thought may prefer pure colour.

By looking at a colour wheel and thinking of a rainbow, we see how the colours merge one into the next – from blue to red, creating violet, through cool and warm reds towards yellows,

347

creating orange, warm yellows, then cool yellows, green yellows, then green, and back to the blues.

In this painting I wanted to make good use of complementary colours so that the bright red of the blooms appeared even brighter against the green background. The complexity of so many flowers called for a simple washy green with a hint of blue sky and some dark green among the leaves at the base of the plant. Initially the flowers were painted with Quinacridone Red and darkened on the shadow side with Quinacridone Magenta. The stamens were hardly visible, so they were hinted at with tiny dabs of paint using the fine point of my smallest brush. The tiny stamens take time and concentration to place correctly, but without them the painting would be incomplete.

Colours are produced by the absorption and reflection of components of white light. In plants, different pigments absorb and reflect light at different wavelengths. The pure colours are called hues. These are the maximum intensity. With white added they become tints, and with grey added they become shades. There are almost always several hues present, but from a distance these may merge and not be evident unless closely examined. Gertrude Jekyll made use of this when designing borders so that they appeared longer than they were.

Painting 2

I really do not like pink and red close together as in these flowers, but nature has a way of making these colours exciting, and also the green of the leaves acted as a softener. This closer view was painted at a different time of day than Painting 1, which meant the shadows were reversed. The same colours were used with a bias toward magenta in the shadows and the stamens. The same colour of the creamy yellow throat was used in the veins of the leaves, with the shadowed areas darkened with a little Magenta. The magenta stems linked to the colour of the flowers so that all was harmonious.

The Gardener

Phyga means flight and *helios* means the sun. This is an erect, evergreen, hardy South African shrub with showy scarlet tubular bell-shaped fuchsia-like flowers from midsummer into early winter. Phygelius is unrelated to the fuchsia, being closer to foxgloves and penstemons. As well as yellow and red hues, there are now peach, pink and magenta flowers.

Phygelius spreads by sending out suckers, which can be cut back and replanted if required. The plants should be pruned back each spring. The seeds, which it produces freely, should be sown in warmth in spring and the seedlings transplanted to a warm border.

PHYSALIS

Physalis alkekengi (bladder cherry, winter cherry, ground cherry, Japanese cherry, husk tomato)

The Painting

These deliciously brilliant-orange seed heads are a delight and were simple to observe and paint. A bright Winsor Orange was applied first as a base wash with a drier orange applied to the top and base of the seed heads. When dry, the stripes of the veins were added using a fine brush. The background seed heads were left suggested with the same orange and the unripe seed was a wet mix of green with a little orange dropped into it. The stems were of the orange and the green used in the leaves, and the two colours were mixed together for the shadow areas.

The Gardener

The Greek word *physa* means bladder, from the inflated calyx. Physalis is native to Europe and Asia and is a member of the nightshade family, Solanaceae. A finely hairy perennial with invasive, creeping underground stems, physalis sends up new shoots some distance from the main plant. It is best planted where spreading is not a problem. It has an erect leafy stem bearing solitary violet, yellow or white drooping flowers, becoming a bright orange strongly veined lantern-shaped envelope (from which it gets its name) surrounding a red berry, which becomes visible when the lantern dries during spring. Despite the poisonous leaves and unripe berries, the ripe fruits have had a variety of medicinal benefits, including anti-inflammatory, expectorant and cough suppressant, and it is used to treat fevers, malaria and bed-wetting.

Physalis needs a sunny position in fairly rich soil. The richer the soil the more flowers and fruit will be produced. Plants should be divided every three years, which provides more plants, or they can be propagated by seed, which have a long germination period and are best started with heat in a propagator. The resulting plants will bloom in their first year.

The lanterns can be cut and dried for decoration, extending physalis's season of beauty indoors into the winter.

Physalis peruviana is cultivated and grows wild across the world. It is closely related to Chinese lantern, tomato, eggplant, potato and other members of the nightshade family. It is not related to the gooseberry family. It is an annual in temperate locations, and perennial in the tropics. It has many common names – Cape gooseberry has been cultivated in England since the late eighteenth century and in South Africa and the Cape of Good Hope since the nineteenth century. Another suggested story is that the name Cape is derived from the husk covering the fruit, and not the Cape of Good Hope. The name Jew's cherry comes from the Middle Ages, based on the shape of the lantern surrounding the fruit, reminiscent of the Jewish head coverings of that time. Other names are Inca berry, Poha berry, Aztec berry, pineapple ground cherry, giant ground cherry, Peruvian ground cherry, husk tomato, Pok Pok, Ras Bhari, Aguaymanto, Uvilla and Uchuva. In France it is called *amour en cage* – love in a cage.

Propagation is by seed. It grows readily from seeds – about 100 to 300 in each fruit. Sow indoors in a small container and place in a propagator.

Keep the seeds moist and transplant them when the temperature is warm. Physalis flowers from July to October, with the seeds ripening from August to November. The flowers are hermaphrodite, having both male and female organs, and are pollinated by bees and the wind. Stem cuttings can be taken, but they have a lower success rate than from seed.

Cape gooseberry is similar to bladder cherry, but distinguished by the whitish, purple-spotted flowers, violet anthers and heart-shaped leaves. It has yellow fruits with numerous seeds, which germinate all over the garden and in the compost. The fruits are edible, juicy and rich in vitamins, welcome in summer and autumn. They are made into fruit-based sauces, pies, puddings, chutneys, jams and ice cream, eaten fresh in salads and fruit salads. While still in the husk they are popular in restaurants as a decorative, exotic garnish for desserts.

YUCCA
Yucca recurvifolia (soapweed, Spanish dagger, Spanish bayonet, Adam's needle)

The Painting

I first made a detailed drawing of the flower heads and used masking fluid, as I wanted to retain the white of the paper. A dilute yellow was used to suggest inner shadows between the flowers and a washy blue behind the flower head. I used a mix of Prussian Blue, Ultramarine Blue and yellow to make a yellow-green. When dry, more green was added with some violet, which intermingled with the green. This green was brought down in between the yucca leaves and a touch of violet was added at their base. The masking fluid was removed and a very dilute blue was added discreetly in places on the shadowed side of the flower heads.

The Gardener
The yucca gives an exotic, tropical look with its rosettes of long, sword-shaped spiky evergreen leaves, which grow from the ground when young but later emerge from the top of the main trunk in terminal clusters. It puts up a tall spine of densely borne creamy-white bell-shaped flowers and will continue to flower if in good health. I have known them to flower in the autumn and into winter in sheltered areas in my garden. I am exceptionally lucky in living in the country with the garden surrounded by beautiful countryside. Plants have to tolerate hot, dry summers, and being on top of a hill it is well drained, with wind from all directions. Yuccas enjoy these conditions in warm, sunny positions. They are propagated by division of suckers.

The yucca is of the lily family, from Mexico and Central America. Some botanists place it with *Agave*, *Coryline*, *Dracaena*, *Phormium* and other genera of similar habit in the family Agavaceae, distinct from

350

Liliaceae and Amaryllidaceae. I cut off the sharp tips of the leaves as they can be a hazard.

When walking our St Bernard, Belle, along the lanes, the grazing cows look up and wander over, keen to investigate. Few wild flowers grow in the fields where the cattle graze, but in the ditches along the lanes grow primroses, verbena, orchids, star of Bethlehem, oxlips and all kinds of herbs. In the lanes the ancient hedgerows tumble with wild roses, sloes, hawthorn, lilac, wild cherries and blackberries. In autumn the berries glow bright with beautiful spindle berries and rose hips, and red squirrels harvest chestnuts, walnuts and hazelnuts. Later, chestnut and walnut saplings appear where the squirrels have previously buried the nuts. I try to capture these treasured moments in my sketchbook. There is a special feeling when looking back on sketches from perhaps years before, recalling the place, weather and events of the time, and hopefully prompting exciting ideas.

DAHLIA
Dahlia

Painting 1

Nature has a wonderful range of colours that can alter with every change of light. This is most noticeable in changeable weather, when the colour and the quality of the light can fluctuate. In cloudy weather, without the sharpness and strength of sunlight, the tones are easier to distinguish. On a sunny day one can work out the direction of the light, but on a cloudy day light appears to come from the whole sky, creating a diffused overall effect. The light can be dull if the cloud is thick, and bright if it is thin. To understand this it is a good idea to paint studies at different times to capture the moods. Strong direct light accentuates form by creating sharp contrasts of tone.

It is largely a matter of evaluating the tones and not depending on colour. It is easy to be diverted by the sheer brilliance of colour in flowers and to lose sight of the tonal values. It is these tonal values which describe form, the delicate roundness of a bloom or the way a petal curls. In order to make a busy garden scene work, there must be a pattern of light and dark shapes. By adding some flower shapes leading up to the canes, the eye is taken directly from the flowers to the top of the painting. This has nothing to do with colour. Colour is far less important than value.

Painting 2

In this painting a careful drawing established the shapes of the petals which were open and upright, while others were curled in the centre where they were just opening. Dilute Lemon Yellow gave the impression of strong light accentuated by a light shadow of complementary blue. The centre was a stronger yellow and the shadows warmer with blue in the foreground shadows. In all, the tones were important in determining the light, shadow and shapes of petals. This dahlia was quite different in shape and format, with the centres a warm tangerine. Once again careful observation was necessary so as to capture the intricate twists and turns of the petals before painting them with Winsor Yellow and Winsor Orange.

Painting 3

In this oil painting I exaggerated the light falling on the dahlia flower by using blue, yellow and red. The power and mystery of light can play never-ending variations, endowing mood, indicating form and texture, emphasising the third dimension and changing an ordinary subject to something stunning. Different angles of perspective, shadow or light, moving backwards or forwards at high or low level, could lead to the creation of a more dramatic painting, especially when there is light against dark and dark against light. The aim is not to describe a scene graphically, but to suggest feelings about it and portray the subject as simply as possible, leaving the interpretation to the viewer.

Some things need to be planned before starting the painting, and deciding the size and shape can be particularly important. It is essential to think about what it was that first attracted me to the subject and how to capture and express it by the use of colour, the play of light, the shapes and the relationship of one area to another. Making preliminary sketches helps to establish the composition.

Just as in good gardening, where the preparation of the ground takes time and determines the success of the project, so getting the sketches of the painting laid in and accurately assessed will benefit the final stages of the work.

352

Oil paint has a thick, buttery consistency and does not change as it hardens and dries, therefore brushstrokes remain as they are applied. Brushwork provides the texture on the canvas surface and can be an important part of the painting. Various brushes give different marks. Short, flat brushes give distinctive square or rectangular marks. Versatile filbert brushes make rounded dabs or long strokes, while round bristle brushes give long, continuous strokes, or when held vertically are ideal for stippling (which is dabbing over the surface). Sable brushes taper to a fine point, so are useful for details in the final stages of a painting. A palette knife can be used for broad impasto as well as for mixing colours on the palette. The pigments should be arranged around the palette in some order for ease of use, and sufficient space should be left in the centre for mixing.

Care should be taken when mixing any colour with white as it lightens the tone but also changes the hue. For example, reds can become pink when mixed with white. For pale tints it is best to start with white and add colour little by little. Adding black to colours can darken the tone, but may muddy colours, so it is best to darken with brown, green or blue. Black mixed with a strong yellow produces an exciting rich olive green.

Although when painting in oils technical ability is essential, that skill should have vibrancy and conviction. Taking risks can create strong, powerful images. Quiet, tranquil subjects still require the techniques of composition in colour and form. In this painting linear information was limited to where it was essential, with some edges implied by overlapping areas of colour, and lastly adding the highlights. Achieving the right balance in a painting means dividing time between the actual painting and the need to look, observe and contemplate.

Painting 4

It was such fun to paint the differing shapes of leaves and flowers and the juxtaposition of colours. This corner of the garden is a riot of colours and shapes of flowers and leaves. The pink anemones echoed the yellow of the sunflowers on the tripod and the cerise of the dahlias. I don't usually like pink and yellow together, but the green in between and the hints of blue here and there lent a feeling of excitement. The blues and greens led the eye harmoniously into the background and complemented the yellow of the sunflowers. The purple morning glory, which twined around the canes, echoed the warm blue of the sky and picked up the blues in the foreground.

The Gardener

Named after the Swedish botanist and pupil of Linnaeus, Dr Andreas Dahl, dahlias were imported into the Botanic Garden, Madrid in 1789, from Central America. The Aztecs called them *cocoxochitl*. It was first imported along with the potato, tobacco, tomato and maize, but the taste was disgusting and no one thought of growing the dahlia for its beauty for another 200 years, when Andreas Dahl bred them for their flowers. By the 1830s, dahlias had become popular throughout Europe. There were three forms to which names were given: *Dahlia pinnata*, with double purple flowers, *D. rosa* with single rose flowers, and *D. coccinea* with single red flowers. All three were sent to Kew from Madrid by the Marchioness of Bute in 1789, but were lost. From Spain they were introduced into France. Empress Josephine was one of the first to cultivate dahlias in her garden at Malmaison and had seeds collected from Mexico. After the end of the Napoleonic wars they were dispersed through Germany, Prussia and Denmark, and later England.

The single-flowered species *D. coccinea, D. merckii* and *D. variabilis* rapidly grew in popularity so that the mid-nineteenth-century Victorian nursery catalogues listed thousands of varieties which had been developed from these original species. The Victorians loved their bright colours and the ease with which they could be cultivated. The favourites in those days were the 'Globe' and 'Ball' types, generally known then as double show and fancy dahlias. Having originally come from Mexico, they were considered too delicate for outdoor cultivation in Europe, but after much cosseting in the greenhouse and a gradual introduction to colder air they became acclimatised. The dahlia is now a hardy plant, which in the south of France flourishes for eight months of the year, from July to February. In modern times, Christopher Lloyd, from Great Dixter in England, has developed them further.

Today dahlias have been propagated to a wide range of sizes, shapes and colours from dwarf bedding varieties to giant, and flowers ranging from tiny pompoms to exhibition blooms and in every colour except blue. The varieties of single dahlias have outer petals with a small fringe of florets in the centre, known as collerettes. They like sun on their tubers, so need room in the flower border. Dahlias have hollow stems and dark-green or purple leaves and have flowers in a vast range of colours and a variety of shapes and forms. There are annual dahlias and half-hardy tuberous perennials. Garden dahlias are grown from tubers or cuttings, with dwarf bedding dahlias grown from seed and treated as annuals.

Planting is simple as they do not require special soil, and some are large, robust types, such as cactus, decorative and pompom, so can be planted singly in the border or where earlier plants have flowered. Within eight weeks of planting there should be a bushy plant. These should be staked as soon as planted as stems are brittle and easily blown by strong winds. It is best to drive the stake in the hole before planting the tuber, to avoid damage. The height of the stake should be a little less than the expected height of the plant. As the dahlia grows there should be at least three outer stakes and string wound round to give support. Smaller collarette dahlia varieties are best planted in the front of the border.

Once the dahlias start to flower they continue blooming for as long as five months. They are gross feeders and need deep, rich soil if the flowers are to develop fully. They need plenty of light and shelter from wind. The top of the flower stem should be pinched out and flower heads removed as soon as they are past their best to stop them setting seed. Deadheading after flowering will speed up their regrowth and encourage more flowers, as will feeding and extra watering in dry weather. If the dead flowers are allowed to remain, there is a check and the flowering season will be shortened as the plants attempt to form seed. Energy that would have been spent turning flowers into seeds is diverted into new growth. An unopened bud is sometimes confused with a deadhead. The bud is round, while a spent flower is nearly conical. The spent flower head should be cut back to the next bud or leaf on the stem to avoid the new flowers being spoiled by being among the dead stems. This is best for the appearance of the plant and keeping the garden looking fresh, but also encourages the plant to produce more flowers.

The dahlia has a broad, soft leaf that picks up dew very easily and becomes almost self-watering. A healthy plant should bear many flowers, and the more they are picked the more they will flower, right up to the frost. As they are only half-hardy they need a good mulch in autumn, or can be lifted and stored in a frost-free place over winter. I leave some in the ground over winter, cutting them down to the ground and mulching with leaf mould. By leaving them in the ground they can continue to plump up ready to give a good show in the following year. As soon as the frost kills the tops of the plants in autumn, they should be cut down and either lifted, labelled and stored in a dry, cool, frost-proof place or left in the ground and covered with bracken or some other form of protection. Those in pots overwinter in the greenhouse.

The flowers consist of a ring of sterile florets surrounding a disc of fertile true flowers. Decoratives have double flowers with no central disc, the florets being broad and flat and pointed at the tips. Cactus types also have double flowers with narrow, pointed florets, which are rolled back for over half their length. Dahlia 'Hillcrest Royal' is one of the most exciting and luxurious of all dahlias. It is a green-leaved medium cactus with voluptuous flowers in deep rich magenta which are produced over a long period on strong stems. The centre of each flower glows purple as the spiky petals unfurl.

Ball dahlias have rounded ball-like blooms and are arranged spirally. Pompom dahlias are similar, but are more globular. Collerettes have wide flowers with yellow centres made up of stamens and a single row of florets round the edge. An inner collar of similar florets surrounds the stamens, lying between them and the petals. Single dahlias have a single outer ring of florets and a central disc of stamens. Anemone-flowered dahlias have double flowers with flat outer florets surrounding a densely packed group of shorter florets. Water-lily types resemble a water lily, but have more petals.

Red dahlias planted among plants with bright-green leaves create a dazzling colour statement, not easily ignored. The red appears more vivacious and the green more vivid. By planting different shades of green, shapes and structures of adjacent plants can be enhanced. Sharp relief is lost if plants are of a similar shade. The impact of green as a backdrop for flowers can be stunning, but the basis of the garden should be well planned. A garden with phormiums, yuccas, agapanthus, aromatic grey foliage and hot colour will have a Mediterranean feel, whereas ornamental rhubarbs and tree ferns will have a jungle look. These effects are vital to the planning for a harmonious garden. Harmony is based on appreciation of the plants' characteristics, from colours and styles of flowers to the colours and textures of branches and trunks. This preserves the balance and impact of individual plants, rather than diminishing them – very much as in a painting, where the blues enhance the feeling of distance and the warmer tones are towards the centre and foreground. Colours range from white to almost black and in almost every colour except blue. There are also bicolour, deep purple with pure-white tips, coffee and cream, scarlet and white, orange and pink, mauve and white.

Propagation is by division of the rootstock or by cuttings. To do this, the old root must be allowed to sprout from the tuber, making sure that a bud is taken on the division. Cuttings from overwintered tubers root readily in spring. The rootstock should be brought into heat at the end of January, and roots, not the crown, covered with soil and lightly sprayed with water to encourage shoots. As soon as the shoot has two joints, it can be cut and potted singly into sandy loam and placed in a propagator. Roots soon form, when the plants should be repotted and put into a cooler position before planting out in May. The cuttings have time to grow roots and will produce a new tuber by the end of the season in autumn. The tops of the cuttings can be pinched out to encourage bushier plants. The taller varieties need staking and tying to support the plant's foliage. Dahlias will thrive in any soil, but a good medium loamy slightly acid soil is best, in a warm, sunny, wind-sheltered position. Dahlias need sun on their tubers to be able to perpetuate themselves year after year, so they need room in the border. Seeds may be sown in March in heat. The seedlings will not be true to the parental type – this is how new types are developed.

Once in bloom in August and September, cut flowers just above a pair of lateral branches, so that more flowers form and carry on until the first frosts. A good mulch of garden compost in hot weather is a great aid to the plants as it tends to prevent loss of water from the soil by evaporation and keeps the plants growing after flowering begins. Hot, dry weather can encourage dahlias to flower prematurely, but there may not be a good display.

Dahlias benefit bees and other pollinators as the pollen and nectar is easily accessible.

The warm days and colder nights of autumn bring out the fiery colours of scarlet, crimson and maroon with berries bright red and yellow. In the mild climate of Pays de la Loire, the colours are not so vivid; but, even so, there is a definite change with a whole range of colourful flowers, such as cyclamens, crocuses, nerines and chrysanthemums.

CHRYSANTHEMUM
Pyrethrum (Michaelmas daisy, Dalmation daisy, big daisy, painted daisy)

Painting 1

This was a very complex subject. To start I spent time on the composition and selected Winsor Red and Winsor Orange, running them together in places. The petals of the main flower were suggested with washy strokes, with thicker paint on the other darker flower heads. Red is a hot colour. While blue-reds are relatively cool, orange-reds are warm, and a light-toned orange red will work well with a deep-toned blue-red.

Painting 2

The more an area is covered with flowers, the greater the impact in terms of colour. If the flowers are separated, their colours are less imposing. When the flowers are densely packed, the overall tints consume the individual flower colours.

The chrysanthemum bloom consists of a large number of florets set in a compact head. There are two kinds: the coloured ray-florets, which are often

356

incorrectly called petals, and the yellow disc florets, which form a cushion in the centre of the blooms. When observing them it helps to understand this as the blooms are very complex.

A thorough knowledge of painting techniques must be learned through practice and experience as there is no easy recipe for success, only hard work, perseverance, observation and passion.

Korean chrysanthemums have stunning colours. I loved painting these beautiful flowers. This painting depended on careful observation and detailed drawing. Each head was drawn individually, but only after the design had been worked out. Once the drawing was established, each petal was painted with pure red. I was especially careful to keep the light on the uppermost parts of the petals and the darks to the base of the petals. Different strengths of red were used so that there was a marked difference between the petals, giving a sense of the depth of the flowers and the light above. Red in all its vibrations and tones can be enhanced by deliberately painting the complementary colour, green, alongside, keeping the brushwork free and loose around the flowers. This appears to intensify the red. The centres of the flowers were added next using a warm yellow and then, when dry, a slightly warmer yellow. The same yellow with a touch of the same red was added using the smallest brush I own – size 3.70 – to suggest a disc shape, and a darker red was added to some petals in shade and to give shape and depth where needed. The Lemon Yellow in the greens also helped to accentuate the red.

The chrysanthemum is a very important symbolic flower in many cultures around the world. I tried to capture the peace, calm and stillness as well as the delicacy of the fragile petals.

Capturing a momentary glow of light which passes through the petals is an inspiration. The stems lead the eye to the leaf that has the most detail, and this detail is surrounded by the strongest glow of light and strongest dark contrasts. This makes it a subtle centre of attention.

The Gardener
The Korean chrysanthemums are similar to singles in that they have a single central eye but are semi-doubles with more than one row of outer petals. They come in crimson, dark purple, apricot, salmon pink, yellow and bronze and flower in mid autumn.

Painting 3

A wonderful flower in the re-flexed group, which has incurved petals. For this painting I sketched the complicated flower head to try to suggest the intricate details of outward turning petals and the inward-facing central discs. I washed in red and, once this was dry, I darkened with stronger colour in between the petals, especially in the centres to suggest depth, and let it dry. When dry, the outer petals, central areas and shadows were painted with a slightly darker, warmer red. All very subtle and delicate with no strong colour or deep shadows.

The Gardener

The botanist who developed plant classifications, Linnaeus, first used the name chrysanthemum. The name chrysanthemum is derived from the Greek and means a gold flower – *chrysos* meaning golden and *anthos* meaning flower. In 1961 the name was changed to *Dendranthema* to avoid confusion with other plant species labelled as chrysanthemums, but this was changed back in mid 1990 as it created confusion.

The Asteraceae family was once called Compositae and comprises many plants, including zinnias, dahlias and marigolds. All are of the aster family; all need long days to form foliage and shorter days to promote flowering. *Aster* is a genus of about 250 species of mostly perennial plants and some annuals. They range from the simplest daisy-like form to the more elaborate types of rayed petals with pincushion-like centres, petals curving up, petals curving down or petals massed tightly together looking like a solid ball. In some types the flowers are small and gathered in loose clusters, and others have one stem bearing one huge single bloom. The simplest type of chrysanthemum produces daisy-like flowers, usually white with a yellow centre, but also in shades of pink or purple.

When the two varieties are closely compared, the difference between the aster and the chrysanthemum is that the chrysanthemum is a heavily cultivated and bred plant which may be perennial or annual, and in colours of orange, red, white, pink, purple and yellow, while asters are limited to cooler hues of blue, purple, pink and white.

Asters do not have a loyal and organised cultural following. The blooms are the classifying feature and rely upon the number of ray florets per flower and the size to delineate to which class they belong. There are more than 175 species, but the aster is not as heavily hybridised as the chrysanthemum.

Chrysanthemums are most numerous in the northern hemisphere, especially in North America, and some in South Africa. The South African shrubby species need greenhouse treatment and a well-drained sandy peat compost, but the tall leafy species, usually called Michaelmas daisies, and their numerous varieties, do well in good garden soil. These grow in sun or partial shade, and because they grow fast, it is best to lift, divide and replant them regularly. The strong-growing kinds exhaust the soil quickly and weaken unless propagated every second or third year and replanted in the border in well-worked and enriched soil.

Ample room should be given so that the plants bloom to their best advantage, and they may need staking to prevent damage from bending and twisting in the wind. It should be remembered that the main stem will thicken out appreciably as the plant grows, so string should be looped around the support and loosely round all the lateral growths. It is best to plant the larger varieties singly at the back of the border early in the season and stake the plant so that it will be supported as it grows and eventually hides the sticks.

The flowering season from July to November has made the name Michaelmas a misnomer. These species are American, but the garden varieties have originated mainly in England and are a feature of the traditional English herbaceous border. The earliest of the American asters were brought to England in 1633, with others following. The Royal Horticultural Society arranged a conference about them in 1891, which brought them more prominently forward, and many new varieties were soon raised. There are over thirteen bloom classes of chrysanthemums, which include cushion, spider, quill, spoon and pompom. The fully double form of *A. novi-belgii,* called 'Beauty of Colwall', in 1907 increased the interest leading to an improved race of the same species with large pink or reddish flowers, and then the dwarf forms, which were used for edging and at the front of the border.

We have no words for scents – we can only liken one scent to another, or contrast them. The honey scent of chrysanthemum could be described as one of the few masculine perfumes of nature.

The chrysanthemum is native to China and has been cultivated in China since 500 BC. Cultivated varieties were introduced from China to Japan about AD 800, where they were further developed by selection and cross-fertilisation. It became the personal emblem of the Mikado, and was represented on the Japanese flag and on their postage stamps. It is one of the most popular flowers in Japanese and Chinese art. The interbreeding of several wild species over hundreds of years by Chinese and Japanese gardeners has produced numerous variations. The precise ancestors cannot be determined with certainty owing to the passage of time since their cultivation began, but it is probable that the dominant ancestor is *Chrysanthemum indicum*, a species with small yellow flowers which grows wild in China and Southern Japan. Other species have been used in the development of modern cultivated varieties, and Japanese horticulturists have endeavoured to prove, from varying shapes of the foliage of cultivated varieties, that three or four wild species, native to Japan, have also contributed to the development of the modern chrysanthemum.

By the seventeenth century the first plants had reached Holland, and England by 1764. In 1789 a purple variety was brought to France by M. Blanchard, a merchant of Marseilles, and then to England in 1795. They were developed by Mr Colvill of Chelsea; and between 1810 and 1830 Mr Sabine, secretary of the Royal Horticultural Society of London, specially encouraged the growing of the chrysanthemum. In 1823 varieties imported from China found to be different from *C. indicum* were named *C. sinense.* The Royal Horticultural Society sent Robert Fortune to China in 1843 on a plant-hunting expedition. In 1846 he sent back from China the Chusan daisy, parent of the present-day pompom varieties, and in 1861 he visited Japan and sent back cultivated Japanese varieties, which were large and had a great range of colour. The Chinese chrysanthemum was mainly of the incurved type and in a limited colour range. These were further developed by Mr J. Salter of Hammersmith and were at the height of their popularity in England when Fortune's Japanese varieties arrived. These were not well received and it was twenty years later, after development by Mr Salter and M. Delaux of Toulouse, that the Japanese type of flower was welcomed by the English public. So successful were Mr Salter's efforts at cross-fertilisation that Mr Fortune, on his return from China, is recorded to have said that European varieties were more numerous than those of China and that many of those raised from seed by Mr Salter would be admired by Chinese florists. M. Delaux at this period also developed from these new Japanese types the first of the early-flowering outdoor varieties, which appeared between 1880 and 1890.

The flowers consist of a large number of florets set in a compact head. The florets are of two kinds – the coloured ray-florets, which are often incorrectly termed petals, and the yellow disc-florets, which form a cushion in the centre of the blooms. In the wild all chrysanthemum blooms are daisy-shaped flowers, from which the double types have evolved with an abundance of ray-florets and very few disc-florets. There are numerous annuals and perennials, ranging from the simplest form to more elaborate. Some have rayed petals with pincushion centres, petals curving up, petals curving down or petals massed tightly together like a ball of colour. Some are in loose clusters; others have one huge single bloom. The re-flexing and incurving Japanese types have a greater range of colour, and this is due to the remarkable development of the Japanese types of horticulture in Europe, the United States and Australia. The single or anemone types arose from hybridisation by European growers and were in general cultivation in 1890. The single-flowered varieties have a disc or cushion centre of yellow tubular florets, with a circle of broad coloured florets consisting of three or four petals. Anemone varieties, *C. anemone*, have the same-shaped centre ringed with petals similar to singles except that the central florets are the same colour as the petals. The quilled and feathery types still grown are probably legacies from the earliest Chinese varieties. Some are not hardy but perennial chrysanthemums. Michaelmas daisies are fully hardy and can be left in their permanent flowering positions. The most popular are the autumn-flowering *C. morifolium,* which grows tall with stiff, erect branching stems, derived after hundreds of years of cross-fertilisation and selection from several species of chrysanthemum that grow wild in China and Japan, and *C. roseum*, generally known as *pyrethrums*. Pyrethrums have white flowers with yellow centres on rigid stems and blue-green leaves, and produce a powerful insecticidal powder which attacks the nervous systems of all insects and inhibits female mosquitoes from biting. When present in amounts less than those fatal to insects, they still act as an insect repellent. They are harmful to fish, but less toxic to animals and birds, being biodegradable, and decompose easily on exposure to light.

C. coccineum, the Persian chrysanthemum, is a perennial plant native to the Caucasus, and has large white, pink or red flowers with leaves resembling ferns. It also contains insecticidal pyrethrum, but is a poor source compared to *C. cinerariifolium. C. frutescens* is actually a shrubby perennial, but is usually raised as an annual. It has white or yellow flowers. It can only be increased from cuttings on non-flowering side shoots in early autumn and rooted under glass. *C. multicaule* has simple golden flowers in late summer. *C. parthenium,* feverfew, is an erect, leafy, branched perennial with numerous white, yellow and gold flowers, and yellowish-green strongly aromatic leaves. Formerly cultivated as a medicinal plant it is also used as an insecticide and vermicide. *C. rubellum,* sometimes known as *C. erubescens,* has masses of pink or various-coloured daisies on long stems, making them excellent for cuttings. *C. maximum,* the Shasta daisy, is tall with white flowers and dark-green toothed leaves. Korean single or double flowers are hardier and can be left in permanent positions. Pompom chrysanthemums produce large numbers of small, tight flowers like powder puffs in white, pink, red, purple and yellow.

Annual chrysanthemums are bred from three wild species – *C. carinatum, C. coronarium* and *C. segetum*. These can be started from seed sown in warmth in March, pricked out in boxes and eventually planted out, or sown outside, in spring. There are both singles and doubles and they range in colour from white to sulphur, yellow, pink and red. They flower from midsummer to mid autumn, June to September. They are useful for filling gaps or between bulbs. They like sunny positions and will thrive in all types of soil so long as it is dry and well drained.

Autumn is an important time of the year for planting trees and shrubs as there is not the urgency about garden tasks that exists in spring and early summer, as growth is not so rapid. The division and replanting of the hardy border plants can be done in autumn, and there are many autumn-flowering plants, such as Michaelmas daisies, that can be dug up and divided by pulling or cutting the roots into pieces. These are then replanted in groups.

All types of chrysanthemum are best propagated by cuttings. Propagation is easy by division in autumn or in spring. The outside sections make the best plants, with the old central stool being discarded. The best cuttings are taken from growths or suckers, coming from beneath the soil, as stem cuttings are more difficult because they frequently develop premature buds. The timing differs according to type. Specimen plants should be taken in November, while decoratives, late- and early-flowering singles and pompoms should be taken in spring. They should be overwintered in a cool greenhouse or frame. Cuttings can be taken from prunings in late winter or early spring. The cuttings should be cut off just below a joint, taking care to ensure that there is a growing point. Any with a hollow stem or a white pithy centre should be rejected. The lower leaves should be stripped off, leaving the stem bare for insertion into the soil. Sand sprinkled on top of the compost, sand and potash mix will lessen the chance of the cuttings damping off. I carefully firm them in to make sure there are no air pockets underneath which could deter rooting, and water them well and label them. Bottom heat and overhead syringing will assist the rooting process. A light syringing of water is helpful, but continuous watering leads to damping off and failure, so no more watering is best until roots have formed about four weeks later. After rooting, the cuttings should be moved to cooler conditions in a frame, gradually hardened off and then potted on. They should then be grown on in cool, airy conditions. When the plants are thoroughly hardened off, the frame can be left open. Although the cuttings are small the plants will get quite large, so need to be planted some distance apart. The best time for planting out is in May, preferably in groups. It is best to have a special bed for early-flowering chrysanthemums. A handful of potash is beneficial when planting and it is a good idea to have a moat around each plant. This will collect moisture and also give small plants a little shelter from wind. Chrysanthemums are greedy plants, so a top dressing in late summer and early autumn is beneficial. Once flowering is over, the stems should be cut down to just above the ground and left to overwinter.

If a profusion of flowers is wanted, then about a week after planting out the growing tip should be pinched out to encourage the plant to grow side shoots. It is important not to remove any stem as this will reduce the number of side shoots produced. Removing the tips of the new side shoots about a month later will encourage further bushing. 'Stopping' means pinching out the growing tip of the plant to make it branch. If the plant is stopped when small and is not allowed to grow on until the natural break bud appears, the side shoots will appear in the leaf axils off the main stem earlier than they would otherwise have done and they will start growing with a gain of two or three weeks. The number of breaks obtained will depend on how many leaves there are left on the main stem after the tip has been pinched out. If a plant is growing strongly, one side shoot usually develops in each leaf axil. The time of stopping has some effect on the time of flowering, and plants that are stopped twice tend to produce flowers with fewer petals than those that are stopped only once. A second stopping, either by removing the first crown bud at the end of each lateral growth or by pinching out the end of each lateral growth before the first crown bud has appeared, will delay the flowering date. Practically all early-flowering varieties produce the largest and best flowers on the first crown buds. Some varieties naturally bloom in August and others not until September, and the time of flowering also varies slightly with the district or locality in which the plant is being grown. The time which normally elapses between the removal of the tip of the main stem of the early-flowering varieties and the production of the first crown bud at the end of a lateral growth is about seven weeks. Left to their own devices chrysanthemums will produce flowers in clusters or sprays. When varieties are in the garden, no disbudding is needed.

A different procedure is required where large blooms are wanted. A chrysanthemum plant, if left to grow naturally, would continue growing taller and taller until the natural break bud was produced at the end of the solitary main stem. Side shoots would then develop in most of the leaf axils on the main stem, the natural break bud would shrivel away and the side shoots would grow as the crown bud. My grandfather grew chrysanthemums, his favourite being the incurved varieties for show at exhibitions, and he provided florists with his magnificent specimens. This meant careful selection of buds, removing all but the best so as to develop an enormous single flower – a perfect globe with every petal upward and curving inward with such regularity that not a single petal seemed to be out of place. He poured love and attention over his chrysanthemums to get large and perfectly shaped blooms. He removed all buds and side shoots except the crown bud on each stem. To produce a perfect specimen bloom meant a lot of skill and attention. They were grown in regimental lines, supported and tied to canes and in a sunny, sheltered environment. To me, these rigid serried lines of blooms, staked and tied, looked far too controlled when growing in the plot, but when cut and gathered the large flowers were magnificent.

Chrysanthemums do not do well under trees, which, although giving shelter from wind, encourage them to grow exceptionally tall and spindly. Good drainage is essential so that the ground is not waterlogged in a wet season. In a drought, watering with cold water should be avoided as they grow better in a soil which is warm and only just moist, rather than in a soil which is sodden with cold water. Later on the plants produce valuable surface roots which must not be destroyed.

COMPOST

I cannot write about Mag's garden and not include her love of making compost. I write from my own experience about making compost, remembering how Mag, even when she was ill, turned the heaps, helping the composting process. The act of decomposition is the action of microorganisms consuming essential quantities of nitrogen, such as in fresh organic material like grass clippings. The nitrogen is returned once decomposition is completed.

Soil is composed of minute particles of inert rock. When organic matter of animal or plant origin falls on to the soil surface, it begins to decompose and is carried into the soil by worms and insects. Bacteria and other microorganisms break it down to form humus, which is essentially well-rotted organic matter with a massive population of living and dead bacteria.

Animal manure is another organic humus maker. It contains plant nutrients in small quantities, but in its raw state it contains acids harmful to plants so it needs to rot down. It is important to ensure that compost is well rotted and of good quality, which will then encourage fertility in the soil. Animal manures and urine are ideal activators. An activator is an organic source of nitrogen, which replaces that consumed through bacterial activity. It is not necessary in the spring and early summer as ample nitrogen will be supplied from lawn mowings and young weeds, but is very useful in autumn and winter.

All vegetable matter from the garden can be added to the compost, but no woody, bony, greasy or badly diseased plants. Apart from soft prunings from the vegetable and flower gardens, soft clippings from shrubs and hedges can be included, layering with lawn mowings and organic manure, including human urine and small quantities of torn paper. A good mixing of various materials in each layer promotes an even distribution of moisture and an even spread of microorganisms. Tree leaves are best rotted separately as they rot slowly. A top blanket helps to generate heat, but this must be porous so that gases can escape. After about three months the centre of the heap should have rotted. This is when the outer material should be turned to the centre, covered and left to rot. In winter it takes six months.

I have a mental picture of Mag turning the heap, which meant she always had good-quality compost.

In autumn late flowers bloom and plants like delphinium and roses have a second flowering as long as they have their old growth and spent flowers cut away. The pruned growth can be composted and eventually used as a mulch as well as potential food for plants. By mulching the plants when the ground is wet, moisture is retained, reducing the effects of drought. Mulches also encourage soil fauna – including earthworms and microorganisms – and help suppress weeds. Even Mag's compost heap was surrounded by flowers.

The best way to help the life of the soil is to give it the remains of living plants, but with the right balance between carbon, nitrogen and other elements. Organic compost spread on the soil helps to deter slugs, which emerge from their hiding places under stones and other locations in the fields and woods which surround the garden. I mulch agapanthus with compost to protect the young leaves from early spring frosts. Compost heaps are the garden's future larder and there is no better way of having the garden relatively free from pests and diseases – far superior to chemical preparations, which can easily destroy nature's subtle balances, perhaps eliminating one pest but fatally leaving the door open for others.

A combination of different textures and nutrients, created by the decomposition of materials, creates the food to produce healthy, productive garden plants with beautiful blooms and bountiful harvests. A healthy compost consists of a combination of brown and green materials, which should be added alternately to keep a good balance, plus adequate moisture to keep the good bacteria working. The brown element consists of dry leaves, cardboard, sawdust and shredded paper, which are carbon-rich and contain less moisture and take longer to break down than green material, which is nitrogen-rich and has more moisture. Green materials include weeds, grass clippings, and kitchen and garden waste. Chicken and horse manure give helpful bacteria which reproduce, quickly assisting the breakdown of elements. Old herbaceous plant stalks need to be chopped into smaller pieces; otherwise they will not pack down and the heap will be too well aired and will not heat. Lawn mowings will pack down, but need to be kept loose and layered so that they don't block air and stop the heap heating properly. The whole heap needs to be wetted and turned with a fork after several weeks so that the outside and centre are mixed, blending the materials together. The natural forces, like water, air and heat, work together. The decomposition of the compost will happen in time, but turning the heap will hasten the process.

Meat, bones and dairy products should never be added to a compost heap as they may harbour harmful bacteria and attract pests.

If the compost heap is in a sunny position, the sun's heat will help create more heat, speeding the decomposition process. It will be much slower if in the shade. The compost should be ready for use in about six months. For more acidic compost I save citrus peelings and teabags in a separate compost for camellias, rhododendrons, azaleas and pieris.

Leaf mould is formed from decaying leaves. The best-quality leaf mould is produced from the leaves of oak, beech and hornbeam. These break down with little assistance; but thick leaves, like sycamore, walnut, horse chestnut, sweet chestnut, holly and laurel, need to be shredded before adding to the leaf container, as they are slower to break down. When mowing the lawn covered with leaves, a lawn mower shreds the leaves and hastens the rotting as well as adding grass clippings, which increase the nutrient value of the leaf mould. It helps if you turn the leaf pile every few weeks to introduce air, which speeds the decomposition. Unlike garden compost, which produces heat from bacteria, it is a cold composting process, as decomposition is primarily by fungi, and is slower. The fungi need moisture to work, but, unlike garden compost, do not need worms or activators. Shredding the leaves makes it easier for the fungi.

Leaf mould improves the quality of the soil. The better water-holding capacity gives a more friable texture, which can hold up to fifty per cent of its own weight in water, helping retain moisture in the soil by reducing evaporation. It also absorbs rainwater, reducing run-off, and in hot weather it helps cool roots and foliage. It also provides an ideal habitat for soil life, including earthworms and beneficial bacteria.

Unlike raw leaves, leaf mould will not steal nitrogen from the soil around plants, so can be used in the vegetable and flower gardens. Leaf mould is a good soil conditioner and a sweet-smelling mulch used around plants. It can be used as a seed-sowing compost and makes a good potting compost when mixed with sharp sand and garden compost in equal parts, and is a good substitute for peat. Fallen leaves are gathered in autumn and stored in a separate leaf-mould container, making sure that there is good airflow. A wire or pallet container works well. By the following autumn, the fungi will have converted the leaves to soft, crumbly leaf mould. The process can be speeded up by shredding the leaves prior to storing.

During spring and summer, the chloroplasts within the leaves constantly combine sunlight, water and carbon dioxide to produce sugars to feed the plants and release oxygen. In autumn, when temperatures fall and daylight shortens, the chlorophyll within the leaves, which gives the leaves their green colour, is reabsorbed by the tree.

I try to balance the sedentary pursuits of painting, drawing and writing, with physical work in the garden. It might not always be as active as turning the compost heap or digging the soil, but there are always plants to tend, seeds to sow, cuttings to take, all the time assessing plants' health, their positions and how they sit together – do colours complement? – and finding inspiration for future paintings. I find this balance of mind and body crucial to being creative in the studio and garden.

My paintings are meditations on Mag's life and also about a shared love of plants, which runs in the family. Our grandfather grew show chrysanthemums and sweet peas and roses for my grandmother, who also had a love of flowers. I loved to buy her violets or anemones on my way home from school. This meant walking instead of catching the bus, so that I had the money for the flowers. The main flower garden was lush, fragrant, colourful and full of scent – the epitome of a cottage garden – with roses round the windows, on the pergola and encircling the seats placed in the curve of the border. These precious moments stay with me, being special for ever.

AUTUMN

Glorious days of sun and showers can be welcome and, with the ground being warm from the summer heat, trigger growth in some plants. In autumn herbaceous perennials can be divided for replanting, when the plants are gradually sinking into dormancy and the soil still warm. This gives the plants the opportunity to make new roots and establish themselves before winter. Cooler nights bring a change in leaf colour – yellow, gold, red and deep plum. As the leaves fall they can be chopped with the lawnmower and composted to provide an invaluable soil conditioner. I avoid adding walnut leaves as these can be a growth inhibitor.

NERINE
Nerine bowdenii (Guernsey lily)

The Painting

Inspiration for the subject invigorates and excites, but the drawing or painting must still be planned. Without planning, failures can occur; however, this might result in stimulating the imagination so it becomes a learning process. The most exciting moments of a painting are the start and the final stages, but the process is more important than the finished piece. Every painting is a learning process – a journey of exploration. With this in mind, I drew the foreground shapes of petals and masked the stamens as I wanted them to be lighter than the background. A light pink was painted over the foreground petals and darkened with a thicker mix when the initial painting was dry. The background petals were suggested with the same pink and, while still wet, a touch of violet was added. The violet was also used in the foreground flowers to suggest depth to the flower. When all was dry, the background was wetted and green, violet and pink added into the wet area and allowed to merge. When this was completely dry, the masking fluid was removed and the stamens painted.

366

The Gardener

Presumably derived from the Greek Nereids, daughter of Nereus, a sea nymph, the nerine originates from South Africa. Nerines flower in early to late autumn, producing beautiful large heads of up to eight blooms. Each has an elegant, narrow flower with backward-arching trumpet-shaped petals of bright glowing pink, which have a spidery effect. They start to flower in late September to November and can last well into winter. They must be given full sun. *Nerine bowdenii* is a member of a genus of twenty to twenty-seven species of bulbous plants, native to South Africa and related to amaryllis and brunsvigia, but with filaments much thicker at the base. Nerines are among the most beautiful of the autumn-flowering bulbous plants, with *N. bowdenii* hardy enough to plant in the open garden in a well-drained sunny position. The shelter of a protected bed at the bottom of a south-facing wall is ideal. They can be planted in August and kept dry until the flower spikes or leaves begin to appear. Then they should be watered, and thereafter they should be watered freely until the leaves begin to turn yellow – a sign that the resting season is beginning, when water should be withheld until the next flowering season.

Nerines are propagated by offsets, which should be treated in a similar way. The seeds are bulb-like and fleshy and are a good way of obtaining new forms, and many fine seedlings and hybrids have been raised and named. The seeds are best sown on the surface of the soil, using fibrous compost and sand.

CALLICARPA
(beauty berry)

The Drawing

Artist's pencils come in various grades ranging from soft 8B to the hardest, 10H, with F and HB being in the middle. Hard pencils make fine lines appropriate for delicate and detailed drawing. Soft pencils are more versatile as they give more varied lines and tones. When sharpened to a fine point they make fluid lines that can be tapered from thick to thin. When blunt, they make broad, grainy marks and the side of the lead can be used to produce solid areas of tone. The marks can be blended and smudged to produce subtle tones and gradations. Pencil lines can be soft and sinuous, vigorous and bold or controlled and crisp. The character of a pencil line will be influenced by the hardness or softness of the pencil lead, the sharpness of the tip, the pressure applied and the speed with which the line is drawn.

Yellow, pink and purple pencils created this drawing. The highlights on the berries are the white of the paper. The stems were darkened to give the illusion of depth as in the leaves. The colours were mixed by placing one colour on top of another until the required tone or colour was achieved. There are a large number of tints available, so there may not be the need to mix. Coloured pencils are versatile, as effects can be bright, heightened colour or soft and atmospheric.

Drawing can be learned. One mark leads to a line, then a shape, which can be developed with shading, giving depth and tone. It's a matter of putting down the first pencil mark, which leads to the next and the image begins to appear. To draw something from life is to brand it in the brain. It is an imprint, exploring every feature, every detail.

Degas said, 'Drawing is not about what one sees, it is about what one makes others see.'

The Painting

The berries were painted first by making sure that the highlights on each was left pure white paper. Some berries were toned down later and the interior of each bunch was darkened. Some of the branches were painted in a yellowy green and others were added after the washy pink background. I didn't make the shadows on the stems too dark as I wanted the main interest to be on the berries themselves.

The Gardener

The common name, beauty bush, should not be confused with *Kolkwitzia amabilis*. It is also known as French mulberry, sour bush, burchberry and purple beauty berry. In Greek, the name *callicarpa* comes from *callos*, meaning beauty, and *carpos*, meaning fruit. The roots, leaves and branches were used by Native Americans for medicinal purposes to treat malarial fevers and rheumatism. The roots were used to treat dizziness, stomach aches and dysentery. In the early twentieth century farmers crushed leaves and placed them under their horse harnesses to repel mosquitoes.

Callicarpa is native to East and South East Asia, Australia, South-East and North America and Central America. Young leaves are flushed bronze in spring, maturing through green to a beautiful rose madder in autumn. The flowers are in clusters, white to pink, and the berries are purple with a metallic lustre and are very conspicuous on the bare branches when the leaves fall. The beauty of this bush is in autumn, when the leaves turn red or violet and, when they fall, the purple berries are revealed on the bare stems, and can continue through winter. *Callicarpa giraldii* 'Profusion' is self-fertile, so can be relied upon for plentiful fruit without the need for multiple specimens. The fruit is high in moisture content and hence an important food for birds and other animals. The lilac flowers bloom on new wood in summer, and pinkish foliage in September is followed by the berries. Callicarpas, which are not self-fertilising, are best pollinated when shrubs are planted in groups or massed together rather than singly, to make sure that the berries will be formed. They are best cut back hard in late winter or early spring when the berries have gone. This ensures bushy plants in the following year.

Propagation is by soft cuttings and by seed.

SNOWBERRY
Symphoricarpos albus

The Drawing

I used coloured pencils for this drawing, choosing my palette, organising the pencils by colour and value. I made sure that the berries stayed as white paper and built up the depth of colour around them so as to have a contrast. I did the same with the veins in the leaves, shading as leaves bent behind others. Edge values are important. A soft edge retires into its surroundings while a hard edge attracts attention, so these need to be placed carefully and not scattered indiscriminately. The drawing process is a matter of seeing and recording. Drawing is the true instant art – it can create a magnificent effect even with just a few dark outlines on white paper, capturing shape, mood and the atmosphere. Attempting to draw what is seen sharpens the ability to observe. It is an exercise of the eye, mind and hand. The eye sees three-dimensionally and the mind translates into two dimensions, which the hand then executes.

The plant was drawn with limited colours: a medium green for the buds and berries and slightly darker for the leaves. Strong pressure was used around the berries to give shape to the leaves, but also to contrast with the white berries. A yellow coloured pencil with a sharp point was used for the veins on the leaves.

The Gardener

The snowberry is an ornamental deciduous shrub of great elegance. The small flowers, in clusters, are borne on short stems, and are bell-shaped, velvety on the inside and tinged with pink on the outside. The flowers are very attractive to bees, flies and wasps, Its waxy white berries are formed in clusters on the branches, and it is for this reason that the generic name derives from the Greek *karpos* and *symphorein*, meaning berries borne together. The snowberry will grow anywhere in full sun, or in dense shade under trees. It will cover large areas in the wilder parts of the garden, and its glory is the mass of large marble-like berries which appear in October and persist for months.

The coral berry is classified into the honeysuckle family, Caprifoliaceae, and is a relative of the snowberry. The genus has red berries, or drupes. The generic name *Symphoricarpos* derives from the way the berries cluster along the branches. It originated from North America as far east as Nebraska and as far south as Mexico. It is regarded as a weed, growing in fields and along roadsides, but is a welcome plant to brighten the winter garden. In summer symphoricarpos has pretty white flowers and grey-green leaves. The berries start white and deepen in colour as they age. It grows well in sun or light shade and is cold-hardy. It can be propagated by rooting suckers and by taking cuttings in autumn.

PHEASANT BERRY

Leycesteria (Himalayan honeysuckle, golden lanterns)

The Drawing

There is something magical about holding a pencil and letting the colour flow. Coloured pencil is a medium about control, discipline and patience – discipline to build shape and form, and patience because it takes time. One needs to be careful to avoid mistakes as they cannot be changed or wiped off.

I look for interesting light-and-dark patterns and strong design, but mostly one that excites. Coloured pencils give the depth needed for the strong colours of the bracts. The edges of the bracts were darkened by building up the colour with extra pressure, and then the point of the pencil produced the sharp edges. I enjoyed this little coloured-pencil drawing, using Magenta for the flower petals, purple for the forming seeds, yellow for the leaf veins and a yellow-green and a blue-green for the leaves.

The Painting

Bright sunlight on foliage creates shadow, intensified colour and transparency. The light showing through the leaves appears to be brighter. The surface texture of the leaf determines the amount of light absorbed or reflected. A shiny, smooth leaf reflects more light than a matt textured leaf. In this painting the seeds are more mature than those in the drawing and appear darker. Colours used were mostly the same as in the drawing, except the leaves were not depicted in so much detail and were more of a washy suggestion. The colours of the leycesteria were exaggerated for greater impact and the green background intensified the contrast. Red and green are opposite each other on the colour wheel. Green is always the predominant colour in the garden and can act as an intermediate, but when red is added it can be vibrant.

The Gardener

Popularly known as the Himalayan honeysuckle, other names are granny's curls, pheasant berry and flowering nutmeg. In 1820 it was named after W. Leycester, Chief of Justice in Bengal and an amateur gardener. Interestingly it does not come from the Himalayas or look like honeysuckle. The soft green, hollow stems put out arching, hanging trails of claret purple and white flowers in summer succeeded by dark-purple berries. The unusual flower heads are long tassels composed of a series of burgundy-coloured bracts intermingled with white flowers at the shoot tips and in the upper leaf joints. The purple colouring persists through summer and into autumn, when the berries ripen from green to pink, to reddish purple, almost to black. In autumn the reddish colour of the foliage intensifies before the leaves drop, exposing green winter stems.

Birds, especially pheasants, are fond of the berries. Propagation is by seed or by cuttings of young shoots in gentle heat in spring, or older stems in autumn. It will grow in sun or shade and the older stems should be cut out each spring, leaving the best stems to flower. New shoots grow readily from the base in spring. It is quick-growing, producing new tall shoots in one season.

BRUGMANSIA
(angel's trumpet)

The Painting
The distinct trumpet shape of the brugmansia in strong light is accentuated by the darker background. Most of the effectiveness of colour comes from the way the eye perceives warm versus cool colours. This is obvious when they are placed side by side, warm next to cool, like the yellow of the brugmansia next to the blue of the background. The two colours were mixed together to produce a neutral colour in the background. The warm and cool colours combined together neutralise without creating mud; also the careful use of tonal values will reveal the form, depth and light, which in turn brings life to the painting.

The alternating pattern of light against a dark background can be interesting. However, it can look completely different depending on the time of day, and especially in sunlight. It is in these circumstances that expression in interpreting the subject with individuality and spontaneity expands the imagination.

The Gardener
Brugmansia is a large perennial shrub with very large pendulous, pointed, trumpet-shaped pure-white or creamy-coloured flowers and a heavy musk-like, sweet-smelling, almost overpowering fragrance, especially on warm evenings. There is also a cultivar 'Golden Queen', which has yellow double flowers, looking like one trumpet inside another. The fruits are smooth and berry-like, containing large brown seeds. It is tender and needs a sunny sheltered place. In warm conditions they begin to flower in late spring. To keep the plant growing strongly they need to be well fed and pruned lightly. They may grow into large bushes, but can be pruned after flowering to the size required. They are naturally evergreen in Peru, but in Europe may be treated as deciduous. Brugmansias enjoy moderate heat in full growth, but should be kept dry and cool and need protection from frost in winter. The roots are hardier and may re-sprout in spring. They can be propagated easily by rooting cuttings taken from the end of a branch during summer. They are best grown in pots so that they can be

moved into shelter in cold weather.

Angel's-trumpet plants are originally from South America. There are no known wild species, which means that humans have cultivated the plant intentionally, perhaps in prehistoric times. Andean priests smoke the leaves in order to see the future and diagnose diseases. The seeds are still used in the Andes as an additive to chicha, a psychoactive maize beer, which is consumed during festivals and rituals. People of Columbia once gave chicha to the wives and slaves of dead nobles in order to cause stupor before they were buried alive with the corpses of their masters. Many Peruvian shamans still believe that ingesting brugmansia allows them to communicate with ancestors and to find treasures buried in graves. Brugmansia is a deliriant, and extreme care must be taken when ingesting any form or quantity. It is one of the most potent naturally occurring hallucinogens in the world. Death can result if too much is consumed. Smoking the dried leaves – an amount similar to a cigarette will have only subtle effects, but a resulting headache is a good sign that one has smoked enough.

Brugmansia is closely related to the annual datura, which has erect rather than pendulous flowers. Datura is commonly known as thorn apple, moonflower, devil's trumpet or angel's trumpet. The American Indians called it white man's plant, and it is believed to have arrived in North America with the Jamestown settlers. Datura was given as a vernacular name in the East Indies, stemming from the Hindu, *dhatura stromium*, an ancient botanic name. The name thorn apple comes from the leathery little fruits, which resemble hard green apples and bear thorns, similar to the Spanish-chestnut fruits. It has naturalised in places. It is a relative of the tobacco plant, nicotiana. All members of the genus are poisonous.

PASSION FLOWER

Passiflora caerulea. Passio means passion and *floris* means a flower – hence passion flower.

Painting 1

Who could not be inspired by these beautiful exotic flowers. The temptation was to include many fabulous blooms, creating a riot of colour. Choosing only one glorious flower, plus the gorgeously coloured fruit, led to a design with the white flower having the most impact, and the yellow of the fruit forming a secondary interest. Here the design is focused on the flower and seed pods, with the dark background creating the contrast needed to make the flowers and pods stand out in the painting. I also painted colour around the pod edges, which adds to the interest. In this painting some edges are softened by blending, which gives the appearance that other blooms and leaves are in the background. The painting is developed from the initial drawing, and the original outlines become less important and eventually obsolete. The darkest darks are laid in, with the lightest light (the flower petals) remaining unpainted paper except for a little hint of shadow where the petals turn in the light. All the other tonal values are between these two tones. The strongest contrasts are those of the flower in the focal point.

Painting beautiful flowers is a pleasure and working with watercolour is exciting, with both intentional and accidental results.

Painting 2

This painting is based more on a circle design, taking the eye around from the fabulous flower and then to the seed pods. The criss-cross of stems also leads the eye around, but the warm colour of one seed pod attracts attention from the others. The variety of colour mixes, arising from some being blended on the paper and some in the palette, give a rich and colourful result despite the choice of limited pigments. Although I have a large variety of pigments, I mainly choose favourite colours and love to create my own variations.

The Gardener

The association between the flower and Christ's Passion was first made by Spanish priests in the plant's native Brazil. The name is an allusion to the parts of the flower which South American missionaries related to the Passion of Christ, with the ten petals representing the Apostles (minus Judas Iscariot and either Doubting Thomas or Peter). The three stigmas represent the nails, and the five anthers below them represent the five wounds – four by the nails and one by the lance. The hand-shaped leaves are the hands of His persecutors and the tendrils represents the whip with which He was scourged. The flower's frilly blue corona, the radial filaments, which can number more than 100 and vary from flower to flower, represent the crown of thorns.

Passiflora is a genus of herbaceous and woody climbers, occasionally shrubs or small trees. There are many different passion-flower species, with considerable variety within them. Some passion flowers are vines, some bushy. It is an extremely vigorous plant with vine-like stems clad in attractive palmate dark-green leaves and questing tendrils, which cling to the structure on which it grows. The fabulous starlike flowers may appear at any time throughout summer and have white petals with a purple-fringed corona centre, with blue-tinged filaments, purple stigmas and five stamens rayed horizontally. It is faintly scented. Passion flowers look like exotic tropical plants, but they can be grown in much milder areas.

The male and female parts are elevated on a column which is called the gynophore, the five stamens below with the ovary, and three styles at the top. The flowers are followed by orange egg-shaped fruits, which are edible but full of seeds and germinate readily. They are technically berries, varying in size from a large pea to a small melon. It is often filled with a pleasantly sweet or acid pulp, which is edible.

Propagation is by seed, by layering stems in spring or by cuttings placed in a cold frame in summer. Propagation from cuttings of young shoots with a heel, taken in spring, should be inserted singly in small pots of sandy soil. They should be placed in a closed propagating frame or under a bell glass, where they will root in due course. Once rooted, the plants grow rapidly and can be repotted and later planted out. They grow rapidly and climb by means of tendrils on to some sort of support. Attention should be given to trailing shoots and cutting away the weakest shoots to avoid overcrowding, but allowing the terminal points of others to hang gracefully. When flowering is over, the main growth may be regulated, thinned and cut back. If trained to a south wall, it grows rapidly and soon covers a large surface. The numerous orange fruits that ripen in summer are as ornamental as the flowers which precede them. They are not particular about soil provided there is good drainage and plenty of water in the growing season. Over-rich soils are apt to produce overly luxuriant growth at the expense of flowers.

AUTUMN CROCUS
Colchicum autumnale (naked boy, son-before-father, meadow saffron, naked lady)

Painting 1

Crocus speciosus has lilac flowers and dark veins with stunningly bright-orange styles. I painted this beautiful flower in stages. I started with a watery wash of Quinacridone Violet on each of the petals, avoiding the stamens and keeping the white of the paper on the central petal. Various parts of the petals were then overpainted with a stronger mix of violet, letting it dry and then adding more violet. The veins in the petals were added using a fine brush when all was dry. I used Winsor Orange for the stamens and then a little Quinacridone Red was added to the tips and base so that they merged. I let everything dry and sometime later assessed the painting and decided to adjust the shadows by adding more violet to these areas of the petals.

The Gardener

Colchicum autumnale is a member of the Colchicaceae or lily family – unlike the true crocuses, which are in the Iridaceae family. The name naked lady comes from the fact that the flowers emerge from the ground long after the leaves have died back. The leaves grow in spring, die back in summer and the flowers bloom in autumn.

It can be very confusing when the name crocus is given to several species. The Latin name *crocus* has supplanted the English one of saffron, which was prized for providing sweet scent, a golden dye and a medicine. Among the autumn-flowering species, the best known is *Crocus sativus,* the true saffron crocus, which was cultivated for centuries for the sake of its stigmata, which when dried became the saffron of commerce from Kashmir to the Bay of Biscay, and at one time was largely grown at Saffron Walden in England. The word crocus is probably derived from a Semitic language, perhaps because saffron was traded throughout the Middle East. Its delicate flowers are pale purple with large drooping stigmas. Saffron is challenging to grow, but *C. speciosus* 'Conqueror' is one of the most beautiful autumn-flowering crocuses, with rich-violet-blue goblet-shaped blooms with a gold flush at the base and large orange-gold stigmas. They will naturalise readily given full sun and good drainage. They flower from September to late October ahead of the foliage.

C. pulchellus has lilac flowers with purple veins. *C. imperati* 'de Jager' is purple on the inside and beige with purple stripes on the outside. *C. goulimyi* 'Mani White' has pure-white flowers.

Crocuses are best planted in clumps in a sunny position around shrubs, in tubs or naturalised in grass, though grass must be kept short before the bulb shoots emerge. So long as they have good drainage they remain hardy and will spread by multiplication of the corms or self-seeding.

Painting 2

The stunning colours were so intense that I decided to glaze (a painting technique to create transparency) with various colours – Permanent Rose, Quinacridone Magenta and Ultramarine Violet – but first I masked out the stamens so as to have freedom to wash over them without fear. Each layer of colour had to dry completely, otherwise the water would cause unwanted marks. This took some time as the atmosphere was damp, even though it was a sunny day. A large brush loaded with plenty of water and pigment created an initial clear wash and, when dry, another layer was added. Glazing creates transparency, which leaves the underlying colours visible. A light touch is necessary, otherwise the underlying colours could be disturbed. When all was dry, the mask was removed and, using a fine brush, the stamens were painted with orange and a dash of rose in the darker areas. The background was glazed with rose and violet and then with violet, rose and green. The green was overglazed with the other colours, giving a deeper tone with a hint of other growth.

A dark background can be most stunning.

The Gardener

One of the fascinations of painting and gardening is to observe the way the changing seasons bring an ever interesting metamorphosis. Some plants are at their best in autumn, especially if other plants have finished flowering or are cut back to reveal previously hidden attributes. One of these delights is the autumn crocus, colchicum, which has delicate flowers with as many as twenty blooms produced from a single corm. The large poisonous bulbs can produce flowers without being planted, but they start to form roots at flowering time in preparation for the leaves in spring. The lance-shaped foliage can smother other low-growing plants. In May the leaves turn brown and shrivel, leaving gaps which can be filled with bedding plants. They are best planted where the leaves are not too obtrusive, in full sun and in rich soil.

These crocuses are now split from their family of lilies into their own Colchicaceae family. They flower in late summer and autumn after producing leaves and fruit in spring and spending the summer in dormancy. This is because they originate from places that are hot and dry in summer, cold in winter and have brief moist, warm springs. They come from Eastern Europe and Asia, from open, sunny, rocky places, but if they are grown under deciduous trees in moderate shade they get a summer drying as the tree roots suck out the moisture from the ground. They flower in the autumn, fading in the light before the tree regains its full canopy.

Colchicums are known to secrete gibberellin – a growth hormone that leads to doubling of chromosomes. It has been recorded that plants growing with autumn crocus are larger and more robust. They look best en masse, but, to increase stock, they can be dug up and spread before growth begins in midsummer. They can also be grown from seed in a cool, shady place, where they will form bulbs a year or two later. As with other autumn-flowering bulbs, such as sternbergias, they are best planted towards the end of summer.

STERNBERGIA
Sternbergia lutea (autumn daffodil, fall daffodil, lily-of-the-field, winter daffodil,
yellow autumn crocus; it should not be confused with colchicum, autumn crocus)

The Painting

It is a true joy to behold such a vivid and exciting colour in autumn. Yellow immediately attracts attention as it draws the eye more quickly than any other colour. I used two yellows – Lemon Yellow for the lighter areas and a warmer Indian Yellow for the shaded parts – to suggest depth and shape, and used a blue-green to surround the petals and so enhance the yellow. I painted a little contrasting purple over the green around the flowers to give impact to the yellow. The addition of the purple over the green darkens the green and gives a link between the green of the leaves and the flowers. The stalks were painted with a mix of the same warm yellow and Ultramarine Blue, adding more or less in different places. The ground colour was a dilute Burnt Sienna, over which more blue was painted in between the flowers, and touches of violet intensified the darks in the centre of the clump and acted as a complementary colour to the yellow.

The Gardener
Sternbergia is a bulbous flowering plant in the family Amaryllidaceae. The upright, thick, deep-glossy-green leaves appear in the autumn, remain through the winter and die away completely

by May. The fragrant flowers appear soon after the leaves and are deep yellow with six petals.

Sternbergia lutea is not a crocus, but is more closely related to the daffodil family, though flowers are similar to the crocus, with bright-golden-yellow flowers in autumn. They are best fertilised annually with a general-purpose fertiliser as the tips break through the soil. They have deep-yellow flowers with six yellow tepals, which is the outer part of the flower, six stamens, and a style with a single stigma, which appears soon after the leaves. In the wild *S. lutea* grows in sunny rock crevices and scorched scrubland. It is hardy and grows in well-drained soil and a hot, sunny border, as it needs a warm, dry period in summer for good flowering, but plenty of water during the growing season. The plants require no water once they flower. They are best planted in clumps and left alone so that they develop further. As the bulbs should be planted fairly deeply, other annual plants can be over-planted in what would be bare earth. Propagation is by lifting and separating the bulbs in spring before the leaves die down in late spring.

PAMPAS
Cortaderia selloana

The Painting
Masking fluid was a must to retain the white of the plumes and stalks, contrasted against the dark background. Touches of dilute violet were carefully applied with a fine brush on the shadow sides of the plumes, and this gave the impression of strong sunshine and a touch of warmth among the cooler greens.

Early morning and late afternoon are the best times for capturing dramatic light. As the light changes so quickly, it is best to make notes as it can be confusing as the sun moves and changes the shadows. The other option is to return to the same place at the same time on the following day so that the light is similar, if not the same.

The Gardener
Pampas grasses are native to South America. *Cortaderia* is derived from the Spanish-Argentinian name, meaning cutter, in reference to the sharp leaf margins; *selloana* is named for Friedrich Sellow, 1789–1831, a German botanist and naturalist from Potsdam, who worked as a plant collector in Brazil. It is named for the pampas plains, where it is endemic. It is considered an invasive species. Pampas grasses grow tall with long, sharp-edged leaves which fold at the midrib, forming dense tussocks of bluish green or silvery grey that can reach three metres in height. Female plants bear pink or silvery-white plume-like panicles of flowers on a tall stem. The feathery seeds are readily dispersed by the wind. They seed

prolifically, with each plant able to produce over a million seeds during its lifetime. The only maintenance is to cut back the old flowering stems in late winter before the new foliage grows. They can grow in a wide range of habitats. They enjoy full sun, but will tolerate partial shade, drought and wind.

In late winter or early spring, the plant should be pruned to the ground. The long and slender leaves have very sharp edges, so care should be taken when pruning. The foliage can be burnt down without harm to the plant.

STRAWBERRY TREE
Arbutus unedo (Killarney strawberry tree, Irish strawberry tree, cane apples, Dalmatian strawberry)

The Drawing

These superb bell-shaped flowers were arranged in a ready-made design, balanced with three clusters, and leaves arranged to balance the whole. I drew the flowers first, with some partially visible. The clusters were linked by the stems from which the leaves grew. All were drawn in ink.

Drawing is a process of selection. What is left out is as important as that which is included. With good accurate drawing comes confidence to be expressive.

The Gardener

The specific name *unedo* is attributed to Pliny the Elder, who allegedly claimed, "*Unum tantum edo,*" meaning "I eat only one." The plant is widespread in the Mediterranean region, North and Western France and Ireland.

The plant is a good bee plant, but produces a bitter honey, and the fruits are food for birds. The fruits are used in jams, beverages and liqueurs such as Portuguese 'Medronho', a type of strong brandy. It has been used for antiseptic, astringent, intoxicant, rheumatoid and tonic purposes.

It prefers well-drained soil and low to moderate soil moisture and is naturally adapted to dry summer climates. Arbutus is an evergreen shrub or small tree and was one of the many species described by Carolus Linnaeus in volume one of *Species Plantarum*, 1753, giving it the name it still bears today. The leaves are dark green and glossy with a serrated margin. The hermaphrodite flowers are white and bell-shaped in panicles in autumn and are pollinated by bees. The fruits are bright-red berries with a rough surface, maturing about a year after flowering and at the same time as the next flowering. The fruits are edible and sweet when red and taste similar to a fig.

WEEPING CHINESE LANTERN

Abutilon megapotamicum (Indian mallow, flowering maple, parlour maple, room maple, trailing abutilon)

The Painting

Subtractive mixtures. Gardens and flowers are a favourite subject, but to create an appealing painting takes more than knowledge of the subject and the technical ability to paint it. It is necessary to look for patterns when designing the composition. When I look around the garden I see shapes and forms where one plant grows tall, another rounded and then groups of architectural plants, and the eye is led to the next, one shape after another, just as in a painting one form leads to another and is balanced and made interesting by design and composition. Painting in the garden is by far the best way to create compositions that capture the feeling and the subtleties and details in shadow areas. Often these paintings are finished on site, and sometimes they are left as sketches and references and inspiration for larger pieces.

To convey a convincing effect of sunlight it is necessary to paint a full range of tones from the darkest dark to the lightest light. In this painting I wanted an explosion of colour, making it dramatic, highlighting petal shapes and contrasting between red and yellow. Pure Quinacridone Red was used for the main petals and, when dry, a richer, thicker red was added to give a sense of shape. Winsor Yellow was used for the inner petals and then a touch of red was added to the yellow for the shaded areas. Ultramarine Blue was washed into the background, and this same blue was mixed with the yellow for the light green, and red was added to darken the green for the shadowed areas and the branches.

When yellow paint is mixed with blue paint, the particles of pigment intermingle. The yellow particles reflect yellow, but also a little orange and green, while the blue ones reflect blue plus a little violet and green. The resultant light reaching the eye is a green that is darker and less intense than either the original yellow or blue. Pigment mixtures like this are called subtractive mixtures because the more pigments are mixed together, the more the light is absorbed or 'subtracted' from the illuminating white light. The green mix appears darker because less light is actually reflecting from it than reflects from yellow or blue alone. Blue light does not illuminate a yellow surface, whereas yellow light reflects all the yellow, tending to make an intense yellow.

The Gardener

Abutilon megapotamicum is in the family of the mallow, Malvaceae, and is native to Argentina and Brazil. Abutilon has beautiful and unusual bell-shaped flowers with yellow petals and a large crimson calyx. It has a very long flowering season, which is at its peak in the summer, but can bloom throughout the year if adequate temperatures are maintained. The leaves are delicately shaped with serrated edges and an elongated pointed tip. They will grow in sun or part shade and in fairly ordinary conditions, responding well to mulch and fertiliser.

Abutilon theophrasti medicus is the Arabic name for a species of mallow easily grown. It may be grown in pots or in the ground as long as there is good drainage, but needs plenty of water. It flowers from the end of May. It is a tall, erect, softly hairy annual with small solitary yellow flowers and heart-shaped long pointed leaves. It is cultivated in China for its fibre and known as jute, which is used in textile manufacture.

Abutilon can easily be increased by cuttings of firm young shoots and placed in a propagator with bright indirect light and high humidity in summer or early autumn, but it is best in early spring and September in compost mixed with some sand. I have many plants which were raised from seeds sown in a greenhouse in spring. Germination should be within a few weeks. They should be grown on and planted out in late spring. They should be watered freely in spring and summer and more sparingly in winter. Long straggly stems should be shortened in spring.

FATSIA JAPONICA
(false caster oil plant, fig leaf palm, glossy leaf paper palm, fatsi, Japanese aralia)

The Painting

It takes much practice to master the medium of watercolour and to be familiar with how the paint will react in different situations. Once I see something interesting, I carefully observe the scene and make sketches, judging all the time whether it will make a good composition. In this painting I thought of the flowers as abstract patterns. Strong bold compositions are a powerful tool. Harmonies of light and dark shapes and well-thought-out colour relations give a sense of depth and look three-dimensional.

The Gardener

Fatsia is a species of flowering plant in the family Araliaceae, native to Southern Japan, Southern Korea and Taiwan. *Fatsia* is the Latinised version of the Japanese name of the plant fatsi, meaning eight, referring to the eight leaf lobes. In Japan it is known as *yatsude*, meaning eight fingers. It is sometimes called aralia, as in the past it was classified in the related genus *Aralia*. Fatsia is often erroneously referred to as the false castor oil plant, which is the unrelated *Ricinus communis*. It is related to ivy as it has been interbred with *Hedera helix*, or common ivy, to produce the hybrid × *Fatshedera lizei*.

It prefers cool conditions and good light with a little shade, avoiding hot sunshine which may scorch its leaves.

This attractive plant is grown for its large, evergreen, leathery, glossy-lobed, palmate and stunningly architectural leaves. In autumn it has globose clusters of pompom-like small creamy-white flowers on branched heads when most shrubs are resting. When pollinated it is followed by black fruits. Each exotic-looking flower forming the head has five tiny petals. It is easy to care for, provided that the leaves are not scorched by sun, or icy easterly winds, and the compost is not too soggy or too dry. In mid to late summer the old leaves droop, turn bright yellow and may need to be taken off the plant. New leaves and buds appear from the base. Because it is a late-flowering evergreen it is useful to insects and is hardy.

It can be propagated by semi-ripe cuttings taken in spring, by suckers or by seed. It can be grown in pots indoors as well as in containers in shady places or under trees. There is a slightly less tough and less common variegated plant, which has cream tips to its leaves, but fatsia is mostly an indoor plant.

BANANA
Musa basjoo (plantain)

The Painting

The intensity of sunlight outdoors is many times brighter than indoor light on a clear day. Light bounces everywhere, even in the shadows. When trying to capture a strong feeling of light, I exaggerate the reflected light rather than the contrast between the highlights and shadows. This way the painting retains the same glowing light quality.

When selecting a scene I need a good arrangement of shapes with a fair amount of contrast in their value, colour or both. Painting is a continuous process of perpetual practice and development in drawing as well as painting. This develops the ability to see and understand the relationship of shapes and design. If the composition doesn't work well, I need to find a new scene with a better design. Elements can always be moved or changed, but the design must have interest and must be a good arrangement.

In this painting there are a few select areas of sharp edges along with bright colours, and high contrast within a limited tonal range. The composition and subject matter are important, but the eye is drawn to the light in the focal point.

To maintain spontaneity and clarity, I like to paint the majority of the painting and then leave it in a place where I will see it later. After a break from the painting I can assess if I should make any changes, additions or improvements not realised at the time of creation.

The Gardener

Named in honour of Antonius Musa, physician to Octavius Augustus, first Emperor of Rome, 63–14 BC. It may have been the world's first cultivated fruit. It is a genus of about forty very large, sometimes gigantic, plants, native of tropical regions of the world.

The large leaves are spirally arranged, growing from the ground, forming a sheath which appears like a stalk. The flowers are half-whorled clusters, each cluster having a large coloured bract. The lower clusters are female, the upper male, the whole issuing from the centre of the leaves at the top of the false stem. I grow them directly in the ground in sheltered locations. They require a strong loamy soil with plenty of manure. They can take any amount of heat and moisture in summer, but need to rest in winter with little or no water.

Musa basjoo, the Japanese banana, gives the garden an exotic feel. It is the hardiest of bananas and withstands winters outside in our mild area if the leaves are tied so that they do not thrash about in the wind, making them ragged-looking instead of majestic, and wrapped in fleece or bracken. The species producing good edible fruit mostly demand great space and much heat, with a minimum night temperature of 17°C, and have therefore little chance of coming to fruition, but *M. cavendishii* is the most compact and the most likely to succeed. Propagation is by taking strong suckers and growing them on in pots until established, when they can be planted in a bed of very rich soil. A stem which has produced a bunch of bananas dies away soon afterwards, but has usually one or more suckers from the base before this takes place.

Archaeologists have found evidence of banana cultivation in New Guinea as far back as 8000 BC. Bananas are produced mainly in tropical and subtropical areas of Africa, Asia and the Americas as well as the Canary Islands and Australia. India is the leading producer of bananas worldwide, though most of the Indian plantations are for domestic use. Bananas are also called plantains, but *ban* refers to the sweeter form of the fruit, which is generally eaten uncooked, while plantain refers to a starchier fruit, which is often cooked before eating. The 'Cavendish' banana, originally native to South East Asia, is the variety sold in stores. This replaced the 'Gros Michel' after it was wiped out by fungus. The 'Gros Michel', being bigger, had a longer shelf life and tasted better. Botanists say that the 'Cavendish' may face the same fate as the 'Gros Michel' within the next twenty years. The correct name for a bunch of bananas is a hand; a single banana is a finger, but it is considered a berry.

CYCLAMEN

Cyclamen coum (Persian cyclamen, hardy cyclamen, sowbread, presumably because pigs like them, but so do other wildlife).
Kyklos, meaning circular, refers to the spiral twisting of the peduncle of some species after flowering.

Painting 1

The artist's palette is full of the fantastic range of colours and textures that decorative plants provide, and the real joy is painting the ever changing picture.

The ratio of water to pigment is an important factor in keeping intensity and transparency. In this painting, pigment was applied to the petals on a wet surface, but to make the edges sharp and well defined I painted them on to dry paper so that the paint did not spread. Painting on to a wet surface gives a softer, muted impression as the paint is diffused into the white of the paper. This is because light is reflected back off the white paper through the thin layers of colour.

Painting 2

When a subject attracts, I try to focus on that first emotional response. Painting is not just about reproducing the image, but it involves looking for something different, extraordinary and perhaps unexpected. Drawing is the foundation of the painting. Although it is possible to paint without drawing, for me the drawing process is essential. In the drawing class at art school it was regarded as old-fashioned to draw from plaster casts of busts. Most students hated the process and didn't have the patience to complete accurate drawings. They were far more interested in the painting classes where we were told to express ourselves. However, for me, the sculptures, busts, casts and days spent in the Natural History Museum and the Victoria and Albert Museum were the fundamental bases for learning to see acutely and accurately. There is no substitute for drawing.

I began this painting by drawing the basic shapes and established a value pattern, being keenly aware of the light on the edges of the petals. In nature there are no outlines, just shapes next to other shapes, and this was part of the design. Remembering the initial attraction of the subject, I changed some elements, simplifying and reducing or enhancing where needed. Understating some minor areas brought out the subtleties of light and enhanced the importance of other areas.

Each petal was painted individually. I wet the petal with clear water, leaving a dry edge, and floated dilute colour into the water and then added a stronger application to the centre of the petal. In places I waited for the paint to dry and then added streaks of fairly dry paint to suggest veins. The leaves were painted in a similar way, running the greens together and then, when dry, adding the much darker green to the centres, with the veins showing the original colour. The dark green was a mix of the yellow-green with a touch of pink, and the flower stalks were the same mix with added pink.

I used a very fine pointed brush with a strong Quinacridone Magenta for the flower petals, which were darkened with a fairly dry pink. The green of the leaves was initially light and then darkened with the same green mix by adding some Magenta. The background was loosely painted to give an impression of more plants and flowers.

The Gardener

Autumn is a turning point in the garden when most hardy plants stop growing and mature plants start forming buds for the next season; however, many flowers continue to bloom if the weather is mild. Hardy winter-flowering *Cyclamen coum*, and late summer-to-autumn- flowering *C. hederifolium* are hardy and do not need cosseting. They are useful in shady north-facing flower beds or under trees and shrubs, and will naturalise in woodland if care is taken to enrich the soil with bonemeal. The leaves are nearly as attractive as the flowers.

C. neapolitanum flowers in the early autumn before the leaves appear, freely producing its crimson or purple white-edged petals, and the leaves, which are often prettily marked, continue well into the following year, forming a pleasant carpet. Since they are low-growing, they are best planted in the front edge of the flower bed, where they can be seen. They are good plants for the rock garden. The seed can be taken by mice.

C. coum is a relative of the primrose, in the family Primulaceae. The genus has about sixteen species with tuberous rootstocks. They are native to the Mediterranean region from Bulgaria to Turkey and in Lebanon and Israel. They are dormant during the summer, starting into growth underground long before they appear above ground. This is when they need moisture – in the autumn, when the weather cools and the rains start. They are precocious, flowering from late winter to early spring. Their dark-green leaves are very dwarf, round, heart-shaped, kidney-shaped or pointed, and can be either plain or marbled, some with a silver speckle or band around the edge, some with silvered or marbled foliage. The dainty flowers carpet the ground with patterned foliage and colours from pure white to deep pink and magenta. The solitary flowers are short and rounded with re-flexed petals, and are unaffected by even the severest frost. The fruit is a many-seeded capsule drawn down to soil level after the flowers fade by the spiral twisting of the peduncle into fantastic shapes. It grows in well-drained poor soils and is a happy companion to hellebores and winter bulbs such as snowdrops and crocuses. The seed is spread by ants, which are attracted to the sugar in the ripe seed. Self-sown seeds are often quicker to flower. Left undisturbed they form large colonies with blooms increasing each year. *C. coum* has the most beautiful flowers, in carmine or white with folded-back petals and the mouth facing downwards.

C. purpurascens has fragrant flowers in late summer and autumn. The flowers range in shades of rose pink to red with deeper blotches of colour. *C. hederifolium* blooms in late summer and autumn, with flowers that appear before the foliage. The flowers continue to bloom through winter into spring. Colours range from white to deep red-pink and magenta. The petals have distinct dark blotches and flared bases. The flowers appear to be delicate, but are in fact tough and hardy. The leaves are heart-shaped, but variable, and often shallowly five-to-nine-lobed, mottled silver-grey, often purplish beneath. They will self-seed freely. The Latin specific name comes from their individual toothed and pointed ivy-like leaves, which last all winter and make excellent ground cover for different areas. They are tough and resilient, coping with shade and dry soils, but will do well in garden compost or leaf mould to keep them moist, preferably on a bank or in a raised bed. Tubers are dormant during early summer and triggered into growth by late summer rainfall.

There are several tuberous varieties characterised by their rounded, often dark-green, kidney-shaped mottled leaves, dull maroon underneath with silvery markings on the upper surface. The leaves may linger into early summer and then wither, reappearing in the cooler, moist autumn. Once established, they will spread by seed, flowering when three years old. They grow from underground tubers and are hardy to -18°C.

Corms will establish themselves slowly, probably because the roots are bound to be injured in the collecting and new ones need to be formed, so the best way to increase them is by sowing fresh seed.

Not only do the cyclamen flowers brighten an area, but the rosettes of foliage also help to hold back weeds from germinating.

The earliest bulbs to flower in the New Year are in fact winter-flowering, but to me they are the first sign of spring. They are very tough, thriving in shade below trees and shrubs and giving a winter thrill with their bright-pink or white flowers.

Most bulbs and corms spend the summer without leaves or roots. The bulb is a store of food for the next season. Chemical changes take place inside during the resting period to support production of leaves and roots.

PYRACANTHA
(firethorn)

The Painting
The berries were drawn carefully, paying attention to composition, placing them in a pleasing arrangement. I then wet the whole of the background, leaving the berries and stalks dry. Ultramarine Blue and Indian Yellow were dropped into the wetted area, neat in certain places, and both colours mixed together to form a strong dark green. All these colours merged and created interesting textures. When dry more dark green – made by adding a little red to the original green – suggested leaves behind the berries. This helped to explain the nature of the plant as well as providing a good contrast to the bright berries. When completely dry, the berries were painted with Indian Yellow and, while

the paint was still wet, a little Quinacridone Magenta was touched on to some berries. This gave shape, texture and colour power. When dry, more red was added where deemed necessary.

The Gardener

The generic name *Pyracantha*, comes from the Greek *pyr*, meaning fire, and *akanthus*, meaning thorn – hence firethorn. As its name suggests, pyracantha, or firethorn, has very sharp thorns. It is a pretty shrub with white flowers in late spring or early summer, and has magnificent red, orange or yellow berries, which mature in autumn. It makes an excellent evergreen hedge, can be grown against a wall or fence or can be a free-standing shrub. There are seven species of pyracantha with either red, orange or yellow berries, which develop from late summer. The flowers and magnificent berries are very decorative. An application of potash encourages flowering and fruiting. Pyracantha flowers mainly on shoots produced in the previous year.

Pyracantha usually responds to heavy pruning when overgrown. It can be trained as an espalier. In spring, after flowering, to make the berries more visible any outward-growing shoots can be pruned, avoiding cutting off future berries. Pruning can be hazardous because of the thorns, which can cause inflammation and severe pain.

Propagate from semi-ripe or hardwood cuttings, or by seed, which needs three months of cold treatment or stratification in order to germinate. Propagation by seed may not come true.

Pyracanthas are good plants for wildlife, providing cover for roosting and nesting birds, and summer flowers for bees, and the berries are a good food source. The berries are mildly poisonous as they contain cyanogenic glycosides, as do the pips of apples, cherries and almonds, and can cause gastrointestinal problems if eaten in large quantities. In Europe, the species *P. coccinea* has been cultivated in gardens since the sixteenth century. The fruit is bitter and astringent, making it inedible when raw, but it can be cooked to make jellies, jams, sauces and marmalades. I prefer to leave them for the birds.

I have its relative, cotoneaster, which is thornless, trained on the side of an archway. A beautiful plant, but this is not a good position for the thorny pyracantha.

As one season evolves into the next, plants adjust to the change. Winter can be seen as an opportunity to revise, recollect and review the garden, as well as protecting plants from cold nights ahead. There is magic in winter as the sun lowers in the winter sky, casting long shadows and intensifying the lovely colours, bringing great pleasure revealed in the glowing low light as nature moves along under the influence of shorter days. There is a passionate, magical sense of charm in fabulous sunsets, frosty mornings and much needed rain. Many plants push up through the ice and snow, and, as the days roll by, remind us that spring is not far away; and as the sun grows warmer there is a feeling that something marvellous is about to happen. Nature never rests and there is always inspiration for the artist, whatever the time of year.

CHRISTMAS CHERRY
Solanum pseudocapsicum (winter cherry, false Jerusalem cherry, Madeira winter cherry, Nightshade, kangaroo apple, *pommier d'amour*)

The Painting

I sketched the leaves lightly in pencil because of how they grow closely, seemingly in a haphazard fashion. The leaves were then painted with a washy cool blue-green and then shadowed areas and veins were added with a darker mix. The contrasting shades of the leaves enhanced the colours of the fruits, which were painted with Winsor Orange, and some of these had a touch of red in places, while for the completely red berries I used Winsor Red with a thicker, darker application at their bases. Some fruits were still green, and for these I used the same green but with some Indian Yellow added to lighten and warm the colour.

I decided against a background as I felt the image was quite strong as it was and I didn't want to detract from or further complicate the image.

The Gardener

I have *Solanum pseudocapsicum*, native to Mexico, Central and South America and the Caribbean. It is a small evergreen shrub, related to the potato and tomato. It has naturalised in many countries, and in some places is considered a weed. It can be confused with the cherry tomato as they are very similar in taste and texture, but Christmas cherries are poisonous; although not life-threatening to humans, they can cause gastric problems.

The small dark-green leaves are dense along the many short branches that grow from woody stems. The flowers, which appear in twos or threes from the leaf axils, are star-shaped with a central core of orange with yellow stamens. Green berries follow the flowers, turning to yellow, orange and then red, and these can last all winter.

Propagation is by seed in spring or by stem cuttings taken in late winter. Seed sown in early spring will flower and fruit in the same year. They should be sown in a pot of moist soil and put into a plastic bag and placed in bright light. Germination takes about two to three weeks. About eight weeks after germination, transplant into single pots. Berries should form in the autumn.

Pruning the stems back to approximately half their length in late winter encourages new growth and keeps the plant trimmed for the next season's growth. The soil should be slightly dry before watering.

Christmas cherries need a sheltered place, but can survive frosts and cold weather. They have been known to live up to ten years. The painting included here is of my plant. It overwintered on the north side of the house (which, strangely enough, is sheltered from frost); it continued to produce seedlings and the fruits graced the winter scene right into spring.

THE ARTIST AND THE GARDENER

We have built a mainly glass extension to the house. The 'garden room' gives us enormous pleasure as we have lunch or coffee watching the birds and butterflies, enjoying the sunshine and appreciating the plants growing and changing as the seasons evolve. Even in winter there is activity, some form of flowers and wildlife to note. Winter is a resting time and without it there would be no appreciation of lengthening days and warming earth with the expectancy of spring. It is an ending and a beginning.

Whatever the time of year, there is always inspiration in the garden for the artist and the gardener. The love of gardening and the love of painting and drawing is like a seed that once sown never dies. Every season brings distinct variations in colours, growth, shapes and shadows, bringing different patterns, different light effects and different moods. Just as with the artist, the gardener must develop the composition, bringing ideas and planning together. A sketchbook is essential for various sketches, colour notes and ideas recorded and used to inspire future paintings.

If gardening is about weeding, watering, hoeing, deadheading, sowing and sheer hard work, then the rewards are seeing the seedlings emerging, watching them grow and blossom with the fabulous perfume of the resulting beautiful flowers. Painting is about appreciating these elements and finding ways of expressing the beauty in line, shape and colour. Drawing and painting are among the most exciting challenges, enormous fun and a consuming passion. There is an element of tedium, repetition and patience needed in gardening and this is what makes the difference between a good and an average gardener. Then there's the first picking of asparagus, the first fruits, and enjoying the changing harvest throughout the season. Then there's the bird life, the frogs and newts, the butterflies, and sitting among the glory of the beauty, drinking in the perfumes and the colours and appreciating everything. Tending the garden is an experience which can have a deep effect through contact with the earth, nature, weather and plants and putting acquired knowledge into practice – much the same as in painting. There is always something to learn, and the best lesson is that there is more to learn, to observe and appreciate. The practices of both gardening and painting give the purist enjoyment of beauty and lift the spirits.

> Blessed are they that see beautiful things in humble places where other people see nothing.
> *Camille Pissarro, 1893*

And in the words of Cowley:

> I never had any other desire so strong as that I might be master at least of a small house and large garden, and there dedicate the remainder of my life only to the culture of them, and the study of nature.

An artist is probably more aware of delicate changes in nature than the average person, but, even so, observation is clearly needed to detect colour harmonies. Painting is a continuous effort to improve and express. The cellist Pablo Casals replied when someone asked him why he still practised so late